Carl Sanders
Spokesman of the New South

Compliments Of

TROUTMAN SANDERS

ATTORNEYS AT LAW

NationsBank Plaza
600 Peachtree Street, N.E. - Suite 5200
Atlanta, Georgia 30308-2216

Carl Sanders, governor of Georgia, 1963–1967.

Carl Sanders
Spokesman of
the New South

by James F. Cook

Mercer University Press
1993

ISBN 0-86554-433-6   MUP/H345

Carl Sanders : Spokesman of the New South

✳

The paper used in the publication meets the minimum requirements
of American National Standard for Information Sciences—
Permanence of Paper for Printed Library Materials,
ANSI Z39.48–1984.

✳

Library of Congress Cataloging-in-Publication Data

Cook, James F.
Carl Sanders : spokesman of the New South / by James F. Cook.
xiii+394pp. 7x10" (18x25.5cm.).
Includes bibliographic references and index.
ISBN 086554-433-6 (alk. paper).
1. Sanders, Carl Edward, 1925– .
2. Governors—Georgia—Biography.
3. Georgia—Politics and government—1951– .
I. Title.
F291.3.S36C66   1993
975.8'043'092—dc20
[B]   93-36314
CIP

Contents

Dedication

To my family,

    May these reflections on my life and career provide you with some interesting reading and furnish you a benchmark by which you can measure your own lives and careers.

Carl E. Sanders

✷

To the memory of

C. L. "Pat" Grant

Democrat, Scholar, Friend

James F. Cook

Foreword

James Cook's biography of Carl Sanders is an engaging story of a prominent public and private career.

Southern governors of the decade of the 1960s had a strong and lasting influence on the image and direction of the states they led. This book is an insightful story of how Carl Sanders's forceful leadership provided a rallying point in the 1960s for the political forces of moderation and racial harmony in Georgia.

I have always been an admirer of Carl Sanders the leader and Carl Sanders the man. As I followed James Cook's chronicling and putting into perspective the political issues of that era, I found myself having an even greater sense of respect for the substance and style of Sanders's leadership during a pivotal period of Georgia's history. His legacy is that at a time of political trial and turbulence he unhesitatingly pointed his state toward the future rather than the past.

Students of politics will be particularly interested in the accounts of the bruising gubernatorial election of 1970, which proved to be Sanders's last election. I find it interesting that following his unsuccessful campaign of 1970, Carl Sanders showed no inclination to "take my ball and go home." Instead he applied to law, business, and community causes the same level of energy and discipline that he earlier focused on politics and public life.

Sanders's story is a civics lesson for us all and an important lesson about the relationship between tenacious hard work and success.

October 1993

Sam Nunn
United States Senator, Georgia

Preface

Writing a biography of Carl Sanders has been a challenging and rewarding experience. Although Sanders has been a public figure since 1954, he is not an easy person to know. A quiet, reserved, dignified man, he has remained the most private of public figures. The public has seen him as an effective legislator, an aggressive campaigner, a forceful executive, and in recent years as a hard-driving corporate executive and the chief partner of a silk-stocking law firm, but it has rarely glimpsed the private man. Formal by nature, he carefully guarded his emotions in public. Despite campaigning for public office six times and expressing his views forthrightly for nearly four decades, he still kept the public at arm's length. To many he appeared distant and somewhat aloof. Bob Coram, who campaigned with Sanders for several months in 1970, cannot remember ever seeing him without a tie. Others expressed amazement that he could campaign in the sweltering heat of the Georgia summer months and never seem to have a hair out of place or even perspire. Columnist Bill Shipp called him the "refrigerator man" and assumed that ice water ran through his veins. With family and intimate friends, however, Sanders allowed himself to be vulnerable, revealing a warmth, compassion, and subtle humor that the public rarely saw. I hope this biography, in addition to explaining Sanders's contributions to his state and nation, will penetrate the public mask to reveal the thought and strength of character of this fascinating man.

Born on May 15, 1925, and reared in a middle-class Southern family, Sanders grew up in a stratified and racially segregated society. Nurtured by his family, the Baptist church, and the YMCA, Sanders had a happy childhood that prepared him well for adulthood. A gifted athlete, he attended the University of Georgia on a football scholarship. During World War II he left Athens to become a B-17 pilot. After the war he completed his undergraduate degree and then earned a law degree. In 1947 he married Betty Foy of Statesboro, and they settled in his hometown of Augusta, where he began a practice of law that soon flourished. Entering politics in 1954, he quickly emerged as a leader in the General Assembly and served as Governor Ernest Vandiver's floor leader and then president pro tem of the Senate. In 1962, a pivotal year, which, according to former President Jimmy Carter, marked a "turning point" in Southern history, Sanders defeated former Governor Marvin Griffin to become governor of Georgia.

Only thirty-seven when elevated to the state's highest office, Sanders was the youngest governor in the entire country. During the four years he served, Georgia experienced some of the most profound political changes in the state's history. In the mid-1960s Georgia abandoned its unique county unit system, reapportioned both houses of its rural-dominated legislature as well as its malapportioned congressional districts, and allowed blacks to serve in its legislature for the first time since Reconstruction. It also witnessed the emergence of the Republican party to challenge the one-party rule of the Democrats and even cast its electoral votes for the Republican presidential candidate in 1964.

Promising to modernize Georgia's government, Sanders introduced a broad program of reform and forced the General Assembly to adopt all of it. He was the last governor who totally dominated the Georgia legislature. By all accounts, Sanders had a successful four-year term as governor that brought substantial progress to his state. By reorganizing several state agencies, luring industry to Georgia, improving the infrastructure, and making Georgia's government more efficient and democratic, Sanders gained much favorable publicity in the national media. He also earned recognition in the Democratic party, for, unlike many Southern governors, he was a national Democrat who developed an excellent working relationship with both the Kennedy and Johnson administrations.

The most outstanding achievements of the Sanders administration, however, were in the field of education. From the beginning he made education his number one priority and directed nearly sixty cents of every tax dollar into education. He brought noteworthy progress to Georgia's public schools, but improvements in the University System, where enrollments doubled, were even more impressive. He opened new junior colleges, established a dental school, appropriated more money for buildings than the University System had received in its previous thirty-one years of existence, and provided such large salary increases to faculty that Georgia advanced from tenth to fourth place among the thirteen Southern states. No previous governor in Georgia's history had ever achieved so much for higher education. And despite such expenditures, he left $140,000,000 in the treasury for his successor, a remarkable feat never before accomplished.

While there was booming prosperity with nearly full employment in the mid-1960s, socially it was a time of turmoil and racial unrest, with numerous marches, protests, and emotional confrontations. Overcoming his heritage, Sanders dealt with racial disturbances in Savannah, Americus, Atlanta, and elsewhere with a combination of firmness and compassion. In contrast to the political leaders of Alabama who stood in the doorway to block integration and used attack dogs and fire hoses against marchers, Sanders insisted that everyone must obey the law and that disputes should be settled in the courts, not in the streets. Consequently, Georgia managed to avoid the kind of tragedies that occurred in Selma and Birmingham. By providing a voice of reason, moderation, and common sense in this turbulent and chaotic period, Sanders emerged as a leader of the New South.

At the conclusion of his term Sanders left office at the crest of his popularity in Georgia. As a proven executive with vote-getting appeal, the handsome young politico seemed poised for national leadership, especially since he had cultivated close ties with President Johnson and the national Democratic party. Rejecting several federal positions offered by President Johnson, Sanders instead started a new law practice in Atlanta. In 1970, when again eligible to serve, he sought a second term as governor. Although highly favored to win the contest, he waged an ineffective campaign and lost to state Senator Jimmy Carter. Embittered by his first political defeat, Sanders never sought public office again. Thus a very promising political career, which seemed destined for greatness, came to an abrupt end.

After 1970, Sanders directed his talents and energies to the practice of law and business investments. Starting from scratch, he built a law firm that grew steadily until it became one of Atlanta's largest and most prestigious firms. Troutman Sanders currently employs more than 175 attorneys and earns more than $40 million annually. Long associated with Augusta businessman J. B. Fuqua, Sanders expanded his investments after leaving the political arena. Achieving success in real estate development and banking, he amassed great wealth and continues to serve on the boards of several companies. As a leader whose contributions in three distinct fields have extended far beyond the boundaries of Georgia, Sanders has few peers. Clearly his formidable record of accomplishment in politics, law, and business makes his life worthy of study.

This biography traces Sanders's life from birth to present. While it emphasizes his political career, it also includes material on his family and his legal and business careers. It is the first full-length study of Sanders and the first to use the extensive collection of papers he donated to the Law Library of the University of Georgia. Technically it is an authorized biography since Governor Sanders commissioned me to write it. He sought a biography of his entire life that would be of particular interest to his family and associates. While insisting that his story be depicted accurately and placed in historical perspective, he clearly did not want a "whitewash" job or a tome so lengthy and scholarly that only academicians would read it. I have attempted to comply with his wishes. Wherever possible I have allowed the events to speak for themselves and have kept scholarly analysis to a minimum. Governor Sanders cooperated fully in the project, provided lengthy interviews, and supported my efforts consistently. Although he must have been tempted on occasion to censor or alter my writing, he made no attempt to do so. After proofreading the entire manuscript, the only changes he suggested were minor ones to correct factual errors. The interpretations are mine alone. Admittedly, one of the pitfalls of doing a biography of a living person is the loss of objectivity, and I confess to gaining greater admiration and respect for Sanders and his family as a result of personal contact. I should add, however, that the interpretations in this book do not differ appreciably from those expressed in my previously published works on Sanders.

This is an old-fashioned biography because in many ways Sanders is an old-fashioned man. He personifies the traditional values of integrity, reliability, and personal responsibility. Deeply attached to his family and region, and imbued with the Protestant work ethic and Christian morality, he adheres to values that are losing favor in America. Despite his understanding of the modern age, considerable involvement in international businesses, and extensive travel abroad, part of Sanders remains fixed in the red clay of Georgia. A "practical dreamer" or an "idealistic realist," he has held on to the past as he has built for the future. So the reader may get a feel for what Sanders was really like, I have allowed him to speak for himself in many cases. I hope this book accurately depicts his thought and character and helps the reader understand one of the modern South's most important leaders.

This book could not have been written without the assistance provided by many individuals. First, I want to thank the Sanders family and their friends and colleagues who graciously granted interviews. I am indebted to Benny Tackett and other staff members of Troutman Sanders for extensive typing as well as to Barbara Walden and Sadie Rush of Floyd College for secretarial help. The library staffs of Floyd College, the University of Georgia, Georgia State University, the Georgia Department of Archives and History, the *Augusta Chronicle-Herald*, and the *Atlanta Journal and Constitution* were invariably helpful. I am especially grateful to my colleagues Philip Dillard, Ralph Peters, and Fred Green, and to Gary Fink of Georgia State University, Hal Henderson of Abraham Baldwin College, Raymond Cook of Valdosta State College, and Willard Gatewood of the University of Arkansas for reading the manuscript and making many helpful suggestions. Finally, a special word of thanks goes to my wife Ida for her patience and understanding.[*]

October 1993   *James Cook*

---

[*]Chapter 12 ("The Special Session") includes material that first appeared in my article "The One Conspicuous Failure: Gov. Carl Sanders and Constitutional Revision," *Atlanta History: A Journal of Georgia and the South* (Summer 1990) and is used by permission.

Chapter 1

Two Lives Intersect

Carl Sanders was frustrated. As a member of the Bulldogs, the University of Georgia's outstanding football team, he was a celebrity of sorts on the Athens campus, but tonight he was despondent. He had argued with his girl friend and had stomped out of her Chi Omega sorority house. It was late October 1945. The chill in the evening air matched the chill in his social life as Carl walked aimlessly down Milledge Avenue, absorbed in his own thoughts.[1]

Known as the classic city, Athens is a beautiful town with many antebellum homes, picturesque gardens, and tree-lined streets. Its residents glory in its heritage and in the University of Georgia which dominates the town. Established in 1785, the University of Georgia reigns as the oldest chartered state university in the country. Like other such schools the University suffered during the war years, as its enrollment dropped below 1,500. But with 2,490 students enrolled in the fall of 1945, the largest class since 1941, it was beginning to recover from the devastating effects of the war. Of the 928 male students, 318 were veterans. One of them was Carl Sanders.[2]

At this time the University of Georgia more resembled a liberal arts college than a university. Its small, friendly campus allowed the socially inclined to know most of the students who matriculated there. The school newspaper, *The Red and Black*, when it was not writing about sports, stressed social activities, plays, dances, and beauty pageants. Fraternities and sororities played an important part in campus life, and the newspaper faithfully listed their pledges, inductions, sports activities,

---

[1]"Governor Carl E. Sanders: An Oral History," interview by James F. Cook, Georgia Government Documentation Project, Georgia State University, Atlanta, June 1988, pp. 13-14.

[2]*Red and Black* (Athens) October 5, 1945.

and even dates for parties. Carl had entered the University of Georgia in the fall of 1942 and had pledged Chi Phi fraternity. The December 4, 1942 issue of *The Red and Black* reported that Carl had taken Elizabeth Bryans to the Chi Phi dance. His fraternity brothers who also attended that dance, included his roommate, Paul "Wink" Lee, and many others who became lifetime friends and associates: Rankin Smith, founder of the Georgia Life Insurance Company and owner of the Atlanta Falcons; Thomas Marshall, chief justice of the Georgia Supreme Court; Jesse Bowles, a justice of the Georgia Supreme Court; and Render Hill, who served for many years in the Georgia General Assembly. The University of Georgia was then, as it had been for many years, the training ground for Georgia politicians.[3]

Politics, however, was not on Carl's mind as he ambled down Milledge Avenue that late October evening. He knew some of the football players would be at the Delta Delta Delta sorority house, so he stopped there. One of the girls thought Carl might enjoy chatting with Betty Bird Foy of Statesboro. She called upstairs: "Hey Betty, will you come down and talk to Carl Sanders?" Betty came down, without realizing she was about to meet her future husband.[4]

The Foys owned a huge farm in Bulloch county in south Georgia. They had farmed in that area for several generations and had prospered by producing cotton and naval stores. Indeed, Betty's grandfather, Washington Manassas Foy, who owned and leased 60,000 acres of farm land, was the largest naval stores, turpentine, and resin dealer in that section of the state. He lent his name to the little town of Manassas, near Reidsville and Claxton. When he died at age forty-one, he left large farms to all of his children. His son Jesse Ponita, called J. P., married Ida Teresa Bird, who was called Doll from birth because her brothers and sisters thought she looked like a doll. One of ten children born to William Andrew and Emma Watson Bird in Metter, Georgia, Doll joined a distinguished family which traced its ancestry back to William Byrd of Westover, one of the wealthiest planters in colonial Virginia, whose beautiful home on the James River is often pictured in American history textbooks. As the Byrds moved south, the spelling of the name

---

[3]Ibid., October 16 and December 4, 1942.
[4]Interview with Betty Foy Sanders, Atlanta, November 7, 1990.

changed to Bird. At the Foy home on South Main Street in Statesboro, Doll gave birth to her first child on August 6, 1926. They named her Betty Bird Foy.[5]

Betty had a wonderful childhood. She roamed the woods, swam in the Canoochee River, and fished in a pond nearly every afternoon. Always fascinated with nature, she loved the outdoors and appreciated the beauty of plants and animals. In the summertime friends from town came out to join in the country fun. They boiled peanuts, had picnics at the river, made playhouses out of bales of cotton, and churned ice cream. Sugar cane grinding became a special time for the whole family. Doll would plan outdoor barbecues in October, usually around the full moon before the weather turned cold. Three wagons took guests on hayrides into the woods to hunt opossum. The hounds treed the opossums, and the hunters usually shot six or eight of them. Then they would all gather at the cane grinding to drink cane juice or hot apple cider. Big iron boilers cooked the cane juice into a syrup. When the festivities ended, everyone took home large bottles of fresh syrup.[6]

When Betty was six the family moved out into the country so they could direct the farming operations more efficiently. Betty attended the small school at Register through the eighth grade. Concerned about the academic inadequacies of the little country school, her parents insisted that she move in with her grandparents in town so that she could attend a better high school in Statesboro. Betty lived with her Grandmother Foy and step-grandfather, Dr. J. E. Donehoo, until her senior year, when her parents returned to Statesboro. Her father's declining health necessitated the move.

Like many young girls, Betty adored her father. A devoted family man, J. P. made Betty, her younger sister Teresa, and Doll feel like they were the stars in his heaven. In the summer months Betty followed him continually. She rode with him in his pickup truck wherever he went. On Saturdays she rode with him to his cotton gin at Claxton where he paid his farm workers. Every July 4, J. P. held a big barbecue for all of his workers. At Christmas he traveled to the bank at Statesboro to fill a sack with coins—pennies, nickels, dimes, quarters, and half dollars. He

---

[5]Interview with Betty Foy Sanders, Atlanta, March 25, 1991.
[6]Ibid.

also bought cases of apples, oranges, and hard candy. When the farmers came to be paid at Christmas, they brought all their children with them. Each child would then put his hand into the money sack and keep all the coins he or she could grasp. Each farmer got a sack of apples and oranges. Most of these black families had worked for the Foys for two or three generations. They respected J. P. and had lived intertwined lives, but class and cultural differences still separated them.[7]

The Great Depression devastated farmers everywhere, including the Foys of Bulloch county. Farmers generally had failed to share in the prosperity of the 1920s, and in the 1930s the price of cotton dropped to five cents a pound, so low it hardly seemed worth planting. Often the expenses of planting and cultivating crops exceeded the income they produced. Savings soon vanished and debts appeared. Land values plummeted so much that banks only reluctantly foreclosed on overdue loans because they had trouble selling the land after seizing it.

The wealth of the Foys declined substantially in the 1930s, but despite the hard times Betty did not suffer. Her parents exposed her to music, dancing, and art. In school she participated actively in sports. Always a tall child, she started playing basketball in the seventh grade at Register. At Statesboro High School she played varsity basketball in grades nine through eleven. She also performed as a cheerleader and marched in the band. A popular student, she enjoyed school thoroughly. Constantly on the go, Betty had many friends and supportive extended family members. It was an exciting period for her and she experienced much joy. But there was sorrow too.

In October of her senior year her father became seriously ill. His blood pressure rose dangerously after a bout with strep throat. The infection settled in his kidneys and caused him intense suffering. In hopes of discovering the source of his ailment, J. P. entered the Mayo Clinic in Rochester, Minnesota, but to no avail. He received further treatment at St. Joseph's Hospital in Savannah, before his physicians decided to operate. Dr. Julian Quattlebaum, a well-known surgeon who had been his roommate at the Sigma Chi House at the University of Georgia, performed the surgery. He found one kidney as big as a football and no longer functioning. The other kidney functioned at only

---

[7]Ibid.

fifty percent. Lacking the modern medicines to combat infection, the doctors could do little. J. P. died on November 12, 1942. He was only forty-two. Betty was then 16, Teresa was 6, and Doll was 38. Though Doll would live another forty-seven years, until October 22, 1989, she never remarried. No one, she felt, could replace J. P.[8]

In this time of crisis, Doll proved that strength and substance lay beneath her fragile exterior. With iron determination she assumed the responsibility of running the complex farming operation. She hired an overseer and kept things going. Having considerable business acumen, she paid off debts and ran the business effectively. After running the farm for eight years, she decided to sell it. Since none of her family was interested in buying it, she sold most of the property to J. G. Altman, retaining only one farm as a keepsake. A convincing talker, she became an insurance agent and later sold real estate. In south Georgia in the 1940s women typically did not do such things. Unconcerned about sexual stereotypes, she became the first woman realtor in Bulloch county. Although she probably would have disavowed militant feminist rhetoric, Doll was an eminently practical woman who recognized her own talents and abilities and simply did whatever she thought needed to be done. While forcefully assuming the economic role in the family that J. P. had filled, Doll still cared for Betty and Teresa and continued to serve her community. The community expected much of prominent families in rural south Georgia, and Doll fulfilled all of the duties society imposed upon her. Her rural community had only one country doctor. It was physically impossible for him to meet all of the needs of the community. Consequently, whenever one of the farmers' family members got sick, Doll did whatever she could to assist the patient and family. When new babies arrived, she took food to assist the family. Highly religious, Doll continued her active role in the Baptist church and instilled high morals in her daughters. And, despite all the demands on her time, she rarely missed a school function involving her girls because she believed Betty and Teresa needed her attention.[9]

Betty had worshipped her father, and his death left a void even Doll could not fill. To overcome her grief she stayed as busy as possible in

---

[8]Ibid.; *Atlanta Journal,* October 23, 1989.
[9]Betty Foy Sanders interview, March 25, 1991.

school, but her senior year of high school dragged on endlessly. While studying or playing ball, she often wondered if the year would ever end. Her classmates, however, saw Betty in a different light. At the end of the year they voted her "Miss Statesboro High School," the "Most Popular Girl," and the "Biggest Flirt."[10]

Betty had planned to attend the University of Georgia, following in the footsteps of her father and grandfather Foy. But under the circumstances her mother urged her to wait a year. Doll wanted her to stay closer to home and get better adjusted before going to Athens. As usual, Doll provided good advice. Betty agreed. She enrolled in Georgia Teachers College in Statesboro, a small state-supported school with 500 students, which later would grow into Georgia Southern University. Although the college was only four blocks from her home, Doll allowed Betty to live on campus so that she could begin to live on her own. A tall, striking girl, Betty was chosen for the May Court, the beauty section of the college yearbook, as a freshman.[11]

After completing her freshman year at Statesboro, Betty enrolled in the University of Georgia in the fall of 1944, shortly after the Allies made their successful landing on the Normandy beaches. With money scarce and gas and food rationed, few students had cars. Females dominated the student population, as total enrollment dropped below 2,000. Assigned a dorm room in Clark Howell, formerly a boys dorm, located on Lumpkin Street near Sanford Stadium, Betty began an eventful phase of her life.

Betty's first few weeks in Athens were exciting. Sociable and unpretentious, she could talk to anyone. She had the rare gift of making people feel at ease in her company. Attractive, friendly, and fashionably dressed in a new wardrobe provided by her mother, Betty attracted favorable attention from all the sororities. She pledged Delta Delta Delta. She thrilled at making new friends from all over the state, including her first roommate at Clark Howell dormitory, Louise Ledbetter, whose family owned Ledbetter Furniture store in downtown Atlanta. Academically, Betty planned to become a dietician. Having completed many of the basic courses at Georgia Teachers College, she was placed

---

[10]Ibid.
[11]Ibid.

in more advanced courses. A few days in a chemistry class, however, convinced her that she had made a mistake. She was lost. Clearly, she lacked the academic preparation for chemistry or physics. Frantically, she telephoned home and cried: "Mother, what should I do?" Doll calmly told her to forget about becoming a dietician and choose her second interest, art. What good advice that turned out to be. The University of Georgia had an excellent art department chaired by Lamar Dodd, an exceptional artist. Betty studied with Dodd, developed her talents, and ultimately became an accomplished artist.[12]

After switching majors, college life improved for Betty. She had tremendous admiration for Dodd and thoroughly enjoyed studying under him. As Dodd and the other professors molded her talents, she could discern steady improvement in her work. In her junior year Betty moved into the "Tri Delt" House on Milledge Avenue. With many friends, numerous sorority activities, interesting courses, and occasional visits to Statesboro, it was an exciting time. Athens became even more exciting in the fall of 1945 when the war ended and more boys appeared on campus.[13]

In contrast to the distinguished heritage of Betty's family in south Georgia, Carl descended from working class people in north Georgia. For many generations the Sanders family had lived in Rex, a small community south of Atlanta in Clayton county. Four generations of Sanders are buried in the cemetery of Rock Baptist Church in Rex, going back to Henry Sanders who was born in 1798. Carl's father, Carl T. Sanders, was born in Rex in 1901. He was the only son of Thomas Monroe and Nancy Jane Born Sanders. His older sister Clarice died in 1932, and his younger sister Alpharetta, called Aunt Flu, was born in 1906 and lived in the ancestral home until her death in 1967.[14]

Carl T. Sanders left home as a teenager to work for the meatpacking firm of Swift & Company in Atlanta. A hard worker, he transferred to Augusta where he became a salesman. The employer-employee relationship must have been a good match because he remained with Swift for

---

[12]Ibid.; *Red and Black*, September 29 and October 13, 1944.

[13]Betty Foy Sanders interview, March 25, 1991.

[14]Carl E. Sanders, "Interviews with James F. Cook, June 26, July 9, 16, 18, 23, 1990" (unpublished manuscript) pp. 1-2.

forty-seven years. In Augusta he met Roberta Alley, an attractive young cashier for S. H. Kress, a department store. A beautiful young woman, Roberta had refined features, a gentle spirit, and a quiet disposition. Carl, by contrast, weighed well over two hundred pounds and stood over six feet tall. Handsome features and thick black hair accentuated his overpowering physical appearance. Roberta (22) and Carl (20) married on September 1, 1921.[15]

Simple, hardworking farmers, the Alleys lived in the Spartanburg area of South Carolina. Roberta's mother, Mary Etta Alley, called Mamie, had been a widow for many years. Roberta's father, Robert Alley, had died when she was young and her mother, poor but proud, raised her by working in her home as a seamstress. After the marriage Carl and Roberta lived with Mamie at 1400 Broad Street in Augusta. The young couple delighted in the birth of their first child on May 15, 1925. They named him Carl Edward. Two years later a second son arrived, and they named him Robert.[16]

In many ways Carl and Bob had an ideal childhood. They were loved and secure—and they knew it. When the children were born, their mother quit working for Kress and became a full-time homemaker. An excellent cook, housekeeper, and gardener, she adored her boys and believed in keeping them busy. Consequently, the boys participated in practically every activity offered in the neighborhood, the school, and their church. Mrs. Sanders set high standards for the boys and made certain that they did their homework, studied their Sunday school lessons, and performed various chores around the house. Mr. Sanders took time to play ball with the boys and take them hunting and fishing.[17]

As a youngster Carl, bigger than most boys his age, had good athletic ability. At age seven he joined the YMCA where he learned to swim, play baseball and basketball, and even to box. The Y in Augusta had unusually good leaders, and Carl flourished under their direction. As he matured, he became an exceptional athlete, and participated in all

---

[15]Carl E. Sanders, "Story of My Life" (unpublished manuscript, 1987) pp. 1-2.

[16]Ibid.; Carl E. Sanders, "My Life" (unpublished manuscript, 1969) pp. 1-2.

[17]Sanders, "Interviews in 1990," pp. 1-34; Charlotte Hale Smith, "Boyhood of Gov. Sanders," *Atlanta Journal and Constitution Magazine*, September 13, 1964, pp. 12, 14, 54.

sports. Later he attended Y summer camps and then served as a counselor for several years. The Y had such a positive effect on his formative years that he maintained his affiliation as an adult.[18]

Carl began to earn his own money as soon as he could. Like thousands of boys in that era, his first job was delivering newspapers, the *Augusta Chronicle*, which meant getting up early in the morning, folding the newspapers, then delivering them on his bicycle. He earned seventy-five cents a week and managed to save fifty cents. Later Carl worked in a grocery store stocking shelves and bagging groceries. Working became a normal part of his life, and during his school and college years he invariably held down a part-time job to earn a little money. Wisely his parents had taught him to become self-reliant, that labor has its rewards, and that success requires diligent effort. In short, he learned to earn his way in life. He would never forget these lessons.[19]

The family moved from Broad Street to a new brick bungalow at the corner of Johns Road and Wrightsboro Road shortly after Carl celebrated his fifth birthday. Although far from elaborate, the comfortable new home was located in a good suburban neighborhood. A boy named Doug Barnard, two years older than Carl, lived across the street. They soon became lifelong friends. Seeing these boys riding their bicycles or playing cowboys and Indians in the woods, few would have predicted that one day Carl would be governor of Georgia and Doug would represent Georgia's Tenth District in Congress for eighteen years.[20]

Doug had a musical talent, and quite often the neighborhood would awaken to his playing the trumpet before breakfast. Carl, who excelled in many areas, was not musically inclined. Playing drums in the Drum and Bugle Corps in grammar school remained his only musical accomplishment. Despite his lack of musical ability, Carl had an aptitude for dancing. His mother enrolled him in a social dancing class offered through the YMCA. The teacher was Mrs. Henri Price, who taught the children the box step, fox trot, and waltz. In addition to learning to dance, Carl and the other boys and girls learned social graces as well. On

---

[18]Sanders, "Interviews in 1990," p. 9; Sanders, "My Life," pp. 5-7.

[19]Sanders, "Interviews in 1990," p. 7; Sanders, "My Life," p. 10.

[20]Sanders, "My Life," pp. 3-4; interview with Doug Barnard, Augusta, February 16, 1991.

the first day in class Mrs. Price grabbed Carl by the ear, led him to a window, and instructed him to throw his chewing gum out the window. She informed him: "We can't have that in dancing classes." Even on the dance floor, Carl exhibited his competiveness and desire to excel. With a Jewish girl named Jane Silver as his partner, he won the Waltz Prize.[21]

Each summer Mrs. Sanders took Carl and Bob to Spartanburg, South Carolina, to visit her relatives. They stayed with her uncle Ed Johnson and his family, who lived on a small farm in the peach country. It was exciting for boys raised in town to experience farm life. They enjoyed riding mules in the barnyard, picking peaches off the trees, and watching peaches being unloaded in the packing house and processed for shipping. They watched freight trains come by, and late at night they heard the mournful train whistles in the distance. They slept on a homemade feather mattress under a tin roof, sat on pine-splintered benches, watched butter being churned, and drank fresh buttermilk—all new experiences.[22]

The boys also enjoyed summer vacations in Rex, with Grandfather Sanders, the chief of police and the local blacksmith. Since both were part-time jobs, he had time to spend with Carl and Bob. He owned his own home, which was located on a hill overlooking the town of Rex, and lived with his daughter Alpharetta (Aunt Flu), her husband Phil Jones, and their son Billy. Phil, an electrician, died tragically in a boating accident when he was in his fifties, and Alpharetta never recovered from his loss. Grandfather Sanders had a Model T which he kept in a shed behind the house, jacked up with the tires removed. Playing in it became a favorite pastime for the boys. They also enjoyed watching their grandfather milk his cow and marveled at the amount of milk she gave.[23]

The railroad which bisected Rex served the town's main industry, a chair factory. A few small stores and a post office stood in the center of town. Social activity seemed to center around the general store. There everyone found time to sit around, chat, and tell tall tales. Roger Born, whose two boys, Harmon and Ivan, were second cousins to Carl and

---

[21]Sanders, "My Life," p. 11.
[22]Sanders, "Interviews in 1990," pp. 5-7.
[23]Ibid., pp. 11-12; interview with Bob Sanders, Atlanta, May 5, 1991.

Bob, owned the general store. The boys played together and remained friends thereafter. Years later, Harmon and Ivan would own the Beaudry Ford dealership in Atlanta. A small river ran through Rex and powered the Rex Mill. Power produced by a large waterwheel ground corn into meal. Below the waterfalls the boys fished, usually catching small perch. Growing up in town, Carl and Bob loved the rustic way of life, and their experiences at Rex reminded them of Tom Sawyer and Huckleberry Finn.[24]

A godly woman, Mrs. Sanders regularly took her sons to Sunday school and church services at Hill Baptist Church. The boys loved and respected her. In later years Carl many times remarked that she was as close to a saint as anyone he knew.[25] His father, by contrast, had little spiritual discernment and did not become active in the church until later in life. One evening at a worship service Carl, about twelve, felt the call of God. The pastor, Dr. Carey Vinzant, made an altar call. Having studied his Bible and grown spiritually, Carl walked forward to be baptized. He had not discussed the matter previously with anyone. He simply decided it was time to make this commitment. Carl's march to the altar surprised his brother, but not desiring to be left out, Bob jumped up and joined Carl at the altar. Bob respected his older brother and knew Carl would not lead him astray. Thus, both boys were baptized.[26]

The stock market collapsed in October of 1929 before Carl had reached his fifth birthday. The family had moved into their new house at 1447 Johns Road when the Great Depression hit. Soon unemployment grew and money became scarce. Mr. Sanders managed to keep his job with Swift, but lost half his salary. It did not take long for his meager savings to disappear. Soon, unable to make his house payments, he had to give up his house. The insurance company which held the mortgage, however, did something unusual. Since no market existed for selling houses, it allowed Mr. Sanders to remain in the house and pay rent. He gladly accepted the offer and rented the house for several years. The Sanders family lived in that house until Carl's sophomore year in

---

[24]Sanders, "Interviews in 1990," pp. 26-27; Bob Sanders interview, May 5, 1991; Sanders, "Story of My Life," pp. 5-7.

[25]Cook, "Sanders: An Oral History," p. 4.

[26]Sanders, "Interviews in 1990," p. 32; Bob Sanders interview, May 5, 1991.

high school. In 1938 Mr. Sanders purchased a house at 2710 Helen Street, his fortunes having improved as increased defense spending stimulated the economy and finally ended the Depression. A story-and-a-half Dutch style house with two bedrooms and a sleeping porch upstairs, it had a long narrow backyard with many shrubs and trees. Although the new house cost less than $10,000, it was larger than the house on Johns Road and was located in a more fashionable neighborhood; "on the hill" as Augustans describe the area.[27]

During the Depression years the Sanders family could afford few frills, but never lacked necessities. They lived in a comfortable home and ate well, especially with meat provided by Swift & Company. Mr. Sanders drove a company car and Mrs. Sanders the family car. The boys, who had a shepherd dog named Blackie and several Persian cats, always participated in sports, and their parents managed to find enough money to buy whatever equipment they needed. Almost every Saturday the boys went to the Rialto to see a "cowboy" movie for ten cents. Thus, through frugal living and practical economies, Mr. and Mrs. Sanders provided the boys with everything they needed during the Depression years.[28]

Carl began school at Monte Sano, a public elementary school built in 1924, which then had fewer than three hundred pupils. With encouragement from his parents he studied hard and enjoyed learning. Many good teachers were on the Monte Sano faculty. Carl's favorite, Miss Emma Wilkinson, taught English in the seventh grade. Many years later, as governor, he took great pleasure in recognizing her as "Teacher of the Year."[29] One year Mrs. Sanders served as president of the Parent Teachers Association. Carl seemed to have vote-getting ability even in grammar school, for the students elected him king of the Halloween carnival.[30]

Carl also must have displayed leadership qualities, since he became the captain of the School Boy Patrol. Wearing a Sam Brown belt and

---

[27]Sanders, "Interviews in 1990," pp. 7-8; Cook, "Sanders: An Oral History," pp. 2-3.

[28]Sanders, "Interviews in 1990," pp. 8-33; Cook, "Sanders: An Oral History," pp. 3-6.

[29]Sanders, "My Life," pp. 4-5; Jack Shepherd, "Gov. Carl Sanders and 'Miss Emma'," *Look* 29 (February 23, 1965): 46-49.

[30]Sanders, "Story of My Life," p. 8.

badge, he assisted the younger students crossing the street to and from school. On one occasion while on patrol duty, he noticed a car going much too fast. The car roared to a stop in front of the school, let out the children, and sped off. Carl took down the license number and turned it over to the local policeman who made a case against the driver for speeding. Carl testified in Recorder's Court against the driver, quite an experience for a boy his age. The driver of the car, Nathan Jolles, was a lawyer late for work. Ironically, years later he and Carl became good friends and his son, Buddy Jolles, later became one of Carl's law partners.[31]

After finishing at Monte Sano, Carl attended Richmond Academy, an exceptional public high school with about 1,000 students. Started in the 1780s, it had a strong military tradition with compulsory ROTC training. The boys wore uniforms four days a week and civilian clothes one day. Both Carl and Bob became officers in the military program. Although Carl enjoyed military training and profited from it, he loved sports even more. As a freshman he made the B varsity football team. Previously Carl had played guard on the YMCA teams, but his coach converted him into a back. He progressed rapidly and soon became first string. In his sophomore year he advanced to the varsity team under coach Wendell Sullivan. Since Carl was left-handed, he played the right halfback or wingback position. Later he moved to fullback in the Notre Dame box and scored many touchdowns. Strong, fast, and agile, he flourished on the football field. At the end of his senior year he made the All-State football team and received the Most Valuable Player award from the Augusta Elks Club. A gifted, all-around athlete, Carl played baseball, basketball, and other sports. Keeping things in perspective, he also kept up with his studies. He belonged to the Gold R Society, which required both scholarship and athletic ability. Having compiled such an outstanding high school record, Carl naturally received football scholarships from many colleges.[32]

The biblical injunction "Train up a child in the way he should go and when is old he will not depart from it" certainly applies to the life

---

[31]Sanders, "My Life," pp. 7-8.

[32]Sanders, "Interviews in 1990," pp. 21-23; Bob Sanders interview, May 5, 1991; undated newspaper clippings in "This Is Your Life," scrapbook, Sanders Personal Papers, Atlanta.

of Carl Sanders. The values formed in his youth would be manifested as an adult. His parents, who always offered encouragement, set an example by their own high moral standards. He dated a number of girls but was not serious about any of them, and, unlike many star athletes, he avoided wild parties and neither smoked nor drank. The Protestant work ethic, instilled in him early in life, remained with him thereafter. Likewise, his religious commitments, which were genuine and deep-rooted, have remained constant over the years. Molded by his family's teaching, the Baptist church, and the YMCA, Carl developed high ethical standards and a fierce determination to excel in whatever he attempted. Extremely competitive, he loved sports where he matched his ability against an opponent. The same energy, drive, and determination that brought him victories and awards in sports would bring him success in many other endeavors. As a mature adult he continued to keep himself physically, mentally, and morally fit, because he was trained that way in his youth. Looking back on his early years, Carl observed: "I had an exceptionally happy and secure childhood [and] I wish all children could be as lucky as my brother and I were." His parents had prepared him well for life away from home.[33]

---

[33]Smith, "Boyhood of Gov. Sanders," pp. 12, 14, 54; Cook, "Sanders: An Oral History," pp. 1-10.

Ida Bird Foy, mother of Betty Foy Sanders.

The Donehoo-Brannen House in Statesboro, home of Betty Sanders's "Grandmother Foy."

Bob and Carl Sanders.

Carl Sanders, Richmond Academy fullback, in 1941.

Chapter 2

Two Lives United

Although Carl had received several college football scholarship offers, for some reason he rejected all of them. How he expected to get a college education without a scholarship is unclear because his family lacked the financial resources to pay such expenses. During the summer of 1942, while serving as a counselor at Camp Dixie in the north Georgia mountains near Clayton, he began to change his mind. Perhaps Wendell Sullivan, his high school coach who had gotten him the summer job, influenced him. Sullivan had graduated from the University of Georgia. Finally, late in the summer, Carl informed the University of Georgia that if they still wanted him he was willing to play. After a brief tryout in Athens, he secured a scholarship from Wally Butts, head football coach. It provided tuition, room, board, laundry, and ten dollars a month spending money.[1]

Carl moved into Milledge Annex, the football dormitory, in August of 1942. As part of the indoctrination into Bulldog football his head was shaved and he was charged one dollar for the haircut. Freshmen had the duty of cleaning their own rooms and the room of a varsity football player. Carl was assigned the room of Garland "Bulldog" Williams, a 215-pound tackle from Arkansas, one of the largest players on the team. Wally Butts was a successful coach and a tough disciplinarian, whose training was so rigorous and demanding that only half of the sixty freshmen survived the season. In addition to the exertions on the football field, brutal "rat courts" harassed freshmen. The varsity players made the freshmen roll dice to determine how many licks they would receive from a leather belt. The pain inflicted by the belt lasted for hours. At one point the whole freshman team, Carl included, threatened

---

[1]Sanders, "Interviews in 1990," pp. 23-24; Sanders, "My Life," pp. 12-13.

to quit. Coach Butts, aware of their frustration and that they had no recourse, came to the dormitory and simply told them they could pack their bags and leave if they wanted to. Since most players had no other way of getting an education, they unpacked their bags and stayed.[2]

Georgians take football very seriously, and in this era the Bulldogs had some of the best teams in their illustrious history. In 1941 the Bulldogs lost only to the Crimson Tide of Alabama and ended the season with a victory over Texas Christian University in the Orange Bowl. Frank Sinkwich, one of the premier running backs of all time, clearly was the team leader. He ranked third in the nation in total offense, and his 1,103 yards rushing led the nation and broke the Southeastern Conference record. Making his record even more impressive was the fact that he played much of the season with a broken jaw.[3] With Sinkwich returning for his senior year, along with outstanding receiver George Poschner and running backs Charlie Trippi and Dick McPhee, Bulldog fans expected great things from the 1942 team. The season began well, and after defeating Kentucky, Navy, Furman, and Ole Miss, Georgia was ranked second in the nation by the Associated Press. Georgia then trounced Tulane, Cincinnati, and Alabama and advanced to number one in the nation.[4] Florida fell 75 to 0 and Chattanooga 40 to 0 before Auburn upset Georgia 27 to 13. The regular season ended with archrival Georgia Tech. Although Tech had an exceptional team and ranked second in the nation, the Bulldogs demolished the Yellow Jackets 34 to 0. In the final AP rankings Ohio State was number one and Georgia was number two. Sinkwich led the SEC in scoring, gained 2,187 yards for a new record, made the AP All America team, and received the Heisman Trophy. The season came to a glorious conclusion when Georgia defeated UCLA in the Rose Bowl 9 to 0.[5]

Carl played on the freshman team and missed the glory of the 1942 team. He performed well until he suffered a severe charley horse in his

---

[2] Sanders, "Interviews in 1990," pp. 34-36; Sanders, "My Life," pp. 13-15.

[3] *Red and Black*, November 27, 1942; *Athens Banner-Herald*, September 1, 6, 17, 1942.

[4] *Red and Black*, August 6, November 13, 1942; *Athens Banner-Herald*, October 13, November 3, 1942.

[5] *Athens Banner-Herald*, November 24, 29, December 1, 3, 11, 1942, January 3, 1943.

thigh that hampered his running. Despite therapy, the pain continued for months. With the injury reducing Carl's effectiveness, his fraternity brother Jim "Chicken" Gatewood emerged as the first string signal caller. Nevertheless, according to *The Red and Black*, Carl was expected to see a lot of playing time on the varsity in 1943. With World War II taking its toll of athletes, he played guard on the varsity basketball team and first base on the baseball team.[6]

The Japanese attack on Pearl Harbor on December 7, 1941, had brought the United States into the war, and as Carl progressed through his first quarter at Athens, the newspapers reported the war news—the German invasion of the Soviet Union, fighting in the Solomons, the tank war in north Africa, and the siege of Stalingrad. With the war continuing and the draft looming ahead, Carl began to consider his military options. He decided he would like to attend one of the military academies, preferably the Naval Academy at Annapolis. With help from his father and some of his friends, Carl sought an appointment through Congressman Paul Brown of the Tenth District. He passed the physical exam and received an appointment as an alternate to the Military Academy at West Point. The principal appointment went to Sewell Elliott of Augusta, then a student at the Citadel. When he accepted the appointment, Carl was left out.[7]

Disappointed, Carl travelled to Atlanta with his roommate Billy Smith to enlist in the Naval Air Corps. The Navy accepted Billy but rejected Carl because he was too young; they sent him home to get his parents' consent. Carl was eager to fly, but, upon further reflection, he concluded it might be better to fly over land than over the oceans. He then enlisted in the Army Air Force at Daniel Field in Augusta and returned to Athens to await his orders.[8]

Carl's orders arrived in May 1943 assigning him to Kessler Field, Mississippi. Growing up in Augusta, Carl was accustomed to hot weather, but the Mississippi heat was unbearable. After six weeks he was sent by train to Lubbock, in the panhandle of Texas. For eight weeks he

---

[6]*Red and Black*, October 16, November 13, 1942, January 15, 1943; Sanders, "Interviews in 1990," p. 36.

[7]Sanders, "Interviews in 1990," pp. 36-37; Cook, "Sanders: An Oral History," pp. 9-10.

[8]Sanders, "Interviews in 1990," p. 37.

was an aviation student at Texas Tech, where he received his preliminary flight training. Since Carl had previous ROTC training, he became a squadron leader. He spent most of his time taking classes in mathematics, navigation, meteorology, and ground training. After passing the aptitude test, Carl advanced to pilot training in Visalia, California. There, in the Fresno Valley, he trained in a PT-19 Ryan aircraft, a low-winged, fast airplane. Like all beginning pilots, he had his share of anxious moments. One of the harrowing obstacles all beginning pilots must face is the first solo flight. His produced the usual trauma, but, overcoming his fear, he managed to get his plane back safely on the ground without mishap. California was a long way from home for an eighteen-year-old Georgia boy, but it had some advantages. When he received an infrequent pass he managed to date a few young Hollywood "starlets."[9]

Carl's previous military training gave him an advantage over the other cadets, and he was selected Wing Commander of the Aviation Cadets, the top military position. It was quite an honor, and after graduation it meant he could choose the type of plane he wished to fly in combat. He chose fighters and was sent to Marana, Arizona, a base in the desert between Phoenix and Tucson. Upon graduating at Marana, he was sent to Williams Field, near Phoenix, for advanced pilot flight training. He trained in AT-6s and P-38s. The advanced training was very difficult and many cadets washed out. Carl had a serious scare. While flying in formation, Carl's plane was hit by another plane which so severely damaged the tail that he could barely control the aircraft. The instructors advised him to bail out. Though tempted to bail out, he thought he might be able to land the plane. He asked for permission to attempt to land it. The instructors agreed. Somehow he managed to land the plane safely. The ensuing hearing placed the blame for the accident on the other cadet. Carl was graduated, received his wings, and was commissioned a 2nd lieutenant. He had just turned nineteen.[10]

After a few days' leave at home, Carl was ordered to Hobbs, New Mexico, for training as a first pilot on a B-17 bomber. Although he had chosen fighters and expected to be trained as a fighter pilot, at this stage

---

[9]Ibid., pp. 37-40.
[10]Ibid., pp. 40-41.

of the war there was a greater need for bomber pilots so his orders were changed. His next assignment was Lincoln, Nebraska, where he picked up his combat crew. His copilot was from Albany, Georgia, the bombardier was from Pennsylvania, and the navigator was from Tennessee. Carl was the youngest of the crew. Their next stop was Dyersburg, Tennessee, for final training before being sent overseas.[11]

One of Carl's first flights in a B-17 was nearly a disaster. Immediately after takeoff, a problem developed in the left outboard engine. The engine caught fire and lost power. Again it was touch and go. Only by the grace of God did Carl get the heavy bomber through the traffic and back safely on the ground. On another occasion the bombardier inadvertently dropped some practice bombs on the town of Humbolt, Tennessee. Fortunately, they injured no one.[12]

Carl had been training for the European theater and fully expected to be sent there. Fortunately for him, Germany surrendered in May of 1945 before his orders arrived. Then, with the surrender of Japan and the end of the war, Carl was given the option of signing up for four years of flying or getting a discharge and returning to school. That was an easy decision to make. Discharged at Fort McPherson in Atlanta on September 15, 1945, he was back at the University of Georgia a week later.[13]

Having missed the 1943 and 1944 seasons, Carl was eager to get back on the football field. Now a twenty-year-old veteran and a solid six-foot 175 pounder, he expected to become the greatest running back in Georgia's history. Since he had been a star on his previous teams, he naturally expected to fulfil that role again. Soon he was in good physical condition and a part of the team, but to his surprise he was not its outstanding player. Although he was an excellent athlete, he found that there were others on the team who were even better. It was a shattering experience for him to realize that he would not star in college football. Putting things into perspective, he refused to quit. On the contrary, he applied himself with increased determination to be the best player he

---

[11]Ibid., pp. 40-42.

[12]Ibid., 40-42, 50-52.

[13]Ibid., pp. 43-44; military record and certificate of service, Personal folder, Box 22, Carl E. Sanders Collection, Law Library, University of Georgia, Athens (hereafter cited as Sanders Collection, Law Library).

could possibly be. Years later Carl looked back on this disappointment as a positive and maturing experience. In learning to cope with disappointment he began to be a man. From football Carl learned valuable lessons that he applied to other aspects of life. He later remarked: "In football—as in the Game of Life—one must keep mentally alert, physically fit, and spiritually inspired. This I vowed to do."[14]

The 1945 Bulldogs had exceptional talent, including quarterback John Rauch, triple-threat back Charlie Trippi, and end Joe Tereshenski. Not only would all of them achieve collegiate stardom, they also would have successful careers in professional football. Carl backed up Rauch at quarterback but actually got more playing time on defense as a sideback. His brother Bob was the starting right tackle. In the Alabama game in 1945 Bob got knocked out and did not remember anything until waking up in a hotel room and seeing Carl crying and holding his hand. Bob then learned he had played a great game. Fortunately, his injuries were not serious.[15] The team won its first two games easily. It then slipped by Miami 27 to 21 and trounced Kentucky 48 to 6 before losing to L.S.U. and Alabama. Chastened by those defeats, the Bulldogs played with greater intensity the remainder of the season. They beat Chattanooga handily and proceeded to shut out their last three opponents—Florida 34 to 0, Auburn 35 to 0, and Georgia Tech 33 to 0. The great season ended with an impressive 20 to 6 victory over Tulsa in the Oil Bowl in Houston.[16]

During the football season Carl met Betty Foy, and soon he lost interest in all the other girls. She was the one for him. They dated regularly thereafter and soon were "pinned." They were a twosome all over campus. With his G.I. bonus Carl purchased his first car, a black Plymouth coupe. Now he could drive Betty to dances, picnics, and other activities. Together they spent much time at the Chi Phi house and the Tri Delt house. Betty was not only strikingly beautiful, she was also friendly and fun to be with. She subsequently became the sponsor of the

---

[14]Carl Sanders, "What Football Taught Me," *Atlanta Journal and Constitution Magazine*, November 3, 1963, pp. 18-20.

[15]Bob Sanders interview, May 5, 1991; Sanders, "Interviews in 1990," pp. 44-45; *Red and Black*, November 9, 16, December 14, 1945.

[16]*Red and Black*, January 16, 1946.

Chi Phis. She also represented her sorority and his fraternity in the Pandora Beauty Pageant. Although she did not win that contest, she later served as Georgia's Maid of Cotton and represented the state in a pageant in Memphis, Tennessee.[17]

With Betty's encouragement, Carl began to think more seriously about what he was going to do when he finished school. When he entered the University of Georgia he had designated chemistry as his major, but like many students he had second thoughts about his choice of a profession. After weighing various options, he abandoned his plans to become a chemist and decided to become a lawyer instead. The field of law appealed to him because the work would not be as structured and regimented as working in business or some other professions. He believed that in practicing law he would have the opportunity to set his own course, follow his own instincts, and act as an individual. Furthermore, if things worked out, the field could be quite lucrative too.[18] Because of his military training, he exempted several courses by examination and was admitted into the law school for the winter quarter 1946. Financially he was in good shape since he received educational benefits under the G.I. Bill and also had his athletic scholarship. He dressed out for spring football training but soon realized that he could not play football and keep up with his studies. There simply was not enough time to do both. Sports had been a major part of his life. He enjoyed playing, and the physical training and discipline of competitive athletics was a positive experience in his development. But now there were new and more important challenges to face. Realizing that his future career and family responsibilities must take priority over football, he contacted Coach Butts and relinquished his athletic scholarship.[19]

Carl made up his lost income from the scholarship in an unusual way. A number of ex-pilots at the University found employment with a Major Garner, who owned several planes and an airstrip near the Atlanta highway. Each week end he put on an air show somewhere in north Georgia. Carl, who thoroughly enjoyed flying, became one of his

[17]Ibid., November 2, 1945, February 8, 22, March 8, May 10, November 1, 1946; Betty Foy Sanders interview, March 25, 1991.

[18]Sanders, "Interviews in 1990," pp. 45-46.

[19]Cook, "Sanders: An Oral History," pp. 11-12.

pilots. Eventually he became the acrobatic pilot, flying a Stearman biplane. Flying stunts and flying the wing walker and parachute jumper was dangerous work, but Carl loved performing such feats. He made ten percent of the gate and usually took home from fifty to seventy-five dollars from each air show. Any extra money Carl made he put in the bank; he planned to buy Betty an engagement ring. Betty, however, never shared his enthusiasm for flying. She worried about him and finally convinced him to quit. He stopped his daredevil flying at a fortuitous time. Shortly after he quit, his successor crashed.[20]

Leaving the football dormitory, Carl moved into a private home on Springdale Street owned by Mr. and Mrs. Johnny McNabb. Sharing three rooms in the boarding house were six law students. Glenn York and Billy Goode from Cedartown shared one room; Frank Cheatham and John Kennedy from Savannah shared the second; and Carl shared an upstairs room with Sam Gardner of Savannah, who was one of his fraternity brothers. By studying hard and going to school the whole year without any breaks, Carl finished the three-year course of study in two years. After completing his second year of course work, he decided to take the bar exam in June of 1947. Not expecting to pass the grueling two-day exam in Atlanta, he took the exam merely for the experience. But, to his utter amazement, he passed it. Among the forty-one who passed the bar with Carl were Denmark Groover, George T. Smith, Pope McIntire, and Thomas Marshall—all of whom were destined to play prominent roles in Georgia politics.[21]

Having passed the bar exam, Carl was now confident that he could establish a practice, earn a living, and support a family. Although he and Betty had become engaged the previous November, no date had been set for the wedding. Betty had finished her degree in June, so now they set the date. They scheduled the ceremony for September 6, 1947, in the First Baptist Church in Statesboro.[22]

Betty's health was a concern that summer. She had lost weight for the Maid of Cotton contest and had not been able to regain it. After her

---

[20]Sanders, "Interviews in 1990," pp. 61-64.
[21]Ibid., pp. 49, 64-65; *Red and Black*, August 15, 1947; Sanders, "My Life," pp. 22-24; interview with Glenn York, Cedartown, Georgia, April 9, 1991.
[22]Betty Foy Sanders interview, March 25, 1991.

graduation in June she was sick with intestinal problems. She was in and out of hospitals but the doctors could not determine exactly what was wrong with her. Her mother wanted to delay the wedding until Betty's health improved, but Carl would accept no delay. He told Mrs. Foy that he wanted to get married, and if he had to he would roll Betty down the aisle in a wheel chair. Faced with such adamant resistance, Doll gave in and proceeded with the wedding plans. She took Betty to Atlanta and hired J. P. Allen & Co. to plan the wedding and Elliott's Studio to do the bridal pictures. Small towns love to entertain, and since everybody in Statesboro knew the Foys, much socializing occurred before the wedding. By September 6 Betty was frail and exhausted, but the wedding went off as scheduled.[23]

The wedding was a lovely affair and was done in all shades of pink. Betty's dress was of blush satin with a medium pink trailing spray of pink roses. The bridesmaids wore deeper faille dresses. Betty's eleven-year-old sister Teresa was the maid of honor. The groomsmen wore winter tuxedos. In planning the wedding the people from Atlanta failed to realize how hot south Georgia could be. In Statesboro it was 103 degrees on September 6, and the packed church was not air conditioned. Despite the sweltering heat, no one fainted. The ceremony went smoothly, and the radiant young couple exchanged their rings and pledged to love each other "till death do us part."[24]

---

[23]Ibid.

[24]Ibid.; undated newspaper clippings in "This Is Your Life," scrapbook, Sanders Personal Papers, Atlanta.

Right tackle Bob Sanders (number 45) and quarterback Carl Sanders (number 19), Georgia Bulldog teammates in 1945.

Lieutenant Carl Sanders.

Betty Bird Foy and Carl Sanders united in marriage, September 6, 1947.

Chapter 3

The Crisis

When two young people deeply in love get married, initially there is much joy and excitement. But along with the happiness, married life inevitably brings problems, too, as the newlyweds become adjusted to their new relationship. In the early years of their marriage Carl and Betty encountered grave problems, difficulties far more serious than the usual problems of adjustment. The problems were not their fault and they could not have been avoided, but the strain on both of them was acute nevertheless. The difficulties began almost immediately after they said, "I do."

Carl and Betty had planned to spend their honeymoon in Miami, but because of Betty's health they decided to stay closer to home. Instead of Miami, they spent a few days at the old General Oglethorpe Hotel near Savannah. Although emotionally joyous, Betty was not well physically on her honeymoon. Soon her physical condition deteriorated as her recurrent fever got worse. She lost weight and became debilitated. Her intestines were blocked. After nine days of marriage her doctor in Statesboro sent her to a hospital. She appeared to be suffering from appendicitis. Surgery removed her appendix, but her condition did not improve. Instead it got worse. The doctors were mystified. Despite running many tests, they still did not know what was wrong with her. Soon gangrene set in and her fever went to 106 degrees. Betty became delirious, drifting in and out of reality. On her sixth day in the hospital, her doctor, John Mooney, called the family in and solemnly told them he did not expect Betty to live through the night. Betty's mother was distraught. Having lost her husband at an early age, she could not bear the thought of losing Betty too. Carl, as always, remained calm and resolute. Holding Betty's hand, he put his face very close to her's to make sure she could hear him, and said quietly: "Betty, this is important. I want you to fight hard tonight. Fight very hard!" That is all Betty remembered that night. Her husband's words kept swimming through her head. She concentrated on them with all her might—"Fight very hard."[1]

The whole town of Statesboro, it seemed, was at the hospital to support the family. Betty's father had helped start the hospital and had served on the first Bulloch County Hospital Board. The hospital itself was built on Foy land near the home of Betty's grandparents. Several people had donated blood since Betty had required several transfusions. While family members and friends paced nervously in the waiting room, Carl took action. He asked Reverend Earl Serson, the preacher who had married them, if he would pray with him. In an empty hospital room they spent most of the night on their knees praying. Carl, who refused to believe that God had given Betty to him only to take her away, prayed as he had never prayed before. He prayed for a miracle. Betty made it through the night. The next morning, though weak and pasty brown in color, she was much improved. The crisis had passed. Betty, it appeared, would live. A miracle had happened. Evidently God had decided that there was more for Betty to do in this life. From that day on, both Carl and Betty have had a deeper appreciation for life itself. And neither has doubted the reality of God or the power of prayer.[2]

Although Betty was no longer at death's door, she continued to have physical problems for the next eight years. Her recovery was slow. In fact she remained in the hospital for six weeks. When she finally got out she weighed only 103 pounds, having lost twenty pounds during her ordeal. Her mother then took her home and nursed her. Carl, lacking one more quarter to graduate, had to return to Athens. By studying furiously during the week, he was able to spend the weekends with Betty in Statesboro. After Betty got stronger she traveled to Athens for visits. Despite the distractions and emotional strain, Carl completed his academic work and received his law degree as scheduled. With remarkable concentration he managed to make two grades of A and a C+ in his last quarter.[3]

[1]Sanders, "My Life," pp. 24-25; Betty Foy Sanders interview, March 25, 1991; Betty Sanders press release, July 1964 folder, Box 34, Sanders Collection, Law Library.
    [2]Ibid.
    [3]Betty Foy Sanders interview, November 7, 1990; Betty Foy Sanders interview, March 25, 1991; academic information obtained from Sanders's University of Georgia transcript, Athens.

During a break the previous summer, Carl had returned home for a few weeks and worked with C. W. Killebrew, a friend of his father, who was the City Attorney of Augusta. His office was in the Southern Finance Building on Broad Street. While working there, Carl became acquainted with other Augusta lawyers who had offices in that building. One of them was F. Frederick Kennedy, who practiced with former judge Henry C. Hammond. When Carl passed the bar exam, he contacted Kennedy about a job. Kennedy offered him a position at $150 a month, when he finished law school. Carl accepted the offer and began practicing immediately after completing his degree in December of 1947.[4]

In theory Carl was a junior partner in the firm of Hammond, Kennedy and Sanders. In reality he was an associate who spent much time in the library doing research for Fred Kennedy. In addition to assisting Kennedy, Carl tried his own cases and got to practice in all the courts in the county. Working with Kennedy and Hammond, he gained valuable experience in his profession and developed useful contacts who later would assist him in politics, but he made very little money. The first year with the firm he earned $2,400 plus a $600 bonus at the end of the year. Even with frugal living and rigid economies, it was hard to make ends meet. By living with Carl's parents Carl and Betty avoided house payments, but the medical bills piled up.[5]

After getting out of the hospital, Betty tried to function in a normal manner, but she was not well. She ran a fever constantly, had fluid in her joints, and hemorrhaged often. To keep her condition from getting any worse, she took new, expensive antibiotics. She also took iron and B-12 injections. She had seen many specialists in Statesboro and Augusta, but they had not been able to diagnose her malady. Through a family connection, she arranged to go to the Johns Hopkins University Hospital in Baltimore for further tests. Johns Hopkins was one of the most prestigious medical centers in the country, but its excellent physicians were as baffled by Betty's illness as were the Georgia doctors. They did, however, prescribe additional medicines which helped Betty to regain her strength gradually.[6]

---

[4]Sanders, "Interviews in 1990," pp. 65-66; Sanders, "My Life," pp. 25-27.
[5]Ibid.
[6]Sanders, "Interviews in 1990," p. 68; Betty Foy Sanders interview, March 25,

Carl's parents were as gracious as they could be, but two families under one roof—and not a particularly big roof at that—created problems. Despite the financial burdens, Betty and Carl decided to get a home of their own. The best accommodations they could afford were a little one-bedroom garage apartment on Williams Street. It was far from luxurious, but at least it was their own. In order to meet the additional expenses, Carl found it necessary to take a second job. After working all day in the law office, he taught law classes at the Augusta Law School, an institution operated primarily for veterans returning to school on the G. I. Bill and servicemen stationed at Fort Gordon. Carl taught corporation law, insurance, and other courses three nights a week from 9:00 to 11:00 p.m. Bolstered with an additional income of $125 a month, they managed to get by.[7]

Betty's health continued to improve as did Carl's law practice, permitting a move to more comfortable accommodations in the Forest Hills Apartments on Walton Way. The new apartment thrilled Betty. Now she had room to display some of her wedding gifts and create a more homey environment. Moreover, the apartment was located in a more fashionable neighborhood and the neighbors were friendly. Doll gave them a dining room suite and a sofa bed for the living room so that she and Teresa would have something to sleep on when they visited. Betty enjoyed meeting her new neighbors and getting to know Carl's old friends as well. She was readily accepted by the Augusta society-conscious group and was soon asked to join the Junior League. Life was looking up, but she still had fevers and knots as big as goose eggs on her arms and legs.[8]

Throughout his life Carl has possessed exceptional stamina, and he has always enjoyed remarkably good health. As a child he had a tonsillectomy, and as an adult he had hemorrhoid surgery; otherwise his body has remained intact. Once he was struck in the head by a golf ball, an injury which required medical attention, but aside from a very occasional cold, he never seemed to get sick or miss work. When he contracted

---

1991.

[7] Betty Foy Sanders interview, March 25, 1991; Sanders, "My Life," pp. 25-26.

[8] Betty Foy Sanders interview, March 25, 1991; interview with Mrs. William "Frenchie" Bush, Augusta, August 29, 1991.

pneumonia in 1991 and missed a few days of work, it was such a rare occurrence that he was utterly amazed, almost dumbfounded, that he had actually gotten ill. Thus he thrived on working days and evenings, and he still found time for many civic and religious activities.[9]

Because of Betty's chronic illness, the doctors had told her that it was very doubtful that she could ever have children. Consequently, the birth of Betty Foy Sanders on May 3, 1952, brought great joy to Carl and Betty. She was born by Caesarian section, and that is when Dr. Virgil Synstricker, chief of staff of the University of Georgia Medical School, finally discovered what was wrong with Betty. He diagnosed her malady as regional ileitis. Apparently she had contracted the disease from raw milk she drank on the farm in Statesboro. The doctors warned her that if she got pregnant again she would have to have major surgery. Soon she became pregnant again, and on October 29, 1953, Carl Edward Sanders, Jr. arrived. There would be no more children and, as the doctors had warned, major surgery was required. The doctors removed part of Betty's lower intestine. Once that was done, her health improved remarkably. No more lumps appeared. The fevers disappeared. And, most importantly, Betty finally began to feel good. It had taken eight long years, but at last she was healthy. After the operation, there was no recurrence of the regional ileitis and, generally speaking, Betty enjoyed good health from that time on.[10]

To accommodate a growing family, Carl and Betty realized they needed more space than their apartment provided. After an extensive search, they found exactly what they needed. In 1951 they bought a new house at 2212 Morningside Drive. It was only the second house constructed in the new Country Club Hills subdivision. It was a gray-painted brick ranch-style home with a black roof and white trim. Surrounded by tall pines and oaks, it was a beautiful home and a good place to raise children. Morningside Drive turned out to be a short cut to the Augusta National Country Club. Its famous golf course became President Eisenhower's favorite vacation spot, and during his presidency

---

[9]Sanders, "Story of My Life," p. 3; interview with Mrs. Benny Tackett, Atlanta, January 23, 1991.

[10]Betty Foy Sanders interview, November 7, 1990; Cook, "Sanders: An Oral History," pp. 14-16; Sanders, "Interviews in 1990," pp. 68-69.

he made twenty-eight trips there. Betty and the children often would sit on the front lawn and wave to "Ike" as he drove by. Over the years Carl and Betty got to know both Ike and Mamie quite well. By coincidence, Ike also suffered from regional ileitis and had surgery at about the same time Betty did.[11]

After Carl had been practicing law for about two years, the elderly senior partner, Judge Hammond, decided to retire. An octogenarian, he was a bachelor and a noted grower of hundreds of varieties of camellias. The firm's other partner, Fred Kennedy, a fine lawyer and a hard worker, was appointed judge of the Superior Court in 1952. Carl, feeling overworked and underpaid, used all his influence to help Kennedy secure the appointment. When Kennedy left the firm, Carl had a dilemma: should he join another law firm or should he practice on his own. Not anxious to start at the bottom of another firm, he decided to start his own firm, knowing all the risks that decision entailed. Securing a loan from a local bank, he purchased all of Kennedy's books and office furnishings. Despite the high overhead, Carl kept the office on the fourteenth floor of the Southern Finance Building.[12]

Soon two young lawyers, Bert Hester and C. B. Thurmond, both native Augustans, joined him as associates. Hester, a recent graduate of the University of Georgia law school, was then teaching law at Fort Gordon. Bert and Carl had first met as children at the YMCA. Carl, then nine years old, pushed eight-year-old Bert into the swimming pool. Naturally a fight ensued. Since they attended different schools (Bert attended Boys Catholic High School), they had not been close friends. Bert's uncle, Charley Bohler, however, was a friend of the Sanders family. An active politician, Bohler later served as tax commissioner for Richmond county. He asked Carl to give Bert a job, and Carl agreed. The other associate, Thurmond, was a cousin of Senator Strom Thurmond of South Carolina and held LL.B. and LL.M. degrees from

---

[11]Betty Foy Sanders interview, November 7, 1990; Andrew Sparks, "Hopes and Dreams of the Sanders Family," *Atlanta Journal and Constitution Magazine*, January 13, 1963, pp. 18-19, 22, 25; Edward J. Cashin, *The Story of Augusta* (Augusta: Richmond County Board of Education, 1980) p. 285.

[12]Sanders, "My Life," pp. 27-28; biographical sketch of Judge Hammond in *Augusta Chronicle*, March 6, 1960.

George Washington University. A few years older than Carl, he had recently been discharged from the Marine Corps.[13]

After a few years Carl made Hester and Thurmond partners so that they received an equal share in everything. At that time Carl was bringing in the bulk of the income, but he believed that making them partners was the way to build a successful law firm. The firm was known as Sanders, Thurmond & Hester. The order of names was based on when they passed the bar exam. A few years later Isaac "Buddy" Jolles joined the firm and the name Jolles was added to the title. Jolles's father, then a respected attorney in Augusta, was the man Carl had helped arrest for speeding when he was a schoolboy patrolman. All four of the attorneys were from Augusta, and all but Thurmond had graduated from the University of Georgia law school. In religion it was truly an ecumenical firm. Sanders was a Baptist, Thurmond an Episcopalian, Hester a Roman Catholic, and Jolles a Jew. The firm started modestly, but it had a solid foundation. From this nucleus it grew and prospered.[14]

---

[13]Undated newspaper clipping in "This Is Your Life," Sanders Personal Papers; Sanders, "My Life," pp. 28-29; interview with Bert Hester, Atlanta, June 5, 1991.

[14]Hester interview, June 5, 1991; Sanders, "My Life," pp. 28-29.

The Sanders home at 2212 Morningside Drive, Augusta.

Chapter 4

Politics Beckons

By Georgia standards Augusta is an old city. Originally established in the 1730s as an outpost for trading with Indians, the town was laid out by George Walton and incorporated in 1789. Located on the Savannah River 110 miles north of Savannah at the fall line, the town grew slowly but steadily in the 19th century. The river, which provided the best means of transportation until railroads were built in the 1830s, was a mixed blessing. Periodically it flooded and inundated much of the city. Serious floods occurred in 1840, 1888, 1908, and 1911. To protect the city from floods a levee was completed in 1919 at a staggering cost of over $2 million, but it was unable to stop the monstrous flood of 1927 when a wall of water forty-six feet high descended upon the city. Flooding remained a problem until the massive Clarks Hill dam, spanning 5,860 feet and measuring 351 feet in height, was built after World War II.[1]

Like most Georgia towns, Augusta had a large black population. The census of 1950 counted 29,518 nonwhites among the city's total population of 71,508. In Richmond county as a whole, blacks constituted approximately one-third of the total population of 108,876.[2] Augusta had more ethnic diversity than is ordinarily found in most Southern towns. A large Irish population had resided there since the early 19th century, and later substantial numbers of Chinese and Greeks arrived. Augusta was exceptional also in having Republican leadership in the Reconstruction era. Georgia's first and last Republican governors, Rufus Bullock and Benjamin Conley, both resided in Augusta.[3]

---

[1]Cashin, *Story of Augusta*, pp. 44, 86, 170, 199, 210, 224, 239, 270-71; Kenneth Coleman, ed., *A History of Georgia* (Athens: University of Georgia Press) pp. 40-42.

[2]Cashin, *Story of Augusta*, appendixes B and C.

[3]Ibid., pp. 106, 139, 150; James F. Cook, *Governors of Georgia* (Huntsville AL:

The Cracker party, an organization resembling on a smaller scale Boss Tweed's notorious Tammany Hall organization in New York City, controlled Augusta politically in the 1930s and 1940s. Catering to working class whites, the Crackers dispensed jobs and services to the faithful. The Cracker policy, as a critical study report put it, was: "Do small favors to as many individuals as possible." Those favors included adjustment of water bills, cancelation of taxes, and reduction of court sentences. The Crackers remained in power, despite the protests of middle and upper class people who considered the system wasteful, inefficient, and corrupt, by providing access to government to their followers, maintaining personal contacts, and controlling the voter lists for the Democratic party primary. As long as the Crackers controlled the voting system, critics could do little. Voter registration remained extremely low, even by Georgia standards, as only fourteen percent registered to vote in the mid-1940s. By maintaining 3,500 votes the Cracker party could control the key positions of mayor and city council. Since many dead and departed citizens frequently cast votes for Cracker candidates, they won elections with ease. Consequently, the few reformers who challenged the Crackers had nothing but frustration to show for their efforts. Not surprisingly, public apathy prevailed.[4]

When the United States Supreme Court ruled the white primary unconstitutional in the *Smith v. Allright* decision in 1944, the Crackers faced a new challenge. Encouraged by the decision, the opponents of the Crackers began to take action. The Junior Chamber of Commerce began a voter registration drive which the Augusta newspapers endorsed heartily. The League of Women Voters joined in the drive, and 3,045 whites and 1,822 blacks became eligible voters during the period December 1, 1945, to March 10, 1946. On March 31, 1946, a newly formed organization, the "Independent League for Good Government," announced a slate of candidates for the state legislature and the county commission. With blacks voting for the first time, a record number of voters turned out. All of the Independent candidates swept into office.

Strode Publishers, 1979) pp. 166-72.

[4]Cashin, *Story of Augusta*, pp. 251-67; Earl L. Bell and Kenneth C. Crabbe, *The Augusta Chronicle: Indomitable Voice of Dixie, 1785–1960* (Athens: University of Georgia Press, 1960) pp. 174-81.

Even Roy Harris, an Augusta attorney and the Crackers' most outstanding leader who seemed to be in line for the governorship, suffered defeat. William Morris, publisher of the *Augusta Chronicle* and member of the Board of Regents of the University System of Georgia, defeated him by 4,855 votes. The Independent victory was a historic election for Augusta, but it was a short-lived triumph. Far from finished, the Crackers recovered quickly and soon became the dominant force in Augusta politics once again. The Independent movement had made a start, but it would take a few more years before the advocates of good government, expansion of city services, and economic growth could obtain enough public support to displace the Cracker machine.[5]

Typical of those drawn to the Crackers was Carl's father. As a meat salesman struggling to make ends meet, he found it helpful to know those in power. After all, a number of city and county agencies bought meat. By developing proper connections with those in power, he hoped to entice those agencies to buy Swift meat from him. Probably no local agency purchased more meat than the University Hospital. As a member of the Hospital Authority, the elder Sanders made a motion to fire the head dietician and replace her with a young, inexperienced college graduate. The motion passed. Critics charged that the dietician lost her job solely because she refused to purchase Swift chickens. A controversy ensued as four other dieticians resigned in protest, as did the new dietician promoted by Sanders's motion, and the superintendent of the hospital, Dr. W. H. Goodrich. Despite threats of moving the Medical College out of Augusta because of the political interference, the Crackers backed Sanders and weathered the storm. As a Cracker stalwart, Sanders later served a term on the county commission.[6]

In contrast to his father, Carl showed little interest in politics. At the University of Georgia many of his classmates, by actively participating in student politics, already had laid a foundation for future political careers. But Carl was so busy with other things that he never considered politics as a vocation. After settling in Augusta and establishing his law

---

[5]Ibid.; James C. Cobb, "Politics in a New South City: Augusta, Georgia, 1946–1971" (Ph.D. diss., University of Georgia, 1975) pp. 30-48; Cobb, "Colonel Effingham Crushes the Crackers: Political Reform in Postwar Augusta," *South Atlantic Quarterly* 79 (Autumn 1979): 507-19.

[6]Cashin, *Story of Augusta*, pp. 262-63.

firm, he became very active in civic affairs. He served on the boards of
the Augusta YMCA, American Red Cross, and the Augusta Community
Chest. He served on the executive committee of the Georgia-Carolina
Boy Scout Council, joined the Augusta Exchange Club, chaired the
Richmond County University of Georgia Foundation Drive, and actively
participated in the Georgia Bar Association. He also served as a deacon
at Hill Baptist Church and taught an adult Sunday school class there for
many years.[7]

That Carl had excellent credentials and would make an appealing
candidate for public office was obvious to Joe Cummings, Sr., an
Augusta attorney and leader of the Independent party. In 1954, when
John C. Bell, one of the local state representatives, relinquished his
position to run for Superior Court judge, Cummings decided that Carl
would be the best man to replace Bell in the state legislature. He dispatched a group of Carl's friends to convince him to become a candidate. The offer surprised and flattered Carl. Intrigued by the prospect of
holding public office, he refused to run, however, without first securing
Betty's support. And he knew she had good reasons to object. Having
endured physical problems for eight years and now with two small
children to rear, she looked forward to a more normal family life without the complications of a political career. Realizing that if Carl won the
election, he would spend six weeks in Atlanta each year in addition to
all the campaigning, she wondered when she would see him. But Betty
also knew her husband. She understood how he loved competition and
how he thrived on new challenges. After considering the matter carefully,
she concluded that Carl really wanted to run. Unwilling to stifle him,
she put her own desires aside and reluctantly agreed for him to become
a candidate. Carl's opponent was R. W. "Billy" Barton, an attorney he
had known for many years. In a hotly contested race, Carl not only won
handily, he also led the ticket in balloting, thus proving that Joe
Cummings was a shrewd judge of political talent.[8]

---

[7]Sanders, "Interviews in 1990," pp. 47-49, 52-56; undated newspaper clippings in
"This Is Your Life"; *Augusta Herald*, November 25, 1957.

[8]Sanders, "Interviews in 1990," pp. 69-70; Cook, "Sanders: An Oral History," pp.
16-17.

Carl had campaigned hard in this race, as he would do in all his political campaigns, but other factors contributed to his impressive victory. In local elections of this type, issues are sometimes less important than image and name recognition. And Carl presented a very appealing image. Young, handsome, intelligent, athletic, he seemed to be the All-American boy. His athletic accomplishments, especially in football, and his military service reinforced that image. Having practiced law for nearly seven years and having started his own firm, he was a successful professional, a local boy who had done well. Growing up in Augusta was another asset. Friends and neighbors he had grown up with remembered him and voted for him. His active civic involvement enlarged that circle of friends and gave him contacts with key community leaders. His law practice brought him into frequent contact with the courthouse folks whose support is vital in a campaign. His father, who knew almost everyone in Augusta, especially political types, campaigned tirelessly for his son, even though he was a Cracker and Carl ran as an Independent. In this initial campaign, Carl had not yet mastered all of the nuances of political speaking and campaigning, but he was articulate, smiled easily, and learned quickly. Finally, no one dressed more stylishly nor campaigned harder. Thus he presented an attractive, clean-cut image, possessed substantial name recognition for a political novice, and was acquainted with many of the power brokers in town. Having so many political assets and no major liabilities, it seemed almost inevitable that he would embark on a career of public service with his initial election in 1954.[9]

Always eager to accept new challenges, Carl found that representing the people of Richmond county in the Georgia House of Representatives was challenging indeed. With 205 members the House was a large, unwieldy body. When Carl arrived no women or blacks served in its ranks and very few Republicans. Since Reconstruction, Georgia consistently voted for the Democratic candidate for president and probably reigned as the most solidly Democratic state in the country. Power continued to rest predominantly with the rural counties, as it had for decades. Since representation was based more on geography than population, the urban counties were grossly underrepresented. House,

---

[9]Sanders, "Interviews in 1990," pp. 69-70.

Senate, and congressional districts were terribly malapportioned and the General Assembly showed little interest in changing them. The prevailing political doctrine held that each of Georgia's 159 counties ought to have at least one representative in the House and the larger counties should have more. Thus 121 rural counties had one representative each, the 30 larger ones had two, and the 8 urban counties had three. Richmond county was in the latter category, and in addition to Carl the county delegation included Lee Chambers, an attorney, and Bill Holley, head of the carpenters union.[10]

Freshman legislators normally exert very little influence in the Georgia General Assembly. The more experienced legislators, accustomed to dominating the proceedings, expected newcomers to remain silent. Actually only a handful of the 205 representatives had much influence in the legislative process, as the governor and his handpicked leaders and committee chairmen ran the show. Since taxes were low and state services minimal, few demands were placed on the individual members. Consequently, for many of the legislators the forty-day session was primarily a time of socializing and taking in the night spots of Atlanta. The legislative session offered a diversion from their drab and prosaic lives. While conducting the affairs of state, plenty of time remained for drinking and partying. One of the more popular diversions was raffling off a prostitute on Sunday evenings at the Henry Grady Hotel. Informality prevailed on the floor of the House. Local delegations and friends of legislators frequently wandered around the legislative chambers while members voted on bills and speakers held forth at the podium. While lawmakers transacted the state's business, some members read newspapers, others chatted with constituents or lobbyists, and others gossiped and repeated the latest joke they had heard. In this pretelevision age, a circus atmosphere oftentimes prevailed as some members enjoyed propping their

---

[10]For general background on Georgia politics, see Coleman, *A History of Georgia*; Cook, *Governors of Georgia*; Numan V. Bartley, *The Creation of Modern Georgia* (Athens: University of Georgia Press, 1983); Harold P. Henderson and Gary L. Roberts, eds., *Georgia Governors in an Age of Change: From Ellis Arnall to George Busbee* (Athens: University of Georgia Press, 1988); Joseph L. Bernd, "Georgia, Static and Dynamic," in *The Changing Politics of the South*, ed. William C. Havard (Baton Rouge: Louisiana State University Press, 1972) pp. 294-365; Neal R. Peirce, *The Deep South States of America* (New York: W. W. Norton and Co., 1974).

feet on their desks, eating peanuts, and flipping the shells on the carpet.[11]

Urbane and immaculately dressed, Carl broke the mold of the typical Georgia legislator. He was not a farmer, and never attempted to look or sound like one. Rather formal and dignified in bearing, his appearance set him apart from the crowd. His political views also made him stand out. Like most southerners, he appreciated traditions and held many conservative views. But he was also a strong believer in efficiency and economy in public affairs and was appalled by the waste and duplication in Georgia's government. From experience and observation he knew that Georgia's system of public education desperately needed improvement. For the state to grow economically and for the people to be prepared for the modern era, Georgia must have better schools, he concluded. It was also apparent that the criminal justice system and the state's highways and airports left much to be desired. Though aware that many changes were needed in state government, Carl did not propose radical changes. Instead he worked quietly within the system. Instinctively he realized that political power rested with the leaders, and only by operating from a position of leadership could he hope to bring about substantial change in the system. To move up the ladder to leadership he had to master the details of the legislative process by serving effectively on committees and becoming friends with as many legislators as possible. Acquiring more contacts and name recognition through frequent speeches to civic and religious groups would also enhance his political standing. By working furiously he accomplished all of these things in short order. His first term in the legislature was a successful learning experience in which he laid a solid foundation for future leadership in state government.[12]

Sanders worked harmoniously with Bill Holley and Lee Chambers, his two colleagues from Richmond county in the House, and together they secured passage of seven local bills. The *Augusta Chronicle-Herald* praised the delegation for its "commendable record" and for exhibiting "an admirable degree of independence" from Governor Marvin Griffin. More important than any of the local bills, however, was Sanders's work in securing a college for Augusta. Establishing a four-year college in

---

[11]Interview with John Harper, Atlanta, May 7, 1991; interview with Roy V. Harris, Augusta, April 10, 1970

[12]Sanders, "Interviews in 1990," pp. 70-72; Sanders, "My Life," pp. 29-30.

Augusta became his "pet project." Since the federal government was in the process of abandoning the Augusta Arsenal, a seventy-two-acre facility that had been in continuous use since 1827, Sanders saw a great opportunity for the community to acquire the property and develop a college. In numerous speeches and articles, he attempted to mobilize public support for the project by pointing out the educational, economic, and cultural advantages a college would provide and explaining that under federal law the city of Augusta or the state of Georgia could acquire the property "at practically no cost." Waxing eloquent, he maintained that the beautifully landscaped arsenal property, located in the Hill Section of Augusta, was such an ideal setting for a college "it has few equals anywhere in this section of the nation."[13]

The first step toward achieving his goal was reached in February 1957 when the Richmond County Board of Education received the deeds to thirty-eight acres of the Augusta Arsenal property, along with forty buildings, to be used as a new home for a junior college. Sanders received a resolution of thanks from the Board for his "unselfish devotion to the project" and a personal commendation from Roy Rollins, Superintendent of Schools. The Augusta Junior College, which was moved to that property, eventually developed into the four-year institution Sanders had envisaged. Sanders's work in securing the Augusta Arsenal property, in addition to his "natural leadership" in church and civic affairs, was one of the reasons the Augusta Junior Chamber of Commerce named him "Young Man of the Year" for 1955.[14]

Sanders resided in the 18th Senatorial District which included Richmond, Jefferson, and Glascock counties. Traditionally the seat rotated among the three counties every two years. In 1956 the seat was scheduled to go to Richmond county. In Georgia's legislature a senate seat is more prestigious and powerful than a house seat because there were only 54 senators compared to 205 representatives. Having made a name for himself as a promising legislator, Carl naturally became a candidate for the Senate. His hard work as a representative paid imme-

---

[13]Undated newspaper clippings in "This Is Your Life."

[14]Ibid.; *Augusta Chronicle*, January 25, November 27, 1956; Roy E. Rollins to Carl E. Sanders, February 13, 1957, "This Is Your Life."

diate dividends when no one ran against him. Thus, after one term in the House, he advanced to the Senate.[15]

Lieutenant Governor Ernest Vandiver, a lawyer and a graduate of the University of Georgia, presided over the Senate. Closely aligned with both of Georgia's United States senators, he had served as Senator Herman Talmadge's adjutant general during Talmadge's gubernatorial term from 1949 to 1955, and his wife was the niece of Richard Russell, Georgia's senior senator and one of the most powerful leaders in Washington. Temperamentally Vandiver was quiet and mild mannered, politically he was moderately conservative. Clearly a man of integrity, he pursued honesty and frugality in government with a passion.[16]

In many ways Vandiver was the antithesis of the governor, Marvin Griffin of Bainbridge. A gifted storyteller and raconteur, Griffin had few equals as a stump speaker. A newspaperman by profession, his humorous and friendly personality was so engaging and likeable it was difficult to resist him. Like Vandiver, he had close ties with Talmadge, having served as the latter's lieutenant governor from 1949 to 1955. An outspoken segregationist determined to maintain white supremacy and rigid racial segregation, Griffin was equally committed to rural domination of state government. Such policies endeared him to the courthouse crowds, especially in south Georgia. As one of the "good ole boys," he had no desire to change the system. On the contrary, he was quite comfortable with the status quo and its rule of the rustics. Although never convicted of wrongdoing himself, his lax and careless administration allowed corruption to flourish all around him. Robert Dubay, Griffin's most thorough biographer, concludes "the Griffin regime is fully deserving of its reputation as one of the most corrupt, amoral, mismanaged, and inefficient administrations in Georgia history."[17]

---

[15]Cook, "Sanders: An Oral History," pp. 19-20; undated newspaper clippings in "This Is Your Life."

[16]Mary Givens Bryan, comp., *Georgia's Official and Statistical Register, 1959–1960* (Atlanta: Georgia Department of Archives and History, 1961) p. 32; Charles Pyles, "S. Ernest Vandiver and the Politics of Change," in *Georgia Governors in an Age of Change*, pp. 143-56.

[17]Robert Dubay, "Marvin Griffin and the Politics of the Stump," in *Georgia Governors in an Age of Change*, pp. 101-12.

Sanders never supported Griffin. Indeed he found his policies repugnant and believed his leadership thwarted progress for the state. While consistently opposing Griffin, Carl was not a member of any political faction, including those identifed with Talmadge, Russell, and Ellis Arnall. He was truly an independent. Unencumbered by any alliances, he studied each issue that came before the legislature, made up his own mind about it, and took whatever action he deemed appropriate. It was soon apparent, however, that his views usually coincided with the views of Lieutenant Governor Vandiver.[18]

In the General Assembly, much of the legislative decision making takes place in the committees. Since committee chairmen wield considerable power, those positions were highly sought after. As an indication of Sanders's rapid rise in stature, as well as his growing friendship with Vandiver, he was appointed chairman of the Defense and Veterans Affairs Committee. Previously this committee had been known primarily for its obscurity, but under Carl's leadership it became newsworthy. What thrust the committee into the limelight was the death of a National Guard pilot who crashed his old F-80 fighter. As a result of his death, all fifty-five jet planes of the Georgia Air National Guard were grounded and an investigation ensued.[19]

As head of the Senate-House committee probe, Sanders took full advantage of his opportunity. He accused Washington of considering "Georgia boys more expendable" than regular Air Force personnel. The Defense Department's failure to furnish the Guard with "safe and adequate aircraft," he continued, had made it impossible for the Georgia fliers to carry out their mission to protect Georgia and the surrounding area. The Air National Guard is charged with the same mission as the regular Air Force, he pointed out, but "right now we'd be sitting ducks in case of enemy attack." Such rhetoric attracted attention both in Georgia and in Washington. Since Richard Russell of Winder chaired the Senate Armed Forces Committee and Carl Vinson of Milledgeville chaired the House Armed Forces Committee, Georgians exerted extraordinary influence on military decisions in Washington. By conducting a

---

[18]Sanders, "Interviews in 1990," pp. 71-77; Doug Barnard interview, February 16, 1991; interview with George T. Smith, Atlanta, April 18, 1991.

[19]Sanders, "Interviews in 1990," pp. 71-77.

lengthy hearing which included testimony from Adjutant General George Hearn, Brigadier General Homer Flynn, and many others, Carl had made a name for himself. And, he got what he was after—a fleet of fifty new F84F Thunderstreak jets for the Georgia Air National Guard.[20]

In 1958, with the gubernatorial election looming in the fall, Governor Griffin proposed adding $50 million to the Rural Roads Authority. Since the money would be dispensed by local county commissions, critics viewed the proposal as an attempt to buy votes for Griffin's hand-picked successor, Roger Lawson, former chairman of both the Rural Roads Authority and the State Highway Board. The measure was introduced in the House and assigned to the State of the Republic Committee, which was dominated by Griffin supporters. Vandiver, who also was a candidate for governor, saw the measure as a "slush fund" for his opponent. He opposed it vigorously and used all his power to defeat it in the Senate.[21]

The legislative debate over the Rural Roads issue continued for weeks and Sanders, working closely with Vandiver in opposition to the appropriation, received much praise for his efforts. As chairman of the Senate committee investigating the Rural Roads Authority, he had a forum for expressing his views. Favoring the construction of roads on a pay-as-you-go basis, he charged that the Rural Roads Authority was wasteful, inefficient, and impractical. He claimed that the costs had skyrocketed from $12,313 a mile in 1955 to $44,000 a mile under the latest phase of the program three years later. Moreover, in Richmond county the priorities had been shifted. A road which had been at the bottom of the list, he discovered, was now to be paved at a cost of $112,800 under the latest bond issue. The priority had shifted, he said, for "reasons unknown to me." The report his committee delivered to the legislature revealed shocking irregularities in the Rural Roads Authority. Calling for the abolition of the Authority, it pointed out that funds had been distributed "indiscriminately," that construction costs were "excessive," and that many roads had disintegrated before they were paid for and

---

[20]Ibid.; undated newspaper clippings in "This Is Your Life"; *Atlanta Journal*, January 29, 30, 1957.

[21]S. Ernest Vandiver, "Vandiver Takes the Middle Road," in *Georgia Governors in an Age of Change*, pp. 157-58.

others were built to serve a "privileged few." The Augusta newspapers commended Sanders's committee for exposing the "first-class boondoggle." With the public aroused by the Sanders probe, the House denied Griffin's proposed rural roads expansion. Lawson then withdrew his candidacy. Essentially, that vote by the House decided the election for governor.[22]

As soon as the 1958 legislative session ended, Carl began to campaign for reelection. Although the Senate seat was scheduled to rotate, no one from Jefferson county emerged to challenge him. His chief opponent was state Representative Bernard Miles, candidate of the Cracker machine. An avid Griffin backer and a strong supporter of the Rural Roads Authority, Miles worked as an inspector for the Highway Department. Since Sanders was an outspoken critic of the Griffin administration and had accused Miles of altering maps and documents to get a particular road paved, the voters had a choice of contrasting candidates. In a hotly contested race Sanders swamped Miles 10,991 to 6,854. Although local issues and personalities were involved, many observers viewed the race as a repudiation of the Griffin administration. Vandiver, who appreciated Sanders's work in the legislature, seemed to share that perception of the race. A week before the Democratic primary election, he made a "nonpolitical" speech to an Augusta civic club. Vandiver's visit clearly aided Sanders's candidacy, which undoubtedly was the lieutenant governor's intention. The Cracker party, still a powerful force in Augusta politics, won four of the six contested positions. Aside from Sanders, the only other victor among the Independents was Representative J. B. Fuqua, who won reelection over a Griffin supporter. Fuqua was one of Sanders's closest friends and business associates. In 1956 they, along with five other investors, started the United States Guaranty Life Insurance Company of Augusta, which grew very rapidly. Sanders was chairman of the board a few years later when it merged with Piedmont Life Insurance Company of Atlanta.[23]

---

[22]*Augusta Chronicle*, January 28, 1958; *Augusta Herald*, January 29, February 20, 1958; Cook, "Sanders: An Oral History," p. 20.

[23]*Atlanta Constitution*, May 16, 1958; undated newspaper clippings in "This Is Your Life."

In the 1958 Democratic primary Ernest Vandiver won an overwhelming victory over Reverend William Bodenhamer, a Baptist minister, whose impact upon Georgia politics was negligible before the election and nonexistent after it. Vandiver carried all but three of the state's 159 counties. The governor-elect, only forty years old, resided in Lavonia, a small town in the northeastern part of the state. He held an LL.B. degree from the University of Georgia, as did the new lieutenant governor, Garland Byrd. Serving as the governor's executive secretary was Peter Zack Geer, a thirty-one-year-old attorney from Colquitt. The new head of the Department of Revenue was Dixon Oxford, a forty-four-year-old businessman-farmer from Dawson. Respected banker William R. Bowdoin, senior vice president of the Trust Company of Georgia, was placed in charge of the Purchasing Department. As a resident of Atlanta, he was one of the few urbanites among the leaders of the Vandiver administration. The most experienced of Vandiver's appointees was James L. Gillis, who was chairman of the Highway Board. Vandiver chose Sanders's close friend William Trotter, a thirty-nine-year-old LaGrange attorney and experienced legislator, to head the Department of Public Safety. He earned his law degree at the University of Georgia as did Robert Jordan of Talbotton, the president pro tem of the Senate, who was a classmate of Vandiver. The key leaders in the House were the speaker, George L. Smith of Swainsboro, and the floor leader, Frank Twitty of Camilla. Rounding out this distinguished group of administrative leaders was another urbanite, Carl Sanders, who was named floor leader in the Senate. Under Governor Vandiver, a new, younger generation assumed political power in Georgia.[24]

The title floor leader is not particularly glamorous, but it meant that in the Senate Sanders would be the governor's eyes, ears, and voice. The floor leader makes more motions, does more talking and listening, and attends more committee meetings than any of his colleagues. As the designated spokesman for the administration, the success or failure of the administration's legislative program depended to a large extent on his political skill. To do the job properly, the floor leader had to have a thorough knowledge of parliamentary rules and procedures and an

---

[24]Vandiver, "Vandiver Takes the Middle Road," pp. 158-59; *Atlanta Journal*, January 17, 1959.

awareness of all pending legislation. Each day the floor leader established the order of business for the day. He introduced legislation, explained it to the members, and answered any questions they might ask. Needless to say, it was a physically demanding job. During the legislative session, Sanders's typical day began at 7:30 with breakfast with a legislator or administrative leader. Meetings and various responsibilities kept him busy all day and well into the evening hours. His work finally ended around 11:00. In addition to his duties as floor leader, Sanders served on the Banking and Finance Committee, the Interstate Cooperative Council of State Government Committee, and was vice chairman of the powerful Rules Committee. He also was named to a new Governmental Operations Committee, which was established to recommend ways the General Assembly could have a greater voice in the preparation of state budgets and the expenditure of tax revenues. Such assignments clearly indicate that Governor Vandiver placed considerable confidence in the abilties of the young senator from the 18th District.[25]

Prior to Vandiver's inauguration as governor, the issue of honesty and integrity erupted, creating a crisis of confidence. Governor Griffin's state revenue commissioner was indicted, and a judge demanded the purchasing records of seven state departments for presentment to a grand jury. Irregularities were uncovered in the education and highway departments, and the state treasurer disclosed that state spending was exceeding income by $12 million a year. It was in this troubled environment that Vandiver took office.[26]

Aware that there was much waste, inefficiency, and corruption in Georgia's government, Vandiver, as lieutenant governor, had appointed a special committee to study the system and propose remedies. Known as the Watch Dog Committee of the Senate, it was headed by Senator Bill Trotter of LaGrange. One of its active members was Carl Sanders. As Vandiver's administration was getting underway, the Watch Dog Committee made its report. It proposed abolishing many agencies,

---

[25]Undated newspaper clippings in "This Is Your Life"; *Augusta Chronicle*, January 10, 25, 1959.

[26]Dubay, "Marvin Griffin and the Politics of the Stump," p. 108; Pyles, "Vandiver and the Politics of Change," p. 147; Lester Velie, "Strange Case of the Country Slickers vs. the City Rubes," *Reader's Digest* 76 (April 1960): 108-12.

including the State Parks Authority, Veterans Resettlement Corporation, Georgia Recreation Commission, and the State Library Committee. It recommended combining many other agencies to achieve greater efficiency. In general, the committee found that state government had grown so large and complex that the problems were beyond the limited time and powers of the committee. To do the job in a more thorough and systematic manner it proposed the creation of a "Governor's Committee on Economy and Reorganization."[27]

Armed with such recommendations, Vandiver was determined to streamline Georgia's government and straighten out its fiscal affairs. Pursuing economy with a vengeance, he immediately ordered most of the state departments and agencies to reduce their expenditures by ten percent. On his first day in office, Revenue Commissioner Dixon Oxford removed 216 employees from the departmental payroll. By such forceful actions, the new administration demonstrated emphatically that it meant business. Economy and frugality in government would characterize Vandiver's four years as governor.[28]

In addition to honesty and efficiency in government, the Vandiver administration also devoted considerable effort to preserving segregation of races in Georgia's schools and colleges. The prospect of integration became a very real possibility when United States District Judge Boyd Sloan ruled on January 10, 1959, four days before Vandiver's inauguration, that the Georgia State College of Business Administration in Atlanta could not deny admission of Negroes on the basis of race and color alone. The decision did not order the admission of the plaintiffs—three Negro women—to the Atlanta school. It did, however, clear the way for the women to seek admission. It also struck down a key regulation of the University System for maintaining segregation; namely, a requirement that applications must be endorsed by alumni of the institution to which they sought admission. In invalidating the requirement, Judge Sloan pointed out that since there were no Negro alumni of any of the white institutions of the University System of Georgia, the

---

[27]Undated clippings in "This Is Your Life"; *Augusta Chronicle*, January 9, 1959.

[28]*Augusta Chronicle*, January 15, 1959; interview with Henry Neal, Atlanta, August 28, 1985.

requirement "upon Negroes has been, is, and will be, to prevent Negroes from meeting this admission requirement."[29]

Judge Sloan's ruling produced a predictable reaction. In Washington Senator Talmadge expressed regret at the ruling and Senator Russell called the decision "shocking." In a prepared statement Vandiver referred to the decision as "regrettable." [30]Since the entire General Assembly professed belief in segregation, it was obvious that new measures would be adopted in the forthcoming session to prevent any integration of the state's colleges. Closing the schools altogether rather than allowing racial integration was a distinct possibility. What the Vandiver administration hoped to do, however, was pass legislation that would ensure maintenance of totally segregated units while satisfying federal courts. As soon as the session began, new bills to accomplish that goal were placed on the docket. In the Senate four measures gained quick approval—three unanimously and the other by vote of 52 to 2. These bills authorized the governor to close a single school ordered integrated instead of closing the entire school district; permitted the governor to close any unit of the University System; set an age limit for students entering college; and allowed the state to hire and pay counsel needed in school integration suits. At the same time the House passed an administration measure 186 to 5 to prohibit independent school systems from levying taxes to operate integrated schools.[31]

A week into the legislative session it was apparent that both the Vandiver leadership team and the legislative program were extremely popular with the members of the General Assembly. Speaker of the House George L. Smith, then in his fifteenth year in the General Assembly, remarked that it was "the best first week since I've been here." Representative J. B. Fuqua of Augusta called the Vandiver program "some of the most constructive legislation in the history of Georgia." Floor Leader Sanders agreed with his friend Fuqua and commented that "everything has gone very well."[32]

---

[29]*Augusta Chronicle-Herald,* January 11, 1959.
[30]Ibid.
[31]*Augusta Chronicle,* January 13, 16, 21, 1959.
[32]Ibid., January 18, 1959.

Everything continued to go well throughout the session as the General Assembly gave rubber stamp approval to the administration's legislative program. The most important new law was the honesty in government bill, which provided stiff prison terms for influence peddling, giving or receiving kickbacks or bribes, and other unethical practices in connection with state business. Vandiver, a staunch segregationist, was pleased with the package of bills designed to uphold segregation. The only segregation bill that aroused any opposition—and it turned out to be minor—was one setting a maximum age for admission to undergraduate programs at twenty-one and to graduate programs at twenty-five. It was adopted because the plaintiffs in college segregation suits had been over those age limits. In the interest of economy and efficiency, a number of bills were passed consolidating or abolishing several minor agencies. To continue such efforts, a committee on governmental reorganization was created to recommend major reorganization to the 1960 General Assembly. All in all it was a harmonious and generally productive session. So completely had controversy been avoided that many veteran legislators and newsmen thought it was the dullest session in years. The only administration bill the legislature rejected was the so-called "Bug" racket bill, which would make mandatory a maximum jail sentence for a second conviction on a lottery charge. Sanders had steered the bill through the Senate 41 to 0, but the House adjourned before voting on it. Vandiver, very angry over the House's inaction, promised to offer the bill again in the next session.[33]

Shortly before the legislature adjourned, Robert Jordan, president pro tem of the Senate, gave up his position in order to become a member of the State Highway Board. Lieutenant Governor Byrd accepted his letter of resignation with regret. To replace Jordan as the number two man in the Senate, Senator John Greer of Lakeland nominated Senator Carl Sanders. The Augustan, he said, was a leader "who has endeared himself to this body." Senator W. J. Crowe of Sylvester and Senator Charles Brown of Atlanta made seconding speeches, after which nominations closed. The Senate then gave Sanders a standing ovation following his unanimous election.[34]

---

[33]Ibid., February 21, 22, 1959.
[34]Ibid.; *Atlanta Journal,* February 20, 1959.

Sanders's rise to political prominence had been little short of phenomenal. Less than five years after entering the House as a little-known freshman, he systematically had advanced to the Senate and to the key positions of leadership—first floor leader and then president pro tem. At age thirty-three and in only his third legislative term, Sanders had become the second most powerful leader in the Senate, outranked only by the lieutenant governor. In rising so rapidly, Sanders clearly possessed unusual political skills. Mastering the legislative process and the details of government came to him quickly and easily. Many observers noted his uncanny ability to grasp almost instantly the complexities of bills. He could analyze provisions of proposed legislation systematically and then discuss their implications with his colleagues. Since few legislators had this ability, many soon looked to him for guidance. His incredible energy and stamina enabled him to work long hours day after day without ill effects. Few of his colleagues had the ability or the desire to put as much effort into the job as he did. Other legislators admired his work ethic, trusted his judgment, and willingly accepted him as a leader. Understanding the rules of the General Assembly and the intricacies of legislation would not have thrust Sanders to the forefront unless he also could get along with other legislators. Somewhat reserved, introspective, and aloof by nature, Sanders would never be a backslapper or a great storyteller like Marvin Griffin, but he trained himself to be more outgoing and friendly. By working cooperatively with others he gained their friendship and respect. Leadership came to Sanders instinctively, and when placed in authority in committees and later as floor leader he clearly was in charge but never became a tyrant. Avoiding threats and insults, he attempted to sway his colleagues with logic and persuasion, and his soft, mellifluous voice with its pleasant southern accent could be very convincing and ingratiating. After proving himself at the lower levels of power, Sanders gained the confidence of the Senate, which then entrusted him with more power. Finally, his political views were close enough to the mainstream of the General Assembly that the rank and file trusted his judgment and believed he would uphold southern traditions and the southern way of life. The main issues Vandiver stressed—honesty, efficiency, and economic growth—were issues Sanders was keenly interested in. Since their views coincided on many points, he supported Vandiver enthusiastically, and Vandiver found in Sanders an able lieutenant who could be trusted with increasingly important responsibilities.[35]

---

[35]Sanders, "Interviews in 1990," pp. 76-87; Barnard interview, February 16, 1991; George T. Smith interview, April 18, 1991; telephone interview with Ernest Vandiver, August 26, 1991.

Chapter 5

The Integration Crisis

Throughout his political career Carl Sanders seemed to lead a charmed life. Things fell into place for him as if fate had ordained his success. Invariably, he appeared in the right place at the right time. Consequently, his advancement to positions of leadership had been smooth and rapid. Whether his political rise resulted from fate, hard work, or "luck," as many observers described it, is debatable. But his career certainly benefitted from many fortuitous events, and none was more helpful than the 1960 Senate race.

Under the existing system of rotation, it was virtually impossible for a senator to remain in office long enough to amass much political clout. Only the senator from Fulton county could succeed himself; all the others had rotating districts. Thus the Senate was a lame duck body on the day it was elected, and the House, where seniority prevailed, usually overshadowed it. Sanders had been extremely fortunate when Jefferson county supported him and allowed him to serve a second consecutive term. In 1960, when the Senate seat rotated to Glascock county, it appeared that Sanders would have to relinquish his Senate seat and with it his position as president pro tem and run for a seat in the House. Late in October 1959 the Glascock County Democratic Executive Committee met. The chairman of the committee was E. E. Griffin, a friend of Sanders. In deference to Sanders, and with Griffin's prodding, the committee waived its right to nominate a senator. This tradition-shattering decision, enabled Sanders to serve a third consecutive term in the Senate. Since a completely new Senate, except for the Fulton district, normally was elected every two years, his seniority was exceptional. His reelection without opposition meant he not only retained his Senate seat and his position as president pro tem, but he also was in line for the lieutenant governorship in 1962. Governor Vandiver, Lieutenant Governor Byrd, and most of the press praised the Glascock county decision. In commending the Glascock committee, the *Atlanta Constitution* observed that the decision was "a fine example of common sense." Sanders later acknowledged the impact of the decision by observing "If E. E. Griffin hadn't done what he did, I wouldn't have been governor of Georgia."[1]

The 1960 legislative session, like its predecessor, was completely dominated by the Vandiver administration. On the whole, it was a rather uneventful session. Vandiver stressed economy and reorganization and no new taxes, and got from the legislature virtually everything he asked for. The most important bill adopted was the Withholding Act. It deducted state taxes from the paychecks of every worker in Georgia and was expected to produce $2 million in revenue. The state's mental health program was thoroughly revised and a new insurance code was adopted. Teachers received a salary increase of $200 and other state employees received modest raises from the budget increase of $44.5 million.

The ominous threat of racial integration, however, hung over the heads of the legislators. In 1958 the NAACP brought suit against the Atlanta Board of Education to force the desegregation of Atlanta's public schools. Federal District Judge Frank Hooper ordered segregated school practices abandoned in Atlanta and directed the Atlanta Board of Education to produce a compliance plan by December 1, 1959. Hooper approved the Board's pupil placement plan on January 16, 1960, and ordered the desegreation of Atlanta schools to begin September 1961, provided the legislature adopted laws making it possible. The legislature talked about desegregation at great length, but failed to act. In campaigning for governor, Vandiver had promised that Georgia's schools would not be integrated while he was governor. His popular slogan, which he later regretted using, was "No, not one will enter." Both the governor and the legislature seemed to believe that somehow the federal courts would allow Georgia's public schools to be operated on a segregated basis. The only legal alternative to integration was to close down the state's public schools.[2]

---

[1]Sanders, "My Life," p. 31; *Atlanta Constitution*, October 30, November 2, 1959, May 24, 1964.

[2]*Augusta Chronicle*, January 10, February 20, 21, 1960; Vandiver, "Vandiver Takes the Middle Road," p. 159.

A few courageous voices called for token integration rather than eliminating public education. The most outspoken leader of this persuasion was former Governor Ellis Arnall. Declaring that "this state cannot afford to turn a million children into the streets," he promised that if the schools are shut down he would be a candidate for governor in 1962, and "I am satisfied the people of Georgia will elect me governor."[3] Since he had been elected governor in 1942 on the issue of removing political interference from the schools, his threat carried weight.

One who took his threat seriously was James S. Peters, chairman of the State Board of Education and patriarch of the Talmadge faction. In a letter to Roy Harris of Augusta he pointed out the political consequences of closing the schools. With dire foreboding he explained that such an eventuality might give Arnall the issue he needed to capture the governorship and might also lead to the downfall of Senator Talmadge and others. Fearing the worst, he predicted "we would lose control of the government and entrench Ellis Arnall and the integrationists in the control of state government for years to come." Though a staunch segregationist, Peters concluded that some form of integration was inevitable. Consequently he advised accepting token integration as the better political alternative to closing the schools. Harris, the most unyielding of the diehard segregationists, was unmoved by Peters's arguments. In an effort to embarrass Peters, he released his private letter to the press and suggested that perhaps Peters had outlived his usefulness as head of the State Board of Education. Although Harris had helped Arnall get elected governor in 1942 and had served capably as his speaker of the house, he later turned against Arnall and became his bitter enemy. Dismissing Arnall's threat to win the governorship, he remarked: "No human agency can breathe life into that body."[4]

Peters's comments evoked widespread discussion and controversy. While most of the state's leaders insisted that the schools would remain segregated, two prominent bankers publicly supported Peters's stand. William R. Bowdoin, senior vice president of Trust Company of Georgia and former state purchasing agent, urged "full consideration" of Peters's proposal in this hour of crisis. Declaring that school closings

---

[3] *Augusta Chronicle*, January 19, 1960.
[4] Ibid., January 17, 18, 19, 1960.

would be disastrous to Georgia business and industry, he urged businessmen to stand up and be counted on the issue. Bowdoin found
nothing in Peters's statement indicating a weakening of his well-known
position against integration, and his "realistic view" recommended itself
to practical people.[5] Mills B. Lane, president of Citizens and Southern
National Bank, Georgia's largest bank, expressed similar views. He
believed a solution would be found and added that shutting down the
schools was not a solution. The economic consequences of closing
schools, he stated, were "very serious."[6]

In consultation with his chief of staff Griffin Bell, Governor
Vandiver decided that as a means of ascertaining public opinion on the
school issue a prestigious study commission should hold hearings
throughout the state. Vandiver contacted John A. Sibley, one of the
most respected men in the state, who agreed to chair the commission.
The seventy-one-year-old Sibley was then chairman of the executive
committee of the Trust Company of Georgia and president of the
University of Georgia Alumni Association. A bill establishing a school
study commission was drawn up, and little-known Representative George
Busbee of Dougherty county, who later became governor, steered it
through the House 167 to 2. The Senate passed it a week later and
Vandiver signed it. Officially the General Assembly Committee on
Schools, it was popularly known as the Sibley Committee. Consisting of
five representatives, three senators, three school and college officials, and
eight prominent citizens, it was charged with finding out how Georgia
citizens wanted the state government to respond to the segregation-
integration crisis and Judge Hooper's order.[7]

In organizing the committee Sibley bluntly told the members that
the Supreme Court decision of 1954 made segregated schools illegal and
"regardless of whether we like it or not, we are all bound by it." The
committee's duty, he said, was to determine whether the people want to
accept private schools and tuition grants or whether to maintain public
schools on an integrated basis. Thus, Georgia faced the choice of

---

[5]Ibid., January 21, 1960.

[6]Ibid., January 23, 1960.

[7]Ibid., January 29, February 5, 1960; *Atlanta Journal and Constitution*, February
14, 1960; Vandiver, "Vandiver Takes the Middle Road," pp. 159-60.

abolishing public schools or changing its laws. No more important question had arisen in the last fifty years, he asserted.[8]

Charged by law to hold hearings in each of the state's ten congressional districts and submit its report by May 1, the committee got busy right away. It tentatively scheduled meetings for Americus, Washington, Cartersville, LaGrange, Douglas, Sandersville, Sylvania, Moultrie, Atlanta, and Gainesville. The first hearing at Americus set the tone for the others that followed. Of the fifty-seven witnesses who testified from twenty counties, only nine expressed reservations. The rest were emphatically for segregation at all costs. Six of the seven Negro witnesses who testified said they wanted segregated schools. A Negro clergyman from Columbus termed the Supreme Court ruling "preposterous," based as it was on sociology. If the Third District was representative of Georgia, then the state's public schools soon would be closed.[9]

The second hearing was held at Washington where more than 300 people jammed the Wilkes County Courthouse and ninety-nine witnesses expressed their views. Roy Harris, the flamboyant lawyer from Augusta recently appointed by Vandiver to the Board of Regents, argued that a system of voluntary segregation developed by white and black leaders would work. Georgia Brooks, an elderly Negro woman, declared that the schools will never integrate because "I don't believe the Good Lord will put us in no such mess as that." Tenth District Georgians expressed some sentiment for local options, but preferred closing schools to integrating them by a margin of two to one.[10]

At the midpoint after five hearings had been held, the Sibley Committee found more support for segregation at all costs than for saving the schools with local options. The last five hearings included emotional and unruly outbursts in Savannah and Atlanta, but generally gave greater support to the local option alternative. As expected, Sibley proved to be the ideal chairman. He conducted the hearings fairly, kept the speakers on the subject, calmed emotions with his gentle humor, and displayed the patience of Job.[11]

---

[8]*Atlanta Journal,* February 17, 19, 1960; *Atlanta Constitution,* February 18, 1960.

[9]*Atlanta Journal,* February 26, 1960; *Atlanta Constitution,* March 4, 1960; *Augusta Chronicle,* March 6, 1960.

[10]*Augusta Chronicle,* March 8, 1960; *Atlanta Constitution,* March 8, 1960.

[11]*Atlanta Journal,* March 15, 1960; *Atlanta Constitution,* March 24, 1960.

Just as the people who testified at the hearings expressed divergent views, so the committee itself was badly divided. A majority of eleven including Sibley rendered a majority report, and a minority of eight presented a minority report. The majority report, which received most of the attention because of Sibley's prestige, recommended a constitutional amendment allowing local school districts to decide whether to continue public education. It further suggested giving pupil placement powers to local boards of education. The minority report argued that the hearings did not support abandoning Georgia's policy of total segregation. It bluntly stated that "enforced integration in the schools of this State would cause serious civil turmoil, bitterness, rancor, and internal strife, inflicting much harm on the people of Georgia and accomplishing nothing for the welfare of its citizens." Both the majority and minority agreed that a constitutional amendment should be adopted providing that no child should be compelled against his parents' will to attend integrated schools.[12]

If the Sibley Committee had done nothing more than provide a forum for Georgians to express their views regarding the schools, it would have been worthwhile. But it accomplished much more. In telling the people that the Supreme Court decisions were the law of the land the Sibley Committee performed a valuable service. It also clearly indicated that state laws in conflict with federal laws were unenforceable. Sibley personally urged the people not to exhaust themselves in futile defense of laws already declared illegal when doing so might cost them the public schools. The better policy, he said, "is to protect, preserve and reserve the rights the people now have under the law." The *Atlanta Constitution* expressed the views of many when it editorialized that Sibley provided the state with "straight thinking and leadership of the highest order."[13]

During the legislative session Governor Vandiver had consistently emphasized his commitment to segregated education, and President Pro Tem Sanders loyally supported the governor and also stated his belief in segregated schools. Sanders, however, differed from Vandiver in stressing the importance of keeping the schools open. He understood that closing

[12]*Atlanta Journal,* April 28, 1960; *Atlanta Constitution,* April 29, 1960.
[13]*Atlanta Constitution,* May 2, 1960.

the schools would be utterly disastrous for the state. Consequently, he urged the people of Atlanta not to panic because of Judge Hooper's order and often asserted that somehow the schools would be kept open. He also forcefully supported the creation of the study committee. When asked by the *Augusta Chronicle* what should be done, he replied: "I think we ought to study this problem. . . . A representative study commission to go into the counties, to talk personally with the people and get a representative feeling of the communities should be formed. This study committee should report back to the General Assembly and then let the General Assembly take appropriate action." Being a skillful politician, he carefully refrained from explaining what the appropriate action might be.[14]

In recognition of Sanders's noteworthy political and civic accomplishments, the Georgia Junior Chamber of Commerce named him one of the five Outstanding Young Men of Georgia for 1960. He received the award at a gala banquet in Savannah. In response to that award the Georgia Senate then passed a resolution congratulating him and praising his many fine achievements and "his progressive and dynamic leadership in state and governmental affairs."[15]

The integration issue continued to be the main political topic in Georgia and other areas of the South. Although Atlanta public transit had been integrated in 1959, practically all other public facilities remained rigidly segregated. Emerging new leaders, however, expressed dissatisfaction with current conditions and demanded more rapid progress in civil rights. The "sit-in" movement began on February 1, 1960, in Greensboro, North Carolina, when four black students refused to leave a segregated lunch counter. The idea spread quickly to neighboring states. On March 9 Atlanta University students published in the city's daily newspapers "An Appeal for Human Rights," a full-page advertisement announcing their intention to use every legal and nonviolent means to secure full citizenship. Atlanta Mayor William Hartsfield praised the Appeal as "a message of great importance to Atlanta" and commended the students for "the promise of nonviolence and a peaceful approach." Governor Vandiver, by contrast, foolishly labeled it a

---

[14]Ibid., January 26, 1960; *Augusta Chronicle*, January 17, 18, 1960.
[15]*Augusta Chronicle*, February 19, 1960.

Communist-inspired piece of rabble-rousing and claimed no injustice existed in Atlanta. A week later some two hundred black collegians conducted a sit-in at several public places in downtown Atlanta, including several cafeterias in federal office buildings. Seventy-seven demonstrators were arrested in Georgia's first sit-in. Soon the movement spread to other cities and towns, and in short order previously segregated facilities were integrated by direct action. In Atlanta protests continued throughout the year until business leaders finally worked out an agreement with the students. By the terms of the agreement, formal desegregation of the restaurants, lunch counters and restrooms in all major department and variety stores took place, without incident, on September 27, 1961.[16]

Atlanta provided the most outstanding leader of the civil rights movement in Dr. Martin Luther King, Jr. Born on January 15, 1929, he was a graduate of both Morehouse College and Crozier Theological Seminary, and received his doctorate in theology from Boston University. His first pastorate was in Montgomery, Alabama, where he gained national attention by leading the successful bus boycott. In 1957 he helped establish the Southern Christian Leadership Conference (SCLC), and as its president traveled widely throughout the South lecturing on desegregation and nonviolent tactics. In 1960 he returned to Atlanta, serving as associate pastor with his father at Ebenezer Baptist Church. The SCLC financed, and King supported, the sit-ins. Although usually aloof from the Atlanta situation, on October 19, 1960, King joined the student demonstrators in a sit-in at Rich's, the South's largest department store. His arrest and imprisonment at Reidsville State Prison attracted national attention—the kind of publicity business leaders in "the city too busy to hate" hoped to avoid. By adding his enormous prestige to the student sit-ins, King played a significant role in integrating businesses in his hometown, but his most productive efforts occurred outside of Atlanta, and indeed outside of Georgia. The next year he

---

[16]Bartley, *Creation of Modern Georgia*, pp. 196-98; Virginia H. Hein, "The Image of 'A City Too Busy to Hate': Atlanta in the 1960s," *Phylon* 33 (Fall 1972): 205-21; Jack L. Walker, "Sit-Ins in Atlanta: A Study in the Negro Revolt," in *Atlanta, Georgia, 1960–1961: Sit-ins and Student Activism*, ed. David J. Garrow (Brooklyn: Carlson Publishing, 1989) pp. 59-93; Ronald H. Baylor, "A City Too Busy to Hate," in *Business and Its Environment: Essays for Thomas P. Cochran*, ed. Harold Issadore Sharlin (Westport CT: Greenwood Press, 1983) pp. 145-59.

helped coordinate "freedom rides" and led a desegregation and voter
education drive in Albany, Georgia, which proved disappointing.[17]

In preparation for the 1961 legislative session, President Pro Tem
Sanders and House Floor Leader Frank Twitty toured the state in a
prelegislative forum. Sponsored by the Georgia Chamber of Commerce
and local chapters, the tour included thirteen stops. At each forum on
the "eggs and issues" tour, Sanders and Twitty delivered speeches
discussing the current political issues and then responded to questions
from the audience. Since the tour was sponsored by the Chamber of
Commerce, the audiences invariably included prominent businessmen
and local political leaders.

Sanders and Twitty soon discovered that most Georgians wanted to
discuss integration. Sanders reiterated the position he had taken earlier;
namely, that the General Assembly is "not going to close the public
schools." Never a diehard segregationist, Sanders was a Southern
politician in frantic search of a legal solution that would keep the schools
open, and he did not explicitly rule out integration. He told the forum
in Atlanta the legislature "will fight to keep the schools open." When
asked later to elaborate, he replied: "I personally do not think any of the
schools will be closed." Twitty, an experienced legislator from Camilla
in south Georgia, surprised Sanders by agreeing. In the early forums he
had acknowledged that a few schools might be closed for a short time
before the problem could be solved, but he subsequently agreed with
Sanders that the General Assembly would respond to the problem in a
way acceptable to Georgians. In telling the people that the schools ought
to be kept open under any circumstances, Sanders and Twitty were
practically unique among Georgia's elected leaders.[18]

At the last forum held in Augusta, Twitty suggested that the
legislature might accept local option after the federal courts had knocked
down Georgia's school segregation laws. He seemed to think this would
be politically feasible after constituents were convinced the legislators had

---

[17]Walker, "Sit-Ins in Atlanta," pp. 75-90; Martin Luther King, Sr., *Daddy King:
An Autobiography* (New York: William Morrow and Company, 1980) pp. 152-67;
Bradley L. Rice, "Martin Luther King, Jr.," in *Dictionary of Georgia Biography*, Kenneth
Coleman and Charles Stephen Gurr, eds., 2 vols. (Athens: University of Georgia Press,
1983) 2:577-79.

[18]*Atlanta Journal*, November 15, 1960.

done everything possible to keep Georgia's public schools segregated. Sanders, who had carefully avoided advocating integration, was grilled directly by local segregationist Hugh Grant, founder of the Georgia State Rights Council. Grant pointedly asked him: "Do you favor token integration as a last resort?" Sanders replied: "Mr. Grant, I don't favor any kind of integration, but I favor public schools." The audience of business and civic leaders applauded wildly. Sanders's position, modest though it was, received favorable comment in the press and thrust him into the forefront as a moderate on the race issue.[19]

Gradually, almost imperceptibly, public opinion in Georgia began to change regarding closing the schools. In addition to Sanders, Twitty, and the prominent bankers, others slowly and reluctantly reached the conclusion that the schools must remain open. Ivan Allen, Jr., Atlanta civic leader and future mayor, stated, "Atlanta's public schools must stay open."[20] Atlanta ministers, public school groups, and university faculty issued manifestos calling for open schools. Atlanta mothers, concerned about schools for their children, formed an advocacy group called Help Our Public Education. By 1960, HOPE had 30,000 members in several Georgia cities. But aside from Sanders and Twitty, very few elected officials were willing to take that stand. The highest ranking elected officials—Governor Vandiver, Lieutenant Governor Byrd, Senators Russell and Talmadge—and the rank and file of the General Assembly seemed firmly committed to segregation at all costs. Roy Harris, Executive Secretary Peter Zack Geer, and former Governor Marvin Griffin appeared to be in competition to determine which one was most committed to maintaining segregation.

As a result of earlier court decisions, it seemed likely that the crisis over integrating the schools would occur in Atlanta, but suddenly the focus shifted to Athens, home of the University of Georgia. On January 7, 1961, Federal District Judge William A. Bootle ordered that two qualified black applicants to the university be allowed to register "now" for the winter quarter. "Now" was the last day for registration, and it was also the first day the General Assembly convened in regular session. The two students seeking admission, Charlayne Hunter and Hamilton

---

[19]Ibid., November 18, 1960; *Atlanta Constitution*, November 20, 1960.
[20]Pyles, "Vandiver and the Politics of Change," p. 149.

Holmes, were ideal pioneers to challenge the system. Both had compiled outstanding academic records at Turner High School in Atlanta; Holmes, the valedictorian, ranked first in the class and Hunter was third. When the University of Georgia rejected them on a variety of pretexts, but careful never to mention race, Holmes went to Morehouse College in Atlanta where he maintained a B+ average, and Hunter studied journalism at Wayne State University in Detroit. Judge Bootle ruled that the two plaintiffs were qualified for admission "and would already have been admitted had it not been for their race and color."[21]

Backed by the court order, Holmes and Hunter completed their registration and thereby ended 175 years of segregated education at the University of Georgia. The rapidity of the court action left the state's political leaders in a state of utter shock. On January 9 Governor Vandiver, obeying the state law as he understood it, closed the university, stating, "It is the saddest duty of my life." He also indicated that he would ask the General Assembly to repeal the section of the 1956 appropriation act which required the cutoff of funds from schools which have been integrated.[22] The following day Judge Bootle enjoined the governor and the state auditor from interfering with the operation of the university, and the U. S. Supreme Court unanimously refused to delay the lower court order. Vandiver responded by sending a scathing protest to Judge Bootle over the "sweeping nature of these orders attempting to take over state legislative and executive processes and the prerogatives of the State Board of Regents."[23]

These events produced turmoil in Athens as emotions ran wild. After a basketball game which Georgia lost, fifty angry students appeared in front of Hunter's dormitory carrying a sheet inscribed "Nigger Go Home." After thirty minutes of chanting "One-two-three-four, we don't want no nigger whore" and throwing firecrackers and rocks, the students

---

[21]*Atlanta Constitution*, January 10, 1961; Calvin Trillin, *An Education in Georgia* (New York: Viking Press, 1963); "Break in Georgia," *Time* 77 (January 13, 1961): 64; Clarence N. Stone, *Regime Politics: Governing Atlanta, 1946–1988* (Lawrence: University Press of Kansas, 1989) pp. 46-47; Paul E. Mertz, " 'Mind Changing Time All Over Georgia': Hope, Inc. and School Desegregation, 1958–1961," *Georgia Historical Quarterly* 77 (Spring 1993): 41-61.

[22]*Augusta Chronicle*, January 10, 1961.

[23]Ibid., January 11, 1961.

rushed toward the building. In the ensuing action, they broke windows, hit reporters with rocks, and injured one policeman. Only the effective leadership of Dean of Men William Tate prevented the disturbance from becoming a major catastrophe. By wading into the crowd, confiscating identification cards, calling students by name, and punching some of the leaders, he blunted the assault. The police arrested several students and used tear gas to disperse the crowd which had grown to nearly 2,000. Shortly after midnight, the president of the University of Georgia, Dr. O. C. Aderhold, announced that he had suspended Hunter and Holmes from the university "for their own safety." The mayor of Athens criticized Governor Vandiver for failing to provide adequate assistance. He charged that state patrolmen sat in their station and refused to aid the thirty-six city policemen in quelling the disorder. The mayor had requested state troopers at 10:00 p. m., but none arrived until after midnight when local police and firemen had already restored order. Clearly it was not the governor's finest hour. Two days later Judge Bootle ordered the reinstatement of Holmes and Hunter, and Vandiver, stung by the mayor's criticism, promised they would be protected.[24]

When the students returned, Athens had the appearance of a police state, as local police, Georgia Bureau of Investigation officers, and Federal Bureau of Investigation officers patrolled the streets. To decide what to do next, Vandiver assembled over fifty of his top officials at the Governor's Mansion to discuss the matter. The vast majority still favored unyielding resistance to the federal courts. Peter Zack Geer had even publicly commended the rioters at Athens for their "character and courage" in not submitting to "dictatorship and tyranny."[25] Of those assembled, only Sanders and Twitty urged the governor to keep the schools open. Their advice carried weight with the governor. After several agonizing days and nights of soul-searching and prayer, Vandiver

---

[24]Ibid., January 12, 13, 14, 1961; "Shame in Georgia," *Time* 77 (January 20, 1961): 44; "The Negro in College," *Newsweek* 57 (January 23, 1961): 50-51; Charlayne Hunter-Gault, *In My Place* (New York: Farrar, Straus & Giroux, 1992) pp. 169-91; Thomas G. Dyer, *The University of Georgia: A Bicentennial History, 1785–1985* (Athens: University of Georgia Press, 1985) pp. 303-34.

[25]"Shame in Georgia," p. 44.

accepted their position.[26] In an increasingly polarized situation, Sanders's moderation assumed more and more the appearance of a racial liberal.

On the evening of January 19 Vandiver gave the most courageous speech of his career to a somber joint session of the legislature. Reversing his previous position, he stated firmly: "We meet together to proclaim to the whole world that public education will be preserved." Profoundly disturbed by the riot, he decided that the state must not defy, by "any thought, suggestion, hint, or encouragement" federal court orders to integrate. He asked the General Assembly to repeal the cutoff funds laws for the University of Georgia and the public schools. He also asked for open school laws and local option laws, as the Sibley Committee had recommended. With obvious emotion he told the legislature the school crisis threatened to "blight our state." Like a cancerous growth it was devouring progress and "denying the youth of Georgia their proper educational opportunity."[27]

In seeking a realistic solution to the problem, Vandiver, in the words of Representative James Mackay of DeKalb county, took Georgia off the low road and onto the high road. The legislature readily followed his leadership. They interrupted his speech twenty times with applause and subsequently passed his recommended legislation with few dissenting votes. The crisis passed, and Vandiver thereafter proved to be a forward-looking governor on civil rights questions. Because of his leadership, Georgia was spared the violence and embarrassment that Alabama, Mississippi and other southern states experienced. Had Vandiver maintained the rigid defense of segregation that his rhetoric demanded or followed the advice of Geer, Harris, and other diehard segregationists, the state would have suffered additional turmoil, bitterness, and economic loss. Fortunately, for the future of Georgia, he reluctantly came over to Sanders's way of thinking and kept the schools open.[28]

Getting the legislature to approve the education bills was easily accomplished. The administration proposals included a local option bill to allow local school districts to close public schools to avoid integration.

[26]Vandiver telephone interview, August 26, 1991; Sanders, "My Life," p. 32.

[27]"Retreat in Georgia?" *Newsweek* 57 (January 30, 1961): 51; "Grace in Georgia," *Time* 77 (January 27, 1961): 64-65.

[28]Ibid.; Pyles, "Vandiver and the Politics of Change," p. 150.

A second bill provided tuition grants for pupils who do not wish to attend integrated schools, and a third bill revised appeal procedures to the State Board of Education. In addition, there was a constitutional amendment to allow freedom of assembly—that is, children of different races could not be forced to attend the same school. The measures passed overwhelmingly and Vandiver signed them on January 31.[29]

The biggest controversy in the 1961 session was not education; it was the budget. Traditionally the governor had prepared the budget and secured its passage by the General Assembly without major changes. Since the General Assembly did not have a budget director or a budget staff, the legislators had little choice but to accept whatever the governor recommended. Some of the legislators, however, were chaffing under the system and seeking more legislative independence. Moreover, Vandiver was under consideration for the position of Secretary of the Army in the Kennedy administration. If he accepted the position, then Lieutenant Governor Garland Byrd would become governor, a prospect some House leaders did not relish. Although Vandiver publicly announced that he would not accept the position if it should be offered, apparently some House leaders were not convinced. Consequently, when Vandiver went to Miami for a short vacation, a group of House leaders, including Speaker George L. Smith, Floor Leader Twitty, and Appropriations Committee chairman Jack Ray, decided to act. They quickly amended the governor's proposed budget of $405 million by cutting some programs and adding a larger raise for teachers. The new House budget also provided for an annual appropriation and reduced the governor's discretionary power over surplus funds. Assuming the Senate would join their move for independence, they passed their budget 172 to 8 and sent it to the Senate.[30]

An irate Vandiver turned to the Senate to block the House measure which he felt unduly restricted his authority. Working closely with Sanders and Byrd, a new budget was proposed, raising the House budget of $406.2 million to $412.4 million for fiscal 1961–1962 and setting the 1962–1963 budget at $420.1 million. Unlike the House version, it left

---

[29]*Augusta Chronicle*, February 1, 1961; *Acts and Resolutions of the General Assembly of the State of Georgia, 1961* (Atlanta: State Printers, 1962) pp. 31-38.

[30]*Augusta Chronicle*, January 4, February 22, 1961; Sanders, "My Life," pp. 33-34.

the governor in control of budgetary matters. The new budget bill passed the Senate 42 to 11. The administration forces then pressured the House to accept it, which it did by vote of 137 to 65. Legislative power over budgetary matters was stifled by Vandiver and would not be achieved until several years later when Lester Maddox became governor. Vandiver did, however, make one concession to the House. He agreed to the establishment of a committee to study budgetary matters and make recommendations to the General Assembly by December 1. A committee of five senators, seven representatives, and five members appointed by the governor was approved on March 28. In the end, the 1961 legislature granted bus drivers a $200 raise, teachers a $300 raise, and themselves a $400 raise. One of the more important measures of the session was the passage of a $100 million highway reconstruction program financed through the sale of bonds. Overall the legislative session was widely praised by the press. The *Augusta Chronicle* editorialized that it had "probably packed more important action into its 40-day session than has any of its predecessors, certainly any in recent years."[31]

As president pro tem of the Senate, Sanders had played a pivotal role in the historic session. He worked closely with Vandiver and Byrd on all administration measures and received much credit for resolving the school crisis. His tour with Twitty had influenced public opinion, and it was his package of educational bills that the legislature adopted. Moreover, his job had become so demanding that he secured his own office and secretary in the Capitol. With 10,000 letters coming in during the session, he could no longer work out of the lieutenant governor's office. His stature was such that the media had for many months asserted that he was a leading candidate for lieutenant governor in 1962. Some newspapers suggested that Twitty and Sanders should run as a team. Clearly the young senator, having found his niche in politics, aspired to higher political office. But which office, governor or lieutenant governor, would he seek in 1962?[32]

---

[31]Ibid., March 1, 3, 8, 1961; *Acts and Resolutions, 1961*, pp. 297-98.

[32]*Augusta Chronicle*, March 23, 1961; *Atlanta Constitution*, October 15, 1959, April 13, 1961; *Atlanta Journal*, March 23, 1961.

Chapter 6

Governor
or Lieutenant Governor?

Since Governor Vandiver had accomplished most of his agenda, the public expected little from him in 1962, his last full year in office. It was also an election year, which reduced the likelihood of much new legislation being passed. Legislators seeking reelection jockeyed to keep their names in the news, and those aspiring for higher office even more frantically tried to enhance their public image. The latter category included Lieutenant Governor Garland Byrd, seeking the governorship; Executive Secretary Peter Zack Geer, Senator Culver Kidd of Milledgeville, and Senator Carl Sanders—all seeking to become lieutenant governor. Other legislators also tested the political waters to see if they had a chance of advancing, and former Governor Marvin Griffin, with his campaign for governor well underway, already had emerged as the frontrunner in the gubernatorial race.

As soon as the 1962 legislative session opened, both Byrd and Sanders presented their pet projects. Byrd told the Senate that budget control legislation was the most important issue it would take up. If the legislature does nothing but pass the budget proposals it will be a successful session, he asserted. Sanders made a speech in which he introduced a constitutional amendment to put a ceiling on the bond-issuing way of paying for improvements, a practice, he noted, that had put the state a half a billion dollars in debt. His measure called for limiting debt retirement funds to 12 percent of the state's annual income. This would mean a ceiling of $48 million for debt retirement with the present state income of around $400 million. It also would place a twenty-year limit on bonds and revenue certificates and would make it mandatory for the General Assembly to appropriate one year's debt retirement money before a state authority could issue any bonds.

Although admitting that he did not expect them to pass, Sanders also introduced two other amendments. One would extend the Senate term from two to four years. The other would provide a system of staggered terms under which half of the Senate would be elected every two years. He also indicated that he would soon introduce a bill to reorganize the State Highway Board in order to remove roadbuilding from politics. Still pending from the 1961 session was his bill to put county roads under a program of state maintenance.[1]

Governor Vandiver, of course, had his own ideas about the state's needs. In a twenty-eight minute address to the General Assembly he emphasized the need for the legislature to have greater control over the budget. Now convinced that the General Assembly deserved greater authority in budgetary matters, he explained that handling the state's money in the past had been a hodgepodge affair. Reasserting the legislature's "sovereign prerogatives over the public purse," the Governor declared, would bring "responsibility and accountability to state fiscal administration." To accomplish those ends Vandiver proposed two constitutional amendments, the first requiring a biennial appropriations bill, and the second limiting appropriations to income. He also sought a law to limit authority spending to 15 percent of the total state budget. Finally, he called for the creation of a modern budget bureau which would prepare the proposed budget. Previously governors had had dictatorial control over the budget, but under his proposal the legislature would have the final word. In defending his proposal he pointed out that "nearly one dollar out of every four has been spent by executive decree" and as a result "the General Assembly has ceased to perform its function in the government."[2]

Since the Vandiver program gave more power to the legislature and severely limited the governor's control over the state's pursestrings, it passed easily. Sanders, having served on the budget study committee, agreed completely with the governor's budget proposals and worked for their adoption. Vandiver disagreed with Sanders on the Highway Board; consequently, the Board was not revised. By accepting a minor compromise, Sanders did, however, gain his support for the state taking over the

---

[1]*Augusta Chronicle*, January 6, 9, 1962; *Atlanta Journal*, January 8, 1962.
[2]*Augusta Chronicle*, January 11, 1962.

maintenance of rural roads and the measure was adopted. Sanders's proposals for changing Senate terms and elections failed to get executive support and, as he expected, were rejected. The General Assembly passed a tax relief bill for new industry, reaffirmed the open schools policy, and provided more home rule for cities. It discussed but failed to equalize state officials' pay, and it refused to deal with reapportionment. On the whole, political observers generally regarded the 1962 legislative session as productive, especially since the governor was a lame duck.[3]

Georgia legislators had little time to relax from the legislative session when a federal court suddenly thrust a new issue upon them. On March 26 the United States Supreme Court ruled in the Tennessee case of *Baker v. Carr* that the question of apportionment of a state's legislature was subject to judicial review. In a single stroke the justices had cut away the rationale used to deny court review of Georgia's county unit system. On the same day the Supreme Court handed down the Baker decision, a suit was filed in Atlanta enjoining state officials and Democratic party officers from holding the 1962 primary on a unit basis. The suit, filed by attorney Morris Abram and known as *Gray v. Sanders*, was scheduled to be heard by a three-judge federal panel on April 27.[4]

Since one vote in Echols county, Georgia's smallest county, was worth ninety-nine votes in Fulton county, Georgia's largest county, the state's county unit system obviously could not stand judicial scrutiny. Governor Vandiver was in Europe when the Baker decision was announced, and when he returned he proceeded cautiously to ascertain public opinion. Sanders, by contrast, immediately called for a special session of the legislature to reapportion the House and redistribute the county unit vote. Unless Georgia acted quickly, the courts will make the decision, he stated. "Our unit system can be defended," he argued, "but there must be some reapportionment." He asked, why wait to be forced? If the legislators wait until a court ruling forces their hand, "it would be like trying to put the pieces back together after the bull has been through the china shop," he said. On this issue, as in so many other in-

---

[3]Ibid., February 18, 1962.

[4]Peirce, *Deep South States of America*, p. 316; Jack Bass and Walter DeVries, *The Transformation of Southern Politics: Social Change and Political Consequence Since 1945* (New York: Basic Books, 1976) p. 152.

stances throughout his political career, Sanders intuitively grasped the essential point and forthrightly stated his position without waiting to determine which way the political winds were blowing. Typically, his position was a middle ground, between the extremes of those unwilling to alter the system at all and those who wished to abolish it altogether. His forceful and courageous leadership, unique among his colleagues, earned lavish praise from the *Atlanta Constitution*, even though that newspaper believed the county unit system was indefensible. Vandiver, after meeting with his advisors, called for a special session to meet April 16.[5]

Before the General Assembly reconvened, Sanders outlined his plan for reapportionment. He proposed increasing the House from 205 to 229 members and raising the unit vote from 410 to 458. Under his plan counties with population from 1,000 to 20,000 would have one representative and two county unit votes. Counties with population from 20,000 to 50,000 would have two representatives and four county unit votes. The most populous counties would get one representative and two unit votes for each 50,000 population. The net result would be 119 two-unit counties and 40 counties with four or more units. Fulton county would have 26 units; DeKalb 14; Muscogee and Chatham 10; Richmond, Bibb, and Cobb 8; and Floyd and Dougherty 6. Sanders claimed his reform would be fair to all counties regardless of size. In praising his plan the *Augusta Chronicle* editorialized that it "is the fairest one that may be expected to gain legislative approval."[6]

The Sanders plan did not receive universal endorsement. In fact, legislators introduced eighteen apportionment bills on the first day of the session and planned to offer more. On the third day of the session the House State of the Republic Committee heard a prophetic testimony. Gainesville attorney William B. Gunter bluntly told the committee the county unit system is "absolutely untenable in the courts." The system is either right or wrong constitutionally, he declared. If it is valid, adding forty more unit votes "is not going to make it any more valid." It is merely "whistling in the dark and playing politics," he stated.[7]

---

[5]Ibid.; *Atlanta Constitution*, April 4, 1962; *Augusta Chronicle*, April 4, 6, 1962.
[6]*Augusta Chronicle*, April 13, 1962.
[7]Ibid., April 18, 19, 1962.

Ignoring Gunter's sound analysis, the legislature continued to debate the proposals and add new ones. At the end of the first week House Speaker Smith presented a plan which added 135 unit votes to be distributed among the more populous counties. Smith explained that his plan had been worked out with Roy Harris and Attorney General Eugene Cook and had Vandiver's support. His plan dealt with county unit votes only and did not provide for reapportioning the House. Reapportionment, Smith insisted, could be done later. The House adopted his plan by vote of 159 to 29.[8]

The Smith-Vandiver plan went nowhere in the Senate. Lieutenant Governor Byrd, already an announced candidate for governor, rejected it and came up with a plan of his own. His measure, which would increase the number of units to 930 and apportion them according to population, called for distributing a county's units on the basis of the number of popular votes a candidate receives. Even though a similar distribution plan had already been rejected by the House when Frank Twitty declared that no court would uphold it, the Senate followed the leadership of the lieutenant governor. In view of the political situation, it appears that having one's name attached to a plan was the most important priority.[9]

With time running out, the General Assembly needed to reach an agreement. Vandiver and legislative leaders attempted to compromise their differences, but for a while it appeared an impasse had been reached, with neither side willing to yield. Finally, with the federal court already hearing arguments in *Gray v. Sanders*, Vandiver addressed a joint session and succeeded in getting a compromise passed. Adopted 147 to 37 in the House and 40 to 12 in the Senate, it was essentially the Smith-Vandiver plan. Byrd reluctantly accepted the compromise and carried the Senate with him. The bill increased the unit vote to 547 and gave Fulton county 40 unit votes.[10]

The General Assembly, with the utmost difficulty, finally had agreed to a minor adjustment in the county unit system. It had not tackled the more serious problem of reapportioning the House, as Sanders had

---

[8]Ibid., April 20, 25, 1962.
[9]Ibid., April 24, 25, 1962.
[10]Ibid., April 28, 1962.

proposed. Nor had it provided equal representation to the urban areas. The new measure clearly was more democratic than the old system, but the urban areas remained grossly underrepresented. The largest county had been underrepresented 99 to 1 compared to the smallest county under the old system; now the disparity between Fulton county and Echols county was 14 to 1. With candidates scrambling for votes in the primary only five months away, that was the best the General Assembly could do. Unfortunately, its efforts were seriously flawed.[11]

The federal panel of judges Griffin Bell, Elbert Tuttle, and Frank Hooper heard lawyers argue that the revised county unit system still discriminated against James O'Hear Sanders, the man who filed the suit, and other urban voters. One day after the legislature passed the new law, the federal panel overturned it. For practical purposes, the ruling ended the county unit system which had dominated Georgia's elections for more than half a century. The court found the system "invidiously discriminatory" and unanimously granted a temporary injunction restraining the use of the county unit system in the Democratic primary. The new law was an improvement in meeting constitutional standards, the court said, "but still misses the mark." Attorney General Eugene Cook immediately appealed the ruling, and one year later the United States Supreme Court upheld it by vote of eight to one. Thus, Georgia's unique county unit system was banished into oblivion.[12]

As expected, the decision produced an immediate and varied reaction. Some rejoiced that at last democracy had come to Georgia's cities, while others lamented the intrusion of federal courts into state affairs. Senator Talmadge assailed the decision as "appalling," and Marvin Griffin termed it "a sorry mess." Georgia Democratic party chairman James H. Gray of Albany, a defendant in the suit, took issue with the fact that presiding judge Elbert Tuttle was a Republican. He remarked: "As far as I am concerned, if Judge Tuttle, a Republican, wanted to run the affairs of the Democratic party in the sovereign state

---

[11]Charles Boykin Pyles, "Race and Ruralism in Georgia Elections 1948–1966" (Ph.D. diss., University of Georgia, 1967) p. 111.

[12]*Augusta Chronicle*, April 28, 29, 1962; Peirce, *Deep South States of America*, p. 316.

of Georgia through court edict, he can do so without my help."[13]
Governor Vandiver cautiously withheld comment until he could study
the opinion. Both Garland Byrd and Sanders said they were not
surprised by the ruling. Sanders expressed regret that the legislature had
been unable to satisfy the court and responded to those who had been
criticizing him, stating: "This decision today obviously disproves the
claim by some candidates in Georgia that the session was premature and
the crisis was manufactured. They were either not informed or were
trying to mislead the people when they made such statements."[14]

The *Gray v. Sanders* decision produced a fundamental change in
Georgia politics. The county unit system, which had emerged after the
Reconstruction era, had been incorporated into state law in 1917. It
insured rural domination of state politics by diminishing the urban vote.
Consequently, political power resided in the rural counties and their
"courthouse crowds." Successful candidates appealed almost exclusively
to the rural counties and some, such as Eugene Talmadge, deliberately
ignored the urban areas altogether. The system not only discouraged
urban candidates from seeking office and largely disfranchised urban
voters, it also bred corruption in small counties where "courthouse
crowds" manipulated and falsified vote totals. The court decision meant
that Georgia candidates for statewide office henceforth would go after
popular votes rather than concentrating their efforts on cultivating rural
political chieftains. The change was profound indeed.

The first beneficiary of the change was Carl Sanders. As an urbane
lawyer from Augusta, his appeal was much greater in the cities than in
the countryside. Moreover, his chief political interests—education,
industrial expansion, and efficiency—were issues that primarily concerned urban voters. While he worked effectively with rural legislators,
he was more comfortable discussing issues with business executives and
chamber of commerce types than with poor sharecroppers in Lowndes
county. Sanders clearly was an urban candidate, and now each vote in
a city would count just as much as a vote in a rural county.

By necessity statewide campaigns begin long before the elections take
place. For many months Sanders had been organizing a campaign to run

---

[13]*Augusta Chronicle*, April 30, 1962.
[14]Ibid., April 29, 30, 1962.

for lieutenant governor in 1962. Though never formally announcing his candidacy, he let it be known that he planned to run, and the newspapers invariably referred to him as a candidate for lieutenant governor. Leasing a 250 horsepower airplane, he flew it all over the state giving as many speeches to civic clubs as he could possibly work into his schedule. When he returned home after each meeting, he made a card file on the people he had met. In this manner he built up a sizeable number of contacts throughout the state. As president pro tem with six consecutive years of service in the Senate, he was perceived as the frontrunner. Possessing enormous self-confidence, Sanders believed he could defeat Peter Zack Geer, Senator Culver Kidd, or anyone else who might enter the race.[15]

Yet, as Sanders campaigned throughout the state and increased his popular following, he began to wonder how he might fare in the race for governor. As he assessed his chances, he concluded that both Marvin Griffin and Garland Byrd, the leading candidates for governor, had serious handicaps. Though Griffin was a skilled campaigner with a loyal following, his administration had been notoriously corrupt. Byrd, a competent lieutenant governor and Vandiver stalwart, was honest, but his campaign had generated little enthusiasm among the voters. Perhaps Sanders's more decisive leadership would be more appealing to the voters, he reasoned. As Sanders pondered such matters, Peter Zack Geer, anxious to get Sanders out of the race for lieutenant governor, promised him an appointment to the appellate court if he did not run. That was a tempting offer for a young lawyer, but Sanders rejected it.[16]

A new and startling development occurred when an obscure former motorcycle policeman in Atlanta named Carl F. Sanders suddenly announced that he was entering the race for lieutenant governor. Geer immediately denied having anything to do with the candidacy of Carl F. Sanders, and in a recent interview he emphatically reiterated that view, but it seems apparent that some of his friends induced the new candidate to enter the race in order to cause confusion. Carl E. Sanders was in Dublin when he learned of the ploy. His immediate reaction to

---

[15]Sanders, "My Life," pp. 35-36.
[16]Ibid.; Geer denied making the offer, telephone interview with Peter Zack Geer, September 5, 1991.

the press was, "If he's going to run for lieutenant governor, I guess I'll have to run for governor." His statement generated much publicity, and he began to think more seriously about seeking the top position. Sanders also considered this factor: What if Griffin became governor and he became lieutenant governor? Could he work four years under a man whose leadership he detested?[17]

Since the deadline for announcing was May 5, Sanders weighed the factors and tried to make a decision while the special session was meeting. During the last week of the session literally hundreds of delegates came to see him, and each one told him the same thing: "We're backing you for lieutenant governor and you are going to win, but we can't support you for governor." His family, on the other hand, saw things differently. Betty had urged him to run for governor all along. She knew her husband and understood that he would be dissatisfied as the number two man, especially if Griffin were governor. At a meeting at J. B. Fuqua's house, his father also advised him to seek the governorship. Still undecided, Sanders, accompanied by Henry Neal, a close personal friend from law school, went to a Wednesday evening prayer service at the First Baptist Church in Atlanta. The guest preacher that evening was Reverend John Haggai, an evangelist and friend of Sanders. No one can explain exactly what happened with any degree of certainty, but when the service was over Carl had made up his mind. He would be a candidate for governor. The next day he told Garland Byrd what he intended to do. Then he took the back stairs down to the Governor's Office and explained his decision to Vandiver. Remaining noncommittal, the governor indicated that his entry into the race might split the votes and elect Griffin, a prospect Vandiver abhorred. Sanders then held a press conference at his home in Augusta and announced that he would be a candidate for governor in the Democratic primary on September 12.[18]

That Sanders made this crucial decision in church after prayer was not surprising, for he was a man of prayer and deep Christian convictions. Early in his life he even considered going into the ministry but de-

[17]Sanders, "My Life," pp. 36-37; Geer telephone interview, September 5, 1991, and follow up letter, Peter Zack Geer to James F. Cook, September 9, 1991; *Atlanta Journal*, March 23, 1961; *Augusta Chronicle*, March 24, 26, 1961.

[18]Sanders, "My Life," pp. 37-38; Henry Neal interview, August 28, 1985; *Atlanta Journal and Constitution*, April 22, 1962.

cided that was not his calling. Essentially a private person, he did not publicize his conversion experience and religious faith, as some of his successors have done, but his beliefs were firm and abiding. In a 1955 newspaper article discussing the separation of church and state, he made one of the clearest statements of his beliefs. "There can be no worthwhile government without God," he declared. Ideas come from the "infinite wisdom which created the human eye, . . . the limitless source of all ideas," he argued, and we must draw upon that "fabulous resource." "A communion between leaders of state and the source of wisdom is to be desired above all things," he stated, and for a leader to succeed, he "must be a man of God with a consciousness of his dependency upon the Almighty." Throughout his political career Sanders acknowledged his belief in Christianity and his dependency upon the Almighty.[19]

In 1962 Sanders had a commendable record of service in the legislature, but he had less name recognition than Griffin or Byrd and fewer contacts in the counties. With practically no political commitments and no financial backers, he began the race as an underdog, far behind his opponents who had been campaigning for four years and had received strong political and financial endorsements. Sanders realized it would be an uphill battle all the way. He also understood the political peril his decision entailed. If he should lose, his political career might be over. The safer course would be to serve as lieutenant governor for four years and then run for governor, as his immediate predecessors, Griffin and Vandiver, had done. But following tradition and seeking the easy way was not for Sanders. Always a fierce competitor, he had previously set high goals for himself and through diligent effort had managed to attain them. Supremely self-confident, he was undeterred by the odds. Years later he confessed that had he known then how difficult it is to campaign for governor he probably would have avoided the race. But in his ignorance and naivete he boldly accepted the challenge. As had happened so often in the past, things almost miraculously fell into place for him. When he announced his candidacy on April 21 the county unit system was in effect. One week later the federal court threw it out. He may have assumed the court would rule as it did, but he had no assurance of that result. And he certainly had no indication that Garland Byrd, an

---

[19]Sanders, "My Life," p. 50; undated newspaper clipping in "This Is Your Life."

apparently healthy thirty-eight-year-old candidate, would have a heart attack a month later and be forced to withdraw from the race. Fate, it seemed, continued to smile on the political aspirations of Carl Sanders.[20]

---

[20]*Atlanta Journal,* May 18, 1962; Sanders, "Interviews in 1990," pp. 81-86; Sanders, "My Life," pp. 39-40.

Carl Sanders, William Holley, and Lee Chambers—
the Richmond county delegation to the Georgia House of Representatives in 1955.

Chapter 7

Carl versus Old Marv

In addition to Carl Sanders, the candidates for governor in the 1962 Democratic primary included former Governor Marvin Griffin, Lieutenant Governor Garland Byrd, and three lesser candidates—Mrs. Grace Wilkey Thomas, an Atlanta attorney; Hoke O'Kelley, a Loganville farmer and perennial candidate; and Cecil Langham, a Warrenton masonry worker. Ed Smith, a Republican from Columbus, also became a candidate, but he died in an automobile accident during the campaign. At the onset of the campaign most observers considered Sanders a long shot, and expected him to come in third, well behind Griffin and Byrd. The complexion of the campaign changed remarkably, however, when Byrd suffered a mild heart attack, and his doctors insisted that his recovery required rest. Convinced that the stress of the campaign would be more than his heart could withstand, he reluctantly dropped out of the race. His unexpected withdrawal essentially narrowed the field to Griffin and Sanders. Now Sanders could focus on Griffin exclusively and show the voters the stark contrast between the two candidates. Additionally, Byrd's withdrawal freed many politicos from their previous commitments and, although Byrd did not endorse Sanders (or Griffin), most of his supporters gravitated to the Sanders camp. That group included such key political figures as Governor Vandiver, State Highway Director Jim Gillis, and a host of state senators who previously had endorsed the lieutenant governor.[1]

Byrd's unexpected departure aided the Sanders candidacy enormously, as did the *Gray v. Sanders* ruling overturning the county unit system and changing the rules of the game. While no one knew how it would affect the outcome of the race, it obviously encouraged urban voters to

---

[1]Sanders, "Interviews in 1990," pp. 81-85.

become more involved since their votes now counted equally with others; it cast a pall of doom on the rural counties when they realized that suddenly by judicial decree their political power had been greatly diminished. Since Griffin's strength had always been in the rural counties of south Georgia and Sanders had greater appeal in the cities, the decision aided the underdog considerably.[2]

Georgia politics in the 1960s was still personal. The voters expected the candidate to spend time in their community, chatting with people from all walks of life, shaking as many hands as possible, and giving a few speeches—in short, making them feel that he was their friend, that he understood their needs, and planned to do something about them. Since Georgia was the largest state east of the Mississippi River, campaigning on a personal basis was a formidable task. Moreover, in addition to its personal emphasis, Georgia politics also had a strong local and county orientation. Only Texas had more counties than Georgia's 159, and the candidate for statewide office was expected to visit all of them and cultivate their leaders.

A further complication to campaigning was the geographical location of the state's urban areas. Only Atlanta and Macon were centrally located, the other urban areas were on the periphery of the state—Augusta and Savannah on the eastern extremity, Valdosta on the Florida border, Albany in the southwest corner, Columbus on the Alabama border, Rome in the northwest, and Gainesville and Athens in the northeast. Driving from Rome to Savannah or from Gainesville to Valdosta, a distance of 300 miles, took the better part of a day on the inadequate highways of that day. The location of the cities also posed problems in getting radio and television coverage of campaign activities. The powerful Atlanta stations covered a wide area with a substantial population, but the others did not. Consequently, to reach the voters, careful coordination with the media was required. In sum, the candidate conducting a statewide campaign in Georgia faced serious logistical obstacles.

With less than five months remaining from the end of the special session until the Democratic primary on September 12, little time

---

[2]Peirce, *Deep South States of America*, p. 316; Albert B. Saye, *A Constitutional History of Georgia, 1732–1968*, rev. ed. (Athens: University of Georgia Press, 1970) pp. 417-18.

remained for Sanders to convince a majority of Georgia's voters that he should be governor. Given such a short time to organize and conduct a statewide campaign, the pace, by necessity, was frantic. In organizing his campaign, Sanders naturally turned to those he knew best, his friends in Augusta. J. B. Fuqua, a prosperous businessman well on his way to becoming one of Georgia's most successful business entrepreneurs, was then completing his third term in the legislature. As one of Sanders's closest confidants, he played a pivotal role in the campaign and was particularly helpful in fund raising. Immediately after embarking on his "daring gamble," as the *Macon Telegraph* described his candidacy for governor, Sanders went to see Mills B. Lane, who ran C & S National Bank, and asked for his support. As one of the key "movers and shakers" in the Atlanta Establishment, Lane wielded immense influence in the business community. The "Big Mules," political writer Bill Shipp's term for the power elite in Atlanta, consisting of Lane, Mayor Ivan Allen, Coca-Cola's Bob Woodruff, retailer Richard Rich, newspaper mogul Jack Tarver, and a few others, had little enthusiasm for Byrd and wanted no part of Griffin. They were searching for a candidate to back when Sanders switched to the governor's race. After investigating the young Augustan, Lane and his friends agreed to help. "You're in business," Lane told him, and the Sanders campaign was off and running. With the Big Mules in his camp, raising money for the campaign was no longer a major problem. Initially, local businessmen in Augusta who knew Sanders, such as banker Bill Weltch, raised substantial funds; later, as the campaign progressed, other sources throughout the state provided funds. Late in the campaign, when it appeared that Sanders might win, contributions flowed in faster as individuals and businesses doing business with the state wanted to be on the next governor's good side. Sanders estimated that his campaign collected $750,000, which was more than he had anticipated and enough to amply finance the campaign.[3]

Doug Barnard, Sanders's boyhood friend and neighbor, having gone into banking developed skills in advertising and public relations. Barnard's employer, the Georgia Railroad Bank, gave him a "casual leave

---

[3]Interview with J. B. Fuqua, Atlanta, Ga., April 4, 1991; Sanders, "My Life," pp. 38-39; Bill Shipp, "Carl Sanders: The Man, The Legend, The Era," *Georgia Trend* 7 (June 1992): 20; *Macon Telegraph*, April 22, 1962.

of absence" so that he could help with advertising and promotions and coordinate radio broadcasts. Whenever Sanders spoke, Barnard tried to get local people to sponsor the broadcast and feed it into urban areas. He normally flew to Atlanta with Fuqua on Sunday afternoon, worked at the campaign headquarters at the Dinkler Plaza Hotel Monday through Wednesday, then returned home to work at the bank on Thursday and Friday.[4]

The press secretary of the campaign was another Augustan, John Harper, a transplanted South Carolinian. He had become acquainted with Sanders when he was a young reporter for the *Augusta Chronicle*, and in 1962 he had advanced to executive editor. Tall and articulate, with a sardonic sense of humor, Harper helped write speeches and kept a steady flow of materials going to campaign workers, newspapers, and radio and television stations. Sanders and his team used the media, including television, effectively to get his message to the people.[5]

After an initial period of confusion, a workable campaign organization emerged. The chairman was Wyck Knox, Sr., of Thomson, a respected businessman and former chairman of the Georgia School Boards Association. Serving under him were two cochairmen: Charles Pannell, an experienced legislator from Chatsworth, coordinated activities in the northern part of the state, and Walter Dyal, the county commissioner of Telfair county, coordinated activities in the southern part. Dividing the state into smaller units, the staff assigned a coordinator to each of the ten congressional districts and named a county chairman for each county. The firm of Harry Segal developed advertising for the campaign.[6]

One of the most important leaders in the Sanders campaign was Jim Gillis of Treutlen county, the powerful state highway director. Originally committed to Garland Byrd, he joined the Sanders camp when Byrd withdrew and brought his close friend Walter Dyal with him. Gillis's knowledge of Georgia politics and long experience in campaigning were invaluable assets since Sanders and many of his key advisors were

---

[4]Barnard interview, February 16, 1991.

[5]Harper interview, May 7, 1991.

[6]Margaret Spears Lyons, "A Comparison of Carl Sanders's Gubernatorial Campaigns: 1962–1970" (master's thesis, University of Georgia, 1971) pp. 157, 162.

relatively young and inexperienced and amateurs at statewide campaigning. In addition to his knowledge, Gillis also had excellent contacts with county commissioners through his work as state highway director, and in 1962 county commissioners had considerable political clout. At age seventy, Gillis was the "old pro" of the inner circle.[7]

Marvin Griffin had, for practical purposes, been campaigning for reelection ever since he left office in 1959. Though embarrassed by the corruption of his administration, he remained a formidable candidate and clearly was the favorite at the beginning of the campaign. With a storehouse of anecdotes and a wonderful delivery, he was a master campaigner on the stump. He had many friends, a host of contacts on the local level, especially among the courthouse crowds, and name recognition. He claimed to have brought progress to the state while he was governor, especially in improving highways and education. Griffin lamented the demise of the county unit system and racial segregation and attempted to blame Sanders for bringing about the changes. Stressing his well-known opposition to integration, Griffin threatened to put Martin Luther King, Jr. so far back in the jail that "they'll have to shoot peas to feed him." He urged the white people of Georgia to give him a majority because his opponent had "the unqualified support and backing of Ralph McGill, Martin Luther King, and the Atlanta political machine." To handle integrationist agitators, Griffin said, "There ain't but one thing to do and that is cut down a blackjack sapling and brain 'em and nip 'em in the bud." To bolster his segregationist image—as if his own record and rhetoric were not enough—Griffin had Governor George Wallace of Alabama participate in his opening campaign rally.[8]

Sanders could not match Griffin's flamboyance, colorful phraseology, or humor, and, wisely, he did not attempt to do so. Instead, he campaigned the only way he knew how—being himself. In a serious, forthright manner he discussed the issues he deemed important. His platform, which he called a "Program for Progress," promised "an administration of complete moral integrity, free from the costly evils of

---

[7] *Official Register, 1965–1966,* p. 313; Peirce, *Deep South States of America,* p. 319; Sanders, "Interviews in 1990," pp. 84-85.

[8] "Out of the Smoke House," *Time* 80 (September 21, 1962): 25; "Politics," *Time* 80 (August 24, 1962): 11-12; *Atlanta Journal,* May 6, 1962.

cronyism, waste and double dealing at the taxpayers' expense." For Sanders, education was the number one priority, and he pledged to raise teachers' salaries, embrace a strong junior college program, and gear higher education to respond to "space age requirements." Asserting that highway reform was long overdue, he called for a thorough reorganization of the Highway Department. In addition, he promised to work strenuously to lure new industry to the state, continue the improvements in mental health, create a Department of Youth, and appoint only "capable, honest, respectable citizens to office." Since the Griffin campaign offered little more than stale racism, the contrast was striking.[9]

A product of the prewar Deep South, Sanders naturally was imbued with the racial customs and values of his region. Augusta was a typical southern town, where white supremacy was taken for granted and the races were rigidly segregated. Sanders attended all-white schools from the first grade through law school, worshipped in an all-white Baptist church, played only with whites at the YMCA, and lived in an exclusively white neighborhood except for the blacks who worked as domestics or did yard work. His circle of close friends was entirely white. Most of the blacks he knew did menial work and manual labor, attended "colored" schools, and lived in their own neighborhoods. Growing up in that environment, Sanders was comfortable with segregation, for he had experienced nothing else. Yet, unlike many of his contemporaries, he never developed a strong aversion to blacks. Or if he did, he abandoned such prejudice at an early age, for lifetime friends, such as Doug Barnard and Mrs. William "Frenchie" Bush, recall that in his early youth he had learned to accept both Catholics and blacks.[10] Sanders himself believes that he never harbored racial prejudice, and he points out that he has associated with blacks all his life and has worked with blacks since delivering newspapers as a boy. By 1962, integration no longer was a political issue for Sanders; the courts already had decided that matter in *Brown v. Board of Education* and other cases, and now the law must be obeyed. Criticizing the Supreme Court and promising to preserve white supremacy and racial segregation, as the Griffin camp frequently did, accomplished nothing, Sanders maintained. Such rhetoric, he felt,

---

[9]Complete platform in *Atlanta Journal and Constitution*, July 1, 1962.
[10]Barnard interview, February 16, 1991; Bush interview, August 29, 1991.

was entirely negative. It simply aroused emotions and misled the people. He would have been delighted to avoid the subject altogether in the campaign, but Griffin, by making race his chief issue, forced Sanders to respond.[11]

While serving in the General Assembly, Sanders, like all the other members, professed his belief in segregation, but he did not defend the system with the same intensity as Marvin Griffin, Roy Harris, Richard Russell, Herman Talmadge, and a host of other politicos. In fact, he seemed to understand that the system was eroding and someday would collapse. Nevertheless, since Georgia politics in 1962 demanded a commitment to segregation, he put aside such reservations and pledged "to maintain Georgia's traditional separation." But he carefully added that "violence in any form will not be tolerated." By avoiding blatant racism and downplaying racial questions Sanders projected a moderate image on the race issue. He understood that the forces converging on the South and a growing national mood for change doomed blind resistance to failure. He was a segregationist, but, as he quaintly put it, "I'm not a damned fool." By recognizing the futility of Griffin's diehard approach and opposing it, Sanders emerged as the voice of reason to many Georgians.[12]

During the campaign Martin Luther King, Jr. conducted a civil rights campaign in Albany, which turned out to be one of the least successful efforts of his career. Repeated marches and protests made little headway as Albany officials refused to negotiate with "individuals who are violating the law." Nevertheless, as the protests continued, the community became edgy and the potential for violence increased. Sanders attempted to end the racial disturbances in Albany and praised the local citizens for remaining calm in a time of trouble. He commended the people of Dougherty county for their respect for law and order and criticized King for violating laws he considered unjust. Sanders repeatedly denounced violent demonstrations and called for disagree-

---

[11]James F. Cook, "Carl Sanders and the Politics of the Future," in *Georgia Governors in an Age of Change*, pp. 171-72; Cook, "Sanders: An Oral History," p. 43.

[12]Cook, "Carl Sanders and the Politics of the Future," pp. 171-72; Earl Black, *Southern Governors and Civil Rights* (Cambridge MA: Harvard University Press, 1976) pp. 14-15, 68, 178; Ben Hibbs, "Progress Goes Marching Through Georgia," *Saturday Evening Post* 236 (February 16, 1963): 70.

ments in law to be settled in the courts. "Whether it be Marvin Griffin or Martin Luther King, I will not tolerate agitators nor permit violence or bloodshed among our citizens regardless of color or creed," he declared early in the campaign. Two days before the election, when two black churches in Terrell county were burned, Griffin disregarded the available evidence to argue that the fires probably were faked. Sanders responded by denouncing lawlessness. "There is no act more cruel and more destructive to American ideals than the burning of a church," he stated, and "such despicable acts are caused by the preaching of hatred." In distancing himself from King's tactics and denouncing violence, Sanders expressed his sincere beliefs. He also enhanced his standing among the voters of south Georgia. In the election he would carry much of south Georgia, including Dougherty county.[13]

Sanders formally opened his campaign with a rally in his wife's hometown of Statesboro. Throwing into the crowd duplicates of "rebate and commission checks" paid in the Griffin administration, he asked: "Is this the kind of government you want?" The crowd, estimated by police at 6,000 to 8,000, shouted back, "No." The youthful senator then proceeded to lambast the Griffin administration's record of "corruption, cronyism and crime." Pledging to banish forever the "peddlers of dishonesty, hate, violence and deceit," Sanders promised "there will be no more rigged bidding, fictitious companies, forged bids, or clearing-house operation carried on in the State Capitol as there were in my opponent's administration."[14]

In addition to the checks, Sanders provided two other effective innovations. Since Roy Harris of Augusta was known as one of Griffin's staunchest supporters, Sanders distributed copies of the August 9, 1954 issue of Harris's weekly newspaper in which Harris wrote: "I still say you can't trust Marvin Griffin. You can't trust him intellectually and you can't trust him politically." After quoting that statement, Sanders then declared, "Today, my friends, these two men are in the same bed." The third innovation was using big black briefcases to take up campaign contributions. For several weeks Griffin had been charging that some fat

---

[13]*Atlanta Constitution*, July 13, 31, August 2, 1962; Black, *Southern Governors and Civil Rights*, pp. 178-80.

[14]*Atlanta Constitution*, July 8, 1962.

cats were trying to buy the governor's office for Sanders. By using the briefcases to collect money from the crowd, Sanders defused the attack and laughed it away. It would be a bitter, hard-fought contest, and Sanders would get in his share of licks. In assessing the opening rallies of Sanders at Statesboro and Griffin at Americus, Eugene Patterson, editor of the *Atlanta Constitution*, concluded that judging the first round was easy: "Sanders climbed all over him."[15]

Corruption in the Griffin administration was an issue Sanders continued to stress throughout the campaign. Rarely did he make a speech without alluding to it, and the evidence was abundantly available. According to a grand jury, the state government under Griffin was characterized by the "perfidious conduct of state officials heretofore inconceivable to the minds of citizens." Among those convicted by the courts were a former director of state parks, a former member of the State Board of Corrections, an employee in the Revenue Department, three former sales tax officials, and others. One educated estimate placed the cost of corruption at $30 million. By continually reminding the voters of Griffin's past misdeeds, Sanders kept the former governor on the defensive and thoroughly disrupted his campaign. In response to the accusations, Griffin feebly admitted his errors and promised not to make the same mistakes a second time. His promises to put honesty and morality in government not only fell flat, they were not even taken seriously. Surveying his integrity pitch, the *Macon News* concluded in an editorial: "The miracle is that everyone who remembers the Griffin administration shenanigans didn't fall right down laughing." Corruption was a ready-made issue that hung like a millstone around Griffin's neck, and Sanders exploited it skillfully.[16]

Griffin, running a negative campaign, fired many misleading volleys at Sanders, but the youthful challenger proved to be an elusive target. Unlike Griffin, his record was free of scandal and corruption and his clean-cut, wholesome image deflected Griffin's charges. Griffin's repeated attempts to hold Sanders responsible for integrating the schools and ending the county unit system convinced few voters because the charges were so patently false. Georgians understood that Sanders, as a leader in

---

[15]Ibid., July 8, 9, 1962.
[16]*Augusta Chronicle*, September 6, 1962; "Politics," *Time* (August 24, 1962): 11-12.

the Senate, had acted courageously in confronting issues forced upon the state by federal courts. When that charge failed to make headway, Griffin depicted Sanders as the puppet of the Atlanta Establishment in general and Mills B. Lane in particular. Sanders did, of course, have the backing of Lane and Atlanta businessmen, but the charge failed to stick because Sanders also gained widespread support from businessmen throughout the state as well as Atlanta bankers who competed with Lane's C & S Bank. Moreover, since independent thought and action had characterized Sanders's public career, it was hard to visualize him as the tool of anyone, even the powerful Lane. John Sibley, perhaps the most respected man in the state and a conservative banker who competed with Lane, dispelled any credence that charge had when, on August 13, he thoroughly castigated Griffin at a Sanders fund-raising dinner. Outraged at the Griffin campaign, the esteemed old gentleman stated: "No amount of race baiting, misrepresentation, or abuse, a field in which the ex-governor is a master, can obscure the issue, or cover up the wholesale corruption and thievery of the Griffin administration." Sibley went on to explain that it was not Mills B. Lane alone, but a great company of responsible Georgia businessmen who supported Sanders, and it was not Ralph McGill alone, but a majority of Georgia editors who urged Georgians to vote for Sanders. When those charges failed to dent Sanders's armor, Griffin then linked Sanders with the Vandiver administration. The accusation was true, as Sanders readily admitted, and it was a serious miscalculation on Griffin's part. Failing to realize that the Vandiver administration remained popular with the majority of Georgians despite integration and reapportionment, Griffin merely enhanced Sanders's standing among the people by his criticism of the Vandiver administration and incurred for himself greater opposition from Vandiver.[17]

At the beginning of the campaign Sanders did not have a detailed strategy worked out, but he resolved to campaign harder than any of his opponents. At age thirty-seven and in top physical condition, he embarked on a speaking schedule designed to wear down his opposition. He knew that the fifty-five-year-old Griffin, who liked to relax and imbibe in the evenings, could not keep pace. As the campaign pro-

---

[17]*Atlanta Constitution*, May 22, July 14, August 14, 15, 1962.

gressed, Griffin's energy began to wane. Eventually, he had to cancel engagements because the pace was too hectic for him. Sanders, however, drawing on his athletic training, pushed himself to his physical limit and managed to campaign vigorously from beginning to end. He nearly pushed himself too hard. For several weeks after the primary he was unable to slow down and relax. Having conditioned his body to the strain of the campaign, it took a long time for his adrenalin to stop flowing so that he could once again relax in a normal fashion.[18]

Sanders correctly concluded that his biggest obstacle was not Griffin, it was simply that he was not well known by the voters. Determined to overcome that problem, he traveled 80,000 to 90,000 miles in the campaign and routinely gave five or six speeches a day, and sometimes as many as eight. With Betty at his side, he crisscrossed the state on a whirlwind schedule to meet as many people as possible. Flying his small single-engine airplane, he campaigned in every county, every town, and every pig path in the state. When airports were not available he landed in pastures, and sometimes it was necessary to drive cows out of the way so that he could land and take off. No one in Georgia had ever campaigned in such a fashion before, and his herculean efforts soon bore fruit.[19]

Starting far behind Griffin, Sanders consistently added friends and new supporters as he took his message to the people. Handsome, trim, and earnest, he spoke with conviction and assurance, and whatever he lacked in eloquence he made up for in sincerity. As the people of Georgia met Sanders, heard his speeches, and shook his hand, more and more of them concluded that he was a man of integrity and character who genuinely believed his rhetoric and who had the competence to carry out his progressive platform. At the midpoint of the campaign, Jim Gillis marvelled at the support Sanders had gained in south Georgia and predicted a 200,000 vote margin of victory for him.[20]

Though Carl continued to remind Georgia voters of the record of the Griffin administration, which, he cried, had made Georgia "the laughing stock of the nation," on the whole he maintained a positive

---

[18]Sanders, "My Life," pp. 40-41.
[19]Sanders, "Interviews in 1990," pp. 86-89.
[20]*Atlanta Journal and Constitution*, August 5, 1962.

tone in the campaign. In promising the voters an honest, efficient, frugal administration that would improve education, lure industry to Georgia, and reform several state agencies so that they delivered services more effectively, his emphasis was on the future, not the past. Progress was his favorite theme. The Sanders campaign, he said, "is one which looks to the future. It's one of moving ahead." Believing that Georgia was on the threshold of unprecedented economic advancement, he promised prosperity, progress, and opportunity through strong executive leadership which would make Georgians proud of their governor and state.[21]

Only three days after Sanders announced his candidacy, his home-town newspaper, the *Augusta Chronicle*, warmly endorsed him as "the ablest man in Georgia's political arena," and "a shining example of integrity," whose "competent leadership" must not be lost to the people of Georgia.[22] In rapid succession other newspapers followed the lead of the *Augusta Chronicle*. On the eve of the primary the *Atlanta Constitution* reported that at least seventy-five newspapers backed Sanders, including fifty-four weeklies and several from south Georgia towns including Adel, Fitzgerald, Baxley, Statesboro, and Cairo. Of the twenty-five dailies making endorsements, twenty-one endorsed Sanders. Daily newspapers in Dalton, Rome, Thomasville, Marietta, Valdosta, Athens, Waycross, Gainesville, Griffin, Columbus, Savannah, Macon, Augusta, and Atlanta supported him. By contrast, only four dailies—Albany, Moultrie, Brunswick, and Cartersville—endorsed Griffin. Sanders may have started the campaign as an urban candidate, but by the end of the campaign he was a Georgia candidate, having gained the allegiance of people from all walks of life and having endorsements from all parts of the state. Eugene Patterson, the astute editor of the *Atlanta Constitution*, described Griffin as "thrashing deep in the wells of desperation and raising great, hollow cries from the hole he is in," while Sanders "has the look of quiet strength and sureness that comes to a man who has gone to the people seeking his own certainty and found in them a confirmation of himself."[23]

---

[21]Cook, "Carl Sanders and the Politics of the Future," p. 172.

[22]*Augusta Chronicle*, April 24, 1962.

[23]*Atlanta Constitution*, September 10, 1962; list of newspapers endorsing Sanders by August 29, folder 1962 memorandums, box 23, Sanders Collection, Law Library.

Sanders became confident of victory about two weeks before the primary when he sensed a groundswell of support shifting to him. Earlier, he was shocked when he encountered Harry Reasoner and a CBS Television crew doing a documentary on him since he was going to win. The pollster Louis Harris was with them and his polls indicated Sanders would win. Having little experience with political polls at that time, Sanders remained skeptical. After the election, however, he found out that Harris had predicted the outcome with uncanny accuracy. Though confident of victory, Sanders maintained his hectic pace of campaigning to the end. On election day, September 12, he and Betty cast their ballots in Augusta early in the morning and then started toward Atlanta. Campaigning along the way, they stopped at Martinez, Evans, Lincolnton, Thomson, Warrenton, Gibson, Stapleton, Wrens, and Louisville. Arriving in Atlanta at 5:30 Carl, Betty, and the children took a room at the Americana Hotel, where they watched the returns on TV and attempted to relax. The initial returns were favorable. Soon Sanders had a comfortable lead which quickly became a rout. By 11:00 p.m. Sanders held a commanding two to one advantage and his joyous supporters clamored for him to make a statement. By then his headquarters at the Dinkler Plaza was so jammed that a big crowd of well-wishers, unable to reach the Sanders celebration on the fourteenth floor, simply started another party in the lobby. Finally, at 11:40 Carl and Betty decided to make an appearance. As they neared the elevator, a hotel guest, a middle-aged woman, stopped him. "Who's going to be governor?" she asked. "It looks like I am," Carl replied.[24]

When the votes were tabulated officially, Sanders had won a smashing victory. He captured 494,978 votes to Griffin's 332,746. He also won the county vote 86 to 73 and the county unit vote 256 to 154.[25] His strenuous campaigning had produced the desired results. By addressing the state's needs in a calm and realistic manner and offering a positive vision of the future, Sanders appeared to many as a voice of reason and common sense in a time of change and uncertainty. When given a clear choice between a traditional rural-oriented, race-baiting

---

[24]*Atlanta Constitution*, September 13, 1962; *Augusta Chronicle*, September 12, 13, 1962; Sanders, "Interviews in 1990," pp. 90-91.

[25]*Official Register, 1961–1962*, p. 1436.

former govenor and a younger, more sophisticated, urban-oriented
proponent of the new politics, Georgia voters chose the latter by an
overwhelming margin. Griffin's strength was confined to the rural
counties, especially in southwestern Georgia, whereas Sanders ran
strongest in the city counties and north Georgia. Indeed, over half of
Sanders's statewide vote came from the eleven city counties. His victory
over Griffin marked a turning point in Georgia's political history. He
was the first popularly elected candidate for governor in the Democratic
primary in fifty-four years, he was the first man from a city to be elected
governor of Georgia since the 1920s, and at age thirty-seven he was the
youngest governor in the country. Sanders's election personified the
meaning of the term "The New South," and he became its leader in the
eyes of the nation. Ralph McGill, that wise observer of the Georgia
scene, saw the election as bringing great credit to the people of Georgia.
He reminded his readers that Thomas Jefferson was of the opinion that
the American people, if supplied the facts, would act always with
common sense and good judgement. By electing Sanders, McGill
concluded, the people of Georgia "have eloquently sustained the great
Virginian."[26]

---

[26]*Atlanta Constitution*, September 13, 1962; Bernd, "Georgia: Static and Dynamic,"
in *The Changing Politics of the South*, pp. 333-34.

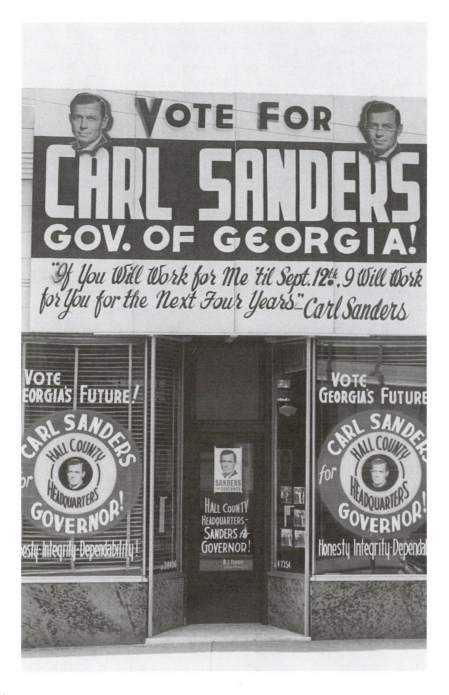

Carl Sanders for Governor Hall County Headquarters in 1962.

Carl Sanders campaigning for governor in 1962.

Marvin Griffin, governor of Georgia 1955–1959.

*Betty and Carl Sanders celebrating his victory
in the Democratic primary in 1962.*

Carl Sanders's parents savoring the Augusta Chronicle
account of their son's victory over Marvin Griffin.

Chapter 8

Assuming the Reins of Government

In the course of the campaign Betty Sanders began to see politics in a new light. Not politically inclined, she would have been just as happy if Carl had never sought public office. Unlike her husband, she did not need the fame, power, and adulation that comes with political success. Nor did she relish campaigning. Lacking Carl's competitive nature, she could not derive the same satisfaction and pleasure he seemed to get from a campaign. To her, campaigning was hard, exhausting work with very few rewards. And sometimes it was quite distasteful. Some of the dirty tricks commonly practiced in Georgia campaigns bothered her and offended her sense of fair play. At one of the first rallies in the campaign, one of Carl's aides had laboriously put up Sanders posters one evening in preparation for the rally only to find them gone the next morning, replaced with Griffin posters. Even more upsetting to her was criticism of Carl, especially when she knew the charges were false. She feared public speaking and tended to freeze up before large crowds. Fortunately she had to do little public speaking. On the occasions when she did, it took all of her courage to stand before the crowd, smile, appear relaxed, and read the prepared speech. Observers commented that she always did a credible job, but for Betty it was an ordeal. She enjoyed flying even less than public speaking, and landing a fragile plane in a cow pasture was not her idea of fun. Despite such feelings, she had campaigned with Carl, spending a good portion of two months in that hated airplane, simply out of love for her husband. He needed her, so she went. They were a team and they campaigned as a team. Carl publicly praised her and acknowledged her contributions to the victory.[1]

---

[1]Betty Foy Sanders interview, November 7, 1990; Sanders, "My Life," p. 40;

Now that the campaign was over and the victory achieved, she reflected on what had happened. She realized that her own ideas about politics had changed substantially in the course of the campaign. Although campaigning at such a whirlwind pace had left her and Carl physically drained, it had been an exhilarating experience. Carl, beginning with only a handful of close friends, had organized an effective campaign, much of it based simply on instinct and guesswork, but it succeeded. The young amateurs had defeated the old "pros." Carl had offered himself to the people, and they had accepted him. While they were campaigning, everything was so busy and confusing Betty sometimes wondered if they were accomplishing anything. But, somehow, through this hectic process of shaking hands and giving speeches, Carl had conveyed a message. He had a vision for what Georgia could become, and his campaign convinced the people that it was attainable. He promised Georgians honest and intelligent leadership, and they sensed that indeed he would provide it. During the campaign, thousands of Georgians simply got to know Carl. Their votes indicated they trusted his judgment to lead them for the next four years. For Betty, that was a sobering and humbling thought. American democracy, despite all its flaws, somehow works. At least in this instance, the best man had won, she reasoned.[2]

While Betty had no doubt that Carl would be an exceptional governor, she wondered about the next four years. How could she maintain a normal family life living in the Governor's Mansion? How would the change affect the children? What would be expected of the First Lady? Would she, a girl from the small town of Statesboro, be able to fulfill all of her duties? Such thoughts flashed through her mind from time to time and left her with a sense of uneasiness and apprehension.[3]

Little time for reflection or apprehension existed, however. After a few days of rest at Ponte Vedra, Florida, with their friends Bob and Mary Anne Richardson, the hectic pace resumed. The City of Augusta welcomed the Sanders family home with a gala celebration. Since Carl was the first Augustan to be elected governor since Charles J. Jenkins in

Sanders, "Interviews in 1990," pp. 158-60.
    [2]Betty Foy Sanders interview, November 7, 1990.
    [3]Ibid.

1868, the city rejoiced in his success. The festivities began with a massive parade down Broad Street. Schools and businesses closed early so that all could participate, and an estimated 40,000 Augustans lined the streets and cheered the governor-nominee and his family. At the conclusion of the parade more than 1,000 people gathered at Bell Auditorium to honor the Sanders family and local campaign workers. In presenting the Sanders family with an inscribed silver service, Mayor Millard Beckum said, "We had a remarkably good candidate. The merchandise was saleable and the sales managers were excellent. They knew how to get the merchandise before the customer." Governor and Mrs. Vandiver, who had ridden in the parade, also appeared on stage. Vandiver praised Sanders as a leader who "has the character, ability and courage to be a great governor of the Empire State of the South." Stepping down from the platform after greeting well-wishers for more than an hour, Carl remarked, "I have to slow down now and take some time to think."[4]

Carl, the most self-assured of men, had few of Betty's doubts about the future, but he did need time to think. Campaigning had required certain skills and an enormous expenditure of physical energy. Now that marathon was over and he needed to employ different skills in governing the state. Carl had to shift gears, so to speak. Having conditioned himself to campaign rigorously day after day, he experienced difficulty adjusting to a slower pace. Instead of constantly going and talking, he now needed to sit still and contemplate. He needed to assemble a team of leaders and make plans for the forthcoming legislative session. Realizing that the decisions he made at this time might well determine the success or failure of his administration, he was anxious to begin the process. Before he could concentrate on those matters, however, a new issue required his attention.

A week before the primary, a three-judge federal court had ruled that the Georgia legislature must be reapportioned before January 1963. Judges Elbert Tuttle, Griffin Bell, and Lewis Morgan unanimously agreed that the only way reapportionment could be done under the state constitution was for a special session to reapportion the Senate on a pop-

---

[4]*Augusta Chronicle*, September 25, 1962; Sanders, "Interviews in 1990," pp. 165-66.

ulation basis. The court also warned that if the legislature failed to eliminate the "invidious discrimination" before the 1963 legislative session
convened, it would fashion its own plan. The court scheduled another
hearing for October 5, apparently expecting action by that time.[5]

Both Governor Vandiver and Attorney General Eugene Cook favored
legislative action over a court-imposed plan, and both stated publicly
that those were the only alternatives. Sanders previously had stressed the
importance of Georgians maintaining control of their own affairs, and
he consistently and emphatically expressed that viewpoint. Vandiver,
cautious as usual, took the position that if a special session convened, it
should be called by the legislators themselves through petition. Sanders,
on the other hand, believed that the governor should be a leader, not a
follower of the legislature. In lengthy consultation with Vandiver, he
urged the governor to call the legislature into special session to
reapportion the Senate. Apparently his arguments prevailed, for Vandiver
reversed his position and called for a special session to meet on
September 27.[6]

Technically Vandiver was still governor, but in the reapportionment
issue he receded into the background and allowed Sanders as president
pro tem of the Senate and governor-nominee to take charge. Never
afraid of responsibility, Sanders gladly accepted the challenge.

Before the special session convened, Sanders sent telegrams to all the
legislators asking them to meet with him informally at the Capitol to
discuss reapportionment proposals. He wanted to make sure they would
tackle this difficult issue. Even though reapportionment meant that
many of the senators would be eliminating their own jobs, the legislators
agreed unanimously to act rather than leaving the problem to the federal
courts. The solons recognized that the old system could no longer be
defended. They disliked being coerced by the federal courts, but they
recognized the political reality of the situation. If they did not reapportion the Senate, the courts would do it. Given those unpleasant choices,
they assured Sanders that they would "bite the bullet." Sanders then
presented for their consideration a Senate reapportionment plan organized by Senator Bob Smalley of Griffin. It called for reorganizing

---

[5]*Augusta Chronicle*, September 6, 1962.
[6]Ibid., September 7, 15, 1962.

Senate seats on the basis of about 73,000 persons per district. The legislators generally agreed with the concept but wanted to work out some of the details.[7]

Both key legislators and the press expected a lengthy and bitter session. Frank Twitty speculated that it would last at least two weeks. Surprisingly, the session went more smoothly than practically anyone had predicted. In establishing the Smalley plan as the basis for discussion from the beginning, Sanders took the initiative and maintained it throughout the session. Naturally legislators debated the plan, and some of the discussion became quite bitter, but Sanders maintained control throughout the session. Always pragmatic in dealing with the legislature, he willingly made minor adjustments in the boundaries to accommodate members so long as the districts remained balanced in population. His forceful yet flexible approach was effective with the legislature. Soon the members realized that the Smalley plan, though not entirely satisfactory to anyone, was as good as any they could adopt. They quit haggling and agreed to it. In only seven working days the legislature reapportioned the Senate on the basis of population. Governor Vandiver signed the bill immediately and praised the legislature and Sanders for the extraordinary accomplishment.[8]

The "impossible" bill, as the press dubbed the reapportionment measure, brought a profound change to Georgia politics. That it passed so quickly was truly remarkable. Since the Senate's inception in 1789, representation had been based on geography. Henceforth it would be based on population. Under the old system, counties having only 6.13 percent of the state's population elected a majority of the Senate, but now power rested with the majority of the people. In addition, the rotational system, which had kept the Senate weak compared to the House, was eliminated. Now senators could succeed themselves and be reelected indefinitely. The law invalidated the nominations of the September 12 primary and required a special primary election on

---

[7]Ibid., September 15, 1962; *Atlanta Constitution*, September 19, 1962.

[8]*Augusta Chronicle*, September 28, 29, 1962; *Atlanta Constitution*, October 6, 9, 1962.

October 16. The new nominees would then go on the November 6 general election ballot.[9]

Basking in praise from the special session, Sanders was formally nominated for governor at the state Democratic party convention in Macon on October 17. Some 3,000 leaders of the party gathered to hear the standard political rhetoric. There was plenty of it in the eloquent keynote address by Dr. Noah Langdale, the president of Georgia State College, the rousing nominating speech by Representative Quimby Melton of Griffin, and many others. In accepting the nomination, Sanders reiterated the promises he had made during the campaign; namely, to reorganize the State Highway Department, establish a new Department of Industry and Trade to replace the current Department of Commerce, make education his top priority, avoid a tax increase this year, and have an honest administration. He also emphasized, as he had many times in the campaign, that "violence in any form will not be tolerated."[10]

As was customary, the new governor established his control over the party by staffing the organization with people loyal to him. Sanders named his close friend J. B. Fuqua, now a new state senator, as the state party chairman, and he placed many of his friends and close supporters in key positions within the party. Serving under Fuqua as vice presidents were Charles Pannell, Walter Dyal, Wyck Knox, and Quimby Melton. One of Carl's friends from law school, William Trotter, became National Committeeman and Mrs. Marjorie Thurman was National Committeewoman.[11]

With the party now staffed with people loyal to him, Carl began to assemble his personal staff. One of the key positions was the executive secretary who actually would run the office. Since that person would work closely with the governor on a host of matters, represent the governor on occasion, and handle confidential matters, the job required considerable tact and diplomacy and—above all—the governor's absolute confidence. For that position Sanders wanted a nonpolitician who would

---

[9]Coleman, *A History of Georgia*, pp. 395-96; *Atlanta Constitution*, October 6, 1962.

[10]*Atlanta Journal*, October 17, 1962; Melton's nominating speech in Special folder, box 22, Sanders Collection, Law Library.

[11]*Official Register, 1961–1962*, pp. 1426-31.

be totally loyal to him and would tell him the unvarnished truth. His old friend Doug Barnard had all of those qualities and proved to be an ideal choice for executive secretary. Securing a leave of absence from his bank, he served effectively for nearly the entire four-year term.[12]

For the unpaid position of chief of staff, Carl named Bob Richardson, a respected Atlanta attorney with the firm of Gambrell, Harlan, Russell, Moye and Richardson. John Harper of Augusta, who had served as press secretary during the campaign, continued in that position. Larry Lloyd, who had worked with Carl from the beginning of the campaign, was named aide to the governor. Henry Neal of Thomson became the governor's legal aide and an assistant attorney general. Neal had experience in the job, having served as Vandiver's legal aide for four years. He also was a law school classmate of Carl's and a close personal friend. Serving capably in the Governor's Office for the entire four-year term were Mrs. Judy Clifton Darby as receptionist and Mrs. Eleanor Owens as appointment secretary. Mrs. Joyce Bailey served as the governor's confidential secretary for two years. When she resigned to have a baby, Mrs. Kathryn Frierson, who previously had served as Sanders's secretary in Augusta, replaced her. Another key member of the office staff was Mrs. Benny Tackett, supervisor of the pool of secretaries who performed the routine clerical work. Also serving on the governor's staff were Porter Weaver and Alex Davis, who transported Sanders wherever he needed to go. Weaver, a state patrolman, became the governor's official driver, and he later rose to command the State Patrol. Davis, who took a leave from Eastern Airlines, served as the governor's personal pilot for four years and rendered outstanding service.[13]

Even before the inauguration, press reports already indicated that the Sanders inner circle had a fondness for handball. Sanders, who loved almost all sports, found handball a good way to relax and relieve tension. Neal, Richardson, and Barnard also were handball enthusiasts, and when time permitted, the four of them played a few spirited games at the YMCA during the lunch hour. These were the men Sanders would work with on a daily basis for the next four years. While clearly in charge and having no reluctance to make decisions, Sanders still valued his staff's

---

[12] *Official Register, 1965–1966*, p. 28; Barnard interview, February 16, 1991.
[13] *Official Register, 1965–1966*, pp. 30-37; Tackett interview, January 23, 1991.

advice and trusted their judgment. They worked together as a team, and the staff rendered loyal and effective service.[14]

Having served on an efficiency committee in the Vandiver administration, Sanders firmly endorsed the concept of having an independent agency study and recommend ways of improving the operation and efficiency of state government. Sanders named William R. Bowdoin, senior vice president of the Trust Company of Georgia, to chair the commission which was made an arm of the executive branch. Bowdoin, who had served with distinction as state purchasing agent for Vandiver and had recently served as chairman of the Sanders campaign in the Atlanta area, was the perfect choice for this position. With a solid reputation for integrity and ability, he commanded great respect in both the political and business communities. Formally named the Commission on Efficiency and Improvement of Governmental Operations, the Bowdoin Commission was destined to play a vital role in the Sanders administration.[15]

To carry out the Sanders program in the Senate Carl named Charles Pannell of Chatsworth as his floor leader. Pannell, fifty-one, was a veteran legislator and a former member of the State Pardon and Paroles Board. He had worked closely with Sanders in the legislature and had served on his campaign staff. As assistant floor leaders in the Senate, Carl named Milton Carlton of Emanuel county and Julian Webb of Donalsonville. To get his legislation adopted in the House, Carl knew he had to have a loyal speaker of the house who would work diligently with him. The incumbent, George L. Smith, offered competence but not loyalty. Moreover, he made a crucial mistake when he arrogantly stated that no governor could replace him. For Sanders, that was George L.'s *coup de grace*. Carl found the leader he needed in George T. Smith of Grady county. Although George T. was nine years older than Carl, they had been classmates in law school. Smith had campaigned enthusiastically for Sanders, but he was surprised when Carl chose him to be speaker since he had served only two terms in the House. George L. Smith tried desperately to retain his position, but when the legislature convened, the House elected George T. Smith speaker by vote of 199

---

[14]*Atlanta Constitution*, November 30, 1962.
[15]*Atlanta Journal*, November 28, 1962.

to 0. Working closely with the speaker was the floor leader, Arthur Bolton of Spalding county, forty years old and a fourteen-year veteran in the House. As assistant floor leaders Sanders named George Busbee of Dougherty county, who would later serve as governor, and Jim Andrews of Stephens county.[16]

Hoping to attract more tourists into the state, Sanders demanded improvement in the state parks. He chose Horace W. Caldwell of Albany to provide that leadership. At age sixty-one the new Parks Director was one of the older members of the Sanders team. He had operated the Radium Springs Hotel for many years. In announcing his appointment, Sanders described him as "an outstanding Georgian" with "many years of success as an administrator in the business world."[17] To head the Welfare Department Sanders named Mrs. Orville Schaefer of Toccoa. Wife of a prominent surgeon and a graduate of Brenau College, she had compiled an outstanding record of voluntary and public service. She was on the executive committee of the twelve-member Democratic National Committee and had chaired the women's division of Sanders's campaign. To accept the new position, she had to resign as vice chairman of the State Board of Education. Her appointment received widespread praise in the newspapers.[18]

The positions of Revenue Commissioner and Supervisor of Purchases were sensitive ones since they handled large sums of money on a daily basis. Sanders appointed Representative Hiram Undercofler to the former and Wistar Jay to the latter. Undercofler, a forty-six-year-old attorney from Americus, possessed exceptional ability and integrity. Another graduate of the University of Georgia law school, he had served two terms in the legislature. Jay was a fifty-nine-year-old businessman from Thomasville. Sanders retained many Vandiver appointees in various positions, including Colonel H. L. Conner as director of the Department of Public Safety and Jim Gillis as chairman of the State Highway Board.[19]

In choosing his team of leaders Sanders sought people much like himself—honest, competent, and willing to work hard. That he was a

---

[16]Ibid., November 5, 1962; *Atlanta Constitution*, December 18, 1962, January 15, 1963; *Official Register, 1965–1966*, p. 414; Sanders, "My Life," p. 42.

[17]*Atlanta Constitution*, December 18, 1962.

[18]Ibid., January 4, 1963; *Official Register, 1965–1966*, p. 261.

[19]*Official Register, 1965–1966*, pp. 233, 267, 302, 313.

good judge of character is evidenced by the fact that none of his appointees brought any scandal or embarrassment to his administration, and many served the state with great distinction. Sanders filled many of the positions with classmates from law school and people whom he knew personally from his legislative service. There was considerable continuity with the Vandiver administration in the appointments of Conner, Gillis, Neal, Bowdoin, and others. That was to be expected since Sanders also had played a major role in the previous administration. The University of Georgia, and especially its Lumpkin School of Law, had been a training ground for Georgia politicians, and that tradition was continued in the Sanders administration. In general, youth marked the leadership of the Sanders administration. Gillis, Caldwell, and Jay were obvious exceptions, but for the most part the new leaders were close to Sanders's age of thirty-seven. The new team also was loyal to Sanders and most of the key appointees had worked actively in his campaign. Sanders's confidence in his team was not misplaced, for they would serve him capably for the next four years.

While assembling his staff, preparing his inaugural address, and making plans for the legislative session, Sanders was diverted by a problem at Fort Gordon. Rumors had circulated for months that part of the army operation might be moved to another location outside of Georgia. Anxious to retain the jobs in Georgia, Sanders had corresponded with Senator Russell as early as September 28 about the matter. On October 3 Russell sent the governor-nominee copies of his correspondence with the Secretary of Defense and the Secretary of the Army. He asserted that in addition to Fort Gordon, two other Georgia installations, Moody Field and Hunter Field, also were vulnerable and would have been closed long ago "if I had not happened to be the Chairman of the Senate Committee on Armed Services." The senior senator urged Sanders to "make a successful effort" to get President John F. Kennedy to approve a request for permanent construction at Fort Gordon.[20]

In early November it appeared to Sanders that several units of the Signal Corps were on the verge of being moved from Fort Gordon to

---

[20]Several letters regarding Fort Gordon in Carl Sanders Special folder, box 122, Political Series VI, Richard B Russell Collection, Russell Memorial Library, University of Georgia, Athens.

Fort Monmouth, New Jersey. Following Russell's suggestion, he made an appointment with President Kennedy. Sanders flew to Washington with J. B. Fuqua, where they were joined by Atlanta lawyer Robert Troutman, who was a friend of the President. The three Georgians met with Kennedy for fifty minutes on November 15 and discussed many issues, including Fort Gordon. Sanders, who also met with Vice President Lyndon Johnson and other leaders, described the meeting as a "courtesy call." The press quoted him as saying he came to Washington primarily to meet the President and other party and government officials so that by knowing the Washington officials he will have to deal with he would be better able to serve the state. Sanders returned home the next day and the Georgia press carried a photo of Sanders conversing with President Kennedy in the White House. The *Augusta Chronicle* gave Sanders full credit for convincing the President to cancel the orders which would have moved the units from Fort Gordon.[21]

Since Sanders received all the credit and Russell got none, the senator was furious. Convinced that his influence and previous efforts had more to do with the decision than Sanders's chat with the President, Russell was thoroughly miffed by the press coverage Sanders received. He subsequently sent a terse letter to the Secretary of the Army asking for copies of the relevant orders concerning Fort Gordon. His letter included five paragraphs from the *Augusta Chronicle* which praised Sanders for saving the jobs and said not a word about Russell. It is doubtful that the senator's disposition improved when he received a letter from Sanders dated November 19. Sanders explained that when I "learned that you had already left for Europe" I made an appointment with the President and discussed the Fort Gordon problem with him, and "it now appears that all the Signal Corps classes will remain at Gordon for the immediate future." Sanders added that he had requested the President to include in the Defense budget an appropriation for permanent Signal Corps school buildings, and "we are depending on you to see that the appropriation is made promptly." Sanders and Russell never developed a close friendship, and this event did nothing to improve their relationship. The event did, however, enhance Sanders's

---

[21]*Atlanta Constitution*, November 16, 1962; *Augusta Chronicle*, November 16, 1962.

relationship with both Kennedy and Johnson. Carl admired both men and developed a warm friendship with them.[22]

While political matters occupied Carl's attention, Betty directed her talents and energy to the inauguration parade, reception, and ball. Campaigning may not have been her forte, but entertaining was, and she did it with style. Working with an advisory committee and consulting with Lamar Dodd, her art teacher at the University of Georgia, Betty attempted to make each event a memorable occasion. Whenever Betty entertained, she planned her activities carefully. Resourceful and imaginative, she developed a theme and coordinated the details so that the event would be enjoyable and make a lasting impression.

Tuesday, January 15, 1963, was inauguration day. It was also one of the coldest days of the year as a mass of frigid air had engulfed the city of Atlanta. The festivities began with a three-mile parade led by the governor and his reviewing party through Atlanta to the Capitol. Despite the inclement weather, the crowds lining the streets seemed to enjoy the numerous marching bands, National Guard units, and colorful drum and bugle corps. There were floats representing the Augusta Bar Association and the Augusta Chamber of Commerce and two huge floats depicting the life of Betty and Carl. Adding an unusual twist to the proceedings were ten floats designed by Lamar Dodd representing ten planks in Carl's platform. The first was "Dawn of New Era." Others included "A New Day—Mental Health," "One Georgia," "Natural Resources," "A Mecca for Tourists," "Science Industry," "Highways for Tomorrow," "Forward Georgia," "The Key to Growth," and "Agricultural Prosperity." Betty's artistic influence was evident throughout the event, as she had developed an appropriate theme for the parade.[23]

There was concern that Carl's mother, recently hospitalized from a fall, would be unable to attend her son's inauguration. But this was one event she could not miss. She and Carl's father rode in the parade with

---

[22]Carl Sanders Special folder, box 122, Russell Papers; Cook, "Sanders: An Oral History," pp. 48-49.

[23]*Atlanta Constitution*, January 12, 16, 1963; press releases, January 9, 1963, Carl Sanders Papers, Executive Department Correspondence, Georgia Department of Archives and History, Atlanta; press releases, January 5, 9, 14, 16, 1963, January 1963 folder, box 34, Sanders Collection, Law Library; Inaugural Parade Program, Carl Sanders Special folder, box 122, Russell Papers.

their son Bob and his wife. Betty's mother and other relatives were part of the receiving party, along with the Vandivers, Geers, and other political leaders. The parade ended at the Capitol, where a platform had been erected for the inauguration ceremony.

Reverend T. E. Boehm of Hill Baptist Church, Carl's church in Augusta, gave the invocation. After guests were recognized, Governor Vandiver delivered the Great Seal of Georgia to Secretary of State Ben Fortson. Justice Joseph Quillian administered the oath of office to Carl, after which Fortson delivered the Great Seal to the new governor. Carl then delivered his inaugural address. Peter Zack Geer was sworn in as lieutenant governor. After his address, the traditional ceremony ended with a benediction by Reverend J. Robert Smith of First Baptist Church in Statesboro, Betty's home church.[24]

Carl opened his inaugural address with an impromptu prayer in which he committed his administration to God's work. Setting the tone for his address, he stated: "This is a new Georgia. This is a new day. This is a new era." Calling for teamwork, cooperation, and hard work to solve Georgia's problems, he asserted: "Together we shall walk in the bright gardens of tomorrow." He promised to accomplish better roads, a higher quality of education, more hospitals, more recreational facilities, better airports, new and expanded industries, and "greater opportunities for all." He offered few new phrases or promises; instead, he repeated the essential points he had been making throughout the campaign. One statement, however, seemed to stand out: "If there is to be a star of the show in the four years of my term of office, it will be the Georgia child." It was a somber speech, interrupted only four times by applause. But it was an appropriate speech delivered with obvious earnestness and sincerity, and it was widely praised by the press and the legislators. The *Atlanta Constitution* editorialized that "it was a good inauguration speech, a fine statement of principles."[25]

Everything went according to plan, but there were some near misses. Carl had ordered a new suit from Muse's to wear to the inauguration,

---

[24]*Atlanta Constitution*, January 9, 16, 1963.

[25]Ibid., January 16, 1963; Frank Daniel, ed., *Addresses and Public Papers of Carl Edward Sanders, Governor of Georgia, 1963–1967* (Atlanta: Georgia Department of Archives and History, 1968) pp. 3-7.

and it did not arrive until the last minute. Because of the intense cold weather, electric heaters were placed on the inauguration platform. Without realizing it, Carl had gotten so close to one of the heaters that his pants started to steam. Fortunately, someone noticed that the governor's pants were about to ignite before they actually did.[26]

Betty made the motto of the Great Seal of Georgia, "Wisdom, Justice and Moderation," the theme for the decor for the Inaugural Reception at the Governor's Mansion. "Wisdom" was florally depicted in the living room with attention focused on a mural of the first Executive Mansion in Milledgeville. In the music room she placed an arrangement built around the brass scales of "Justice." The third word—"Moderation"—was symbolized in the overall restraint of the arrangements and was spotlighted in the dining room in a floral arrangement around a silver and crystal columned epergne. Punch was served in the sun parlor where the predominant theme was the state symbols—the live oak, Cherokee rose, and brown thrasher. Carl and Betty greeted guests in a receiving line in front of a huge, symbolic floral replica of the Great Seal with gold drapes forming the background. And the guests kept coming, thousands of them. The schedule called for the reception to last from 4:00 to 6:00 p.m., but the crowds were so large that it was well past 6:00 when the First Family finally got away so they could prepare for the Inaugural Ball.[27]

The excitement generated by the Inaugural Ball was something the city of Atlanta had rarely seen. Hotels were booked solidly from Sunday through Tuesday, rental firms ran out of mink stoles and tuxedos, and hairdressers reported thriving business. Tickets for the ball were in great demand. More than 5,000 people jammed the ballroom of the Dinkler Plaza Hotel and spilled out onto the sidewalks.[28]

The ball began at 9:00 and Carl and Betty arrived shortly before 10:00 with a military escort. Entering on a red carpet, they were introduced with pomp and ceremony and escorted to their seats, where eight United States Marines stood guard. The First Lady was stunningly beautiful in a gown designed by Philip Hulitar. Carl noticed that

---

[26]Sanders, "My Life," pp. 42-43.
[27]*Atlanta Constitution*, January 16, 1963.
[28]Ibid., January 12, 1963.

because the crowd had congregated in one area, that part of the ball-room had become quite warm, so warm, in fact, that some women were about to faint. To avoid a catastrophe, he quickly escorted Betty to the dance floor to formally open the ball and provide more space for breathing. Soon the dance floor was so packed with bodies that dancing was nearly impossible. Couples could not move; they stood, swayed a little, and listened to the music. Dean Hudson's music continued until midnight, but Carl and Betty departed long before it was over.[29]

When the First Family retired that evening, exhilarated but exhausted by the activities of the day, they knew they had made a positive impression on the people of Georgia. The new administration was off to an impressive start. The first day had been a memorable one. Carl and Betty were determined that the 1,460 remaining days in the Sanders administration also would be good ones for the people of Georgia.

---

[29]Ibid., January 16, 1963.

*Governor-elect Sanders and President John F. Kennedy
in the White House, November 15, 1962.*

*Justice Joseph Quillian administers the oath of office
to Governor Carl Sanders, Januay 15, 1963.*

Chapter 9

The 1963 Legislative Session

Carl Sanders served as governor during a period of great change and ferment. It was a vibrant, exciting, youth-oriented age, confident in its ability to improve the world. In the field of civil rights, it was the period of Selma, Birmingham, the march on Washington, Martin Luther King's "I Have a Dream" speech, and the passage of federal civil rights laws. It was also a period of black frustration, which saw the emergence of growing militancy, "black power," and devastating urban riots. It was the age of the New Frontier and the Great Society, the Peace Corps and the War on Poverty, the Beatles and Peter, Paul and Mary, the arrival of the Braves and Falcons in Atlanta, protests and marches, miniskirts and the counterculture, full employment and the war in Vietnam. America would never be quite the same again. As Bob Dylan, who captured the spirit of the 1960s better than anyone, put it, "The Times, They Are a-Changin'."

While much changed in the 1960s, much also stayed as it was. Indeed, many Americans—and certainly most Georgians—considered themselves conservatives and adhered to traditional beliefs and values. In Hollywood, the number-one box-office draw in 1962 was wholesome Doris Day. She was followed in order by Rock Hudson, Cary Grant, and John Wayne.[1] Popular television fare included Ed Sullivan, Perry Como, Ozzie and Harriet, Donna Reed, Lawrence Welk, and "Perry Mason." Westerns, such as "Bonanza," "The Virginian," "Gunsmoke," "Have Gun, Will Travel," and "Wagon Train," presented traditional values to millions of viewers. If the entertainment media reflected American tastes, then conservatism remained a powerful force indeed.

---

[1]*Atlanta Constitution*, January 7, 1963.

Sanders, who had campaigned as a reformer determined to launch the state "into a new orbit of progress and opportunity," seemed to represent the new politics. But while he was an advocate of change and a great admirer of President Kennedy and his New Frontier, he also held many conservative views. He was a fiscal conservative, a staunch believer in law and order, a devoted family man, and a sincere Christian. In his inaugural address he explained his attitude toward change. "Change in government can be dangerous," he stated, "but to refuse to change when the world around you is changing is even more dangerous." Therefore, he believed that "change to achieve efficiency, economy and better government is both wise and justified." At the same time he added: "We revere the past. We adhere to the values of respectability and responsibility which constitute our tradition." He summed up his position by stating, "I tipped my hat to the past, but took off my coat to the future."[2] By demonstrating a responsiveness to new ideas and change in government within the framework of traditional values, Sanders appealed to both camps.

As Ernest Vandiver relinquished the office of governor to Sanders, he remarked that he felt like "a fellow who has just finished his final exam and felt like he passed." Both his political colleagues and the press agreed that Vandiver had given Georgia four years of honest, competent leadership. By any measurement, the condition of state government was better when he left office in 1963 than when he had assumed the governorship four years earlier. Vandiver could proudly state that in his administration services had been greatly expanded, $850 million in new building programs had been undertaken, public education had been preserved, and confidence in state government had been restored. In addition, the Senate had been reapportioned, a budget system had been adopted, and, despite no increase in taxes, $22 million had been left in the treasury. The *Atlanta Constitution* editorialized that he had done "a great job" and leaves office "with the overwhelming respect and affection of the people."[3]

---

[2]Daniel, *Addresses of Carl Sanders*, pp. 5-6; Cook, "Carl Sanders and the Politics of the Future," in *Georgia Governors in an Age of Change*, p. 173.

[3]*Atlanta Constitution*, January 1, 2, 16, 1963.

The press optimistically predicted that the Sanders administration would continue the progress begun under Vandiver. Writing a few days after Sanders won the primary, Gene Britton, a reporter for the *Macon Telegraph*, ruminated about the implications of the election for the future of Georgia. Sanders, he predicted,

> will, undoubtedly, prove to be a wise guardian of public funds, following a precedent set by Ernest Vandiver. . . . On race relations, he will be a coolheaded moderate, not given to breaking tradition, but not given to breaking heads either. He will work to improve Georgia's industrial climate, bring about significant advances in the state's health and welfare programs and, again like Vandiver, do some reorganizing and streamlining of the government to make it work better for the people. He will, in all probability, be a good governor, possibly one of Georgia's best. If Georgians back him in office as they backed him in the campaign, Georgia and Carl Sanders have much to look forward to in the next four years.[4]

The new legislature that would be called upon to enact the Sanders program was quite different from its predecessors. As a result of the reapportioned Senate and the special election, there were eighty-nine freshman legislators in the General Assembly that convened in January of 1963. Many of them represented urban areas, which heretofore had been underrepresented. Democrats maintained overwhelming control of the General Assembly, but a handful of Republicans had been elected from urban areas. One of the new senators from Fulton county was Leroy Johnson, a wise, soft-spoken attorney, and the first black elected to Georgia's General Assembly since Reconstruction. The *Atlanta Constitution* observed a sense "of responsibility, of reason, and of good intent" in both chambers. Unlike the old politicians, the new legislators looked like "sensible executives preparing to make some big decisions" with serious resolve. As the legislators assembled in Atlanta for the 1963 session, they were almost unanimous in predicting a smooth session. Representative James Mackay of DeKalb county expected the legislature to give Sanders a "honeymoon" with his program because the members realize he had a mandate from the people to carry out his program.[5]

---

[4]*Macon Telegraph*, September 17, 1962.
[5]*Atlanta Constitution*, January 14, 15, 1963.

On January 16 the new governor delivered a combined budget message and state of the state address to a joint session of the General Assembly. As a compliment to Vandiver he declared, "The state of our grand old state is excellent!" To move the state forward he asked the legislature to appropriate nearly $1 billion for the next two years. To balance that budget without raising taxes, he urged the legislature to pass a law to collect corporate income tax quarterly, as the federal government does. In explaining his spending plans, he noted that 72 percent of all new spending will go to education. Teachers will receive $100 pay raises the first year and $200 the next year. Some $25 million worth of new schools will be built through the sale of bonds. The University System, he explained, would get an additional $4.3 million the first year and $3.3 million the second year, plus three new junior colleges would be built. "Every boy and girl in Georgia, no matter how rich or poor, should have the opportunity of a college education, and it is my intention to make this possible," he declared. Although Sanders stressed education, he also allocated increased expenditures for mental health and highways.[6]

Sanders's budget proposals were made in accordance with a new constitutional amendment that had set up a budget officer to compile in detail the needs of every department. Thus, it was a comprehensive budget supported by data and careful estimates of expected revenue. Sanders had less latitude in budgetary matters than previous governors, but he welcomed the change which mandated a more responsible and systematic development of the state budget. Although his budget of $465 million for the next fiscal year was $45 million more than the latest appropriation, he believed revenues would be available to balance it, providing "we hold expenditures to the recommended maximums" and "firmly resist unreasonable demands for spending."[7]

After outlining his spending plans, Sanders then called for numerous reforms. Although he was committing over 56 percent of the total budget to education—the highest percentage ever—he nevertheless wanted to create a commission to study the needs of education at all levels. He wanted to make sure that the appropriations were being spent

---

[6]Daniel, *Addresses of Carl Sanders*, pp. 11-18.
[7]Ibid.; *Rome News-Tribune*, January 16, 1963.

in the most efficient manner possible. Since the state constitution had been amended 381 times since its adoption in 1945, he recommended the creation of a constitutional revision commission to revise the existing document or propose a new constitution. To take the highway department out of politics, he called for the establishment of a new ten-member State Highway Board. He also requested the creation of a Department of Youth, a Georgia Mountain Authority to develop the state's scenic mountain and lake attractions, and a police academy. Finally, he advocated rewriting Georgia's election code and adopting two amendments to the constitution: one to extend Senate terms to four years, and the other to allow the merger of counties by majority vote.[8]

Having served in a leadership capacity in the Vandiver administration, Sanders had a solid grasp of the problems confronting Georgia's government, and, as a result of his legislative experience in the House and Senate, he knew how far the General Assembly was likely to go in solving them. Thus, he presented an ambitious but realistic program that addressed many of the state's most glaring immediate needs and also provided the groundwork for some long-range reforms. The legislators received his speech favorably, interrupting it fourteen times with applause. Despite a few criticisms of specific items, legislators in general praised it lavishly. Representative William Killian of Glynn county said it was "the strongest State of the State message I've heard." Representative Quimby Melton of Spalding county called it an "outstanding speech." Representative Henry Milhollin of Coffee county said "I don't think it will be hard to sell his program to the General Assembly." Fulton county Representative Wilson Brooks thought Sanders offered "a splendid program for the state." The praise was not confined to Sanders supporters. Even Representative Marvin Moate of Hancock county, a former speaker of the house and a Marvin Griffin stalwart, called the address "a great speech."[9]

Despite the positive comments from legislators, it remained to be seen how effectively the new leaders would function in the House and the Senate. The new lieutenant governor, Peter Zack Geer, had been a rival of Sanders. Before the session got underway, Sanders met with him

---

[8]Ibid.
[9]*Atlanta Constitution*, January 17, 1963.

and attempted to secure his support. He explained that they could battle each other for the next four years and accomplish very little for the state, or they could cooperate and work harmoniously together to benefit the state. If Geer would support his program, Sanders promised to make sure he received full recognition for his contributions. The meeting produced the desired results. Geer not only offered his support, he delivered it for the next four years, as both men later acknowledged.[10] The House also had new leadership with George T. Smith as speaker and Arthur Bolton as floor leader, and it was in the House that the first test of strength occurred. It came from Representative Denmark Groover of Macon, another of Sanders's classmates in law school but more recently Governor Griffin's floor leader. One of the most brilliant men in the legislature, Groover was also one of the most erratic members. An independent thinker, he often marched to the beat of a different drummer. Perhaps that was to be expected of him since he was a Marine fighter pilot in World War II in Major Gregory "Pappy" Boyington's famed "Black Sheep Squadron." Groover offered an apparently innocuous amendment to the administration's House Bill One, the bill establishing the new Highway Department. He argued that too much power was being given to the director and not enough to the ten-member board. Though couched as a philosophical difference, Groover's amendment was really a test of political power. Floor Leader Bolton and Speaker Smith, anxious to find out where the members stood, decided to call for a vote. The members of the House stood with the governor, as Groover could muster only fifty-two votes. All other amendments were defeated and the House approved the bill 195 to 0. This was Groover's first challenge to Governor Sanders, but it would not be the last.[11]

The other measures of the Sanders program were introduced and proceeded through the legislative process. The Senate quickly approved by vote of 47 to 0 the bill to lengthen Senate terms from two to four years. In the House there was a temporary setback on the constitutional

---

[10]Cook, "Sanders: An Oral History," pp. 53-54; Geer telephone interview, September 5, 1991.

[11]*Atlanta Constitution*, January 23, 1963; *Official Register, 1963–1964*, p. 424; interview with Denmark Groover, Atlanta, September 12, 1989, Georgia Government Documentation Project, Special Collections, Georgia State University, Atlanta.

amendment providing for easier consolidation of counties. Passage required a two-thirds vote, or 137 "ayes," but when first voted on, the measure received only 126 votes. It was an embarrassing defeat for the new team, and Bolton announced there would be a reconsideration soon. After some administration arm-twisting, the House adopted the measure by vote of 159 to 30. The amendment received only token opposition in the Senate, which passed it by vote of 43 to 4. When the legislature recessed after meeting two weeks, Sanders was pleased with the progress of his program. By then House Bill One had been adopted. In signing the bill, Sanders announced that he was reappointing Jim Gillis as state highway director. Under the new law, the Highway Board would choose the director beginning in 1967. Until then, the governor chose the director, and Gillis was Sanders's choice.[12]

Invariably the budget is the most important measure passed by the legislature each session. It is studied in depth and debated at length. After sixteen days of public hearings, the Appropriations Committee approved Sanders's proposed budget and sent it to the House. There Representative Alpha Fowler of Douglas county and Representative Denmark Groover led a fight to reduce the budget by $11 million. Fowler, another graduate of the University of Georgia and a banker by profession, described Sanders's budget as a "fiscal obscenity" and declared: "It's a premeditated walk up a primrose path to hari-kari." Groover cried that he was filled with "stark fear" when he contemplated the spending program and argued that a tax increase would be "irrevocably necessary." Despite their flamboyant rhetoric, the House approved the budget, almost exactly as Sanders had presented it, by vote of 170 to 2. The Senate, after making only slight changes in it, approved it unanimously.[13]

When the General Assembly adjourned on March 15, there was general agreement that the nine-week session had been a very productive one. The *Atlanta Constitution* thought it was "one of the most remarkable legislative sessions in years."[14] While some legislators doubted that revenues would equal expenditures, only a few were critical of the session

---

[12]*Atlanta Constitution*, January 23-26, February 15, 1963.
[13]Ibid., February 27, March 12, 1963.
[14]Ibid., March 16, 1963.

as a whole. One of that small minority was Johnny Caldwell of Upson county. He thought that the session accomplished little and passed too much nonessential legislation. While conceding that the governor's program of a dozen bills was "essentially good," he found the overwhelming majority of the 600 bills introduced in the House and the 200 in the Senate "absolutely unnecessary." A more typical view of the session was that of Howard Overby of Hall county. He declared, "Of all the years I've been coming, this has been one of the better legislatures." Sanders obviously was pleased with the performance of the legislature. In thanking the members at adjournment, he stated, "You have given Georgia her most shining hour."[15]

Sanders had good reason to be pleased. He had set the agenda, kept the legislature on course, and accomplished practically all of his objectives. The only one of his priority measures the legislature failed to adopt was the four-year term for senators. Since senators represented approximately 72,000 people often scattered over a wide area, while their colleagues in the House had as few as 2,000 constituents, it made sense to extend the Senate terms to four years. Unfortunately, the House refused to make the change. In essence, the House decreed that if Senate terms were to be lengthened, then House terms must also be lengthened. Since there was little justification or public sentiment for extending House terms, an impasse was reached. Sanders, who had served in both houses, genuinely believed that four-year terms for senators were justified. He promised to continue the battle in the next session, but once again the House blocked the measure. Sanders was unable to accomplish the change, and none of his successors have fared any better. Two-year terms for both houses have remained unchanged up to the present.

During the session several issues arose which provoked heated legislative debate, but they were not administrative measures. Restricting billboard advertising on interstate highways proved to be a divisive issue. The billboard measure passed the Senate but languished in a House committee. Sanders, arguing that the full House should have an opportunity to vote on the measure, managed to get it out of committee and onto the floor of the House where it was defeated 99 to 73. As a result,

---

[15]Ibid.

Georgia kept its interstates cluttered with billboards and lost a substantial amount of federal money it would have received had the bill passed. Sanders, always eager to get federal funds for Georgia projects, promised to continue the legislative battle, and in a later session succeeded in securing passage of the reform.[16] Perhaps the most controversial issue of the session was the attempt to raise the age of execution for a capital crime. Everyone seemed to agree that the existing age limit of ten was too young, but there was little agreement on how high it should be raised. The Senate favored raising it to eighteen, but the House insisted on sixteen. Finally, near the end of the session, the houses compromised at age seventeen.[17]

Aside from the four-year term for senators, the legislature adopted all of the major issues Sanders presented. It approved his budget along with the changes in collecting corporate taxes, reorganized the Highway Department, created the Department of Youth, and restructed the Welfare Department as the Department of Family and Children Services. It also established an Election Laws Study Committee consisting of three representatives, two senators, and four members appointed by the governor. In addition, Sanders gained legislative support for three commissions which would have a major impact upon his administration and the future of Georgia. A legislative committee agreed with the governor that the state constitution needed to be revised or rewritten. To accomplish that goal, the Constitutional Revision Commission was set up. To study "all facets of public education" and suggest appropriate reforms, the Governor's Commission to Improve Education was created. Finally, and most importantly, the Governor's Commission for Efficiency and Improvement in Government was put into operation. Headed by William Bowdoin, it consisted of seven outstanding business and professional men appointed by Sanders. They served without pay, but the legislature appropriated $290,000 to cover the expenses of the commission. During the next four years, the Bowdoin Commission, as it was usually called, would study numerous agencies and departments of state government and suggest needed reforms in published reports. Sanders backed the Bowdoin Committee enthusiastically and used its findings to

---

[16]Ibid., March 1, 12-15, 1963.
[17]Ibid., March 1, 13, 1963; *Rome News-Tribune*, March 5-7, 11, 14, 1963.

bring about substantial improvement in government. Thus, much had been accomplished in the 1963 session, and a foundation had been established for more substantive reforms in future sessions.[18]

[18]*Acts and Resolutions, 1963*, pp. 10-12, 81-121, 176-79, 218-21, 228-50, 394-96, 402-409, 492-94; Daniel, *Addresses of Carl Sanders*, pp. 26-28; *Official Register, 1963–1964*, pp. 88-93.

Carl Jr. and Betty Foy Sanders being introduced at the Inaugural Ball, January 15, 1963. Also pictured, from left to right, President Pro Tem and Mrs. Harry Jackson, Lieutenant Governor and Mrs. Peter Zack Geer, Governor and Mrs. Carl Sanders, and Speaker of the House and Mrs. George T. Smith.

Governor Sanders at his desk in the State Capitol.

Governor Sanders addressing the General Assembly.

First Lady Betty Sanders.

Chapter 10

Life at the Mansion

A division of power existed in the Sanders household: Carl ran the Capitol and Betty ran the Mansion. It was a good arrangement since both were skilled in their respective jobs. Carl was so busy attending to the affairs of state, working with the General Assembly, traveling all over the state for meetings, dedications, and inspections of trouble spots, and delivering around two hundred speeches a year that he gladly yielded the household responsibilities to Betty. Keeping the Mansion attractive for family and guests, entertaining dignitaries, traveling with Carl and greeting the public, conducting special projects—all were demanding tasks for Betty. Additionally, she was determined to provide a homey and comfortable atmosphere for Carl and their two rambunctious children. Though they operated in different spheres, Betty's responsibilities were as demanding as Carl's.

The Governor's Mansion was a large stone structure located in the Ansley Park section of Atlanta at 205 The Prado. Built more than half a century ago by the grandfather of Rankin Smith, it had long passed its prime when the Sanders family moved in. When Betty first toured the Mansion, she was shocked by its dilapidated condition. Major renovations were needed to bring it up to par, but little money had been spent on maintenance, since the legislature had decided that it should be replaced. Betty was astounded that there was no set of crystal, no table linens—not even for entertaining. The only attractive pieces she found for entertaining were a handsome silver punch bowl and candlesticks from the battleship *Georgia*. Realizing that the First Family is the state's number one public relations firm, she insisted that temporary repairs and modest redecorating be done. Unless such work were done, Betty feared it would be impossible to entertain guests without embarrassing them and herself. With the complete backing of Secretary of State Ben Fortson, her requests were carried out. Fresh paint and wallpaper as well as new linens, towels, and accessories did wonders. Over the years, much of the china with the state seal had been lost or broken, but fortunately Lenox China managed to provide a complete set for twenty-four by inauguration day.[1]

Even though the cosmetic improvements enabled Betty to entertain in an acceptable—if not grand—style, serious problems remained. The twelve-by-twelve-foot kitchen was inadequate when preparing for 300 to 500 guests. For legislative dinners it was necessary to move all of the furniture out of the downstairs to accommodate the crowd of people. Parking was woefully inadequate for almost every event. Over the years tree roots had grown into the pipes causing serious plumbing problems. Rain was always an adventure because the roof leaked in several places. After a heavy rain in February of 1965, a two-foot by four-foot patch of ceiling plaster fell to the floor. Prior to that mishap, the ceiling in the hallway had fallen and had been replastered. One night, a huge patch of wallpaper in the downstairs front guestroom fell completely off the wall onto the floor. On another occasion, when several friends had dined with them, a piece of stone fell out of the wall and almost struck Mills B. Lane as he was leaving. There was little doubt that Georgia's First Family needed a better home. As Ben Fortson, who had been responsible for maintaining the home for many years, remarked, "This old house has just had it."[2]

Although Betty cried when she first toured the living quarters of her new "home," over a period of time she grew to love it. After four years of patting it and knocking it to get it to perform, she came to appreciate the character and charms of the old granite home on the hill, and she cried when she had to leave it.

No one claimed the house was haunted, but it was spooky. Like most old houses, it made strange noises. The doors creaked, the walls rattled, and the windows vibrated whenever the wind blew. Noises came from the attic where squirrels nested, and they could be heard scampering about at all hours. The noises were especially scary to Betty Foy. Only ten years old when she moved into the Mansion in 1963, she could imagine all sorts of frightful things. Often at night, with the house

---

[1]Betty Foy Sanders interview, November 7, 1990.
[2]Ibid.; *Atlanta Constitution*, February 8, 1965.

creaking, she would get so scared she could not sleep. On such occasions she would go into her brother's room or make him sleep in her room. Her scariest experience occurred on a cold December night. A ladder had been propped up against the balcony outside her room in order to install Christmas decorations on the roof. She was always nervous about the balcony, and with the ladder there she imagined people climbing up to get into the house. Listening to the creaks, she became frightened. Then there was a loud noise. She was certain she heard it. She could hear the ladder shaking, and she was convinced that the noise came from someone climbing up the ladder. She ran into her brother's room and told him that someone was climbing up the ladder. He heard the noise too. Together they dashed into Carl and Betty's room. Carl immediately called the troopers' shack where the state patrolmen stayed. No one answered. Betty Foy concluded, "They've done something to the troopers and now they are coming up the ladder." She was right. There was someone on the ladder. But it was not a burglar or intruder. It was instead a state patrolman. In making his rounds he noticed the ladder. Deciding that it was a security risk, he removed it.[3] As a result of such experiences, Betty Foy wrote the following poem when she was in the fifth grade:

> I live in a big stone house on a hill
> With flowers and bushes all pretty and still.
> It's spooky at night and gives me a fright
> Then comes the day and it's sunny and bright.[4]

Despite her fears, both Betty Foy and Carl Jr. enjoyed living in the Governor's Mansion. It was so big and had so many nooks and crannies they felt a sense of freedom. It was hard for anyone to find them when they wanted to hide. They played in the basement, in the attic, on the grounds, and at the troopers' shack. Developing a friendship with several of the state patrolmen, the children continually played pranks on them and stayed underfoot. They enjoyed sneaking into the shack and releasing their pet squirrel. When the surprised patrolman yelled some obscenity, they would run off laughing, having accomplished their

---

[3]Interview with Betty Foy Botts, Atlanta, January 28, 1991.
[4]Carl and Betty Sanders Personal Papers, Atlanta.

mission. Carl Jr. delighted in throwing firecrackers into the shack and scaring the wits out of the unsuspecting patrolman.[5]

The children attended Westminster, a fine private school, and, of course, the harassed state patrolmen drove them to school. That sometimes led to exciting and embarrassing experiences. One afternoon, as the children were beginning to leave school, a boy who had committed a crime on the campus jumped into his car and sped off. The state patrolman who was there to pick up Betty Foy took off in pursuit. He captured the suspect and held him at gunpoint until policemen arrived. Betty Foy was terribly embarrassed by the whole thing. She derived no pleasure from that kind of attention and would have preferred a more inconspicuous routine.[6] Carl Jr., however, was just the opposite. He was thrilled to ride with state patrolmen in an unmarked car. Steve Polk, who later was head of the State Building Authority, was his favorite driver. He had a good sense of humor and got along well with children. Once when Polk was driving Carl Jr., a maniac confronted them and attempted to run them down. Polk managed to get Carl Jr. out of the car and then set out after him. He caught the crazed driver when he wrecked his car on Mt. Paran Road and Highway 41. Carl Jr. loved such experiences. To an adventuresome boy in his preteen years, traveling with a patrolman was invariably exciting, more fun than playing games with boys his age.[7]

Carl Jr. and Betty Foy found the academic level at Westminster more advanced than the public school they had attended in Augusta. As a consequence, they had to study hard to catch up with the other students. As children of the governor, they naturally attracted considerable attention. Betty Foy also attracted attention for another reason: her pronounced southern accent. At recess the students enticed her to talk so they could make fun of her unusual pronunciation. It amused them to hear the little "country bumpkin from Augusta" say "bawl" the water and other words that sounded funny to sophisticated young Atlantans. At first Betty Foy also received gifts, such as candy, trinkets, or dollar bills from her male classmates. The boys, it seems, were vying to become

---

[5]Betty Foy Botts interview, January 28, 1991.
[6]Ibid.
[7]Interview with Carl Sanders, Jr., Augusta, February 15, 1991.

her boyfriend so they could get to the Governor's Mansion first. Her parents discouraged such gifts, and after a while the novelty wore off.[8]

Since there were only a few children from the neighborhood who attended Westminster, Betty Foy spent a lot time with her German shepherd named Midnight. In fact, she spent more time with Midnight than with any of her classmates. Sometimes she would visit other children, and occasionally other children would come to the Mansion and play. But Midnight was always available, and he was Betty Foy's constant companion. The state patrolmen also were fond of Midnight, and he often accompanied them as they made their rounds of the house and grounds. As Midnight grew older, he suffered hip dysplasia, an ailment common to German shepherds. It became increasingly painful and eventually Midnight had to be put to sleep. That was a sad day in the Sanders household. They had another dog, a tiny Chihuahua named Chico. According to Betty Foy, he was "the meanest Chihuahua that's ever walked the face of the earth." He stayed in the basement and was so ferocious that only a few people could pet him. Little Chico could not replace Midnight in Betty Foy's affection. She grieved over the loss of Midnight for a long time. Betty Foy loved animals in general, and especially dogs and horses. She had learned to ride a horse at an early age when she lived in Augusta. When she was twelve, her parents bought her a beautiful seven-year-old thoroughbred mare named Hossnik. Betty Foy thoroughly enjoyed riding Hossnik, and some of her closest friends were girls she rode with. After a few years, however, when Betty Foy became interested in boys, there was not enough time for boys, studying, and Hossnik. Her grades dropped and Hossnik was sold.[9]

Both of the children were outgoing and energetic. Carl Jr. had a mischievous streak which could be discerned by a twinkle in his eyes, and Betty Foy was effervescent, even at that early age. Although she was popular and was included in everything, she sometimes wondered if people really liked her as an individual or if they invited her to things because she was the governor's daughter. Despite such concerns, on the whole they were happy-go-lucky types and had few worries. They had a good network of love and support from their parents and other family

---

[8]Betty Foy Botts interview, January 28, 1991.
[9]Ibid.

members, and they knew they were loved. Betty Foy was Daddy's little girl. If things did not work out with her mother, she could usually get her way with her father. Mrs. Sanders was the main disciplinarian, but, if necessary, Carl could use his belt. He did not use it often, but when he did he meant business. The children learned what was permissible, and by staying within acceptable limits wisely avoided encountering Carl's belt, except on rare occasions. Looking back from the vantage point of twenty-five years of hindsight, both Betty Foy and Carl Jr. have fond memories of their years in the Mansion. They understand that there is a price to pay when you are a public figure. While acknowledging some negative aspects of living in the proverbial fishbowl, they agree that the positive aspects, especially the opportunity to travel and meet interesting people, including national leaders, far outweighed the negatives.[10]

Living in the Mansion required some adjustment from all concerned. The state provided a staff of two maids, one houseman, and a chef, which relieved Betty of the duties of cooking, cleaning, and washing. Instead of those burdens, Betty spent much of her time planning, supervising, and coordinating. The diminutive cook Ben Cruz and his large wife were welcome additions to the household. But Betty was aghast when she learned that state prisoners, including convicted murderers, performed much of the manual labor in the Mansion. Fearing that her family would be unsafe with convicted prisoners roaming about, she insisted that they be removed and other help hired to do the work. To please his wife, Carl readily agreed. So did Ben Fortson, who was responsible for such matters. While granting her request, wise old Ben was convinced that Betty would regret her decision. He knew from long experience how the system worked. The prisoners were brought to the Mansion early each morning. They worked all day and then were transported back to jail at night. Since working in the Mansion was more pleasant than languishing in jail, the prisoners worked diligently. They understood that if their work or behavior caused any concern, they would remain in jail. They also knew that if they made a favorable impression on the governor, there was a chance he would pardon them. Consequently, they were excellent workers. The replacements that were

---

[10]Betty Foy Sanders interview, November 7, 1990; Betty Foy Botts interview, January 28, 1991; Carl Sanders, Jr. interview, February 15, 1991.

hired to appease Betty did not perform as well as the prisoners. Not only did they work at a slower pace, sometimes they did not show up at all. After a few weeks of painful experience, Betty learned why prisoners had been used for many years. Reluctantly, she called Ben Fortson, and prisoners were used thereafter.[11]

While attempting to rear Betty Foy and Carl Jr. as "normal" children in the abnormal environment of the Governor's Mansion, Betty was called upon to perform many other duties too. She was an active First Lady, and her positive accomplishments contributed to the success of the Sanders administration. Always involved in civic activities, she expanded her efforts as First Lady. She was an active member of the Georgia Legislative Forum for Women and the Governor's Commission for Better Education. A lover of beautiful flowers, she worked with the Garden Clubs of Georgia and the Georgia Federation of Women's Clubs in their beautification programs. Fighting cancer was one of her top priorities. For three years she was honorary chairman of the American Cancer Society's Earlier Treatment Education Program. In that capacity she sent letters to individuals, did radio spots, and worked with women's civic organizations regarding the "Conquer Uterine Cancer" program. In general, she did all that she could to publicize cancer education, including the need for frequent examinations and early treatment. Some 5,000 Georgians died of cancer each year, she pointed out, and one in four deaths could be prevented. As a result of her dedicated leadership, she was named Atlanta's 1965 Woman of the Year in civic affairs.[12]

A noted hostess, she was contacted by Georgia Power Company to put together a book of her favorite recipes. Working with Mirion Bennett of the Advertising Department of Georgia Power Company, Betty carefully chose recipes utilizing Georgia products, especially peaches and pecans. Their labors produced an attractive little book, *Favorite Recipes of Georgia's First Lady*, which appeared in April 1965. It included a portrait of Betty, a foreword by her, numerous illustrations, and twelve recipes plus one favorite menu, representing a sample of delicacies most frequently prepared and enjoyed at the Mansion. Some 10,000 copies

---

[11]Sanders, "Interviews in 1990," pp. 57-60.

[12]American Cancer Society folder, Woman of the Year folder, box 40, Sanders Collection, Law Library.

were printed initially. Betty considered the book a means of advertising
Georgia, and she seldom missed an opportunity to publicize her native
state. She gave away hundreds of the books as gifts. Later, four of her
recipes were reprinted in the March 1966 issue of *McCall's*.[13]

Betty's talent for entertaining was legendary. Despite the inadequacies of the old Mansion, she and Carl entertained a host of distinguished
visitors to Georgia during their four years. The most prominent visitor
at the Mansion was Mrs. Lyndon Johnson, who made a quick trip to
Atlanta on May 11, 1964. Betty and Carl, along with Mayor and Mrs.
Ivan Allen, greeted Lady Bird at Atlanta Municipal Airport. Her hectic
schedule included a tour of the Communicable Disease Center, a short
speech at a groundbreaking ceremony there, a private luncheon with the
president of Emory University, a main address at the Emory University
Convocation, a tour of the Atlanta Art Museum, a reception at the
Governor's Mansion, and the return flight to Washington.[14]

According to Betty Carrollton, women's editor for the *Atlanta
Constitution*, the reception for the First Lady was "the most eagerly
anticipated social event of the year." It did not disappoint Lady Bird or
the seven hundred guests who attended. Mrs. Johnson wore a three-piece
white suit and around her neck was a gold chain from which dangled a
gold silhouette of the map of Georgia. She was proud of the silhouette
and explained that "Betty Sanders gave it to me when she was our guest
in Washington last February." Greeting the guests in the reception
room, Betty wore a sleeveless overblouse and slightly flared skirt of
cream silk with a peach print, matching peach stole and shoes, and a
spray corsage of Tropicana roses. In planning major social events, Betty
always developed a theme and coordinated all aspects of the event with
great precision. The mood and motif of the elaborate reception were
unquestionably Southern and specifically Georgian. Floral arrangements
in varying colors of the Georgia peach highlighted the decor theme, and
refreshments featured various state products, with emphasis on the
peach. Betty served peaches in an ingenious array of dishes. There were

---

[13]McCall's Article folder, First Lady Cookbook Information folder, box 40, Sanders
Collection, Law Library.

[14]*Atlanta Constitution*, May 12, 1964; press releases May 9, May 11, 1964, May
1964 folder, box 34, Sanders Collection, Law Library.

peach cookies, iced cake garnished with peaches, peach-shaped peach ice cream served in silver baskets lined with magnolia leaves, peach punch, and even peach-shaped candles on the serving trays. At each end of the main banquet table were large pyramids of fresh peaches which impressed Mrs. Johnson. She commented on the beauty of the peaches and observed that "all the food looks too dressed up to eat." Then she quickly added, "I won't let that deter me for long." Lady Bird also admired portraits of Carl and Betty painted by Elizabeth Shoumatoff of New York. Since her husband was very dissatisfied with his official portrait, Lady Bird inquired about the artist. Betty informed her that the artist's work already was hanging in the White House. She had done three portraits of Franklin Roosevelt and was working on another when he died. The last work is known as the unfinished portrait of Roosevelt. The reception for Mrs. Johnson was a grand success. As Lady Bird was leaving the festive setting she remarked, "It has been a very busy, very exciting day, and I've loved every minute of it."[15]

In addition to her renown as a hostess, Betty also was known for her love of hats. Hats were in fashion in the 1960s, and Betty was a style setter. Indeed she was recognized by the National Millinery Institute for her outstanding taste in hats. Consequently, when the Women's Committee of the High Museum of the Atlanta Art Association decided to hold a flea market sale of hats in 1965, Betty was named to chair the event. She wrote letters to three hundred celebrities asking them to donate hats and explaining that all of the proceeds of the sale would go to the new $8 million Atlanta Cultural Center, which was being built as a tribute to the 106 artists and community leaders who were victims of a tragic plane crash at Paris, France in 1962. Her letter produced an overwhelming response. Hats began to arrive from all over the country. For a while it was hard to get around in the Mansion because hats were everywhere. Hats were donated by Hubert Humphrey, Bobby Jones, Roddy McDowell, Bob Hope, John Wayne, Natalie Wood, Steve McQueen, Bobby Dodd, Vince Dooley, Olivia de Haviland, Joan Crawford, Mamie Eisenhower, Lyndon Johnson, Richard Russell, Herman

---

[15]Ibid.; undated newspaper clipping in Foy Newspaper Collection, Sanders Personal Papers, Atlanta.

Talmadge, and numerous foreign embassies. Needless to say, the flea market was a financial success.[16]

Looking back on her tenure as First Lady, Betty remembers how busy she was those four years. It seemed that some major project requiring her time and energy came up each week. She would no sooner complete one activity than another would begin. Since Atlanta was a rapidly growing city located in the heart of the South, a steady stream of visitors came to the capital city. The city began as a rail center, and it continued to be a transportation center. In the 1960s the interstate highways were under construction and three of them—I-75, I-85, and I-20—converged on Atlanta. In addition, Atlanta's airport had already become one of the busiest in the nation. So many planes landed in Atlanta that jokes already were being told about it. It was said that if you were going to heaven, you would first have to transfer in Atlanta. Since Carl and Betty were personal friends of the Kennedys and Johnsons, numerous federal officials visited Atlanta. Betty and Carl, eager to lure new industry to the state and enhance Georgia's image, frequently entertained corporate executives and foreign dignitaries as well as federal officials. Even more frequent were delegations from the state. When the mayors from all over the state came to Atlanta for the Georgia Municipal Association meeting, Betty hosted a tea for their wives. Groups of all ages and sizes came to the Mansion. There were groups of farmers, retired people, county commissioners, sheriffs, legislators, and a host of others. One of the biggest challenges for Betty's hospitality was the annual dinner for the legislature. The Governor's Mansion simply was not big enough to accommodate so many people. After struggling through the ordeal two years, Betty and Carl moved it to the more spacious Grand Ballroom of the Marriott Hotel in 1965 and 1966.[17]

Entertaining diverse groups of people effectively is a talent few people possess. Those who do it well have a special ability or knack that sets them apart from others, much like a professional athlete who performs athletic feats better than the rest of us. The Bible includes

---

[16]Flea Market folder, Hats Received folder, box 40, Sanders Collection, Law Library.

[17]Mayor's Day folder, Legislative Dinner 1964 folder, Legislative Dinner 1965 folder, Legislative Dinner 1966 folder, box 40, Sanders Collection, Law Library.

hospitality as one of the spiritual gifts, and Betty had it in abundance. She made people feel welcome and comfortable in her home, regardless of their age, background, or social standing. While she could entertain senators, diplomats, and executives with aplomb, she was equally adept at entertaining orphans at Christmas. Each year the Mansion customarily had been covered with Christmas decorations. Betty, easily discerning ways of improving the decorations, made some changes. She placed a twenty-five-foot tree decorated with 1,500 colored lights on the roof. Another 1,500 lights were placed on the foundation of the Mansion. Two six-foot decorated trees mounted on masonry columns flanked the driveway entrance. A large sign reading "MERRY CHRISTMAS TO ALL" was prominently displayed and highlighted by flood lights. The cost for all of her new decorations for Christmas came to the modest sum of $434.42. When the Christmas decorations were completed, Carl and Betty invited one hundred or more children from local children's homes to a Christmas party at the Mansion. The first year 150 children came from the Methodist Children's Home, the Baptist Children's Home, and Hillside Cottages. Carl read Christmas stories, the Atlanta Boys Choir sang, and "Stars and Strings" marionettes performed. After some hilarious antics from organ grinder Garland Parnell and his trained monkey Tricky Bob, Santa appeared and refreshments were served. Each year a different group of children was invited and different entertainment provided, but the result was the same: the children had a grand time, and so did Carl and Betty.[18]

Sending out Christmas cards was another project that Betty was involved in. Since she and Carl mailed 12,000 cards, it was a formidable undertaking. As a trained artist, Betty wanted the cards to recognize some aspect of the state's political history and to be artistically attractive. Inside the card she placed the Georgia state seal followed by a traditional Christmas message from Governor and Mrs. Carl Sanders. The 1963 card featured an original drawing of the State Capitol by Charles W. Schmidt. For the 1964 card Betty contacted Professor Vincent J. Dieball of the Art Department at the University of Georgia. He recommended a talented graduate student named Ken Williams, who did a beautiful

---

[18]Christmas 1963 folder, Christmas 1964 folder, Christmas 1965 folder, box 40, Sanders Collection, Law Library; *Atlanta Constitution*, December 16, 1963.

etching of the Governor's Mansion. Inside the card was the state seal and the inscription "From our home to the homes of our friends, we extend holiday greetings as we honor the anniversary of the birth of our Lord." Professor Dieball and Professor Lamar Dodd were pleased with the card. Betty liked it and so did Ben Fortson. After 12,000 of the cards were mailed, a secretary in Ben Fortson's office, looking at an enlarged version of the etching, noticed something peculiar. Near the top of the scene, hidden in the foliage above the roof of the Mansion, was one tiny but clearly discernible word—GOLDWATER. The young artist, it seems, had a sense of humor. Knowing that Carl was a staunch Democrat who had campaigned vigorously for Johnson in the recent presidential election and would mail the card to other Democrats, he evidently thought that it would be fun to include the name of the Republican presidential candidate in the card. The writing was so small it was barely visible. In fact, no one noticed the word GOLDWATER until Fortson's secretary discovered it. The young artist's professors were not amused. They were astounded and embarrassed by the "joke." Betty was mortified. Since the cards had already been mailed, there was nothing she could do about it. Carl was more philosophical. He laughed about it and told Betty the card would become a collector's item. After the Goldwater fiasco, Betty was unwilling to take any chances with graduate students and their sense of humor. For the 1965 card Professor Alan Tiegreen of Georgia State College did a drawing of Georgia's old State Capitol at Milledgeville. For the 1966 card Betty did composite sketches of the five homes for Georgia governors, from Oglethorpe's tent at Savannah to the new Mansion. Her original drawing from which the card was made currently hangs in the Georgia Department of Archives and History in Atlanta.[19]

The hectic pace of public life took its toll on Betty. Lacking the stamina of Carl, she was unable to function at his pace for an extended period of time. Very few could. She needed a break, some relaxation, some time to herself. Carl broke his routine with exercise at the YMCA and playing golf, but she did neither. Her physician advised her to slow down and get more rest. During their second year in office she told Carl

---

[19]Christmas Cards 1963, 1964, 1965 folder, box 40, Sanders Collection, Law Library.

that she was getting "people-pooped." Having to deal with people every day and every night had become a strain, and she was tired. Betty had met a local artist named Ouida Canaday. She suggested to Carl that resuming her art studies under Canaday's direction might be a good way to break her routine and provide some needed relaxation. Carl agreed. Canaday agreed to come to the Mansion and give Betty private lessons once a week. The art lessons not only were therapeutic, they opened the way to a new career for Betty. Having done little art work since college, she was "rusty." But resuming where she had left off in college, she honed her skills and continued to develop her talents. Painting became a means for Betty to express herself. And Betty was particularly eager to express her feelings about her native state. Painting became her "soapbox," as she put it. Working with Canaday, she resolved to use her art to leave a gift to the state. In the intervening decades she was able to fulfil that pledge many times.[20]

A project that consumed much of Betty's time and energy was the construction of the new Governor's Mansion. Before the Sanders administration began, the legislature had decided that the old mansion should be replaced. As soon as the 1963 legislative session was completed, Carl and Betty began to think seriously about the project. They met several times with Ben Fortson, who was well aware of the old mansion's numerous shortcomings. The state appropriated $1 million for the land and structure and chose Tom Bradbury of Atlanta as the architect. The first order of business was to find the proper location. Betty and Bradbury looked at several old homes that were available and found some of them quite appealing. The beauty and charm of the Swan House, a European villa on Andrews Drive which was available for $400,000, was especially tempting. Despite its appeal, they rejected it as well as several others because they were convinced that a Southern style home would be more appropriate for the governors of Georgia. Finally, they decided on an estate on West Paces Ferry Road owned by Robert Maddox, a former mayor of Atlanta. The elderly Maddox was in failing health and could no longer maintain his large Tudor home and lovely gardens. The state paid $225,000 for the seventeen-acre site in the most

---

[20]Betty Foy Sanders interview, November 7, 1990; *Statesboro Herald,* September 29, 1985.

exclusive residential area of Atlanta. Maddox, who was pleased that his property would be the home of the future governors of the state, died shortly after making the transaction.[21]

Before designing the new mansion, Bradbury visited several other state mansions and historical sites. Betty wrote former governors' wives for suggestions about priorities for the future home. Gradually ideas began to take shape. Bradbury did preliminary drawings. On several occasions he took his plans to the Mansion where Carl, Betty, Fortson, and Ernest Davis, the state budget director, would gather around the dining room table and discuss them with him. Out of these meetings an agreement was reached. The new mansion would be done in the Greek revival style with thirty Doric redwood columns twenty-four feet high. At 25,000 square feet, it would be the second largest gubernatorial mansion in the country, surpassed only by Louisiana's. P. D. Christian's bid of $1,045,000 was the lowest to construct the mansion, and it was accepted.[22]

Before the Maddox home was removed, Betty was asked to chair a flea market and auction for the Women's Committee of the Atlanta Art Association. The sale and auction was held on October 3 and 4, 1963, at the Maddox home. The flea market was a great success as large crowds came to see knights in armor and bejeweled ladies, and to get one last view of a grand old home before it was razed. The proceeds, which totalled $60,000, went toward the construction of the Atlanta Memorial Cultural Center.[23]

After the property was cleared and the construction had begun, Betty and Carl decided that a steering committee should be named to make sure that the furnishings and grounds were tastefully done. Some seventy of Georgia's most prominent citizens were appointed to the Mansion Fine Arts Commission. At its first meeting at the Governor's Mansion on August 30, 1966, Henry Green of Madison, an expert on early historical furniture, was named chairman and Betty was chosen honorary

---

[21]Betty Foy Sanders interview, March 25, 1991; New Mansion folder, box 40, Sanders Collection, Law Library.

[22]Ibid.; *Atlanta Journal*, March 26, 1964, June 27, 1965.

[23]Atlanta Art Association (1963–1964) folder, box 40, Sanders Collection, Law Library.

vice chairman. Subcommittees were established to utilize the expertise of the members. Mrs. Mills B. Lane, Jr., chaired the Gardens and Grounds Committee, Mrs. Albert Thornton chaired the Furniture and Furnishings Committee, Edward Shorter of Columbus chaired the Painting and Sculpture Committee, and Franklin Garrett, the respected historian of Atlanta, chaired the Books, Manuscripts and Historical Documents Committee. A talented and enthusiastic group, it was dedicated to making the new mansion one of the best in the nation.[24]

The new mansion was designed to be more than simply a home for the First Family of Georgia. It was to be a facility where prominent visitors could spend the night in privacy and comfort. It was also designed to accommodate meetings and even large receptions. The governors who have lived in it from Lester Maddox to Zell Miller have regarded it as a facility for the people of Georgia. Thus it has been a busy place, housing the governor and his family and providing a beautiful setting for a host of meetings and other activities. For the past quarter of a century the new Governor's Mansion has served as a showplace and a symbol for Georgia, and Georgians are proud of it. Betty, who had worked so hard to make it a reality, was quite pleased with the finished product, but she was troubled by one thing. She thought the entrance to the Mansion needed a fountain made of white Georgia marble. Convinced that a fountain would enhance the appearance of the facility, she decided to build one. When Betty resolved to do something, she usually did it. The legislature had allocated no money for a fountain, but Betty was undeterred. To raise the necessary funds, she organized an exhibit of twenty-six of her original paintings which reflected her affection for the state. The paintings, which captured the natural beauty of the state, were all done while she was First Lady. She took the exhibit to ten Georgia cities, where the paintings were viewed by Georgians ranging from elementary schoolchildren to art critics. Her friends arranged receptions in each of the cities and contributions were received. On December 5, 1966, one month before the Sanders administration ended, Betty announced that her "Portrait of Georgia" exhibit

---

[24]New Mansion folder, box 40; press release August 23, 1966, August 1966 folder, box 35, Sanders Collection, Law Library; Betty Foy Sanders interview, March 25, 1991.

had reached its goal of $20,000. In thanking the people for their contributions, she said, "I feel that the fountain, a perfect circle embellished only by a carved Greek key design around its rim which matches the trim for the Mansion, will serve as a reminder of the people's pride in our State's rich heritage." That beautiful fountain, viewed by thousands each year, is one of Betty's proudest legacies to the state.[25]

---

[25]*Atlanta Constitution,* December 6, 1966; press release December 5, 1966, December 1966 folder, box 35, Sanders Collection, Law Library.

The old Governor's Mansion at Christmas.

Georgia's First Family.

Carl Sanders landed a 112-pound sailfish.

Betty and Carl Sanders celebrating his thirty-eighth birthday.

The new Governor's Mansion, built during the Sanders administration.

Chapter 11

"Rendezvous
with Responsibility"

Carl Sanders is usually regarded as one of modern Georgia's reform governors, a category that includes Hoke Smith, Richard Russell, Ellis Arnall, and Jimmy Carter. Although he attempted to reform his state in diverse ways during his tenure as governor, his efforts fell into three broad categories. His first goal was to raise the standard of living of all Georgians, the second was to provide a program of education that would give every Georgia child a first-rate education, and the third was to improve the image of Georgia so that it would be recognized nationally as a progressive and solid state. Sanders well understood that these goals were related. In order to have better-paying jobs, Georgia must have a better-trained work force. If the two goals of better jobs and better schools could be achieved, Georgia would be well on the way to obtaining the national image he desired.

During this period many industries were leaving the rustbelt of the Northeast to relocate in the warmer climate of the sunbelt, where wages and taxes were lower and unions were weaker. Sanders, determined that Georgia should get its share of such industries, established the goal of attracting a billion dollars of new and expanded industries in Georgia during his four-year term. Many lucrative high technology research grants and projects also were available, but Georgia and the other southern states received very few of them. They went primarily to California, Massachusetts, and the states with proven research universities. Sanders desperately wanted Georgia to attract more high tech industries and government research grants, and to that end he established the Governor's Commission for Scientific Research and Development. But he knew Georgia was unlikely to get many such investments unless the state's educational system, and especially its universities, were greatly improved. Consequently, he emphasized repeatedly that education was going to be the top priority of his administration. For Sanders, education was the "common denominator of progress." Impressed by the educational accomplishments of California and other states, he saw no reason why, in a reasonable period of time, Georgia could not have a system of higher education "as good as any in the country."[1]

Setting goals is easy, accomplishing them often is not. Sanders, however, seemed to have a natural aptitude for thinking ahead, making long-range plans, and developing reasonable strategies for achieving goals. Those who have known him well and worked with him for years consistently comment on how orderly his mind worked and how systematically he planned ahead. Thus, he did not immediately embark upon major reforms at the onset of his administration. Instead, he proceeded more deliberately, first laying a foundation and then generating public support for his programs before presenting them to the legislature. He used study commissions extensively to prepare the way for significant reforms. In his first legislative session he gained approval for the Governor's Commission for Efficiency and Improvement in Government, the Governor's Commission to Improve Education, and the Constitutional Revision Commission. In addition to these commissions, he established several more during his first year as governor. In May he appointed the North Georgia Mountains Commission and the State Election Laws Study Committee. In June he staffed the State Recreation Commission and the Commission for Scientific Research and Development. In July he named one hundred prominent Georgians to the Governor's Commission on the Status of Women and twenty members to the Congressional Apportionment Committee. Two months later he announced the appointment of the Governor's Council on Physical Fitness chaired by Garland Pinholster of Oglethorpe College. In December he established the Governor's Special Committee for Statutory-Constitutional Coordination. As the need arose, he created others, including the Nuclear Advisory Committee. Obviously some of these commissions were more important than others, but together they reflect the varied interests of the

---

[1]Press releases March 8, April 15, box 34, Sanders Collection, Law Library; Sanders, "A Time for Progress," in *Georgia Governors in an Age of Change*, 187-88; John Pennington, "Carl Sanders: The First Year," *Atlanta Magazine* 3 (January 1964): 56.

Sanders administration. Critics charged that there were too many study commissions and that some of them were unnecessary, but Sanders believed that all of them served a purpose. Even those that had minimal influence on legislation or administrative reform, such as the Council on Physical Fitness, made positive contributions by utilizing the expertise of competent Georgians, coordinating and disseminating information, and publicizing areas of concern. Often they were an effective means of generating public interest and legislative support for reforms Sanders desired. Moreover, he was adept at luring outstanding individuals to serve on these commissions, and the commissions helped develop a new image of Georgia as a more progressive state.[2]

Of these various commissions, none contributed more to the success of the Sanders administration than the Governor's Commission for Efficiency and Improvement in Government. Composed of seven outstanding business and professional men who served without pay, it was headed by William Bowdoin and usually called the Bowdoin Commission. Dr. M. W. H. Collins, Director of the Institute of Law and Government at the University of Georgia, served ably as the executive director. Sanders instructed the commission to "study the organization and operation of the agencies, departments, boards, commissions, and public authorities of the state," and to "submit to him and to the General Assembly reports of findings with recommendations for a thorough modernizing of Georgia's governmental structure and procedures." During the four years of its existence, the Bowdoin Commission studied various aspects of Georgia's government and encouraged agencies to do self-studies. Whenever possible, it utilized Georgia personnel and research agencies, but it did not hesitate to go outside the state to secure competent researchers and consultants. To ensure objective study and recommendations by the consultants, it released consultants' reports simultaneously with the commission reports, even though they were not always in total agreement. Altogether the commission prepared and distributed more than thirty studies of departments or areas of state government. Its recommendations dealt with administrative policies, personnel changes, training, long-range

---

[2]Press releases March 8, May 7, June 19, 29, July 17, 26, September 17, December 19, 22, 1963, box 34, Sanders Collection, Law Library.

planning, funding, and related matters in order to provide Georgians "with the most efficient and economical state government possible."[3]

Governor Sanders supported the Bowdoin Commission enthusiastically. He used his "clout" to see that its recommendations were implemented, and later suggested that his successor establish a similar commission. By the end of his administration, many of the Bowdoin Commission recommendations had been carried out, and others were implemented later. In his book *Georgia's Third Force*, published in 1967, Bowdoin noted that of the fifteen major recommendations in the area of prison reform "all but one have been implemented either fully or partially" and that of the more than eighty recommendations relating to the state Highway Department and its administration "approximately 75 percent have now been implemented fully or partially."[4]

The commission reports, coming out in a steady stream, received favorable publicity from the media, identified obvious weaknesses in government, proposed reasonable remedies, and gave Sanders an agenda for reform as well as leverage to use against recalcitrant department heads and the General Assembly. Taking full advantage of this opportunity, Sanders achieved impressive results, especially in the Merit System, the Board of Education, the Highway Department, the Department of Agriculture, the prison system, and the mental health program. Although much remained to be done in modernizing Georgia's government, as Bowdoin readily acknowledged, substantial progress was made in the Sanders administration.[5]

Some of the Bowdoin Commission recommendations were easy to implement, such as the first report on personnel management. It called for the establishment of an executive management seminar for top executives of state government and the hiring of a qualified training advisor for the State Merit System to initiate and continue a comprehensive training program for both officials and employees. These actions were taken immediately. Others which upset entrenched bureaucracies

---

[3]Ibid., January 21, 1963; Cook, "Carl Sanders and the Politics of the Future," in *Georgia Governors in an Age of Change*, p. 175.

[4]William R. Bowdoin, *Georgia's Third Force* (Atlanta: Foote & Davies, 1967) pp. 18, 22; *Athens Banner-Herald*, January 12, 1967.

[5]Bowdoin, *Georgia's Third Force*, pp. 11-35.

or required additional funding from the legislature were more difficult to accomplish, but Sanders never wavered in backing the Bowdoin Commission and attempting to implement its recommendations.[6]

The second report, which fell into the difficult category, was also one of the best and most needed studies. Joseph Ragen, Director of the Illinois Department of Public Safety, was chosen by the Bowdoin Commission to study Georgia's prison system. A recognized penologist, he previously had studied twenty-three state prison systems. In May 1963 he published a 106-page report which clearly documented numerous inadequacies in Georgia's penal system and suggested appropriate remedies. Despite improvement in recent years, Georgia's prison system remained woefully inadequate and unprofessional, as Ragen discovered when he observed the state's facilities. His thorough report provided an outline for statewide prison improvement and reform which Sanders attempted to implement. One of Ragen's most important recommendations called for the abandonment of a proposed prison in Hart county. He pointed out that its location, far from any metropolitan center, was utterly impractical and unduly expensive. Indeed, he estimated that the proposed facility would cost the taxpayers of Georgia $5,000,000. He also recommended closing the Rock Quarry prison for incorrigibles because it was "unfit for the housing of human beings"; constructing a new maximum security prison in a central location with an adjacent classification, diagnostic, and reception center; and establishing an industrial training program. Sanders, heartily endorsing these and Ragen's other recommendations, made prison reform part of his administrative legislative package in 1964.[7]

Prison reform was only one of many far-reaching reforms he proposed to the 1964 General Assembly. In addition, he sought passage of a package of educational reforms, a revised state constitution, a thorough revision of state election laws, and congressional redistricting. Sanders, who had an excellent relationship with the legislature, had gained approval for practically everything he asked for in 1963. Though

---

[6]Ibid.

[7]Ibid., pp. 18-20; Joseph E. Ragen, "Report and Observations on Inspection of Facilities and Operation of the Georgia Penal System," 1970 Georgia Penal System folder, box 26, Sanders Collection, Law Library.

impressive, that was not exceptional because Georgia governors usually received full cooperation from the legislature the first year, the honeymoon session. In subsequent years, however, they generally faced stiffer resistance. Moreover, the Sanders legislative agenda for the second session was so ambitious it was certain to encounter strong opposition from legislative factions. It was obvious that Sanders's leadership would be tested, and there was considerable doubt that the forceful young governor would be able to steer these bold and controversial measures through the legislature. He knew that the session would not be easy. He would have to battle for each of his reforms. He also realized that if he failed to get major aspects of his program adopted, it would be politically damaging and possibly disastrous for him. But Sanders was a gambler. As he saw it, to achieve great things great risks must be taken. Convinced that the measures he was proposing were needed and that Georgia would benefit from their adoption, he pushed ahead, confident that the people were behind him and that the legislature would follow his leadership.[8]

During the previous year Sanders had already faced several unpleasant situations and had come through them unscathed. When reports of irregularities in the Game and Fish Commission reached him, he forced the director, Fulton Lovell, a Vandiver appointee, to resign while an investigation took place.[9] When travelers going to and from Florida complained that Long county was a speed trap, he took appropriate action. He had the State Patrol conduct a thorough investigation which uncovered serious irregularities in traffic enforcement. Long county, it seems, was more interested in raising money for the county by fining out-of-state motorists than in maintaining traffic safety on Highway 301. Fleecing tourists was not the image Sanders wanted Georgia to project. By promptly suspending the county's powers for six months and placing traffic control in the hands of the State Patrol, the governor solved the problem.[10] When the Ragen Report revealed that mismanagement in the

---

[8]Daniel, *Addresses of Carl Sanders*, pp. 28-36.

[9]Cook, "Sanders: An Oral History," p. 57; *Atlanta Journal*, June 27, September 10, 1963.

[10]H. L. Conner to Sanders, October 24, 1963, report on Long county traffic enforcement; press relaease October 25, 1963, October 1963 folder, box 34, Sanders Collection, Law Library.

prison system was even worse than anticipated, it was clear that the Prison Director was not doing his job properly. Unfortunately, the director was a friend of the governor and a political supporter. Although it pained him to do it, Sanders removed him to a lesser job.[11] For Sanders, the needs of the state came first. Those who could not—or did not—perform at an acceptable level of competence had to go, regardless of personal connections. By such actions Sanders had demonstrated that he could make tough decisions when the situation demanded it.

After one year as governor, Sanders had made an extremely favorable impression upon the people of Georgia. Both officials and ordinary citizens seemed comfortable with his ideas and style of governing, and most of the press was favorably disposed toward him. Even many former political opponents acknowledged that he was doing a good job. In evaluating his first year in office, journalist John Pennington observed that Sanders appears "too good to be true." While admitting that the governor had made some mistakes, Pennington concluded that "he has instituted more reforms than any governor of recent history. He has tackled old and cantankerous problems with vigor and routed scoundrels with actions that in the past would have been considered political heresy."[12]

One of the most appealing aspects of Sanders's leadership was the zest and enthusiasm he brought to the job. No one, not even his bitterest political enemies, ever accused him of laziness or lack of effort. By routinely putting in twelve and fourteen hour work days, it was obvious that he was devoting his best efforts to the job. During his first year in office he delivered two hundred speeches throughout the state. Considering all of the other demands on the governor's time, that was an amazing feat requiring tremendous stamina. Fortunately, the state had an airplane for the governor to use, and Sanders kept it busy. Although capable of flying it himself, he rarely did so. Instead, he found that his time in the air could be used more efficiently by reading materials, preparing speeches, or taking a quick nap. Sanders realized that he could not keep up that pace of speech making for four years, but he felt it was important to communicate with the people directly, especially at the beginning of his administration. "I feel like people have more confidence

---

[11]Pennington, "Carl Sanders: The First Year," pp. 55-56.
[12]Ibid., pp. 44, 55.

in the state when they get to see the governor in the flesh," he explained.[13]

In many ways, the governor is the symbol for the state. Sanders's strenuous speaking schedule was part of his effort to enhance the image of the state. What better way was there to erase Georgia's image as a rural, racist, reactionary state than for its urbane and progressive young governor to get wide exposure? Unlike many politicians, he did not attempt to change his image or the content of his speeches to appeal to different audiences. Always poised and well groomed, he delivered essentially the same message whether he was addressing wealthy executives in Atlanta or poor farmers in Hahira. His speeches were designed to convey a new image of Georgia and a new concept of the state's potential. He stressed growth, new industries, economic advancement, space-age technology, and a unified Georgia. The Sanders administration had a feeling of "official boundless optimism," the governor later wrote. Recalling those years, he explained why there was such optimism. "We were in a period of peace. Inflation was low. The economy was strong. President Kennedy said we were going to the moon. I honestly felt like we could do anything in Georgia that could be done in any other state in America if we just worked hard enough. It was a positive, exciting time."[14]

In addition to creating a new image for the state, the governor's speeches also called attention to his legislative agenda. Periodically he addressed the topics that concerned him and by doing so kept those issues before the public and generated public interest in them. At various times he focused on prison reform, constitutional and election code revision, the merit system, and a host of other issues. None, however, received more attention in late 1963 than education. Addressing civic clubs at a luncheon in rural Americus on September 13, he stated: "The Sanders Administration has cleared the ground and started plowing and we hope to have the whole farm ready for seeding and fertilizing when the General Assembly meets next year." The governor then explained that "the crops we want to put in are a Master Plan for Education, a new State Constitution, a new State Election Code and a program of

---

[13]Ibid., p. 46.
[14]Sanders, "A Time for Progress," p. 187.

economy and efficiency in all phases of State Government."[15] Two weeks later he outlined ten goals for improving education to the Governor's Commission to Improve Education. The governor appeared on radio several times to explain his Master Plan for Education. It was, he said, a long-range, ten-year program based on the findings of the Bowdoin Commission and the Governor's Commission to Improve Education. Together these study groups had made ninety-seven recommendations, and Sanders called for the implementation of all of them.[16]

On December 28, two weeks before the legislature convened, he addressed the people of Georgia in a statewide radio broadcast that stressed education. He first presented unpleasant facts about the status of education in Georgia: one out of every five people in the state is a functional illiterate, Georgia ranks fiftieth in the nation in dropouts, and forty percent of the state's young men and women are rejected for military service because of illiteracy. To complicate the situation, the state's school population was growing at the rate of 24,000 new children each year, and the colleges already were packed, the high schools and grammar schools overcrowded, and the vocational programs totally inadequate. Georgia needed jobs, new industries, and higher salaries, the governor asserted, and all of them could be achieved only by education. After outlining the specific proposals he would present to the General Assembly, he concluded that education was "the most important battle in the history of our State." Education, Sanders declared, "is the keystone to our liberties and our freedom." Appealing to the practical side of Georgians, he explained the alternatives. Without education citizens wind up on welfare rolls or in jail, and it is much cheaper to educate people for jobs than to pay their welfare or confine them in the penitentiary. In conclusion, he asked his listeners to contact their representatives so that Georgia could win the battle for education and progress.[17]

A week later Sanders appeared on a statewide television and radio broadcast drumming up more support for his programs to improve education. He described the situation as a "modern crisis which involves

---

[15]Press release September 13, 1963, September 1963 folder, box 34, Sanders Collection, Law Library.

[16]Press release September 29, 1963, September 1963 folder; undated radio script in December 1963 folder, box 34, Sanders Collection, Law Library.

[17]Ibid., December 28, 1963.

the very survival of Georgia in spaceage competition." The response to his speech was gratifying. His office reported that of the seven hundred telegrams it received only two of them were not in favor of his educational program. Endorsements also came from the Georgia Education Association, the Georgia School Boards Association, the Georgia Municipal Association, and even Representative Denmark Groover. Clearly Sanders had plowed the ground and was now ready to plant the seeds of education with the General Assembly.[18]

In view of such preliminary emphasis on education, it was not surprising that Sanders stressed education in his state of the state address to the General Assembly on January 15, 1964. After praising the General Assembly and declaring that "the state of the state has never been better!" he devoted the bulk of his speech to education. Solemnly he stated that this may be the most critical session of the General Assembly in this century. "We must enact and implement a new Master Plan for Education in Georgia," he declared. Based on the recommendations of the Commission to Improve Education and the Bowdoin Commission, he proposed a comprehensive program of reforms. Specifically, his program called for uniform minimum standards for all public schools, an equalized tax digest, a realistic teacher salary schedule, more vocational training, an increased allotment for textbooks, and, most importantly, more local support for education. Since Georgia was sixth from the top in state financial support and seventh from the bottom in local support for education, Sanders insisted that local governments make a greater contribution. The state was paying 85 percent and the counties only 15 percent of the costs. Sanders proposed increasing the local support one percent per year for five years to establish a new state/local ratio of 80/20 percent.

Sanders frankly admitted that the state could use $150,000,000 to implement his program. But he quickly added that although that amount was needed, it was unrealistic to expect it. Instead, he proposed raising $30,000,000 in new revenues. With this increased funding, he maintained, the state would be able to raise teachers' salaries, hire more teachers, finance extensive construction of new facilities through the sale of bonds, create an honors program for outstanding junior students, and

---

[18]*Rome News-Tribune*, January 7, 8, 1964.

complete the state's educational television network. These objectives, he added, cannot be accomplished through local support alone. To raise the additional revenue, he proposed five measures. They included a three-cent tax increase on cigarettes, a fifty cents per gallon tax increase on distilled spirits, the elimination of the vendors' commission on collection of retail sales tax, a one percent increase in the corporate income tax, and an increase in the tax on beer of twelve cents a case. These measures, he concluded, "are realistic and fair, and they will make possible the improvements we so desperately need in education."[19]

After devoting two-thirds of his speech to education, he then briefly addressed other topics. He called for the passage of the following measures: a sheriffs' salary bill to eliminate the evils of the fee system once and for all, a bill effectively regulating billboards on the highways, a congressional redistricting plan, and a new state constitution. If there was not enough time for "deliberate consideration" and adoption of a new constitution, he promised to call a special session later in the year for that purpose. Altogether it was an extremely ambitious program that Sanders had presented to the legislature. He called it a "rendezvous with responsibility."[20]

Sanders's intensive preparations before the session convened paid handsome dividends with the legislature. It was quickly apparent to the legislators that his education package addressed serious problems in a reasonable and comprehensive manner. More importantly, it won widespread public support. Consequently, the Senate passed the Master Plan for Education in a week's time by vote of 47 to 0. Two days later the House approved it 190 to 6.[21] The legislature is always reluctant to increase taxes, but Sanders convinced the members that additional revenue was essential. His tax proposals were adopted with only minor changes. The billboard control law generated little enthusiasm among the legislators when it was presented. Some, including Denmark Groover, opposed it vigorously, arguing that it took away property rights from landowners without compensating them. Betty Sanders and many women in garden clubs, appalled at the proliferation of unsightly

[19]Daniel, *Addresses of Carl Sanders.* pp. 28-36.
[20]Ibid.
[21]*Atlanta Daily World,* January 23, 25, 1964.

advertisements along Georgia's interstate highways, urged passage of the measure. The governor supported the bill for economic rather than aesthetic reasons, since Georgia stood to gain $3,000,000 in federal grants if billboards were curbed. In urging the members to pass the bill, Sanders pointed out that his wife was very insistent that the highways be beautified. If the bill did not pass, he claimed he would be in serious trouble at home and would not be able to face Betty. Whether the members were more concerned about the governor's domestic happiness or the merits of the bill cannot be determined, but they passed the bill. Celestine Sibley of the *Atlanta Constitution* gave most of the credit for the adoption of the billboard bill to Betty Sanders.[22]

Reg Murphy, political editor of the *Atlanta Constitution*, was impressed with Sanders's skill in getting bills passed by the legislature. According to Murphy, his standard approach was to outline in general terms what should be done. This causes an uproar which produces confusion and the possibility of doing nothing. Then someone offers a compromise that seems passable. "The governor buys the compromise, pushes it for everything he is worth, and it gets passed." As an example, Murphy cited the sheriffs' salary bill. Many different bills were proposed and all of them were attacked. Finally it was suggested that the problem could be solved by simply setting a two-year deadline and telling all counties to begin paying sheriffs' salaries by then. The compromise worked, and the bill became law. Murphy characterized Sanders's talent as a "muddle-through-to-the-compromise approach," but he admitted it achieved impressive results.[23]

While Murphy had insight into the governor's style, it would be more accurate to say that Sanders presented broad goals that he was determined to achieve but did not rigidly insist that they could be achieved in only one way. Flexible and pragmatic, he recognized that different approaches were possible and was not too particular about which one was used as long as his goal was accomplished. For example, one of his goals was to raise $30,000,000 in new revenue. While he preferred the tax package he proposed, he made it clear that if the

---

[22]*Atlanta Constitution*, February 19, 1964; Betty Foy Sanders interview, November 7, 1990.

[23]*Atlanta Journal and Constitution*, February 23, 1964.

General Assembly preferred raising the sales tax to obtain the revenue he would not object. For Sanders, raising the revenue was the essential point: how it was raised was less important. The same thing happened with reapportionment. He clearly wanted a reapportionment bill adopted in the 1964 session. He insisted that it was the duty and responsibility of the elected officials of Georgia—not the federal courts—to reapportion the state's congressional districts. Yet he knew that if the state did not provide reasonable districts based on population, the court would intervene. Thus, he prodded the legislature to resolve the problem, but he kept his hands off the specific bills. After the House and Senate had thrashed out the problems, he would then intervene and "try to pass the fairest bill we can agree on."[24]

With one week remaining in the forty-day legislative session, no consensus had emerged on congressional reapportionment. Many plans had been introduced, but the General Assembly was deadlocked and its members were tired and bitter. A new dimension to the problem was added on February 17 when the United States Supreme Court ruled in *Wesberry v. Georgia* that Georgia's congressional districts would have to be redrawn so that "as nearly as is practicable one man's vote in a congressional election is to be worth as much as another."[25] This bombshell decision stunned the legislature. Now there was no choice; the districts must be redrawn. Since Georgia's districts were terribly unbalanced, ranging from a population of 272,154 in the smallest district to 823,680 in the largest, there would have to be major adjustments. The immediate reaction of legislators, aside from criticizing the court for its intrusion into state rights, was that the issue was so complex and politically charged that it should be dealt with in 1965 or in a special session. Governor Sanders, however, had other ideas.

With only four days remaining before mandatory adjournment, Sanders insisted that the General Assembly act on the issue. The legislature tackled reapportionment once again as Sanders directed, but despite diligent efforts it failed to reach an agreement as the session drew to a close on February 21. Furthermore, it appeared that no agreement would be possible since the members were badly divided over the various

---

[24]*Rome News-Tribune*, January 14, February 5, 1964.
[25]"Redrawing the Lines," *Time* 83 (February 28, 1964): 19-20.

proposals. The House and Senate tried to resolve their differences in a conference committee, but after fifteen hours of rancorous debate and maneuvering, they remained deadlocked. By then the legislators were exhausted, angry, and frustrated. The governor's floor leader, Arthur Bolton, along with practically everyone else, had given up hope. Despite all the negative feelings and the yelling and screaming that had filled the legislative chambers throughout the night, Sanders persisted. He still believed a solution was possible. He strode to the rostrum of the House at 10:45 p.m.—one hour and fifteen minutes before automatic adjournment. "I have heard from my advisors that this House is in no mood to do anything," he said. "I don't believe that!" He urged the members to try once more to come up with some plan they could vote on. Somehow, his plea worked. Eighty minutes after his dramatic appeal, both houses had agreed upon a reapportionment bill.[26] In football terms, quarterback Sanders had thrown a "Hail Mary" pass for a touchdown to win the game as the clock expired.

The closing minutes of the 1964 legislative session provided some of the most controversial, emotional, and bizarre actions that have ever occurred under the gold dome of Georgia's capitol. At 11:50 Representative Denmark Groover attempted to stop the clock. He leaned over the balcony, grabbed the base of the clock, tore it loose from the wall, and smashed it to pieces on the floor below. He later offered to pay for the clock, claiming that he did not intend to destroy it, only to stop it. Nevertheless, the next day photos of the less-than-sober Groover hanging precariously over the balcony to reach the clock appeared in newspapers throughout the country.[27] According to observers, the Senate passed the bill with two minutes to spare at 11:58 by vote of 35 to 7. The House, however, did not approve it until after midnight when the session was legally supposed to end. While opponents yelled and cursed and Representative James "Sloppy" Floyd cried in desperation that "the tactics used here are unconstitutional, Communist, and everything else—and I don't like it worth a damn!," the House approved the

---

[26] *Savannah Evening Press*, February 22, 1964; *Rome News-Tribune*, February 16, 23, 1964; Cook, "Carl Sanders and the Politics of the Future," pp. 177-78; *Acts and Resolutions, 1964*, pp. 478-82.

[27] *Valdosta Daily Times*, February 22, 1964.

reapportionment bill by vote of 113 to 69 at 12:11.[28] Actually, there was no written bill. The House had voted on a map with the congressional districts drawn in crayon. Sanders quietly instructed an aide to go to the clerk's office when it opened the next morning and write a bill that conformed to the map. By such unorthodox measures, Georgia's congressional districts were reapportioned. The reapportionment bill did not achieve total equality among the ten districts, but it did greatly reduce the disparities. Under the new bill, the districts ranged in population from 329,738 in the Ninth District to 455,575 in the Sixth District. Sanders cautioned that the bill might not stand up in court, but he was extremely pleased that redistricting had remained in the hands of the General Assembly.[29]

Despite the chaotic ending, the 1964 legislative session had adopted much important legislation; indeed, it was one of the most productive legislative sessions in modern Georgia history. In addition to the Master Plan for Education, the tax package, congressional reapportionment, the sheriffs' salary bill, and highway billboard curbs, it also approved a $41.3 million supplemental appropriations bill, a package of prison reforms, and an effective water pollution bill. Many legislators acclaimed it the most fruitful session in recent years, and the press had lavish praise for both the governor and the General Assembly. The *Atlanta Constitution* described the legislature's performance as "quite remarkable" and praised Sanders "not only for a splendid program but for providing the strong leadership necessary to gain its approval."[30] Similar praise came from the *Savannah Morning News*, which stated that reapportionment "represented a personal victory for Sanders, who laid his personal prestige on the line by getting embroiled in the explosive issue."[31] Sam Hopkins of the *Atlanta Journal and Constitution* claimed that "Never before have such far-reaching pieces of educational legislation passed the General

---

[28]Cook, "Carl Sanders and the Politics of the Future," pp. 177-78; "Redrawing the Lines," *Time*, p. 19; *House Journal 1964* pp. 2313-21; *Senate Journal 1964*, pp. 1345-47.

[29]*Savannah Evening Press*, February 22, 1964; *Atlanta Journal*, October 8, 1978.

[30]*Atlanta Journal and Constitution*, February 23, 1964; *Rome News-Tribune*, February 23, 1964.

[31]*Savannah Morning News*, February 22, 1964.

Assembly."[32] Eugene Patterson, editor of the *Atlanta Constitution*, described the session as "extraordinarily productive—perhaps unprecedentedly so." He stressed the emergence of Sanders as a leader. When the session began, Sanders was "untested"; when it was over, he looked "like a pro." According to Patterson, he proved his strength in the education bill. It was the make-or-break issue of his administration. Facing tremendous pressures, Sanders lowered his head, and, with a minimum of compromise, butted the program through. "Thereafter," Patterson concluded, "the young man clearly was of political age."[33]

Sanders himself was delighted with the results of the session. He had set a full agenda, kept the legislators focused on his issues, and succeeded in getting most of his program enacted into law. Aside from revising the constitution and the election code, everything he sought became law, and those two measures would soon be addressed in a special session. Sanders worked cooperatively with the General Assembly and had genuine admiration for the legislators. Believing that the members were extraordinarily capable and dedicated to improving the state, he praised them then and continued to extol them years later. In addressing the General Assembly at its closing, he stated, with obvious pleasure and pride, that the program they had adopted "has neither precedent nor equal in the annals of legislative accomplishment in Georgia." Like many politicians, Sanders had a penchant for florid prose, but he was probably speaking from the heart when he declared "history will register this as the most productive session of the General Assembly in the twentieth century."[34]

---

[32]*Atlanta Journal and Constitution*, February 23, 1964.
[33]*Atlanta Constitution*, February 25, 1964.
[34]Daniel, *Addresses of Carl Sanders*, pp. 36-37.

Governor Sanders in the cockpit of the state-owned Twin Beechcraft H 18.

*Governor Sanders meeting with J. W. Crosby,
president of Thiokol Chemical Corporation.*

Governor Sanders dedicating a new Sunbeam plant.

Governor Farris Bryant of Florida and Governor Sanders of Georgia dedicate a segment of Interstate 75 linking their two states.

Chapter 12

The Special Session

In addition to education, reapportionment, and industrial expansion, Governor Sanders made governmental reorganization a high priority in his administration. Utilizing the findings of the Bowdoin Commission, he continually sought ways of making existing departments and agencies operate more efficiently. But he also was concerned that the whole structure of Georgia's government rested on a shaky foundation. The state's constitution, adopted in 1945, was relatively young but already had been amended 381 times. Many of the amendments dealt with trivial local matters, but the result was a confusing and unwieldy document. One newspaper editor accurately described it as "outmoded, inefficient, and unworkable, . . . a hodgepodge of amendments and provisions that are not in line with modern demands of government."[1] Sanders expressed similar sentiments on many occasions and was particularly concerned that "Nowhere is there to be found a complete copy of the Georgia constitution as it now exists."[2] For one trained in law who liked things done in an orderly and systematic manner, Georgia's constitutional situation was intolerable. If Georgia was truly to become a modern and progressive state, then it must have a new constitution, the governor reasoned.

The General Assembly agreed that constitutional changes were needed, and it approved the governor's proposal to establish a Constitutional Revision Commission of twenty-eight members presided over by the governor and composed of both private citizens and political officeholders. The commission was authorized to "revise the present Constitution, either by amendments thereto, a new Constitution, or in such other manner as the Commission shall decide." To that end it could hold

---

[1] *Carroll County Georgian* (Carrollton), May 2, 1963.
[2] Daniel, *Addresses of Carl Sanders*, p. 121.

hearings, propose legislation, employ clerical staff, and distribute reports. The commission's final report, however, had to be completed by December 1, 1965, at which time the commission would be abolished.[3]

On April 23, 1963, Sanders announced the appointment of the Constitutional Revision Commission. In addition to the governor, the officeholding members were the lieutenant governor, speaker of the house, attorney general, secretary of state, legislative counsel, and state budget officer. Speaker George T. Smith appointed Representatives Arthur Bolton, George Busbee, and Harry Mixon. Lieutenant Governor Peter Zack Geer named Senators Charles Pannell and Julian Webb. For the remainder of the positions, Governor Sanders selected seventeen prominent Georgians representing various disciplines and occupations. Altogether it was a distinguished body composed of many of the state's most respected political and professional leaders.[4]

Subsequently, the Constitutional Revision Commission was divided into a Policy Committee, a Drafting Committee, and thirteen committees to study specific areas of government. The Policy Committee, which would oversee the whole process, was chaired by Sanders and included Pope McIntire, Speaker Smith, Representative Bolton, Representative Busbee, Lieutenant Governor Geer, and Senator Pannell.[5]

In swearing in the commission, Sanders cautioned the members against adopting radical changes such as reorganizing the government or developing a new concept of state government. Rather, he insisted, "our task is to fit the constitution to the facts as they exist here and now." Anticipating some of the difficulties involved in constitutional revision, he added that any new method must be a real improvement and not just a change "which will send us on a completely unknown journey and create new and more serious problems."[6] This was sound advice, but unfortunately not all involved in the process would heed it.

Sanders wanted the new constitution to include a smaller legislature, a unified judicial system, and increased home rule. He also believed it

---

[3] *Acts and Resolutions, 1963*, pp. 402-409.

[4] Press release April 23, 1963, Carl Sanders Papers, Executive Department Correspondence, Georgia Department of Archives and History, Atlanta; *Official Register, 1963–1964*, p. 89.

[5] *Atlanta Journal*, May 7, 1963.

[6] *Savannah Morning News*, May 7, 1963.

should be a simpler and more understandable document that would not require frequent amendments. Furthermore, the governor insisted that the process be completed quickly so that the new document could be voted on by the people in the 1964 general election. Any delay beyond that point would place it on the 1966 ballot, and Sanders did not want the constitution to become an issue in the governor's race. Consequently, he prodded the committees to move as rapidly as possible. Arguing that the state could not afford to wait, he insisted that the work be completed in time for the 1964 session of the legislature.[7]

As the committees studied their areas of concern, new ideas for changing the constitution in substantial ways emerged. The Georgia League of Women Voters proposed reducing by half the 205-member House of Representatives.[8] Dr. William Cornelius, professor of political science at Agnes Scott College, argued in a public hearing that the governor should be allowed to succeed himself, while Dr. Albert Saye, professor of political science at the University of Georgia, maintained that one term was sufficient.[9] Dr. Cornelius later proposed that the governor should appoint the attorney general and that the new constitution should provide for public defenders paid from state funds. Dr. Saye urged an increase in the sales tax from three percent to four percent.[10] The Georgia Bar Association sought a unified judicial system with appellate judges "removed as far as possible from partisan politics."[11] Early in August, Attorney General Eugene Cook presented to a subcommittee an extensive home rule plan that would allow counties and cities greater autonomy over local affairs.[12]

Since federal courts were beginning to mandate reapportionment of congressional and legislative districts, commission members felt pressure, and many reapportionment plans were offered. Representatives Arthur Funk and Bart Shea of Chatham county offered contrasting plans. Funk wanted a Senate of 159 members—one senator from each county—and

---

[7]State Constitutional Revision Committee, Scrapbook, 1964, Legislative Department, Georgia Department of Archives and History, Atlanta.

[8]*Atlanta Journal,* June 7, 1963.

[9]Ibid., July 20, 1963.

[10]*Augusta Herald,* July 18, 1963; *Valdosta Times,* July 22, 1963.

[11]*Atlanta Journal,* July 23, 1963.

[12]*Savannah Morning News,* August 4, 1963.

a House of 100 members based on population. Shea, on the other hand, proposed a House of 54 members and a Senate of 159—both based on population.[13] Dr. Cornelius urged reducing the size of the House, reapportioning the legislature on the basis of population, and putting the legislators on a minimum salary of $4,000.[14] Representative Mike Egan, an Atlanta Republican, wanted the House reduced to no more than 110 members.[15] Representative James P. Wesberry, an Atlanta Democrat, also favored a smaller House based on population, but he recommended that the terms of senators and representatives be extended to four years.[16]

Governor Sanders tried to avoid the extremes so that the committees could reach a consensus. He well understood that drastic changes were not likely to be approved by the General Assembly or the people. By bluntly opposing the increase in the sales tax and the proposal to allow the governor to serve two successive terms, he nipped those ideas in the bud. He also opposed a salary increase for the governor, stating, "I knew what the governor's salary was when I ran and I am perfectly satisfied with it."[17]

Working simultaneously with the Constitutional Revision Commission was the Election Laws Study Committee, a nine-member committee established by the General Assembly and staffed by the governor in April 1963. It was chaired by Secretary of State Ben Fortson. Shortly before Christmas 1963, it proposed sweeping changes in the election code. "Our state has never had a comprehensive set of election laws," the committee reported. The laws had been haphazardly accumulated over a century and "are the worst in the nation."[18] Upon receiving the Election Laws Study Committee's report, Sanders appointed a special committee to study changes that would be needed in Georgia's code provisions and statutes as a result of a new constitution. Called the Governor's Special Committee for Statutory-Constitutional Coordina-

---

[13]*Moultrie Observer*, August 9, 1963.

[14]Ibid.

[15]Ibid.

[16]*Savannah Morning News*, August 10, 1963.

[17]Ibid., November 14, 1963.

[18]Ibid., December 22, 1963; *Acts and Resolutions, 1963*, pp. 492-94.

tion, it consisted of twenty-one lawyers with Elliott Levitas as chairman and Representative Mike Egan as vice chairman.[19]

The Sanders scenario called for the various committees to complete their work by September 1, 1963. Their reports would then be combined and revised into a new constitution by the full Constitutional Revision Commission, which would submit the document to the legislature when it convened in January 1964. The General Assembly would then have a complete legislative session to debate and approve the measure. The last step would be for the people to approve the new constitution in the general election in November 1964. Unfortunately, those deadlines were not met, and revisions continued to be made throughout the 1964 legislative session. As noted previously, the 1964 session had a full agenda without considering a new constitution or a revised election code. The Master Plan for Education, prison reform, congressional reapportionment, and other issues took priority during the forty-day session. Realizing that there was inadequate time for legislative debate on additional issues, especially one as controversial as a new constitution, Sanders wisely adjusted his plans. Three weeks after the productive but chaotic 1964 legislative session ended, enough time for tempers to cool and constituents to be heard from, Sanders called a special session of the General Assembly to meet May 4 for the dual purpose of revising the constitution and revamping the state's election laws.

At the end of March the Constitutional Revision Commission finally completed its work and submitted the new constitution to public inspection. Included in the 101-page document were several judicial reforms. The state supreme court would be able to assign judges to overcrowded court calendars, and chief judges would be named in multijudge districts to assist in the battle against delays. For businessmen there was a "free port" provision to attract new industries and a change of taxation of inventories. The new constitution also encouraged the development of area school systems across county lines. It provided for extensive home rule for local governments. Specific pay amounts for officials were removed so that constitutional amendments would no longer be necessary to award pay raises. The governor was still limited to one four-year term,

---

[19]Press release December 19, 1963, Carl Sanders Papers, Georgia Department of Archives and History.

but legislative terms were increased from two to four years. The speaker of the house would be elected by voice vote. The size of the legislature would remain unchanged, with a Senate of 54 members and a House of 205 members. The Senate districts were to be based on population; the House was to consist of one representative from each county, plus 46 additional representatives apportioned by the General Assembly.[20]

The first major step in the process had now been accomplished, but two more steps remained—securing approval by the General Assembly and by the people. Writing the new constitution by the commission, though extremely important, was probably the easiest of the three obstacles to overcome. It was a formidable achievement, and Sanders clearly was the dominant force in the process. He had made constitutional revision a priority, secured legislative approval of the Constitutional Revision Commission, appointed competent people to serve on it, chaired the Policy Committee, encouraged the committees to complete their work, eliminated the most controversial or divisive proposals, and managed to secure a document that generally satisfied his desire to update and clarify the existing constitution. The result was not perfect—no constitution is—but Sanders was convinced that it was "far better than the constitution now in effect."[21]

The task of securing legislative consent would prove daunting. Columnist Reg Murphy of the *Atlanta Constitution*, noting the different needs of the rural and urban areas, doubted that an acceptable package could be put together that would satisfy the necessary two-thirds of the legislators. The outlook for adopting a new constitution, he wrote, could only be described as "bleak."[22] Other skeptical voices were raised. The *Savannah Evening Press* suggested that the matter was so complex that more time was needed for study.[23] The *Augusta Herald* generally was negative. It seemed to agree with Senator J. Taylor Phillips of Macon that the new constitution was too long and restrictive and probably would be defeated by the General Assembly.[24] The Georgia League of

---

[20] *Atlanta Constitution*, March 28, 1964.
[21] *Savannah Morning News*, April 21, 1964.
[22] *Atlanta Constitution*, March 31, 1964.
[23] *Savannah Evening Press*, April 8, 1964.
[24] *Augusta Herald*, April 10, 1964.

Women Voters labeled the document a "collection of lengthy and over-detailed directives and prohibitions to the legislature."[25] The *Thomaston Times* probably expressed the view of many Georgians when it editorialized that "we stand in fear and trembling at the thoughts of an entirely new Constitution although we will admit the hundreds-time amended version on the books is antiquated."[26]

Despite modest reapportionment efforts to satisfy federal courts, Georgia's legislature remained woefully malapportioned in 1964. Rural politicians continued to dominate Georgia's government as they had done for many decades. The chief criticism of the productive 1964 legislative session came from urban interests. The executive director of the Georgia Municipal Association called the legislative performance "punitive and vicious."[27] According to Reg Murphy, the rural-dominated House consistently pursued a simple policy: "Anything cities want, it kills."[28] Like the majority of the legislators, the governors usually resided in rural areas or small towns. Vandiver, for example, lived in Lavonia, Griffin in Bainbridge, Herman Talmadge in Lovejoy, and Ellis Arnall in Newnan. Indeed, it can be argued that Sanders was the most urban-oriented governor Georgia has elected since the county unit was adopted in 1917. In the General Assembly, few of the key legislative leaders resided in metropolitan areas or had urban constituencies. In the House, Speaker George T. Smith made his home in Cairo; Floor Leader Arthur Bolton lived in Griffin; and Assistant Floor Leader George Busbee resided in Albany. In the Senate, Lieutenant Governor Geer was from Colquitt; Floor Leader Milton Carlton lived in Swainsboro; and Assistant Floor Leader Julian Webb resided in Donalsonville. Rural legislators were reluctant to tamper with a system that served them well. Consequently, securing their approval would not be easy. It would require all the persuasiveness and political skill that Sanders possessed.

The plan for the special session called for the Senate to consider the election laws while the House considered the new constitution. Before going to the floor of the House, the constitution was first to be submit-

---

[25]Ibid.

[26]*Thomaston Times*, April 2, 1964.

[27]*Savannah Morning News*, February 23, 1964.

[28]*Atlanta Constitution*, February 21, 1964.

ted to a Special Committee chaired by Speaker Smith and composed of about forty members of the House Rules, Judiciary, and Special Judiciary Committees. After the session convened, there would be two weeks of hearings beginning on May 5. The Special Committee would then submit the constitution to the full House, where it would be considered section by section. If the constitution was approved by a two-thirds vote, it would go to the Senate where the routine would be repeated—committee, public hearings, discussion, and vote. Sanders optimistically predicted that the special session would accomplish these tasks in thirty days.[29]

A confident Sanders opened the special session on May 4 with an uplifting address. In exhorting the legislators to adopt the new constitution and codify the general election laws, he lavishly praised them for their past performances. "History will record the year 1964," he pronounced, "as the most productive legislative year . . . of all time!" The governor then outlined the efforts that had been expended in writing the new constitution and pointed out why it should be adopted. The new document was a third shorter and considerably more flexible than the present constitution, he noted. The number of articles had been reduced from sixteen to nine and hundreds of local amendments had been brought forward as statutory law rather than as part of the constitution itself. More than twenty sections of the present constitution had been eliminated, more than seventy-five substantive provisions had been changed, and home rule had been provided for. The new constitution, the governor declared, "is more understandable and easier to work with" and "compares favorably with any Constitution of any state." Therefore, the governor concluded, the legislature must overcome any obstacle to progress and provide for the citizens a constitution "in tune with the times."[30]

As soon as the new constitution reached the floor of the House, representatives sought to change it in various ways. Urban legislators wanted a smaller House reapportioned on the basis of population, while rural legislators insisted on a House with at least one representative for each of the state's 159 counties. Representative Robin Harris of DeKalb

---

[29]*Savannah Morning News*, April 21, 1964; *Atlanta Journal*, May 4, 1964.
[30]Daniel, *Addresses of Carl Sanders*, pp. 37-42.

county proposed abolishing the office of lieutenant governor or prohibiting him from presiding over the Senate or succeeding himself.[31] Representative Denmark Groover of Bibb county, who caused Sanders much anguish throughout the session, moved to delete the Highway Board from the constitution.[32] Members disagreed over the length of legislative terms. Some wanted four-year terms for all, others preferred two-year terms, and still others agreed with Sanders, who favored the pattern common in many states of two-year terms for members of the House and four-year terms for senators. Speaker Smith predicted that the biggest fight would be over whether to allow cities to begin sharing state aid. He was correct. Counties then received $9.5 million a year, but the cities did not share in this largess. When the Special Committee voted against allowing state gas tax revenues to go to cities as well as counties, urban representatives were furious. Urban representatives threatened to block the whole constitution unless they got relief. The president of the Georgia Municipal Association proposed the elimination of the automatic appropriation of motor fuel taxes to the Highway Department and the elimination of any mention of the direct grants of such taxes.[33]

As tempers flared and criticism mounted, Sanders tried to smooth the troubled waters with compromises. He pledged increased financial aid to cities the next year and reminded legislators that "there is no way to draft a document to please everybody." Sanders pleaded, "I am trying to do what I think is best for the people of Georgia, and if I get burned, I'm just going to get burned."[34] Some were certain that he was getting burned. One disgruntled legislator muttered "Carl Sanders is governor, but he ain't king," and a Sumter county legislator observed, "Carl Sanders just ain't as popular now as he was during the regular session."[35]

The House was split into two rival camps. One group, led by Speaker Smith, Representative Arthur Bolton, and Representative George Busbee, sought what they called a "modern" constitution. Opposing them was a faction led by Representatives George L. Smith, Denmark

---

[31] *Columbus Ledger*, May 8, 1964.

[32] *Savannah Evening Press*, May 9, 1964.

[33] *Atlanta Journal*, May 4, 8, 10, 1964; *Savannah Evening Press*, March 31, 1964; *Columbus Ledger*, April 1, 1964; *Tifton Gazette*, March 27, 1964.

[34] *Rome News-Tribune*, May 10, 1964.

[35] *Columbus Enquirer*, May 14, 1964.

Groover, and Roy McCracken that favored the existing constitution. Sanders, working with both groups, generally tried to stay in the middle. In doing so, he managed to anger both sides.

Relations between the two factions deteriorated to the point that Sanders seriously considered giving up on the constitution, adjourning the General Assembly, and sending the members home. A crisis came when rural lawmakers stuck with an amendment offered by Representative George Brooks of Oglethorpe county. It stipulated that no county's share of gasoline tax grants ever should be taken from it and that the total distribution to the counties would be frozen at a minimum of $9.3 million. Reluctantly the governor agreed with the proposal, but only if rural lawmakers would also allocate $9.3 million to municipalities. Sanders had worked closely with the Georgia Municipal Association for years and was sympathetic to the needs of urban Georgians. In fact, in the 1962 campaign he had promised the G.M.A. that he would attempt to secure for the cities an appropriation equal to the amount the counties received. This was his opportunity to fulfil his campaign pledge, and he made the most of it. Sanders conferred with both factions at great length, and finally, late at night, the impasse was resolved. The rural legislators yielded to the governor. The next day the House voted 177 to 3 to guarantee cities $9.3 million in yearly street and traffic control grants. Sanders did not want either proposal in the constitution. But since rural legislators insisted on the counties getting their money, he demanded that the cities be included, too. Clearly the compromise was a major victory for the governor and the cities. It was a major development because it marked the first time the state government had seriously considered the needs of Georgia's cities. Elmer George, the executive director of the G.M.A. from 1957 to 1983, was extremely pleased with the result and considered it a start toward a partnership between the cities and the state government. Once again Sanders had, to use Reg Murphy's phrase, muddled through to a successful compromise. Had an agreement not been reached, Sanders probably would have terminated the special session. The crisis over revenue marked a turning point in the deliberations. The atmosphere changed dramatically. The anger and hostility that nearly had destroyed the session suddenly was replaced by a new mood of harmony and good will. Representative

Busbee, amazed at the transformation, remarked after the vote, "I have never seen better feelings between urban and rural legislators."[36]

Other controversies arose as the House debated the constitution article by article, but none were as serious as the highway revenue dispute, and they were resolved easily. Cedartown banker W. D. Trippe, arguing that a new constitution must be drafted by a constitutional convention, claimed the whole procedure was illegal and threatened legal action. Fortunately for Sanders, Attorney General Eugene Cook ruled that the legislature had the legal right to write a new constitution.[37] Representative Groover tried to remove from the new constitution a provision that would let the legislature help finance rapid transit for Atlanta and other cities, but his attempt was defeated by a vote of 85 to 59.[38] Home rule generated much controversy in the House, but Sanders insisted that it be included. Eventually, administrative forces prevailed and they acknowledged Representative Groover's help in getting the measure adopted. Finally on May 29, the House approved the last article and the whole constitution by a vote of 161 to 9.[39]

Action then shifted to the Senate, which took up the measure on June 1. The Senate resolved itself into a Committee of the Whole to consider HR 6 (the proposed constitution). After two weeks of debate, the Committee of the Whole recommended passage of HR 6. On June 17 the constitution was read a third time, and the Senate approved it unanimously.[40]

Although both houses had approved the new constitution, substantial differences remained because the Senate had added 151 amendments to the House version. The House quickly agreed to thirty of the Senate amendments but rejected the remainder. To reconcile the differences, a Conference Committee of six members was established. Lieutenant Governor Geer appointed Senators Julian Webb, Milton Carlton, and John Gayner. Speaker Smith named Representatives Arthur Bolton, Den-

---

[36]Ibid., May 24, 1964; *Augusta Chronicle*, May 21, 1964; *Atlanta Constitution*, May 21, 22, 24, 1964; telephone interview with Elmer George, March 13, 1992.

[37]*Savannah Morning News*, May 28, 29, 1964.

[38]*Valdosta Daily Times*, May 28, 1964.

[39]*House Journal, Extraordinary Session, 1964*, pp. 566-68; *Athens Banner-Herald*, May 31, 1964.

[40]*Senate Journal, Extraordinary Session, 1964*, pp. 574, 653.

mark Groover, and Frank Twitty. Several basic issues divided the two bodies. The House version provided for an elected state school superintendent; the Senate version had an elected Georgia State Board of Education that would appoint the superintendent. The House version provided two-year terms for both senators and representatives; the Senate version gave senators four-year terms. The Senate version pledged that the 1965 General Assembly would reapportion the House on a population basis; the House version did not.[41] This difference became moot, however, when a federal court ruled that both houses must represent population, not geography.

By June 23 the Conference Committee had produced a compromise package. It recommended four-year terms for both senators and representatives, continued election of the school superintendent, and appointment of the Georgia State Board of Education by the governor as was currently done. The size of the House would range from 162 to 216 members with apportionment by the General Assembly. The terms of state supreme court, court of appeals, and superior court judges were set at six years, as the Senate desired. The House accepted the Conference Committee report 152 to 16, and the Senate approved it 43 to 9. The General Assembly also approved the new election code. The code, since it was statutory and not constitutional in nature, would not require a vote by the people. On June 25 Sanders adjourned the special session with high praise for the General Assembly. The legislators, he said, were "the most dedicated group of public servants that I have ever had the pleasure or privilege to know or work with."[42]

Before the special session ended, constitutional revision became hopelessly embroiled in the larger debate over legislative reapportionment. A bombshell decision from the federal appeals court nullified the constitutional revision part of the special session and left the state's political leadership angry, frustrated, and bewildered. In the case of *Toombs v. Fortson*, United States circuit court judges Elbert Tuttle,

---

[41]Ibid., pp. 699-700; *House Journal, Extraordinary Session, 1964*, pp. 1004-16, 1024-25; *Rome News-Tribune*, June 17, 1964.

[42]*Senate Journal, Extraordinary Session, 1964*, pp. 767-90, 799-800; *House Journal, Extraordinary Session, 1964*, pp. 1091-1113; *Atlanta Journal*, June 23-25, 1964; Daniel, *Addresses of Carl Sanders*, pp. 42-43. The entire revised constitution is printed in *Acts and Resolutions, Extraordinary Session, 1964*, pp. 234-333.

Griffin Bell, and Lewis Morgan ruled that the new constitution could not be placed on the November ballot since the General Assembly that proposed it had not been apportioned in accordance with federal constitutional standards. The court, however, let stand the new election code passed by the legislature.[43] When the court issued its temporary ruling, there was concern that it would demand the immediate reapportionment of the House. Governor Sanders wanted to delay further reapportionment until the 1965 legislative session. In an unprecedented move, he appeared before the three-judge panel on June 19 pleading his case. As always, he argued that the legislature—not the courts—should handle reapportionment. "The subject needs careful study," he asserted, and the legislature ought to be given a chance to do it "in an orderly fashion." Reapportioning the House, he told the judges, could not be done in the "flick of an eye."[44] The governor's impressive testimony convinced the judges to delay the reapportionment of the House until the 1965 legislative session but did not salvage his constitution.

The decision of the three judges was bitterly assailed at the time, and their reasoning has continued to puzzle observers ever since. Lieutenant Governor Geer thought the court decision was "faulty" and declared that the judges had gone "beyond the scope of the U. S. Supreme Court reapportionment decison in throwing out Georgia's constitution revision." He predicted that it would be reversed on appeal. A baffled Representative Bolton could not understand the logic behind the decision. Nor could Representative Groover, who remarked, "I don't see how you can legally pass an election code if you can't legally pass a constitution."[45] Nor could Sanders, who, like Geer, Bolton, and Groover, was a first-rate lawyer. The governor was furious. He could see all his efforts being nullified by a force over which he had no control. The power of the people, he complained, had been usurped by the federal court. He was certain that the court erred. It seemed ridiculous to him that the court would accept the election code but reject the constitution written by the very same malapportioned legislature.[46] He later succeeded

[43]*Atlanta Constitution*, June 25, 1964.

[44]Daniel, *Addresses of Carl Sanders*, pp. 72-77.

[45]*Atlanta Constitution*, June 20, 1964; *Savannah Evening Press*, June 20, 1964.

[46]Press release June 24, 1964, Carl Sanders Papers, Georgia Department of Archives and History; Cook, "Sanders: An Oral History," pp. 34-36.

in getting the decision overturned on appeal by the United States Supreme Court, but it was to no avail. By the time the court had rendered its verdict, it was too late to get the new constitution on the general election ballot in November 1964. Consequently, the momentum for constitutional revision had been lost, and the people of Georgia would never vote on his constitution.[47] The federal court's ruling had destroyed it. The whole process seemed to have been a dismal failure—a monumental waste of time, energy, and more than $1 million of taxpayers' money for the special session.

Despite the disappointment at the time, the experience was not entirely negative. Practically everyone agreed that the new election code was a positive accomplishment. The *Atlanta Constitution* editorialized that it was "a progressive step in the direction of honest voting and broadened voter participation." The newspaper commended Sanders, the Special Committee that wrote the draft, and the legislature for adopting it.[48] Even the generally skeptical *Savannah Evening Press* admitted that the new election code made it easier to vote and harder to cheat.[49] In addition, observers acknowledged that the experience of trying to write a constitution was educational and should prove beneficial in the future. Senator Leroy Johnson predicted, "The work on the Constitution can be used to good advantage when a new one is written later."[50] Eighteen years would pass before Senator Johnson's prediction came true and Georgia finally adopted a new constitution when George Busbee was governor. Busbee had served as a key legislative leader for Sanders, and the bitter experience of 1964 significantly influenced his cautious but ultimately effective approach.[51]

After more than a quarter of a century of hindsight, it is apparent that Georgia needed an updated constitution and that Carl Sanders attempted to provide one. He did a masterful job of generating public interest in the endeavor. Constitutional revision became his issue, and

---

[47]Saye, *A Constitutional History of Georgia*, p. 429.

[48]*Atlanta Constitution*, June 24, 1964.

[49]*Savannah Evening Press*, June 23, 1964.

[50]*Atlanta Constitution*, June 26, 1964.

[51]"Governor George Dekle Busbee: An Oral History," interview by James F. Cook, Georgia Government Documentation Project, Georgia State University, Atlanta, November 1988, pp. 51-52.

he mobilized support for it. In directing the work of the Constitutional Revision Commission, incorporating modest public involvement in the process, and securing legislative approval of the document, Sanders did all that reasonably could be expected of a chief executive. He set the agenda, urged committees to meet deadlines, and kept the process on course. By firmly opposing proposals to increase the sales tax and to allow the governor to serve two consecutive terms, he eliminated potential controversies before they developed. He was also wise in securing court approval to delay reapportioning the House until a later session. Given the conservative nature of the Georgia electorate and the rural domination of the General Assembly, especially the House, Sanders was forced by political necessity to compromise on many issues that he regarded as nonessential. As a result, the document was not exactly what he wanted, being longer and more detailed than he preferred. But without such concessions the House would not have approved the document. Despite its flaws, the proposed constitution seems to have been a reasonable compromise between the rural and urban elements that reflected a consensus of the people of Georgia and their elected officials.

Observers at the time generally agreed with Sanders that the proposed constitution would have been an improvement over the existing one. But there was a noticeable lack of enthusiasm for the change. The conflicts, compromises, concessions, and court rulings apparently had taken their toll. Even the *Atlanta Journal*, usually supportive of Sanders, was critical. "Instead of the brief and basic charter we expected, it was full of statutory provisions and expedient concessions," the paper observed. The *Journal* doubted that the constitution would have been approved, and it praised the federal court for saving us "further expense and bother."[52] Had the court not intervened, it is impossible to determine whether the constitution would have been approved by the people, but it is clear that approval would not have come easily and might have been impossible to obtain.

In an administration noted for many successes, constitutional revision stands out as the one conspicuous failure for Sanders. The experience was disappointing, and it cost him some political support. However, it could have been much worse. If the people had voted

---

[52] *Atlanta Journal*, June 20, 1964.

against the constitution, Sanders would have suffered a major political defeat. One of his inner circle, looking for the silver lining, rationalized, "Why, it's one of the finest things that ever happened. Look at it this way: Citizens very likely were going to vote against it in November.

"So which is better—getting slapped by three federal judges or getting voted against by a million or so citizens?"[53]

Viewed in that light, perhaps Sanders was lucky after all.

[53] *Atlanta Constitution,* June 21, 1964.

Speaker of the House George T. Smith discusses strategy with Governor Sanders.

Chapter 13

J.F.K. and L.B.J.

Carl Sanders found a kindred spirit in John F. Kennedy. Despite the obvious differences between the Massachusetts Roman Catholic and the Georgia Baptist, they had much in common. Both were young, handsome, and articulate. Both had beautiful wives and two children. Both were veterans of World War II. Both were talented leaders who enjoyed serving the public and had advanced rapidly to higher political offices. But more important than these superficial similarities was their vision for America and their understanding of the American political system. The president's concept of a New Frontier struck a responsive chord with the governor. Like the president, Sanders was a visionary, a planner, an organizer. Neither was content with the status quo. Both believed that America could do better in educating its youth, developing its technology, reducing racial tensions, providing jobs for its people, making its cities more livable, its people more healthy and physically fit, and its political system more democratic. What was needed to make these dreams a reality, they believed, was forceful and courageous leadership. Sanders was convinced that Kennedy was providing that kind of leadership on the national level, and he resolved to assist him in any way possible on the state level.

Sanders first met Kennedy at the 1960 Democratic convention in Los Angeles. Although he was immediately attracted to the Massachusetts senator, they did not become well acquainted until 1962. Shortly after his election as governor, Sanders met with the president in the Oval Office. Despite the president's busy schedule, he extended the meeting beyond the scheduled fifteen minutes and then had photos taken. They not only discussed a wide range of political issues, they also began a friendship which deepened with subsequent contact.[1]

---

[1]Barnard interview, February 16, 1991; *Atlanta Constitution*, November 16, 1962;

Although Kennedy and Sanders were visionaries, they were also political realists, having learned how the system works through the rough experience of campaigning and governing. Clearly there was a natural rapport between them, but their friendship also brought political advantages to both of them. As a northern Roman Catholic with moderately liberal views, Kennedy needed to bolster his support in Protestant, conservative Deep South states like Georgia. Sanders, striving to raise the economic level of his state, needed every federal dollar he could get. Sanders understood that every state had economic needs that could justify federal grants. Since there never was enough revenue in the federal treasury to meet all legitimate needs, it was vitally important to have access to the sources of power. Sanders was convinced that if he had the opportunity to present his case to the proper authorities, then Georgia would get its share of the federal largess. In his initial meeting with the president, the governor explained how important the jobs at Fort Gordon were to the Georgia economy. Kennedy responded favorably to the governor's arguments, and shortly afterwards the press was informed that the signal corps would remain at Fort Gordon. Subsequently the Kennedy administration provided permanent buildings as well.

Sanders made a point of meeting personally the members of the president's cabinet and top administrative personnel in Washington that he would be dealing with as governor. He seldom missed an opportunity to develop personal ties with federal officials, for he wanted Georgia to have a harmonious relationship with the federal government. In January 1963 Sanders brought most of his top lieutenants from Georgia to Washington for a reception honoring him which preceded the Democratic Party's Second Annual Inaugural Salute. The next morning Sanders visited President Kennedy again. Among those attending the reception were Attorney General Robert Kennedy and his wife Ethel. Sanders quickly developed a warm relationship with Bobby Kennedy and corresponded with him regularly. At a breakfast meeting in Atlanta on April 26, the attorney general discussed Georgia's economic and political needs with the governor. In May Sanders was back in Washington meeting with the Georgia congressional delegation and seeking $200,000 in federal funds for an Army Corps of Engineers study of the possibility

Cook, "Sanders: An Oral History," pp. 48-49.

of building a canal across south Georgia which would connect the Atlantic Ocean and the Gulf of Mexico. While in Washington he had an extended meeting with President Kennedy and explained that Georgia was in a "strategic location" for space operations. The governor pointed out that Georgia had potential missile-launching sites on the coast and that Georgia Tech offered expertise in the space field. Meanwhile a delegation from the University System of Georgia met with officials of the National Aeronautics and Space Administration to develop a program so that Georgia could make "a major contribution to the space program." Although Sanders did not secure all the assistance he sought, the gears of government in Washington and Atlanta meshed smoothly during his tenure as governor.[2]

While Sanders sought the positive support of the federal government for Georgia projects, he took precautions to avoid the negative involvement of the federal government. Convinced that Georgia was capable of handling state matters, he did not want federal courts reapportioning Georgia's legislature, nor did he want the Justice Department intervening in racial matters. Since his record of moderation in racial matters stood out in stark contrast to the performances of Ross Barnett, George Wallace, and other diehard segregationist governors of the era, Sanders had little trouble convincing both the president and the attorney general that blacks would be treated fairly under the law while he was governor and that he would continue to work toward improving race relations.

Sanders, always conscious of Georgia's national image, was determined to keep racial protests to a minimum while he was governor. In trying to devise a suitable strategy, he discussed the matter at length with his friend J. B. Fuqua, who was then chairman of the Democratic party in Georgia. Fuqua, after several meetings with the president and attorney general, became the unofficial liaison between the state government and the federal government. This policy worked extremely well and isolated Sanders somewhat from unpleasant activities and tedious details. One part of the agreement with the Kennedy administration called for the attorney general, whenever he received a complaint from any county in

---

[2]*Atlanta Constitution*, January 19, May 28, 1963; press releases March 4, April 26, 1963, box 34, Sanders Collection, Law Library; Sanders to John F. Kennedy, May 28, 1963, K (1) folder, box 19, Sanders Collection, Law Library.

Georgia about a civil rights violation, to contact Fuqua first. Fuqua would then try to resolve the problem before it reached the newspapers. Quite often either he or Sanders would know some prominent person in the local community who could remedy the problem with appropriate action. As a result, Georgia had fewer racial disturbances than her neighboring states, and the Sanders administration avoided many potentially embarrassing situations. Fuqua believes that his role as liaison was "one of the most constructive things" he did in the Sanders administration.[3]

Despite his respect for Kennedy, Sanders did not agree with every aspect of the president's domestic program, especially his commitment to passing a major civil rights bill. Sanders had no qualms about the major thrust of the civil rights bill, but he objected strenuously to the public accommodation portion of it. In fact, he felt so strongly about the matter that he testified against that section of the bill before the Senate Commerce Committee on July 30, 1963. In emphasizing the importance of private property rights, Sanders maintained that the federal government had no authority, constitutional or otherwise, to "dictate the actions of the private property owner in determining the use or disposition of his property." The proposed bill, he argued, was unwise, indeed unnecessary, and would not accomplish its stated purposes. He was appalled that anyone would want to bring the mighty force of the federal government down to the local level and "thrust it into the four walls of the store, the shop, the plant, the warehouse or other facilities of private business." Rather than federal coercion and lawsuits, Sanders favored voluntary change by men and women of good will. He believed the voluntary approach was working in Georgia and other areas, and in the long run would accomplish more than federal intervention. To support his position he quoted the Atlanta Chamber of Commerce and the editors of both the *Atlanta Journal* and the *Atlanta Constitution*—all of whom opposed the Public Accommodations Bill. In conclusion, Sanders found the bill to be "a destroyer of rights" and "a breeder of division." Its passage, he feared, would imperil "the peace, the tranquility, and the future strength and freedom of our nation."[4]

---

[3]Fuqua interview, April 4, 1991.

[4]Statement of Governor Carl E. Sanders, Appearance before Senate Commerce Committee, July 30, 1963, July 1963 folder, box 34, Sanders Collection, Law Library.

Sanders's forceful opposition did not prevent the passage of the civil rights bill, nor did it jeopardize his friendship with Kennedy. Indeed, the president agreed to participate in a ceremony in Atlanta on October 7 commemorating the 75th anniversary of Georgia Tech. Mayor Ivan Allen, who made the arrangements, was delighted when Kennedy accepted the invitation, but Sanders and Fuqua were startled when they read about the president's planned visit in the *Atlanta Constitution*. Surprised that they had not been consulted, they were concerned that the controversy surrounding civil rights and the emotional debate on the civil rights bill might produce unfortunate consequences. What if Kennedy's presence in Atlanta provoked a demonstration, Fuqua reasoned. It could be politically embarrassing to both Kennedy and Sanders. Concerned about such possibilities, Fuqua told Sanders, "We just can't let this happen. It's not the thing to do politically."

Sanders agreed with Fuqua's reasoning but could see no way out of the dilemma. "I can't uninvite the president of the United States," he exclaimed.

"I can," replied Fuqua, who then offered to go to the White House and explain why the president should cancel his visit. Unable to think of a better alternative, Sanders reluctantly told him to go ahead. Fuqua then arranged to enter the private entrance of the White House so that he could avoid the press room and having his name appear on the list of visitors. He explained the problem to Kennedy who quickly agreed to cancel the trip if they could figure out a way to get him out of it. The president called in his press secretary, Pierre Salinger. After much discussion, they finally decided to announce that the president was so busy with the civil rights bill and other matters that he would have to cancel some of his engagements. Shortly thereafter he cancelled his appearance at Georgia Tech.[5]

Sanders and Fuqua were grateful that the president followed their advice. And it was probably fortunate that he did, as emotions continued to rise over civil rights. On August 22, six weeks before Kennedy's proposed visit to Atlanta, the famous March on Washington took place which culminated in Martin Luther King, Jr.'s inspiring "I Have a

---

[5]Allen to Johnson, May 29, 1963, K (1) folder, box 19, Sanders Collection, Law Library; Fuqua interview, April 4, 1991.

Dream" speech. On November 22, six weeks after the proposed visit, Kennedy flew to Dallas. Because of the close working relationship between Atlanta and Washington a potentially embarrassing situation was averted.

Astute members of the press concluded that something out of the ordinary had happened. Margaret Shannon, an investigative reporter for the *Atlanta Journal*, was especially curious to find out why the president had canceled his visit. Checking her sources, she discovered that Fuqua had been in Washington and had visited all of Georgia's congressmen. Convinced that he had been involved in the decision, she finally confronted him. When she asked him pointedly if he had "uninvited" the president, he replied evasively: "Oh, no one would uninvite the president."[6]

Sanders was playing golf in Augusta when he heard the tragic news that Kennedy had been assassinated. The country had lost its leader; Sanders had lost a friend. In a press release, Sanders called upon all who love their nation and cherish their liberty to deplore this "despicable act" which has tarnished the heritage of all Americans and ended a life distinguished by its "unstinted service to mankind." On behalf of four million Georgians, he expressed "the profound, heartfelt sympathy of our people" to the entire Kennedy family. Sanders and his wife also sent personal condolences to Mrs. Kennedy and flew to Washington to view the bier in the East Room of the White House. At a special memorial service at Hill Baptist Church in Augusta, Sanders commented further on the death of the president. "The bitter harvest of Friday grew from the seeds of discord, distrust and destruction which are sown by those who now profess innocence of this tragic deed," he said. "The price has been the death of a disciple of peace." To achieve the victories Kennedy sought, he urged the people to "take a fresh new look at religious principles and teachings" and to "turn to God for comfort, for strength, for guidance."[7]

---

[6]Fuqua interview, April 4, 1991.

[7]Sanders to Mrs. John F. Kennedy, November 22, 1963, K (1) folder, box 19; press release November 22, 1963, box 34, Sanders Collection, Law Library; *Atlanta Journal*, November 25, 1963.

To Sanders, President Kennedy's death was truly a national tragedy. In a wide-ranging interview conducted at the end of his governorship, Sanders stated that he admired Kennedy "more than any man I met in government."[8]

Sanders's grief over the loss of Kennedy was assuaged by the fact that Lyndon Johnson was his successor. Sanders had first met Johnson at the Democratic convention in Los Angeles in 1960 and immediately was impressed by the powerful Texan. In the intervening years their paths crossed many times, and a warm friendship and mutual respect developed between them. Sanders and Fuqua had enjoyed the hospitality of the LBJ ranch in Texas on more than one occasion. Johnson not only liked Sanders personally, he also admired his political skills and apparently saw in him the potential for national leadership. The new president's respect for the governor was evident when he delivered his first major address to Congress. At the president's request, Sanders heard the speech from a very prestigious location—sitting next to Mrs. Johnson in the executive gallery. And after the speech, Johnson rearranged schedules so that he could have a lengthy meeting with Sanders and Fuqua in the White House.[9]

The same direct and personal communication between Atlanta and Washington that had existed under Kennedy continued under Johnson. On January 3, 1964, for example, Burke Marshall, an assistant attorney general in the Justice Department, alerted Sanders to the possibility of racial violence in Baker county at a forthcoming election. Acting on that information, Sanders sent several state officers into the county to observe the primary election. Fortunately there was no violence. Sanders thanked Marshall for his "thoughtful suggestion," which he considered "a true expression of federal-state cooperation in the best interest of both governing agencies."[10]

On May 4, 1964, Sanders was working in his office, making final preparations for the special session of the legislature that was scheduled to convene in ninety minutes, when at 9:30 he received a telephone call

---

[8] *Atlanta Constitution*, November 7, 1963.

[9] Ibid., November 28, 1963; Sanders to Johnson, December 3, 1963, Lyndon B. Johnson Presidential file (2) folder, box 19, Sanders Collection, Law Library.

[10] Marshall to Sanders, January 3, 1964, Sanders to Marshall, January 17, 1964, M folder, box 19, Sanders Collection, Law Library.

that he would never forget. A presidential aide informed the governor that President Johnson was traveling in the South and wanted to stop in Georgia. Suddenly the president himself grabbed the telephone and explained to the startled Sanders that most of his emphasis on poverty programs had been in the North. He wanted people in the South to know that he was interested in their problems, too. To dramatize his commitment Johnson wanted a tour of Appalachia. Sanders assured the president that such a tour could be arranged. He invited Johnson to stay in the Mansion and have breakfast with the legislature. The president accepted the breakfast invitation but rejected the Mansion because he traveled with such a large entourage. President Johnson telephoned on Monday; he was scheduled to arrive in Atlanta the next Thursday evening, leaving very little time to prepare for the executive visit.

When Sanders's staff learned what had happened, they were panic-stricken. How could all the details be worked out in such a short period of time, they wondered. A flurry of activity ensued. Doug Barnard and John Harper were on the telephone immediately trying to clarify the details. Pandemonium reigned as Benny Tackett, Yvonne Redding, and the other secretaries frantically made the local arrangements. If preparing for an unexpected presidential visit in three days was not enough strain for the staff, there was the special session of the legislature to keep up with and an announced visit on Monday by Senator Edward Kennedy of Massachusetts. By working furiously day and night and doing without sleep, the staff managed to make all the necessary preparations so that the visit went smoothly.[11]

Traveling with the president, in addition to the host of news media and vigilant Secret Service personnel, was a large entourage that included his daughter Lynda Bird, Secretary of Health, Education and Welfare Anthony Celebrezze, Secretary of Agriculture Orville Freeman, Federal Housing Administrator Robert Weaver, Chairman of the Tennessee Valley Authority Aubrey Wagner, and Undersecretary of Commerce Franklin D. Roosevelt, Jr. Secretary of Labor Willard Wirtz joined the group later. The president's plane, scheduled to arrive at Atlanta

---

[11]Barnard interview, February 16, 1991; Tackett interview, January 23, 1991; interview with Yvonne Redding Lowe, Cedartown, July 2, 1991; *Atlanta Constitution*, May 5, 1964.

Municipal Airport at 8:40 p. m., landed nearly two hours late. Waiting to greet him were Governor and Mrs. Sanders, Mayor and Mrs. Allen, Senator Herman Talmadge, seven of Georgia's ten congressmen, and other officials. Despite the late hour, huge crowds lined the streets of Atlanta to cheer the presidential motorcade as it proceeded from the airport to the Dinkler Plaza Hotel.[12]

The next morning the legislature joined the presidential party for breakfast at the Dinkler Plaza. Another motorcade took the president from the hotel to the Atlanta Municipal Airport for a short flight to Gainesville where Johnson delivered a speech. He then visited a poverty-stricken area near Gainesville and endorsed an old friend, Ninth District congressman Representative Phil Landrum, who was being challenged by a young state senator named Zell Miller. The president was in his element waving to throngs of cheering admirers, pressing the flesh, interacting with politicians, and making headlines. He poked fun at the marksmanship of both Sanders and Fuqua. Both, it seems, had experienced difficulty in bagging a deer at the LBJ ranch.[13] Johnson was then at the peak of his popularity, and the crowds were even larger than expected. An astonished Herman Talmadge remarked that it was "the biggest crowd of people I have ever seen anywhere." In a note thanking the president for the visit, Sanders estimated that "over 750,000 Georgians had the opportunity to see one of America's greatest Presidents." With understandable exaggeration he claimed that Johnson's visit was the "outstanding experience of my life." Sanders added that he and Betty were pleased to count him as "one of our personal friends." The visit clearly was a great success that accomplished everything that Johnson could possibly have hoped for. In a personal thank you to "Dear Carl," Johnson described his reception in Georgia as "incredible and very inspiring" and thanked Sanders for his well-spent efforts.[14]

Lyndon Johnson had barely left Georgia when Lady Bird Johnson arrived for an announced visit. She toured the Communicable Disease

---

[12]*Atlanta Constitution*, May 6, 8, 1964; itinerary for President Lyndon B. Johnson, press release May 7, 1964, box 34, Sanders Collection, Law Library.

[13]*Atlanta Constitution*, May 9, 1964.

[14]Ibid.; Sanders to Johnson, May 8, 1964, Johnson to Sanders, May 12, 1964, Lyndon B. Johnson Presidential File (2) folder, box 19, Sanders Collection, Law Library.

Center, Emory University, and the Atlanta Art Museum. The First Lady was honored at an elaborate reception at the Governor's Mansion, which was described in chapter ten.

Betty and Carl corresponded regularly with Lyndon and Lady Bird Johnson. They also spent time with them at the Democratic Party Convention in Atlantic City in July. Carl, serving as chairman of the Rules Committee, took the opportunity to make detailed suggestions to the Platform Committee on foreign policy, fiscal responsibility, transportation, agricultural and rural development, and other issues. He repeated his opposition to the public accommodations section of the Civil Rights Law and called for a new program of federally guaranteed loans to all capable students who would not otherwise be able to attend college. He also strongly endorsed Johnson's nomination for president. Johnson was grateful for Sanders's staunch support and described his service at the convention as "invaluable."[15]

Under President Johnson's Great Society, federal funds became available for a wide range of programs, and Governor Sanders made sure that Georgia received its share of them. The governor created a special committee headed by Mrs. Orville Schaefer, Director of Family and Children Services, to coordinate federal programs in the state. He also worked closely with Georgia's area planning and development commissions. Such efforts enhanced Georgia's chances of securing federal assistance, and at the end of his term Georgia won a prestigious national award for "Intergovernmental Cooperation."[16]

Determined to raise the living conditions of Georgians, the governor eagerly sought federal aid in order to achieve that goal. With a cooperative administrative in Washington allowing federal dollars to flow into the state in a steady stream, considerable economic gains resulted. When hurricane Dora struck the Georgia coast, inflicting heavy damage to Jekyll Island and the Savannah area as well as flooding in other parts of the state, Georgia received more than $4 million in federal assistance.

---

[15]*Atlanta Journal,* July 30, 1964; undated press release in August 1964 folder, box 34; Johnson to Sanders, September 8, 1964, Lyndon B. Johnson Presidential File (2) folder, box 19, Sanders Collection, Law Library.

[16]Press release March 8, 1964, box 34; press release December 6, 1966, box 35, Sanders Collection, Law Library.

Georgia was one of the first states to receive a grant from the Department of the Interior under the Water Resources Act. Particularly helpful for Georgia were Hill-Burton grants for hospital construction, the Higher Education Facilities Act, Economic Development Administration grants for water and sewer projects, Department of Interior grants for parks and recreation area, and grants from the Department of Health, Education and Welfare. Collectively these funds, along with extensive federal aid for highways and the military, made a substantial impact on the Georgia economy.[17]

Passage of the Appalachian Regional Development Act of 1965, making thirty-five Georgia counties eligible for federal assistance for economic development, was of special interest to Sanders. He had testified to a Senate committee that Johnson's Appalachia and antipoverty programs were "wise investments, not wealth-consuming expenditures." When the bill was passed by Congress, he congratulated the president on "your great victory" and pointed out that "the people of these states are the winners."[18] Taking full advantage of the opportunities this law offered, he secured numerous grants for an economically deprived area of Georgia. When the Appalachian Regional Commission was established in April 1965 to administer the federal-state programs of development in the eleven-state mountainous region, Sanders was elected cochairman. Under his leadership Georgia became a pacesetter in this program and established a number of "firsts." The first grant for a school under this act went to a vocational-technical school in Jasper. The first funds for the construction of a hospital went to Gainesville. Another first came in April 1966 when $200,000 was awarded to Georgia counties for the purchase of special teaching equipment in elementary and secondary schools. Several Appalachian grants were awarded to Georgia for sewage treatment plants, hospitals, libraries, and schools. In one month—May 1966—Georgia was granted over $1 million in Appalachian funds. The projects included sewage treatment plants at Canton, Summerville,

---

[17]Press releases September 25, 29, October 19, 1964, January 15, 1965, May 24, 29, June 2, 8, August 10, 25, 31, October 18, 28, 29, 1966, box 35, Sanders Collection, Law Library.

[18]*Atlanta Constitution*, January 22, 1965; Sanders to Johnson, March 3, 1965, Lyndon B. Johnson Presidential File (2) folder, box 19, Sanders Collection, Law Library.

Trion, and Vogel State Park, libraries at Carrollton, Calhoun, and Canton, and $217,708 for the new junior college at Dalton. Two months later a delighted Sanders announced that the Appalachian Regional Commission had approved $1,356,600 in funds for four Georgia projects: a hospital in Rome, nursing homes in Commerce and Ellijay, and a vocational-technical school in Carrollton. Grants provided by the Appalachian Regional Development Act certainly provided an economic boost to the northern counties of Georgia.[19]

While President Johnson was waging a War on Poverty in America, he also was escalating the war in Southeast Asia. Sanders backed Johnson's efforts in both wars with equal enthusiasm. In October and November 1965 he took a four-week tour of the Far East, including lengthy stops in Japan and Vietnam. He returned to America convinced that "we must defeat this Communist threat and affirm the stand which our Country has made." As a staunch anticommunist, Sanders was utterly appalled when the United States Supreme Court struck down the federal sedition law which required individual Communists in the United States to register their identity. Although he normally refrained from public criticism of Supreme Court decisions, he made an exception this time. To Sanders, the decision was "insane." "You don't furnish your mortal enemy with a loaded weapon," he argued. He failed to see why the Supreme Court allowed Communists to use our Constitution, which they repudiate, as the basis for their protection. As long as American boys were being sent to the far corners of the world to give up their lives fighting Communism, Sanders expected the government, including the Supreme Court, to do just as much here at home to destroy the Communists.[20]

Despite mounting criticism of the war in Vietnam, Sanders's support of the war effort remained firm. To counteract the "false impression" that a "handful of radicals" had portrayed to the rest of the world, he helped organize "Affirmation Vietnam." He hoped that it would show

---

[19]*Atlanta Constitution*, April 20, 1965; press releases March 4, August 18, 1965, February 11, April 7, June 7, August 10, 1966, box 35, Sanders Collection, Law Library.

[20]Press releases October 18, November 16, 1965, January 4, 1966, box 35, Sanders Collection, Law Library.

Americans on the battlefield, as well as America's allies and enemies, that "our resolve in Vietnam is strong and we will not back down." He signed a proclamation making February 12, 1966, "Georgia Affirmation Viet Nam Day." A rally was held that day in Atlanta Stadium, featuring General Lucius Clay, Secretary of State Dean Rusk, singer Anita Bryant, and Governor Sanders. Unfortunately, heavy rains dampened the spirits of the participants and a disappointing crowd of only 15,000 attended.[21]

Long before Vietnam became an emotional issue, President Johnson lost much of his public support in Georgia. Extremely popular when he visited the state in May 1964, Johnson's standing among Georgians steadily declined over the next six months. His liberal domestic program, and especially his forceful backing of the Civil Rights Law of 1964, caused the erosion of his popularity among white Georgians. The growing militancy of black activists, the increasing violence of civil rights protests, and the urban riots of 1964 turned thousands of Georgians against the Johnson administration. Many disgruntled Democrats found the conservative views of Senator Barry Goldwater, the Republican presidential nominee, more appealing than Johnson's liberalism. One Georgia congressman, a Democrat, was quoted in August as saying "it would be poison now to say you had even heard of Lyndon Johnson in Georgia."[22] Consequently, most of Georgia's political leadership quickly distanced themselves from the unpopular president.

Like President Johnson, Governor Sanders also suffered a loss of popularity. Writing in early August 1964, Reg Murphy observed that Sanders was at "a low ebb politically in much of Georgia." He cited three reasons for his decline. First, he was identified with the Democratic administration which sponsored the Civil Rights Act, and as a supporter of Johnson when the tide was running strongly for Goldwater; secondly, there was resentment at the barring of Governor George Wallace of Alabama from speaking at Jekyll Island facilities; and thirdly, governors traditionally experience a sharp slump in popularity a couple of years after their election.[23] Other commentators made similar observations.

---

[21]Ibid., January 4, February 11, 1966; *Atlanta Journal and Constitution*, February 13, 1966.

[22]Transcript of an interview of Sanders by Ed Blair, August 4, 1964, August 1964 folder, box 34, Sanders Collection, Law Library.

[23]*Atlanta Constitution*, August 3, 1964.

Oddly, Sanders was not responsible for barring Wallace from speaking at Jekyll Island, but the public blamed the governor nevertheless. An independent agency had blocked Wallace from speaking at Jekyll because federal law prohibited political campaign speeches at a National Guard armory. Sanders had been responsible for killing a move by some legislators to have Wallace address the special session of the legislature when the new constitution was being debated. He did not object to Wallace speaking in Georgia, but he was unwilling to provide him with a forum paid for by the taxpayers of Georgia.[24]

Sanders, no doubt, could have enhanced his popularity by joining the Goldwater bandwagon or simply by playing no role whatever in the 1964 presidential election. The latter choice was the safe and expedient policy, and the one most of Georgia's leading Democrats selected. Both Senators Russell and Talmadge announced that they would vote Democratic, but neither took part in the campaign. None of Georgia's ten congressmen—all of them Democrats—campaigned actively for Johnson. Lieutenant Governor Geer sat on the fence, as did Secretary of Agriculture Phil Campbell, Treasurer Jack Ray, and Comptroller General Jimmy Bentley, although Bentley reluctantly announced he would vote Democratic. In fact, of all of Georgia's top elected officials—and all were Democrats—only Sanders campaigned for President Johnson's election with any enthusiasm. He came out fighting for Johnson even before he was nominated at the convention in August, and his support never wavered throughout the campaign.[25]

Ordinarily presidential campaigns are perfunctory affairs in Georgia since the state invariably cast its votes for the Democratic candidate. In 1964, however, things were different. The Republicans, sensing a possible victory, campaigned aggressively, and their efforts forced national Democrats to pay more attention to Georgia. As a result, Georgia became a political battleground as both parties struggled to convince the undecided. Lady Bird and Lucy Johnson conducted an effective whistle stop campaign through south Georgia with stops at Savannah, Jesup, Waycross, Thomasville, and Valdosta. At some stops

---

[24]*Savannah Evening Press*, July 28, 1964; Sanders, "Interviews in 1990," pp. 109-10.

[25]*Macon Telegraph*, November 1, 1964.

the First Lady was heckled, as was Hubert Humphrey, the vice presidential candidate, when he spoke in south Georgia. There were anti-Democratic demonstrations in Moultrie, Tifton, and Savannah. President Johnson was booed in Macon and Augusta. Such activities led observers to comment that it was one of the bitterest presidential campaigns in the history of the state. Reg Murphy claimed it was "the closest, hardest-fought campaign in Georgia history." On the eve of the election, the outcome was still in doubt. Sanders, having been in the thick of the campaign, had observed the anti-Johnson hostility, yet he remained confident of a Johnson victory. At least he maintained that public posture. At a news conference shortly before the election, he predicted a Johnson victory by 50,000 to 100,000 votes.[26]

The governor's prediction, however, was far off the mark, as Goldwater carried Georgia by a wide margin. He swept the south and central Georgia lowlands and also won most of the urban counties. Johnson garnered the black vote, but received only 46 percent of the total vote. From a historical perspective, Sanders's prediction seemed quite reasonable. After all, Georgia was possibly the most solidly Democratic state in the country. Until Goldwater broke the tradition, the state had not voted for a Republican presidential candidate since 1868. Since Reconstruction, all of Georgia's governors and United States senators had been Democrats. No Republican had represented Georgia in Congress in the previous eighty-nine years, but that tradition also ended abruptly in 1964 as Howard "Bo" Callaway defeated Garland Byrd in Georgia's Third Congressional District. Party loyalty finally had broken down in Georgia primarily because of the Kennedy-Johnson support of civil rights. Although it was not so apparent at the time, Georgia's support of Democratic presidential candidates had declined consistently since 1952, and that trend would continue thereafter. Adlai Stevenson took 70 percent of Georgia's vote in 1952 and 66 percent in 1956, and Kennedy won 63 percent in 1960. Johnson's total dropped to 46 percent in 1964, but the Democrats did even worse in 1968 and 1972, as Humphrey got 27 percent and George McGovern only 25 percent.[27]

---

[26]Ibid.; *Atlanta Journal*, October 9, 1964; *Atlanta Constitution*, November 1, 1964.

[27]*Atlanta Constitution*, November 4, 1964; Peirce, *Deep South States of America*, p. 312.

An alarming number of Georgians were abandoning the Democratic party, but Carl Sanders was not among them. He had done all that he possibly could to ensure the election of the Democratic nominee, and he remained steadfast in his support of the president even as he sadly watched the election returns come in. Pleased by Johnson's overwhelming national victory, he was disappointed by the outcome in Georgia and chagrined that other Georgia Democratic officeholders had not done more for the party. Had they campaigned as vigorously as he had, perhaps the outcome would have been different. Instead, they had placed a higher priority on their own careers than on the needs of their party. Like Russell, Talmadge, and the others, Sanders also understood the political realities and he, too, had future political aspirations to consider. He certainly understood the risks involved, and as a result of Johnson's failure to carry Georgia, the governor's prestige plummeted. Indeed many observers concluded that he had sacrificed his political future in Georgia by supporting an unpopular president. Some doubted that he could recover. Sanders, however, had no regrets. He made it clear on election night that if he had it to do over again he would still go all out for Johnson. His reasoning was simple. "I'm a Democrat," he said. "I've been a Democrat all my life and whatever the outcome of this election is, I still couldn't do otherwise than support the Democratic ticket."[28]

By enthusiastically backing President Johnson in the 1964 campaign, Sanders suffered a severe lost of prestige, but the political courage and party loyalty he demonstrated made him stand out as a giant among pygmies when compared to Georgia's other Democratic officials.

---

[28]*Atlanta Constitution*, November 4, 1964.

President Lyndon Johnson and Governor Sanders exchange small talk during breakfast, May 8, 1964. (Courtesy of the Atlanta Constitution.)

Senator Hubert Humphrey greets former Governor Adlai Stevenson warmly as Governor Sanders looks on at the Democratic National Convention in Atlantic City, New Jersey, August 27, 1964. (Courtesy of the Atlanta Constitution.)

*Governor Sanders campaigning for the Johnson-Humphrey ticket
in 1964 at the DeKalb County Democratic Headquarters.*

Chapter 14

1965

In the weeks following the 1964 presidential election, Carl Sanders's popular support dropped to a new low. As one who had enjoyed strong public support from the people of Georgia for many years, both as a legislator and as governor, this was a new experience for him. "A majority of the people are completely down on him," was the way one lawmaker described the situation. According to a United Press International poll of the General Assembly, an overwhelming majority of the legislators believed that the governor's standing had dropped. The legislators cited a number of reasons for his decline. One Republican senator found Sanders "personally vain in image." A Democratic House member objected to the governor "trying to tell people how to vote." Another complained that he was "turning the party over to Negroes." But a broad consensus attributed his problems to "Wallace and L.B.J." Sanders's opposition to the former and support of the latter had cost him dearly.[1]

As Sanders prepared for the forthcoming legislative session, he knew that his leadership would be challenged. Since he was politically vulnerable, his political opponents undoubtedly would flex their muscles and attempt to control the legislative agenda. If they succeeded in taking the initiative away from the governor, it would be extremely difficult for Sanders to provide any leadership for the remainder of his term. He would continue to occupy the executive chair, but he would be a figurehead, a "lame duck," while the important decisions would be made in the House and Senate. Sanders, however, had no intention of allowing such a scenario to develop. He believed that the governor should be the leader of the state and that the legislature simply was incapable of providing effective executive leadership. Certain that

---

[1]*Atlanta Constitution*, December 21, 1964.

Georgia had prospered under his leadership, he was determined to provide for the next two years the same kind of forceful executive leadership that he had given the state the past two years.

Sanders was not one to second guess himself, dwell on the past, or concern himself with matters over which he had no control. On the contrary, he looked to future. Rather than worry about things that might have been different in the past, he focused his attention on the tasks before him and carefully developed strategies for accomplishing them. Always a realist, he acknowledged that he had suffered a setback. But, as he analyzed the situation, there was no reason why he could not recover. He may have been knocked down, but he was not knocked out. Soon he was back on his feet and once again taking the offensive.

Defeats are not pleasant, and certainly Sanders did not enjoy losing. But sometimes defeats, though painful, can be beneficial too. Eugene Patterson, editor of the *Atlanta Constitution* and an astute observer of the Georgia political scene, claimed that was the case with Sanders. The bad beating the governor had suffered had instilled new wisdom in him, wrote Patterson. Gone from the Sanders rhetoric were the frothy declarations and the overly optimistic orations. Now, observed Patterson, he is "quieter, calmer and clearer in the eye." He analyzes facts with "realistic bluntness." He has the toughness of a bloodied fighter. He relaxes and handles himself better. "My impression is that he's a stronger man for what he has been through."[2]

The toughness Patterson observed was apparent at a meeting of the Georgia Democratic Executive Committee early in January 1965. Addressing the party leaders, Sanders acknowledged that the party had a few problems and clearly did not get out enough voters in the recent election, but then he stated emphatically: "I would do what I did all over again, without any regrets, without any apologies to anyone. I am prouder today to be a Democrat than I have ever been." Having analyzed the situation, Sanders had found nothing in his behavior to be ashamed of and saw no reason to be repentant or to change his policies. The 106 Democrats in attendance seemed to agree, for they responded to his blunt remarks with uproarious applause.[3] The governor's tough-

---

[2]Ibid., January 6, 1965.
[3]*Savannah Morning News*, January 7, 1965.

ness (and political acumen) also was demonstrated at the same time in the struggle for the position of speaker pro tem in the House. Five strong candidates were vying for the job. Sanders could have avoided the issue altogether, but instead, working closely with Speaker George T. Smith and Floor Leader Arthur Bolton, he quietly threw his support to veteran legislator Maddox Hale of Dade county. His efforts succeeded. Hale was accepted as a compromise and the others withdrew. To secure future support from the powerful defeated candidates, Sanders made sure that they received choice committee assignments. By quietly working behind the scenes and consulting with each of the candidates, Sanders had avoided a potentially damaging floor fight at the beginning of the legislative session. These actions reveal the governor's political astuteness and his determination to lead. Regardless of the public perception, he had put the defeat behind him and moved on to confront new challenges.[4]

On January 12, 1965, Sanders delivered his combined state of the state and budget address in the crowded chamber of the House of Representatives. The aisles and galleries were packed with legislators, state officials, friends, and the press. The governor's thirty-minute speech was carried on radio and television. Sanders wore a conservative dark blue suit. Mrs. Sanders, sitting behind him and smiling radiantly, wore a cream wool-jersey dress and a sombrero-shaped hat to match, which was immediately dubbed "an LBJ cowboy hat." Sanders had spent much time working with his staff preparing this address. In politics, timing is crucial. His administration was at a crossroads. If he was going to lead the state for the next two years, now was the time to assert leadership. How this speech was received might well determine the success or failure of his administration. Calmly and confidently he strode to microphone.

At the midpoint of this administration, "the state of our state is excellent!" Sanders proudly declared. He supported that assessment with an impressive list of accomplishments. In 1964 Georgia's increase in per capita income ranked third in the nation and her capital investment for new and expanded industry more than doubled. Continuing the theme of economic growth, he pointed out that 19,300 new jobs had been created and that agricultural production had reached an all-time high. The state had made extraordinary progress in highway construction, airport

---

[4]*Atlanta Constitution*, January 8, 1965.

development, and tourism, which had become a $350,000,000 industry. Sanders then cited the accomplishments of specific agencies. The Revenue Department has been "reorganized, automated, and is collecting more revenue today than ever before." The penal system has been revamped and a greater emphasis has been placed on rehabilitation. The Game and Fish Department, the Department of Education, and the Department of Public Welfare (renamed the Department of Family and Children Services) have all been reorganized for more efficient delivery of services. A constitutional Highway Board has been approved by the people, the new Master Plan for Education is well underway, a new Water Quality Control Board has been established, the Public Health Code has been completely rewritten, and the new Department of Industry and Trade has embarked upon a revitalized program. Sanders also called attention to the passage of the comprehensive election code, the elimination of speed traps, and improvements in both the State Merit System and the field of mental health. He hastened to add that these "magnificent accomplishments" had been achieved within a balanced budget.[5]

For the next two years the governor proposed expenditures of $583,000,000 in fiscal 1966 and $628,000,000 in fiscal 1967. His budgets provided increased appropriations for many agencies, including over $15,000,000 in direct grants to municipalities, but the greatest emphasis was placed on education. Both teachers and college professors would receive substantial salary increases, and 679 new faculty members and more than 2,000 new teachers would be hired. In addition, Sanders's budget called for developing a statewide educational television network; funding the Governor's Honors Program, new scholarships, and new loans; opening six new junior colleges; and converting Augusta College, Georgia Southwestern College, and Armstrong College into four-year institutions. In four years, Sanders intended to invest over $1.2 billion in educating Georgians, which was nearly $400,000,000 more than the total appropriated in any previous four-year period in Georgia's history. For higher education he offered by far the largest building program in the history of the University System. Sanders did not exaggerate when

---

[5]Ibid., January 13, 1965; Daniel, *Addresses of Carl Sanders*, pp. 43-52.

he concluded that his budget "provides the greatest emphasis on education our state has ever known."[6]

After outlining his budget, Sanders briefly addressed the controversial topic of reapportionment. Since the court had ordered that the House of Representatives be reapportioned this session, the legislature had little choice but to comply. If the legislature failed to act, it was apparent that the court would. Sanders, expressing confidence that the General Assembly would adopt an acceptable plan, offered to provide any help the legislature deemed proper, but he wisely added "I will not presume to suggest any plan of action."

Lest there be any doubt about where the political power rested or how Sanders intended to govern in the remaining two years of his term, he stated: "This administration will become a lame-duck administration at high noon on January 10, 1967 . . . and not one minute before!" He delivered this key pronouncement in the same low-key tone that he used throughout the speech. It was not a threat or a plea, it was simply a statement of fact that he was still in charge. And the message was heard.[7]

The address was not especially eloquent but it was extremely effective. In a calm, businesslike manner, he had addressed the major issues facing the state and had set forth a comprehensive plan of action. As usual, he had presented his ideas forcefully, but not so emphatically that the General Assembly would be alienated. In fact, the legislators were so pleased by the tone and content of his address that they interrupted it with applause twenty times, and when it was over they gave Sanders a standing ovation. His budget, despite increased expenditures, was widely perceived as affordable and responsible. The *Savannah Morning News* called his budget "a work of art which can lead this state into what the Governor called a 'Golden Era of Growth and Greatness.'" While noting that the budget called for record expenditures, "the likes of which Georgia has never before experienced," it added that "it does not appear wasteful to any degree." Many legislators praised the governor's emphasis on education and his pledge to stay clear of a specific plan for reapportionment. Other solons agreed with Senator Ford Spinks of Tifton who remarked: "I think history is going to record Carl as

---

[6]Ibid.
[7]Ibid.

being the most progressive governor of our time." Based on the reaction to the speech, there could be little doubt that Sanders was well on the way to regaining the popularity he had lost. A remarkable change in public perception had occurred in a short period of time. On November 4, immediately after the general election, Sanders would have experienced difficulty getting elected dogcatcher of Augusta; two months later he was clearly in charge of Georgia's government. Perhaps the press (and some legislators) had exaggerated the impact of Johnson's defeat in Georgia on the governor's public standing. But more importantly, Sanders refused to be cowed by it. Exercising the considerable political power he possessed, he continued to govern as if nothing had changed and soon the issue faded from public view.[8]

A few days after presenting his program to the General Assembly, Sanders led a happy delegation of 135 Georgia Democrats to Washington for the inauguration of President Johnson. Travelling in a special ten-car inauguration train, the delegation consisted of most of the top officials in state government as well as several of Sanders's closest friends and supporters, including J. B. Fuqua, Mills Lane, Bill Trotter, Wyck Knox, Sherman Drawdy, and Julius Bishop. Despite bitterly cold weather, the Georgians were in a festive mood and enjoyed excellent accommodations at the Sheraton Park Hotel. The delegation also received special treatment at the inaugural ball as a tribute to Sanders's all-out support for President Johnson. Sanders was honored to be included in a special prayer session with Johnson just before he took the oath of office.

Georgia's entry in the inaugural parade, a red, white, and blue miniature train, was a popular float. Since Mrs. Johnson had campaigned by train in Georgia, the state used the Lady Bird Special as its theme. Behind the locomotive and coal car were two coaches and a caboose—all loaded with attractive young ladies. The Georgia entry also included the Dalton High School band and the Georgia Military Academy marching unit. Governor and Mrs. Sanders led the way in a white convertible. In the campaign the Lady Bird Special was a flop, as five of the eight states Mrs. Johnson visited voted Republican. But the

---

[8] *Savannah Morning News,* January 13, 1965; *Atlanta Constitution,* January 13, 17, 1965.

Georgia version in the parade was a smashing success, and it was greeted with cheers and applause all along the inaugural route.[9]

While Sanders was in Washington enjoying the political festivities, the United States Supreme Court overturned the lower court ruling banning a vote on Georgia's new constitution. Sanders was elated by the verdict. It vindicated his judgment and the work of the General Assembly. His immediate reaction was to submit the proposed constitution to the voters in the 1966 election. After more careful study, however, he changed his mind. He learned that much of the enthusiasm for the constitution had waned during the interval. Thus, getting it adopted by the people would be a hazardous undertaking. Unwilling to interject the constitution in a bitter gubernatorial race, he reluctantly put it aside as a lost cause.[10]

The General Assembly that convened in 1965 was quite different from its predecessor. There were sixty-eight new members in the House and twenty new senators. While the Democrats still controlled the legislature, the Republican party had gained eleven seats, and now held nine seats in the Senate and seven in the House. Joining Senator Leroy Johnson in the Senate was a second black lawyer from Atlanta, Senator Horace Ward, who had spent six futile years trying to break the color barrier at the University of Georgia Law School. Breaking the sexual barrier was Mrs. Janet Merritt of Sumter county, who was the first woman to serve in the House in several years and only the eleventh woman ever to serve in that body. Not only was the personnel different, but the leadership was too. Milton Carlton, Sanders's floor leader in the Senate, had been defeated, and J. B. Fuqua and Wyck Knox, both stalwart Sanders supporters, did not seek reelection. Their leadership would be missed. Sanders picked Julian Webb, an experienced attorney from Donalsonville, as his new floor leader. In the House Sanders relied on the steady leadership of Speaker George T. Smith and Floor Leader Arthur Bolton, both runaway picks as the most influential legislators, according to a poll of House and Senate members and the press corps conducted at the end of the session.[11]

---

[9]*Atlanta Constitution*, January 17, 18, 21, 1965; list of the Georgia delegation who went to the inauguration, B folder, box 19, Sanders Collection, Law Library.

[10]*Atlanta Constitution*, January 19, 1965.

[11]*Savannah Morning News*, January 7, 10, 1965; *Atlanta Constitution*, March 8,

The first bill Sanders wanted the new legislature to approve was his $4,000,000 supplemental appropriations bill. His hopes for a quick passage were dashed when Senators Jimmy Carter of Plains and Bobby Rowan of Enigma fought to eliminate $500,000 from the bill. That Sanders had regained his political clout was evident when the Senate approved his supplemental budget by vote of 35 to 12. It was the first significant legislation passed in the 1965 session.[12]

After meeting twelve days, the legislature recessed for two weeks. The General Assembly recessed, but political bickering did not. A storm of controversy erupted when the Bowdoin Commission delivered to Governor Sanders a three-volume report on the Highway Department. It declared that Jim Gillis "has attained exclusive and complete control within the department over county contract awards." The Commission urged the State Highway Board to take charge of operations and stop assuming that it is merely an "advisory board." In calling for major changes in administration and tighter supervision of contracts, it did not accuse Gillis of any wrongdoing. Instead it blamed a system that needed to be modernized. Nevertheless, critics emerged to defend Gillis and lambast the Bowdoin Commission. Former Speaker George L. Smith of Emanuel county saw an opportunity to embarrass the Sanders administration which he could not resist. Charging that the Bowdoin Commission had overspent its budget, he called for a full-fledged study of its expenditures. Following his lead, Senator Hugh Gillis of Soperton, son of the Highway Director, claimed that the Commission had overspent its budget by $78,000. "Figures don't lie," he declared. Representative James "Sloppy" Floyd of Chattooga county was another vocal critic, as was Representative Bill Laite of Bibb county, who demanded that the Bowdoin Commission be abolished.[13]

As a result of such charges, Bowdoin appeared before the House and Senate Appropriations Committees. He produced figures to show that his commission was operating within its budget. Attorney General Eugene Cook backed him up. The hearing, which was supposed to embarrass the Bowdoin Commission, embarrassed its critics instead. It

1965; "The Legislative Elite," *Atlanta Magazine* 5 (March 1965): 60-66.
    [12]*Savannah Morning News*, January 21, 22, 1965.
    [13]*Atlanta Constitution*, January 30, February 1-3, 1965.

lasted thirty-one minutes. The highlight came when Representative Laite admitted that he had not read the highway report when he criticized the Bowdoin Commission. He apologized to Bowdoin for "popping off" and "jumping to conclusions too fast." According to a high-ranking member of the House, the "whole thing has developed into a fight between George L. Smith and the governor." Working skillfully behind the scenes, Sanders won that confrontation and left his critics looking foolish.[14]

In February, Sanders enjoyed a brief respite from the political battles when he traveled to Atlantic City, New Jersey, to receive the 1965 Golden Key Award. Sponsored by six national education associations, this prestigious award was presented to Sanders at the annual convention of the American Association of School Administrators for his outstanding record of promoting education. Accompanying the governor was a host of state leaders in education and the teacher he picked to share the award. Miss Emma Lonsdale Wilkinson of Augusta, his seventh grade teacher, was his choice. "Miss Emma," still active at age seventy-five, received a check for $1,000. Over the years Sanders received countless awards and tributes, but this award, coming from leaders in the field of education, was special to him.[15]

The most important bill passed in the annual legislative session ordinarily is the state budget. Naturally, Sanders's record biennial budget was scrutinized carefully by the House and the Senate, but only minor changes were made in his proposal. The biggest controversy came when powerful Representative George Brooks of Oglethorpe county, a spokesman for the rural interests, sought an additional appropriation for the counties of $9,000,000 in the next two years. With reapportionment of the House mandated by the federal courts, rural legislators knew that their power soon would be diminished. Thus, there was the temptation to grab as much "pork from the barrel" as they could while they still had the opportunity. Arthur Bolton, however, was not swayed at all by their arguments. "This is the height of fiscal irresponsibility," he sternly told

---

[14]Ibid., February 3, 1965.

[15]Georgia Education Association News Release, February 8, 1965, Education 2 folder, box 1, Augustus Turnbull Collection, Richard B. Russell Memorial Library, University of Georgia, Athens; Jack Shepherd, "Gov. Carl Sanders and 'Miss Emma'," *Look* 29 (February 23, 1965): 46-49.

the House. "If we do this today, we ought to get rid of any budget controls," he continued. Debates and parliamentary maneuvering went on for another four hours, but finally the Sanders forces prevailed. The House acted responsibly by defeating the Brooks measure by vote of 125 to 54. The budget subsequently was passed by the Senate with only one dissenting vote, that of Republican Senator H. E. Sanders of DeKalb county. In signing the $1.2 billion measure, Governor Sanders stated, "We now have the finest, best-balanced government in the history of our state." The few changes the legislature had made actually improved the bill, the governor added. With his budget approved, Sanders was then free to exert more influence on reapportionment and other matters being considered by the General Assembly.[16]

Sanders, like everyone else, knew that reapportioning the House would be a sticky issue. To make the districts more equal as the federal court demanded meant that many legislators from small counties would be voting themselves out of office. Realizing how difficult this issue was, Sanders had presented a rather skimpy legislative program so that legislators could concentrate on reapportionment. From the beginning the governor had maintained that the legislature would adopt an acceptable plan, but there were times during the session when he doubted that his prediction would be fulfilled.

Although Sanders personally favored a smaller House and had expressed that opinion publicly on many occasions, he nevertheless quietly endorsed the Reapportionment Study Committee's plan which kept the size of the House at 205 members. He no doubt concluded that it would be impossible to achieve his goal at this time, and the greater priority was for the legislature to adopt a plan that would satisfy the courts. For the past six months, the Reapportionment Study Committee, chaired by Representative George Busbee, had studied the issue. Its plan, introduced at the beginning of the session, immediately produced strong reactions from both sides. Busbee argued that it was a reasonable plan which would be passed by the legislature. His critics disagreed. Senator Dan MacIntyre of Atlanta predicted that the Senate would defeat the plan because it did not reduce the size of the House. Countering those who demanded a smaller House for greater efficiency,

---

[16]*Atlanta Constitution*, February 11, 25, March 1, 2, 1965.

Representative George L. Smith declared: "If you want to see good government, you want to see a large House." Senator James Wesberry of Atlanta opposed it because "it allows too great a discrepancy in the sizes of some proposed districts."[17]

Soon a host of competing plans were introduced. Representative Willis J. Richardson of Chatham county offered a plan to reduce the House to 166 members, and his plan was endorsed by the *Savannah Morning News*. Representative Sam Singer presented a plan which called for twenty seats in each of the state's ten congressional districts. Late in the session, the small county legislators, in a last-ditch effort to maintain rural control of the House, insisted on a plan to keep all existing seats and add forty-seven more seats for urban areas. In supporting the 252-member plan, Representative Dorsey Matthews of Colquitt vowed to fight "to the bitter end."[18]

The House, guided by the Sanders administration, defeated the 252-member plan 116 to 72. Finally, on March 3 after seven grueling hours of debate, the House approved the amended Busbee plan by vote of 141 to 48. Under the new plan, the larger counties got substantially more representation. Fulton received 24 seats, DeKalb (with Rockdale) 12, Chatham 9, Muscogee 7, Richmond 6, Bibb 6, Daugherty 4, Hall 3, and Lowndes 3. For the first time in history, the state's twenty-two largest counties would have a majority in the House. Sanders, whose influence was evident in the passage of the bill, applauded the House for its statesmanship. While most of the press praised the House, the *Savannah Morning News* was critical of the manner in which reapportionment was carried out. Rather than represent the people or make the system more efficient and economical, the members sought to hold on to their seats and introduced plans that ran the gamut from the reasonable to the absurd, it asserted. "When it came to size of House membership, almost the only proposal that wasn't introduced was one that would have made every citizen of the state a member of the House," it editorialized sarcastically.[19]

---

[17]*Savannah Morning News*, January 10, 11, 1965.

[18]Ibid., January 14, 1965; *Atlanta Constitution*, February 12, March 3, 1965.

[19]*Atlanta Constitution*, March 4, 1965; *Savannah Morning News*, March 4, 1965; *House Journal, 1965*, pp. 1505-20, 1596-97.

Sanders urged the Senate to pass the reapportionment bill as soon as possible so that he could sign it and take it to the three-judge federal court for its approval. The Senate complied a week later, but not before causing Sanders some anxiety. The Senate passed a measure extending Senate terms from two years to four years, knowing that the bill had little chance of being adopted by the House. Some urban senators saw an opportunity to coerce the House into passing the desired legislation. They threatened to delay the reapportionment bill until the House approved four-year terms for senators. It was a harebrained scheme that had no chance of success, but it created so much turmoil that Governor Sanders had to cancel a trip to Washington to attend the signing of the Appalachian bill by President Johnson to resolve the matter. He bluntly told the senators: "There is a right time for everything, but this is the wrong time to bargain." When the senators finally realized that their tactics were not working, they capitulated and approved the reapportionment bill. Sanders signed the bill almost immediately after it was approved on March 10.[20]

In urging the legislature to act, Sanders had pledged to take the reapportionment plan personally to the judges, but at the last minute he decided to let others do it. His accompanying letter explained that the legislature had acted in "total good faith," and he hoped that the court would act with "equal good faith and consideration." He further requested that the court render a decision as soon as possible. After hearing arguments from both sides, the court accepted the plan even though the districts were not balanced to the court's satisfaction. In accepting this plan as a temporary improvement, the court insisted that the districts in the House must be brought within fifteen percent of the average by the end of the 1968 legislative session. Everyone seemed pleased by the court ruling. Sanders called the decision "a victory for every citizen of our state."[21]

---

[20]*Atlanta Constitution*, March 6, 9, 10, 1965; *Atlanta Journal*, March 10, 1965; *Acts and Resolutions, 1965*, pp. 127-74; *Senate Journal, 1965*, pp. 951-79.

[21]*Atlanta Constitution*, March 8, 1965; *Savannah Morning News*, March 11, 1965; *Savannah Evening Press*, April 2, 1965; Sanders to Tuttle, Bell, and Morgan, March 10, 1965, March 1965 folder, box 35, Sanders Collection, Law Library.

In addition to achieving his major objectives, the budget and reapportionment, Sanders also secured legislative approval for other matters as well, the most important being the rapid transit bill. It created an eleven-member study committee to continue to push for rapid transit while the five metropolitan Atlanta counties voted to determine if they would participate in the system. Former Governor Vandiver, who had worked hard for the measure, called it "landmark legislation," and Governor Sanders, who also strongly backed the bill, believed that it was one of the most important laws passed during his term. Subsequently the voters in Fulton and DeKalb counties endorsed the concept, and the rapid transit system was begun. Ironically, rapid transit, which has played such a vital role in the growth of Atlanta, was passed primarily by the votes of rural legislators. Sanders tirelessly met with rural legislators pointing out the transportation needs of the rapidly growing Atlanta area. To build all the highways the city required would deplete the budget of the Highway Department, he explained, leaving very little revenue for highways in the rest of the state. On the other hand, large federal grants were available for rapid transit. If Atlanta had a rapid transit system it would not need as many highways, thereby freeing funds for highways elsewhere in the state. Such arguments by the governor convinced rural legislators that supporting rapid transit was good for Atlanta and likely to produce more highways in their area too. The chief opposition to the measure came from suburban counties which feared that MARTA would bring innercity problems to the suburbs, but on this issue Sanders, through skillful politicking, managed to break through the rural-urban animosity and achieve success.[22]

When the legislature adjourned on March 12, Sanders praised the members for conducting themselves so well in a time of "soul-searching and challenge." He noted that despite the great strain they were under, they met their responsibilities with "courage and intelligence" for the benefit of the people of Georgia. It was Sanders's custom to praise the legislature lavishly, but this year he was especially proud of the members. They had approved his record budget and reapportioned the

---

[22]*Atlanta Journal,* March 11, 1965; Sanders, "Interviews in 1990," pp. 173, 193-94.

House—measures that required considerable political fortitude, and such efforts gained the governor's respect and sincere appreciation.[23]

Six weeks after the successful legislative session had ended, Sanders was at the Governor's Mansion having just returned from a trip to New York City when he received a shock. He was informed that his father had died. Flying immediately to Augusta, he learned the sad details. Mrs. Sanders had left him about 4 p.m. to mail a letter and run some errands. Carl's father appeared to be in good spirits when she left, but when she returned three hours later he was not in the house. She found his body in a small tool shed behind the garage at their home. He had shot himself with a .38 caliber pistol. The coroner ruled that the wound was self-inflicted. Everyone agreed that the fatal shot was self-inflicted, but whether it was intentional or accidental is uncertain.

Carl's father had been in ill health since suffering a stroke in December. The stroke was so severe that his personal physician, realizing that he would never fully recover, advised the family to let him go. Carl's mother, however, insisted that everything possible be done to save his life, and she convinced Carl to bring in specialists who performed a tracheotomy and managed to revive him. Three more strokes followed in rapid succession, and it became obvious that he would never be able to work again. Since the elder Sanders had led an active life and had worked for Swift & Co. for forty-seven years, forced inactivity weighed heavily upon him. He recovered sufficiently so that he could walk with a cane but his mobility was greatly restricted. Despite his physical incapacity, his mind remained clear to the end.

Governor Sanders believed that his father, depressed as a result of his physical limitations and unwilling to be a financial or emotional burden on his family, became despondent and took his own life. His assessment may be correct, but Doug Barnard and Bert Hester, who knew Carl's father well, were convinced that his death was accidental. Since he did not have any financial problems or life-threatening health problems and left no suicide note, they believe his death was a horrible accident. Accident or not, Carl's father was dead at age sixty-four. The funeral was

---

[23]Daniel, *Addresses of Carl Sanders*, pp. 52-54.

held at Hill Baptist Church and he was buried in Augusta's beautiful Westover Memorial Park.[24]

A few weeks after Carl's father died, Justice T. Grady Head of the Georgia Supreme Court also died. To fill the vacancy, the first to occur on the high court during the Sanders years, the governor chose Eugene Cook. Cook, sixty-one years old, had been attorney general for twenty years, longer than anyone in Georgia's history. Although he had a problem with alcohol, he was an able jurist. To replace Cook as attorney general, Sanders selected Arthur Bolton, a man of great intelligence and integrity. The appointment of the forty-three-year-old floor leader received widespread praise in the press, and Bolton filled the position with distinction for many years. Sanders swore in both men on June 14.[25]

Throughout the summer and fall of 1965, rumors circulated that Governor Sanders was making plans to challenge Richard Russell for the Senate seat in 1966. Early in the campaign the Russell forces claimed that Sanders had made a "deal" in 1962 that he would not oppose Russell in 1966—in exchange for support of the Vandiver administration in his race for governor against Marvin Griffin. In a press conference in May 1965 Sanders angrily denied making any such verbal promise to Russell. And for more than a quarter of a century he has consistently and emphatically denied the charge. Yet, many politicos at the time assumed that Sanders had reached some type of understanding with the Russell forces in the 1962 campaign, and newspapers alluded to it as well.[26]

Several oral history interviews done in 1971 for the Russell Library at the University of Georgia comment on the "deal." Roy Harris, Sanders's longtime opponent, stated that the political crowd thought Sanders had promised not to run against Russell, but he could provide

---

[24]Barnard interview, February 16, 1991; Hester interview, June 5, 1991; telephone interview with Carl Sanders, February 28, 1991; *Atlanta Constitution*, April 30, 1965.

[25]*Atlanta Constitution*, June 11, 15, 1965; *Official Register, 1965–1966*, pp. 140, 630.

[26]*Atlanta Journal*, May 25, 1965. The rumor that Sanders might challenge Russell circulated as early as March 1963. Responding to an Associated Press story, Pat Young of the Democratic National Committee sought confidential information from J. B. Fuqua regarding Sanders's plans. Fuqua informed him that Sanders "has given no serious thought as to what he might do in 1966." Young to Fuqua, March 6, 1963; Fuqua to Young, March 8, 1963; X-Y-Z folder, box 19, Sanders Collection, Law Library.

no evidence. Wyck Knox, Jr., son of Sanders's campaign manager, had heard talk about the "deal," but he had no personal knowledge of it. Jimmy Bentley, former comptroller general and staunch Russell supporter, was more emphatic. According to Bentley, "Carl Sanders was maneuvering feverishly to run against Dick Russell, and having promised him he wouldn't run—he promised Vandiver and the others that he wouldn't run against Senator Russell." A more objective source was Margaret Shannon, the first woman correspondent for the *Atlanta Journal.* She also heard the reports, and being a good investigative reporter attempted to track down the leads. Eventually she gave up because she was never able to get anything concrete. Despite the lack of evidence, the issue persists.[27]

Governor Vandiver contended that after Byrd dropped out of the 1962 campaign, "Carl came into my office and asked for my support. I agreed to support him with one caveat—I wanted him to protect Senator Russell from any opposition. Henry Neal was there and heard it." Henry Neal, it turns out, had no memory of the conversation Vandiver described and suggested that perhaps it was Peter Zack Geer, then Vandiver's executive secretary, who was present. Geer had no recollection of the meeting either.[28]

What actually was said in 1962 may never be discovered. It is conceivable that Russell backers simply concocted the story in order to discredit Sanders and discourage him from challenging Russell in 1966. It is also possible that the whole controversy stemmed from an innocent misunderstanding. When Vandiver agreed to support Sanders he quite likely expressed a concern about Senator Russell's political future. Sanders, not the least bit concerned about the 1966 Senate race when he was trying desperately to get elected governor in 1962, may well have made some general comment which Vandiver interpreted to be a promise that he would not run against Russell in 1966. Two years later,

---

[27]Roy V. Harris interview by Hugh Cates, February 24, 1971; Wyckliffe A. Knox, Jr. interview by Hugh Cates, February 24, 1971; James L. Bentley, Jr. interview by Hugh Cates, February 18, 1971; Margaret Shannon interview by Hugh Cates, March 31, 1971, oral history, Richard B. Russell Collection, Richard B. Russell Memorial Library, University of Georgia, Athens.

[28]Vandiver telephone interview, August 26, 1991; Neal telephone interview, September 5, 1991; Geer telephone interview, September 5, 1991.

when Sanders began to test the waters for the Senate race, Vandiver probably told others of Sanders's "promise" in 1962, and the rumor then circulated throughout the political community. All of that, of course, is speculation and may be untrue. If Sanders had made such a promise, surely Senator Russell would have alluded to it, but there is no record that he ever did. Professor Gilbert Fite, Russell's thorough biographer, found no record of it, and he discounts the story entirely because Russell had nothing to fear from Sanders in 1962.[29] Furthermore, Sanders did not have to make any concessions to secure Vandiver's support after Garland Byrd withdrew from the race. Vandiver detested Marvin Griffin, and Sanders was his only viable alternative. At that point Vandiver had no choice but to support Sanders enthusiastically; if Sanders lost, Vandiver's enemy would succeed him as governor.

Furthermore, at the time the rumors circulated Vandiver held Sanders in great esteem. Indeed, on March 14, 1965, Vandiver, then laying the groundwork for a gubernatorial campaign in 1966, met with Sanders at the Dinkler Plaza Hotel in Atlanta and promised that if he became governor and a vacancy occured in the Senate, he would first offer the appointment to Sanders "before considering any other person." Jim Gillis, who attended the meeting, recorded the conversation in an affidavit a month later.[30]

Now, with the passage of time and the fading of memories, it seems doubtful that the mystery of exactly what Sanders said ever will be completely resolved, but the available evidence strongly suggests that Sanders made no promise regarding Russell in 1962.

It was to be expected that Sanders would at least consider a race against Russell in 1966 as his term as governor neared its end. Russell was sixty-seven years old and in declining health; Sanders was forty years old, enjoyed excellent health, and was ambitious for higher office. Newspapers often reported that Sanders easily could get an important federal appointment, but they soon concluded that Sanders was leaning toward running for the Senate. Late in June 1965 Charles Pou reported that two mayors and Senator Herman Talmadge had concluded that Sanders

---

[29]Gilbert Fite telephone interview, March 13, 1992.

[30]James L. Gillis, Sr., affidavit, subscribed by Clarice Akin, Fulton county, Georgia, April 13, 1965, Sanders Personal Papers, Atlanta.

was running against Russell. On July 12 Reg Murphy went beyond re-porting rumors and speculation and stated plainly: "In case there is any lingering doubt, Gov. Carl Sanders is running for the Senate."[31]

Murphy exaggerated, but it was obvious for all to see that Sanders was seriously considering the Senate race. The governor, however, remained noncommittal about his future plans. As was his custom, he continued to deliver speeches at a hectic pace throughout the state. By doing so, he increased his contacts and added names to his lists of supporters in each county. Letters offering support began to arrive in his office in a steady stream. It was still much too early for Sanders to announce his plans, or even to make a definite decision. Never one to rush into matters hastily, he simply was laying a necessary foundation for the race so that when the time came to make a decision that option would be available. What to do after leaving the governorship would not be an easy decision to make.

As his political career evolved, several forks had appeared, and eventually Sanders would have to choose one. Accepting a federal appointment from his friend President Johnson was always a possibility. Depending on the position, he could expect to earn a reasonable salary, exert some influence upon national policy, and perhaps use it as a stepping stone to higher office. In addition, no campaign would be required and he could begin the job soon after concluding his term. A second alternative was to resume his law practice in Augusta. Having been governor, his practice very likely would skyrocket and his income would increase proportionately. Sanders enjoyed the practice of law and he would live at home among friends. If politics still beckoned, he could run for governor again in 1970. Both of these options were appealing, but so was the Senate race. In the Senate he certainly would influence national policy. Perhaps he could make a difference in American foreign policy, in the field of education, in civil rights, in the criminal justice system, or other areas that interested him. Perhaps, also, even higher political office might follow a stint in the Senate. Lyndon Johnson often reminded him that the current leaders would not be in office forever. Soon there would be a leadership vacuum. The president pointed out how important it was for capable young southern Democrats to position

---

[31]*Atlanta Constitution*, June 27, July 12, 1965.

themselves for leadership roles on the national level. Before any of that could transpire, however, Sanders would have to defeat Russell. Was it possible for him, or anyone else, to defeat the venerable senator? Among Georgia politicians, Russell's prestige was unequalled. Having been in the Senate since 1933, Russell was more than a senator, he had become an institution. So great was his standing that he had not faced serious opposition since 1936. Defeating Russell would be an enormous challenge, perhaps an insurmountable one. Sanders's career demonstrated that he was not intimidated by challenges, but running against Russell clearly was a decision that he would not make lightly. Thus, as the year 1965 drew to an end, Sanders weighed his options, analyzed his strengths and weaknesses, discussed the possibilities with his family and close friends, and pondered his future.[32]

[32]Gilbert C. Fite, *Richard B. Russell, Jr., Senator From Georgia* (Chapel Hill & London: University of North Carolina Press, 1991); Sanders, "Interviews in 1990," pp. 177-82; Betty Foy Sanders interview, November 7, 1990.

Chapter 15

"A Light in the Darkness"

During the four years Sanders served as governor, civil rights became a national preoccupation. The mild protests and sit-ins of the earlier period gave way to highly publicized marches and demonstrations which often led to bitter conflicts and violence. During Sanders's first year as governor, Birmingham Sheriff Eugene "Bull" Conner brutally beat and jailed Martin Luther King, Jr. and his nonviolent marchers; President Kennedy submitted a civil rights bill to Congress; and over 200,000 marched to the Lincoln Memorial in Washington in support of civil rights. In 1964, President Johnson signed the Civil Rights bill; blacks disrupted the Democratic Convention in Atlantic City; riots occurred in Harlem and Brooklyn; and King received the Nobel Peace Prize. During Sanders's third year in office, King led the civil rights campaign in Selma, Congress adopted the Voting Rights bill, Malcolm X was assassinated, and a terrible riot in Watts left thirty-five dead. By 1966, Sanders's fourth year as governor, militant organizations such as the Student Nonviolent Coordinating Committee had emerged demanding "black power," and riots erupted in Chicago, Cleveland, and other areas.

When Sanders ran for governor in 1962, he did not expect to play a significant role in the civil rights movement and showed little concern about the plight of black Georgians. He received widespread support from blacks because, compared to his opponent, Marvin Griffin, an outspoken racist, Sanders seemed a model of racial enlightenment. Like Griffin, Sanders campaigned as a segregationist, but unlike the former governor, he avoided inflammatory racial rhetoric, promised to keep the schools open, and emphasized that court decisions must obeyed. In the campaign he had not promised to end the Jim Crow system, speed up integration, or appoint blacks to office. Nevertheless, in 1962 he was generally classified as a "moderate" or a "liberal" on the race issue.

By the time Sanders became governor, integration still had made little headway in Georgia. In the field of public education, only the University of Georgia and a few schools in Atlanta had accepted even token integration. In Atlanta and Savannah public transportation and several restaurants and stores were integrated, but outside of Atlanta, Athens, Savannah, and a few other urban areas, Georgia remained rigidly segregated, and the vast majority of the state's elected officials vowed to keep it that way as long as possible.

Upon taking office, Sanders seemed to believe that the changes brought about by the civil rights movement thus far were, for the most part, positive achievements. Blacks, he realized, had been abused in the past, denied basic rights under the "separate but equal" doctrine, and deserved better schools, greater employment opportunities, and equal protection under the law. Fortunately, substantial progress had been achieved in recent years, and Sanders sincerely wanted blacks to continue to advance in the future. He believed that southern racists such as Marvin Griffin, Roy Harris, and Orval Faubus had impeded racial progress and were detriments to the South. By unnecessarily inflaming racial tensions, they had given the South an unfavorable national image. Instead of thwarting progress and exacerbating racial tensions, Sanders believed that government should solve problems, generate economic growth, and build for the future. In his judgment, better leaders, men like Leroy Collins in Florida, Luther Hodges in North Carolina, and Ivan Allen in Atlanta, provided the solutions, not more laws. Rather than dwelling on the past, these men built for the future. By working cooperatively with the federal government, the business community, and responsible black leaders, such leaders were creating a New South with enhanced economic opportunities for all southerners, including blacks. Sanders shared that progressive outlook.

As governor, Sanders's speeches reveal no hostility to blacks, but advancing civil rights clearly ranked low on his list of priorities. His chief concerns were improving education, raising the economic level of the state, and making state government more efficient. Accomplishing these goals would be a formidable challenge in a four-year period; in addition, his administration also faced the difficult tasks of reapportioning the legislative and congressional districts and writing a new constitution. In short, Sanders faced many politically divisive issues without considering civil rights. He probably would have been pleased if civil rights issues had disappeared from Georgia during his four years. Instead of vanishing, civil rights became a major concern which could not be ignored or avoided. It affected practically all Georgians, grew in intensity each year, and by the end of his administration seemed to overshadow all other issues. The race issue surfaced at the beginning of his administration and forced him to act even before he was inaugurated.

In 1962, for the first time since Reconstruction, a black had been elected to the Georgia Senate. Some people thought the ceiling of the Capitol would fall and the walls would crumble when Leroy Johnson, a black lawyer from Atlanta, took his seat as the senator from the 38th District. The governor inevitably sets the tone for his administration, and in this situation everyone wondered how Sanders would react. This was a new phenomenon, and no one quite knew how Sanders would respond. Johnson himself was unsure what the governor would do. He wondered if Sanders would invite him to the inaugural ball at the Dinkler Plaza Hotel. As he pondered that subject, he considered what he could do if the governor invited all the other senators except him, but at the proper time his invitation arrived. Johnson and his wife attended the ball and did enjoy the festivities, while some of the guests were dismayed to see a black couple there. Everything went smoothly, Johnson believed, because Sanders made the decision that "his administration was going to do justice toward all."[1]

As a state senator, Leroy Johnson had many opportunities to integrate facilities, and with quiet determination he took advantage of them. Shortly after the 1963 legislative session began, he decided to eat lunch at the state cafeteria where legislators frequently dined. Senator James Wesberry of Atlanta joined him. Together, they went through the line, selected their food, and sat down at a large table where seven or eight others already were eating. As soon as Johnson sat down, all of the others picked up their food and left. Later that week, Johnson and Wesberry returned to the state cafeteria. After a while the shock wore off, and whites in the cafeteria grew accustomed to seeing a black senator eating with them. On another occasion, Johnson went to the basement of the state Capitol to renew his driver's licence. There he

---

[1]Interview with Leroy Johnson, Atlanta, February 20, 1991.

found two lines of people. At the front of the lines were two tables, one marked "whites" and other marked "colored." Johnson got in the line for "whites." When he reached the front of the line, the licence examiner informed him that he was in the wrong line. Unintimidated, Johnson refused to move. Dismayed by Johnson's persistence, the examiner, after making a telephone call to higher authority, gave Johnson the application. By resolutely challenging the Jim Crow system in this manner, Johnson succeeded in eliminating various racial barriers.[2]

Of all the incidents of this type, none brought Johnson more satisfaction than the time Sanders invited the senators to a luncheon at the exclusive Commerce Club. When Johnson arrived, the maitre d' met him at the door and asked what he wanted. Johnson explained that he had been invited to a meeting of state senators and asked where it was being held. The maitre d' told him where the senators were meeting but haughtily pointed out that blacks were not allowed there. Undeterred, Johnson walked past him and entered the room, with the startled maitre d' following quickly behind him. Johnson spoke to some of the senators who were there, noticed the black waiters and waitresses standing by the wall, and then sat down at the table. Whereupon, the maitre d' proceeded to remove the entire table service in front of Johnson. After the plate, silverware, glass, cup, and saucer had been taken away, Johnson said firmly for all to hear: "Someone had better tell this man that I intend to exercise all of the rights and privileges of a state senator. I intend to have lunch here or I'm going to call the radio station, and we're going to have the worst fiasco we've ever had in this state." Someone telephoned the Governor's Office. In arranging the meeting, it never occurred to Sanders that a state senator would be denied admission. Using all of his persuasive skills, he tried to convince the manager to seat Senator Johnson, but to no avail. The manager simply refused to take the responsibility of integrating the club. Sanders then called Mills B. Lane and asked him to make an exception, but he would not do it either. Finally, the governor went to the highest seat of power in Atlanta, Robert W. Woodruff of Coca-Cola. Convinced by Sanders that it was time to change the policy, Woodruff called Mills Lane and told him that the all-white rule no longer applied. Thereafter, membership in the

---

[2]Ibid.

Commerce Club was open to all citizens without regard to race, creed, or color. Soon the same maitre d' who had removed Johnson's table setting came back into the room. Carefully, he placed a plate, silverware, glass, cup, and saucer in front of the angry Johnson, and then departed. As soon as he left, the black waiters and waitresses, unable to restrain themselves any longer, applauded vociferously.[3]

Neither Johnson nor Sanders publicized events such as these. Instead of calling press conferences and issuing press releases to call attention to their actions, they preferred bringing about change quietly and without fanfare. They sought results, not publicity, and working together they eliminated many vestiges of the Jim Crow system. Johnson made headway by directly challenging the segregated system; Sanders supported his efforts and issued executive orders to remove "whites" and "colored" designations over water fountains, restrooms, and other facilities in state buildings. Johnson recognized that none of the changes he instituted could have occurred without the backing of the governor. He also recognized the political dilemmas Sanders faced and understood how easy it would have been for Sanders to stifle black aspirations. Instead of frustrating black efforts, Sanders brought about constructive change. His courageous efforts earned Johnson's respect and admiration. Johnson knew immediately that neither Sanders nor any of his staff were racists, and soon blacks throughout the state came to that understanding. After the recent experiences with Vandiver, Griffin, and Herman Talmadge, blacks discerned a noticeable difference in the Governor's Office. Indeed, compared to his predecessors as governor, the Sanders administration, as Johnson expressed it, "shined like a light in the darkness."[4]

While Sanders admired Leroy Johnson and developed a warm friendship with him, his relationship with Martin Luther King, Jr. remained decidedly cooler. Sanders knew King's father, Reverend Martin Luther King, Sr. quite well and considered him a friend. He also had a good working relationship with other leaders of the black establishment in Atlanta. They had sought to advance black rights through accommodation with white moderates and liberals. Encouraged by the gains blacks

---

[3]Ibid.; interview with Benny Tackett, Atlanta, June 19, 1991.

[4]Johnson interview, February 20, 1991; Cook, "Sanders: An Oral History," pp. 45-46.

had made in recent years, they carefully avoided issues that might alienate their allies. Skeptical of the direct action tactics of the younger generation, they feared such confrontations might jeopardize all of the progress that they had accomplished in recent years. Their cautious approach coincided with Sanders's policies, but the younger generation of
blacks, impatient with the modest gains, demanded more rapid change.[5]

Although Martin Luther King, Jr. was a native Atlantan, Sanders
actually had very little direct contact with him, and what contact they
had was not cordial. Sanders had grudging respect for King's courage,
eloquence, and leadership. He also gradually abandoned his belief in
segregation and by the mid-1960s shared King's vision of a racially integrated society where blacks and whites could live together in harmony,
but he disliked King's tactics. The governor believed King was trying to
accomplish too much too quickly. He was trying to bring about a radical
transformation in thinking overnight. Sanders understood that changing
deeply ingrained attitudes and prejudices in the South would take time,
and he concluded that King's marches, freedom rides, and protests
ultimately would fail to accomplish his goal of ending the Jim Crow
system and, by antagonizing moderate whites, might even be counterproductive. Moreover, King appeared somewhat hypocritical to Sanders
because his "nonviolent protests" almost always produced violence.

While languishing in a Birmingham jail in April 1963, King received
a public declaration from eight white clergymen who castigated him for
stirring up trouble in Alabama. King responded with his classic "Letter
from a Birmingham Jail," an eloquent expression of the goals and
philosophy of the nonviolent civil rights movement. In explaining why
he had brought his campaign to Birmingham, King expressed grave
disappointment with the white moderate "who is more devoted to
'order' than to justice" and "who constantly advises the Negro to wait
for a 'more convenient season.'" King found the moderate's "shallow
understanding" and "lukewarm acceptance" more bewildering than
outright rejection. In response to the charge that he was an "extremist,"
King explained that he stood in the middle of two opposing forces in

---

[5]King, *Daddy King*, pp. 100-67; Cook, "Sanders: An Oral History," pp. 47-48;
Alton Hornsby, Jr., "The Negro in Atlanta Politics, 1961–1973," *Atlanta Historical
Bulletin* 21 (Spring 1977): 7-33.

the Negro community. One group, he wrote, had become complacent, had adjusted to segregation, and had become insensitive to the problems of the masses; the other force, characterized by bitterness and hatred, included various black nationalist groups, made up of people "who have lost faith in America, who have absolutely repudiated Christianity, and who have concluded that the white man is an incorrigible 'devil.'" In essence, King told white moderates: either cooperate with me or you will have to deal with the likes of Malcolm X or Stokely Carmichael.[6]

In describing the white moderate, King could have used Sanders as his model, for the governor, like so many white moderates in 1963, simply did not understand King. He had little comprehension of the frustration and pent up rage among blacks that would soon emerge in bloody riots. Nor did he recognize the pressures upon King within the black community. He simply regarded King as an extremist whose activities at best retarded progress in race relations and at worst created a backlash among whites, thereby enhancing the popularity of southern racists like George Wallace and Lester Maddox.

As Sanders campaigned for the governorship, intense civil rights protests erupted in the quiet, southwest Georgia town of Albany late in 1961 and continued throughout the summer of 1962. Led by the Student Nonviolent Coordinating Committee and the Southern Christian Leadership Conference, the Albany Movement sought to achieve fair employment, an end to police brutality, and the desegregation of the bus station, the train station, and all municipal facilities. Civil authorities jailed hundreds of protesters, including King who was arrested in December and again in July. Sanders criticized the protesters and praised the authorities. The Albany effort ended in total failure. A fiasco, it accomplished practically nothing. The Albany Movement failed because of friction between SNCC and SCLC and because Laurie Pritchett, the chief of police, shrewdly avoided violence and thereby minimized press coverage.[7]

---

[6]Martin Luther King, Jr., *Why We Can't Wait* (New York: Harper & Row, Publishers, 1963) pp. 77-100.

[7]Adam Fairclough, *To Redeem the Soul of America: The Southern Christian Leadership Conference and Martin Luther King, Jr.* (Athens: University of Georgia Press, 1987) pp. 85-109; David J. Garrow, *Bearing the Cross: Martin Luther King, Jr. and the Southern Christian Leadership Conference* (New York: William Morrow and Company, 1986) pp.

From the Albany experience, King and the SCLC learned to choose their targets more carefully. "Protest becomes an effective tactic," Bayard Rustin explained, "to the degree that it elicits brutality and oppression from the power structure." With Sanders at the helm, Georgia was unlikely to provide the desired brutality and oppression. In order to touch the conscience of the American people, King needed to reveal the worst aspects of the Jim Crow system. Finding Alabama and its feisty governor, George Wallace, more appealing than Georgia for that purpose, King concentrated his attention on Georgia's neighbor to the west and led demonstrations in Birmingham, Selma, and Montgomery. In Alabama, King and his marchers received the brutality they anticipated from Governor Wallace, Sheriff Eugene "Bull" Conner, and other militant defenders of segregation. Their use of billy clubs, fire hoses, and attack dogs against the demonstrators outraged the nation. In addition to the major campaigns in Alabama, King also organized the massive March on Washington in August 1963, and in 1966 he undertook the Chicago Freedom Movement, which resulted in bitter rioting. Georgia, it seems, was spared much turmoil and embarrassment in part because of the moderate leadership of Sanders.[8]

Although King spent little time in Georgia during the Sanders years, the state did not escape racial confrontations altogether. Fortunately, they were mild compared to the bloody protests in Alabama and the riots in Watts, Chicago, Harlem, and Cleveland, but they were serious nonetheless. Two of the most difficult and highly publicized racial conflicts that Sanders faced occurred in Savannah and Crawfordville. In both instances, the key black leader was Hosea Williams, a gifted organizer and activist, who was then beginning a career in civil rights that would keep him in controversy and headlines for the next three decades.

Born illegitimately in poverty in rural southwest Georgia, Williams experienced racial violence in his youth. Once whites tried to lynch him for "messing around" with a white girl. Wounded in action in Europe

---

173-230; Ralph David Abernathy, *And the Walls Came Tumbling Down* (New York: Harper & Row, 1989) pp. 201-29.

[8]Faircloth, *To Redeem the Soul of America*, pp. 108-50; Stephen B. Oates, *Let the Trumpet Sound: The Life of Martin Luther King, Jr.* (New York: Harper & Row, Publishers, 1982) pp. 151-420; Garrow, *Bearing the Cross*, pp. 231-525.

in World War II, he returned to Georgia on crutches. Travelling through Americus, he limped into a bus station to get a drink of water at a white fountain, only to be beaten mercilessly by berserk whites. After earning a bachelor's degree at Atlanta University, he secured a position as a chemist with the U.S. Department of Agriculture in Savannah in 1952. He bought a house and a car, married, and started a family. Joining the NAACP in 1953, he plunged into the civil rights movement. Ambitious and pugnacious, he was a superb grass-roots organizer and had a special appeal to the poor masses because like them he had suffered privation, too. As vice president of the Savannah NAACP in the early 1960s, Williams conducted successful voter education drives and developed an effective political action group. Despite his impressive achievements, his brawling, confrontational style offended the local leaders who refused to promote him. Williams resigned in disgust in 1962. On the day he resigned he became affiliated with the SCLC, whose leaders had been impressed by his efforts. He quickly advanced to the SCLC executive staff, and early in 1964 King appointed him director of voter registration.[9]

Governor Sanders first encountered the mercurial Williams in Savannah in June 1963. As leader of the Chatham County Crusade for Voters, he initiated demonstrations when three movie theaters reneged on an agreement to desegregate. Sit-ins and a fifteen-month boycott of businesses in 1960 and 1961 had produced substantial progress in civil rights in Savannah. City buses, the city park, golf course, and library, as well as the cafeterias in the airport and bus station had desegregated. In 1961 Savannah became the first city in Georgia to open its lunch counters to blacks. Despite such advances, Williams became increasingly frustrated, because restaurants, hotels, theaters, and most drug stores remained segregated. When a segregated drug store refused to serve Williams and his two sons lunch, he went into action. During the next six weeks, Savannah witnessed some of the largest street protests in the South. Williams addressed lunchtime crowds repeatedly and led large

---

[9]Hosea Williams, biographical file for *Official and Statistical Register*, Georgia Department of Archives and History, Atlanta; Oates, *Let the Trumpet Sound*, pp. 287-88; Faircloth, *To Redeem the Soul of America*, pp. 94-95, 143-44, 167-68, 263-64; Paul Douglas Bolster, "Civil Rights Movements in Twentieth Century Georgia (Ph.D. diss., University of Georgia, 1972) pp. 233-54.

marches at night, some reportedly having 3,000 marchers. His provocative oratory and flamboyant style drew enthusiastic responses from the black community, especially young blacks. After a week of demonstrations, about 500 protesters had been arrested. When Negroes attempted to block the doorway of the DeSoto Hotel where the Georgia Municipal Association was holding its annual convention, police arrested over fifty protesters, mostly juveniles. The featured speaker at the GMA Convention was Governor Sanders.[10]

In his address Sanders urged the demonstrators to seek rights in the "courts, not in the public streets." Convinced that the essential conflict was a legal matter, he consistently opposed demonstrations and tried to convince protesters that the courts would resolve their disputes fairly. He repeated his admonition many times, but it seemed to have little impact as the protests continued. Indeed they grew larger as local leaders received support from SCLC, COPE, and SNCC. As many as 7,000 people were involved in a single day of continuous marches. At the request of Mayor Malcolm MacLean, a prominent young lawyer and a graduate of Yale, Sanders dispatched state troopers to Savannah. At the request of Hosea Williams, Martin Luther King, Jr. sent Andrew Young and others to instill nonviolent discipline in the protests. After Williams's arrest in July, Young took over the campaign to prevent it from disintegrating into anarchy. On July 11 the demonstrations reached a climax. Young addressed a mass meeting and cautioned the protesters against causing damage, but things got out of hand. When the police and national guardsmen used tear gas and fire hoses against the demonstrators, the angry marchers went on a rampage of destruction. They threw rocks, broke windows, set fires, and destroyed much of downtown Savannah before their fury subsided. Fortunately, no one was killed and no serious injuries were reported, but property damage was extensive. With hundreds of blacks in jail and the demonstrations out of control, Young suspended the marches. White businessmen, now thoroughly alarmed, were willing to talk with black leaders about additional desegregation. Following serious negotiations, a committee representing one hundred businessmen accepted a desegregation plan covering hotels,

---

[10]Faircloth, *To Redeem the Soul of America*, p. 143; *Atlanta Constitution*, June 25, 1963.

motels, theaters, and bowling alleys. The blacks, in turn, agreed to a cooling off period, and Williams was released from jail.[11]

Sanders was delighted that Williams and King concentrated their activities outside of Georgia, but like a bad headache Williams returned to cause the governor more pain. Williams, urging the SCLC to concentrate on voter registration, proposed a program, "Summer Community Organization and Political Education" (SCOPE), which called for northern students to work in black belt counties. SCOPE got underway in May 1965. In Georgia, about one hundred SCOPE volunteers worked in fifteen counties, where they usually encountered tough opposition from whites. The most serious confrontations occurred in Crawfordville, a village midway between Atlanta and Augusta that had once been the home of Alexander Stephens, the vice president of the Confederate States of America. Crawfordville, the county seat of Taliaferro county, like so many rural southern counties, had fallen on hard times. With practically no industry to hire farmers no longer needed in agriculture, many residents had been forced to migrate to earn a livelihood. As a result, Taliaferro's population fell from 8,841 in 1920 to 3,370 in 1960, and it ranked as one of Georgia's poorest counties.[12]

Direct action began in Crawfordville in 1964 when Calvin Turner, a popular teacher in the black high school, organized an effective voter registration drive. SCOPE workers arrived in the summer of 1965 and assisted in the project already underway. The town bitterly resisted this assertion of black rights, and when the SCLC pressed for school desegregation, whites retaliated by firing their maids and domestic workers. When SCOPE workers were beaten and jailed, the SCLC dispatched Hosea Williams, Andrew Young, and other leaders to Crawfordville to organize mass protests. They marched, picketed, and instituted an economic boycott in an attempt to desegregate the town. With no hotel or theater and very few businesses, there was little to desegregate in Crawfordville. Its state park already had been integrated before the demonstrations began, and 75 percent of the blacks had been registered to vote, as the SCLC acknowledged. What aroused the black

---

[11]*Atlanta Journal,* July 12, 1963; Faircloth, *To Redeem the Soul of America,* p. 144.
[12]Faircloth, *To Redeem the Soul of America,* pp. 258-63; *Acts and Resolutions, 1964,* p. 3373.

community, however, was the local school board's refusal to renew the contract of Turner, then president of the local NAACP chapter and head of the Negro Voters League, and five other teachers who had actively participated in the civil rights movement. Their replacement with other blacks did not assuage their anger. Even more upsetting to blacks was the effort to avoid integrating the public school. All of the white students of Taliaferro county simply had transferred to schools in neighboring counties. Since no white students remained in Taliaferro county, the white school did not open in the fall of 1965. Furious that whites were being bussed to adjoining counties, blacks demanded integration in Taliaferro county schools. As tempers flared and demonstrators marched, many black parents kept their children home in protest. Hosea Williams emerged as the spokesman for the disgruntled blacks. In his uniquely abrasive style, Williams organized the protests, aroused the marchers with fiery rhetoric, and threatened to lead a march to Atlanta 110 miles away, if results were not forthcoming.[13]

Sanders had kept a close watch on events in Crawfordville throughout the summer, and he hoped that local authorities could resolve the matter without additional state involvement. The chances of that happening, Sanders realized, had been greatly diminished when Hosea Williams arrived in Crawfordville. As far as Sanders was concerned, Williams was adept at attracting media attention but offered nothing constructive. He was a Sam Adams, an inciter of riots, an obstacle to progress. Moreover, Sanders saw no reason to recognize Williams as the leader of blacks in Crawfordville. Others, he felt, had a better claim to represent people in Crawfordville than Williams, "a commercial integrationist" who was attempting to "fatten his own pocketbook" and keep his name in print. Having only contempt for Williams, Sanders refused to have any dealings with him.[14]

In addition to avoiding Williams, Sanders launched a barrage of verbal assaults at him, assuming that the best defense is a good offense. Calling Williams a "false prophet," Sanders cautioned those who listened

---

[13]Faircloth, *To Redeem the Soul of America*, pp. 263-64; *The Advocate-Democrat* (Crawfordville, Georgia) June 4, 11, July 30, August 6, September 3, 1965.

[14]Sanders, "Interviews in 1990," pp. 170-71; press release September 24, 1965, box 35, Sanders Collection, Law Library; *Atlanta Journal*, September 24, 1965.

to him to "be prepared to be exploited by him." Regarding his proposed march to Atlanta, Sanders said: "he can march until his heels are up to his knees providing he stays within the law," but I do not intend to see anyone representing a "mass mob." In a press release Sanders asserted that Williams "is attempting to lead some people down a prim rose path to keep his name in print and the money flowing in. Instead of encouraging children to stay in school and helping parents get a better job, he issues marching orders, takes them out of school, keeps their parents away from their jobs, so he can grow fatter and richer."[15]

By the end of September 1965, only 170 of the 515 black students in Taliaferro county were attending school. Deeply concerned about the effects of the boycott, Sanders urged the parents to keep their children in school. Always upholding the law, he pointed out that under Georgia law all students sixteen and under were compelled to attend school. There was no option. The laws of the state, he declared, "will be enforced, and those who violate them—regardless of race—will be brought to justice." Unimpressed by Sanders's pleas or threats, Williams stated that Sanders was "dead politically," and he predicted that Georgia would have a long hot winter. In this battle of words, Sanders retaliated with another public statement in which he regretted that the efforts of one "false prophet" were creating "an emotional issue out of a legal matter." Georgia, he stated, "needs no demagogues, white or Negro, who seek to play racial politics for personal gain. Both races must obey our laws, and both must be protected by these laws." To clarify his statement of the previous day, he explained that it was not his goal to fill the jails with children; rather, his goal was to fill the classrooms with children. In conclusion, he repeated that "Georgia has no second-class citizens" and the "proper recourse for legal grievances is in our courts of law, not in our streets."[16]

To dramatize their plight and attract more media attention, the protesters adopted more militant tactics. First, they sought to get arrested. Having been denied admission to the school buses carrying whites to Warren county, several black students dropped to the pave-

---

[15]Ibid.

[16]Press releases September 29, 30, 1965, box 35, Sanders Collection, Law Library; *Atlanta Constitution*, October 1, 1965.

ment in front of the buses. State troopers asked them to move, and
when they refused the troopers gently hauled them out of the street.
None of the students were arrested or hurt, though their clothing got
wet and muddy. Other students drove to Warrenton, nineteen miles
away, where 112 white Taliaferro county students had transferred. The
blacks were barred from the school grounds by the state police. Since
none of the protesters were arrested, the demonstrations became more
unruly in subsequent days. Several demonstrators who tried to force their
way past state troopers to board school buses were hurled to the ground.
Two of the most violent ones were arrested. To complicate matters,
Calvin Craig, Georgia's grand dragon of the Ku Klux Klan, came to
Crawfordville to pressure Sanders to stop any attempt at integration. He
promised to create enough tension to force Sanders "to do something."
Although Craig and Williams represented opposite extremes of the
political spectrum, Sanders considered both extremists who were
detriments to a successful conclusion to the problems at Crawfordville.
"Georgia doesn't need any Hosea Williamses or any Calvin Craigs," he
stated repeatedly; "they represent the unreasoning extremes of issues."[17]

Since the local officials failed to resolve the disputes at Crawfordville,
Sanders increased his involvement. When the protests began, he sent
troopers to reinforce local law enforcement. Then he dispatched Senator
Leroy Johnson and three other blacks to Crawfordville on a fact-finding
mission and began consulting with local black leaders and county
officials by telephone. His quiet diplomacy eventually produced results.
On October 6, after meeting with the mayor of Crawfordville and the
chairman of the Taliaferro County Commission, Sanders announced that
progress had been made. The state had asked a three-judge Federal
tribunal to accelerate its hearing on the litigation which had been filed
in the Augusta Division of the U. S. District Court involving the school
controversy in Taliaferro county. The elected county and city officials
agreed to "abide completely by the findings and decisions of the Court,"
and so did "other responsible and recognized Negro leaders." When the

---

[17]*Atlanta Constitution*, October 2, 1965; *Savannah Evening Press*, October 4, 1965;
press release October 4, 1965, box 35, Sanders Collection, Law Library.

court met the following week, it appointed State School Superintendent Claude Purcell as receiver of the Taliaferro County Schools.[18]

The court decision satisfied Donald Holloway, the black attorney who represented civil rights interests before the judges. It also satisfied Calvin Turner, the black teacher who was the focus of the initial controversy. But it failed to satisfy Hosea Williams. Sanders, wisely it turns out, had carefully avoided any direct negotiation with Williams. He took the position that since Williams had been neither elected nor appointed to office by the people of Taliaferro county, he was nothing more than a tourist, a visitor, or an observer to the events in Crawfordville. Having no authority to represent anyone in the dispute, he was excluded from the negotiations. By refusing to acknowledge Williams as a legitimate leader of blacks in Taliaferro county, Sanders deeply undermined his power and incurred his wrath. Williams could accept almost any kind of opposition or criticism better than he could accept being ignored. He was furious that a settlement had been reached without his input. He criticized Sanders, Senator Johnson, and other blacks who negotiated the settlement and maintained that only the SCLC could speak for the "movement." He repeatedly demanded that Sanders speak with him and his group, but the governor never did. Exasperated by Sanders's actions, he exclaimed: "How can there be a settlement with us, unless us is there?"[19]

After Crawfordville, Hosea Williams left Georgia and concentrated on racial problems in other areas, but even without his agitating presence other racial disturbances erupted, the most volatile occurring in Sumter county in 1965 and in Atlanta in 1966. In all of these protests, Sanders consistently and emphatically urged all concerned to obey the law. As in Crawfordville and Savannah, he worked cooperatively with local officials and sent in state troopers when they were requested. At the same time, he sought information from responsible blacks and attempted to resolve problems through quiet diplomacy. If such efforts failed, then he insisted that the solution should come from the courts, not from violence in the

---

[18]Press releases October 6, 7, 1965, box 35, Sanders Collection, Law Library; *Atlanta Constitution*, October 25, 1965; Johnson interview, February 20, 1991; *The Advocate-Democrat*, October 15, 22, 29, 1965.

[19]*Atlanta Journal*, October 7, 1965; *Atlanta Constitution*, October 15, 1965; Cook, "Sanders: An Oral History," pp. 46-47; Sanders, "Interviews in 1990,: pp. 170-71.

streets. Totally rejecting the philosophy of civil disobedience, he placed great confidence in the courts. He maintained that racial issues could be settled and progress achieved by patiently working within the legal system. Consequently, he opposed all those who deliberately violated laws to achieve their goals. To Sanders, the law was sacrosanct. No state or nation, he maintained, "can give its citizens the 'right' to break the law. There can be no law to which obedience is optional or selective." Since both Senator Barry Goldwater and Martin Luther King, Jr. had justified disobeying certain laws, Sanders regarded both as extremists and argued that in essence they held the same philosophy—that the end justifies the means. In contrast to them, he reasoned that moderation was a virtue and extremism a vice. Settling disputes in the streets instead of the courts, he believed, would jeopardize civilization itself, which rests on the concept of rule by law. In explaining the importance of obeying the law, Sanders reminded Georgians that "the only safety in society—the only security for property—the only protection for life—the only hope for the future—is undivided, faithful and honest submission to the law whether we like it or not."[20]

While Sanders consistently stressed the necessity of obeying existing laws, he was not anxious to add new civil rights laws. In fact, he opposed the public accommodation section of the 1964 Civil Rights Act so strenuously that he testified against it in Washington. In arguing that federal involvement in state and local matters would not solve the problems and might in the long run exacerbate racial tensions, he disagreed with his friend Mayor Ivan Allen of Atlanta who testified in favor of the bill. His defense of individual private property rights and limited government also put him at odds with civil rights leaders who placed a higher value on human rights than property rights. Sanders wanted—and expected—the law to be colorblind, but he did not want a federal bureaucracy intervening in state and local matters to correct past abuses. While sympathetic to the liberal cause of civil rights, he nevertheless adhered to traditional conservative values and beliefs. Insofar as civil rights was concerned, Sanders agreed with Thomas Jefferson's maxim of "the less government, the better."

---

[20]Cook, "Carl Sanders and the Politics of the Future," p. 180.

Sanders's opposition to the Civil Rights Act cost him support within the black community, and his forceful criticism of rioters at Watts and elsewhere also elicited negative comments from black publications. In general, they noted that Sanders blamed only the civil rights movement for the riots. He neglected to point out the underlying causes of the riots nor did he criticize the public officials who failed to "remove conditions that bred slums, racial injustice and ghettos that are the seeds of such riots." Those criticisms had merit, as did the charge that Sanders was unrealistic in expecting "that illiterate Negroes should know the responsibilities of first class citizenship." Blacks also complained that he did not use the full powers of his office to improve the plight of Georgia Negroes, especially in state employment where only a handful of black clerks, secretaries, and typists could be found.[21]

While blacks wished that Sanders would do more for civil rights, they approved of many of his actions. His firm criticisms of white racist extremists and the Ku Klux Klan, sentiments rarely expressed by Georgia governors, gratified blacks, as did his expressions of outrage over atrocities committed against blacks, such as the burning of a church in Birmingham that killed four Negro children and the murder of Colonel Lemuel Penn near Athens. Sanders's willingness to appear on CBS TV with Bobby Kennedy and Roy Wilkins shocked many whites and pleased many blacks. In contrast to his predecessors as governor, he opened lines of communication with blacks, met frequently with black leaders, and acted on many of their requests. He even spoke at the Hungry Club, a political institution in Atlanta normally the exclusive domain of blacks. Blacks often disagreed with Sanders, but at least he communicated with them and incorporated some blacks into the political process.[22]

Perhaps Sanders's most important contribution in civil rights was his appointment of blacks to office. He appointed two blacks to the Governor's Commission to Improve Education as well as the first blacks to the Georgia delegation to the Democratic National Convention. He also appointed the first blacks to the Georgia State Patrol, the National

---

[21]*Atlanta Inquirer*, August 21, 28, 1965; *Atlanta Daily World*, July 25, 1965; *Atlanta Journal*, May 16, 1965; *Atlanta Constitution*, December 24, 1965.

[22]*Atlanta Constitution*, September 17, 1963, March 31, 1965; press releases July 11, 1964, box 34, July 29, October 18, December 22, 1965, box 35, Sanders Collection, Law Library; *Atlanta Journal*, May 3, 1964; Johnson interview, February 20, 1991.

Guard, and the Committee on the Status of Women. In breaking these color barriers, Sanders demonstrated political courage. The controversial appointments offended many whites, and they were certain to alienate white voters in any future election. But Sanders believed that blacks gradually should be incorporated into the political system. He argued that when qualified blacks applied for positions they should be given equal consideration with white applicants. To Sanders, it was only right and proper for blacks to be included, and he acted on that conviction rather than political considerations. Yet, Sanders appointed no black judges, department heads, or Georgia Bureau of Investigation agents, and blacks criticized him for such omissions. Political reality undoubtedly deterred him. Appointing a black to such a high-visibility position would have been extremely controversial in the mid-1960s and would have jeopardized the passage of his whole legislative agenda. Always a realist, he refused to run that risk. He decided to proceed more slowly on civil rights and concentrate his efforts on other issues he considered more important. For Sanders, many issues surpassed civil rights in importance, and he kept his priorities in order. To keep matters in perspective, however, it should be noted that his predecessors appointed no blacks to those positions and his successors have appointed very few.[23]

In the field of civil rights, Sanders remained a moderate who attempted to steer a middle course between the reactionary racists on the one hand and militant agitators on the other. He never intended to make civil rights a priority in his administration. Indeed, for Sanders it ranked in importance far behind education, industrial development, efficiency in government, and reapportionment. More important to Sanders than civil rights measures was his whole legislative program which, if adopted, would benefit all Georgians, including blacks. Sanders revealed his true feelings at the Southern Governors Conference in September 1965 when, in urging governors to focus attention on industrial development, he remarked that the race issue was "somewhat passé." For Sanders, it was passé, and he was eager to address other matters. But the race issue persisted, and Sanders was forced to confront

---

[23]Cook, "Carl Sanders and the Politics of the Future," p. 179; Pat Watters, "It's Nearly All White in the South," *New Republic* 150 (June 13, 1964): 11-12; *Atlanta Constitution*, March 19, July 29, 1964; Cook, "Sanders: An Oral History," pp. 45-46.

it repeatedly. To militants, such as Hosea Williams, Sanders remained a patrician racist who never really accepted the concept of black equality. Yet, when all factors are considered, Sanders probably advanced civil rights in Georgia as much as was politically feasible at that time, and much more than he had promised in his campaign. To do more, as black critics demanded, would have aroused emotional opposition throughout the state, made the passage of his legislative program more difficult, and severely weakened his chances of holding elective office in Georgia again. That was a heavier burden than Sanders or any other ambitious young Georgia politician was willing to bear. Near the end of his term, neutral observers concluded that he had managed to keep the lid on the race situation and had maintained good relations both with strong segregationists and with fervent integrationists. That was not an easy political feat to accomplish in the mid-1960s.[24]

[Photograph on page 256]

At a ceremony in Atlantic City, New Jersey, in February 1965, Governor Sanders received the prestigious Golden Key Award for his outstanding contributions to education. Pictured with him is Miss Emma Wilkinson, his seventh grade teacher, who also was honored at the ceremony.

[24]*New York Times*, September 13, 1965; *Atlanta Constitution*, January 2, 1966; Black, *Southern Governors and Civil Rights*, pp. 14-15, 68.

*Governor Sanders chats with Marine platoon leader Jerry Vereen
of Moultrie, Georgia, in Danang, Vietnam, November 9, 1965.*

*Governor Sanders greets employees of Minami Kyushu
Coca-Cola Bottling Company, Kumamoto, Japan.*

Chapter 16

The Last Year as Governor

Racial considerations—or, more precisely, the unpopular statements of a black legislator—disrupted the opening of the 1966 Georgia legislative session. In a special post-reapportionment election in June 1965, eight blacks won election to the House of Representatives. With Leroy Johnson and Horace Ward already serving in the Senate, the election meant that Georgia had more black state legislators than any state except Michigan and Illinois. The House accepted seven of the eight new legislators routinely, but it took offense at the public statements of Julian Bond, a twenty-five-year-old light-complexioned intellectual elected from the 136th district. Son of Dr. Horace Mann Bond, dean of the School of Education at Atlanta University, he was the publicity director of Atlanta-based SNCC, a civil rights organization that had grown increasingly militant and had alienated many whites by espousing "black power." Having won eighty-two percent of the votes in his race, Bond clearly had the backing of his constituents, but his association with SNCC upset many Georgia legislators. They found SNCC chairman John Lewis's remarks about Vietnam particularly offensive. Lewis hit a sensitive nerve in the Southern psyche when he stated that civil rights murder in the South was "no different than the murder of peasants in Vietnam," that sixty percent of the draftees are Negroes who do not have democracy at home, and that the United States was violating international law in Vietnam. By urging "all Americans" to avoid the draft and work in the civil rights movement instead, he went beyond freedom of speech and approached treason, according to many critics. Such remarks enraged Georgia legislators. When Bond refused to disavow them, their anger shifted to him. On a nationwide TV program shortly after his election, Bond endorsed SNCC's position on the Vietnam War and expressed sympathy with draft-card burners. Trying to avoid a bitter confrontation, the other newly elected black legislators urged Bond to make a patriotic statement, but he stubbornly refused. As a result, a stern-faced House committee voted 23 to 3 to bar Bond from the House.[1]

SNCC's inflammatory remarks angered Governor Sanders too. A veteran and staunch defender of America's military effort in Vietnam, he disagreed entirely with the statements. In a terse press release he stated, "I have no sympathy with the beliefs expressed in the SNCC statement of yesterday. It was both inaccurate and intemperate in content. In my judgment, this is the time for all Americans to rally around our flag, not kick it."[2] Although Sanders detested SNCC's comments as much as any member of the House, he kept his emotions under control and reacted rationally. He advised members of the House to seat Bond and then ignore him, arguing that Bond would be powerless and inconspicuous in that large body. Denying him a seat would be emotionally satisfying but counterproductive, Sanders reasoned, because Bond would seek redress in the courts and very likely would win. Consequently, seating Bond, distasteful as that might be, would be a better policy in the long run than drawing attention to him and making him a martyr and a celebrity, Sanders argued.[3]

The House, aroused by the firebrand rhetoric of Representatives Jones Lane and James "Sloppy" Floyd, rejected Sanders's perceptive arguments and voted 184 to 12 to deny Bond his seat. As Sanders predicted, Bond appealed to the courts. Rebuffed initially by a three-man federal court which upheld the legislature's decision, Bond persisted with more appeals. Finally, by the end of the year, after winning three elections, Bond received a favorable verdict from the United States Supreme Court. Upon hearing the Supreme Court ruling, a disgruntled representative snorted, "We'll let him have his seat, but we won't like it, and we'll see to it he gets the silent treatment." That, of course, was exactly what Sanders had recommended in January. The House's strenuous opposition to Bond inadvertently made him a national

---

[1]"Times Have Changed," *Newsweek* 65 (June 28, 1965): 24-27; "Georgia Legislature's New Look for 1966," *Ebony* 20 (September 1965): 48-55; Reese Cleghorn, "No Seat for the Negro Who Won," *New Republic* 154 (January 29, 1966): 11-12; *Atlanta Constitution*, January 11, 12, 1966; John Neary, *Julian Bond: Black Rebel* (New York: William Morrow and Company, 1971).

[2]Press release January 7, 1966, box 35, Sanders Collection, Law Library.

[3]Sanders, "Interviews in 1990," pp. 121-23.

celebrity who thereafter earned large stipends on the lecture circuit and even had his name placed in nomination for the vice presidency at the 1968 Democratic convention.[4]

After resolving the Bond affair, the General Assembly concentrated on legislative matters. Governor Sanders set the tone of the session with an uplifting state of the state address. Before offering new bills, he proudly reviewed the many accomplishments of the past three years. With Georgia's economy booming, personal income advancing rapidly, and unemployment dropping to 1.4 percent, the lowest in the history of the state, he reported the condition of the state as "truly magnificent." And, despite unprecedented expenditures in education and mental health as well as substantial commitments to highway construction, law enforcement, tourism, and many other aspects of government, he expected to leave at least $40,000,000 in the state treasury, the largest surplus ever left to a succeeding governor in Georgia's history. The surplus, he added, resulted from "sound fiscal responsibility, economy, and efficiency in government."[5]

Sanders's last legislative program called for passage of a supplemental appropriations bill of $18,555,000, with one-third of the total allotted to education and $3,475,000 for mental health. To generate more income, he sought a one-dollar increase in hunting and fishing fees and the payment of ad valorem taxes on motor vehicles when the tags are purchased. He also offered a package of antigambling measures and four constitutional amendments regarding education. The amendments facilitated school system mergers, simplified the election of county school superintendents, allowed a millage increase for local school financing, and increased the limitation of a county's bonded indebtedness from 7 to 10 percent of the local tax assessment. Sanders also strongly supported an amendment to allow the General Assembly to make direct appropriations for rapid transit systems up to 10 percent of the total cost of the project.[6]

---

[4]Ibid.; "Bond's Word," *Newsweek* 68 (December 19, 1966): 27; "The Bond Issue," *Time* 87 (February 18, 1966): 24; Harold H. Martin, *Atlanta and Environs: Years of Change and Challenge, 1940–1976* (Athens: University of Georgia Press, 1987) p. 464.

[5]Daniel, *Addresses of Carl Sanders*, pp. 54-65.

[6]Ibid.

The *Atlanta Constitution*, though complimentary of the progress made during the Sanders years, noted that Georgia still had a long list of deficiencies. Despite recent improvements, Georgia continued to rank near the bottom in education and mental health. The state's per capita prison population ranked among the nation's highest, its highway system remained inadequate, and city governments throughout the state tottered near bankruptcy. It urged the legislature to approve all that Sanders had recommended "and then some."[7]

The General Assembly, however, responded to Sanders's program with greater enthusiasm than did the *Atlanta Constitution*. Members frequently interrupted his speech with applause, and many commented that it was the best speech Sanders had delivered. One not-so-friendly representative observed, "Whether you like the governor or not, his administration has been a productive and good administration in all fields of endeavor. I thought he outlined a splendid program of progress that all Georgia could be proud of." Although many legislators commented that the expected surplus showed that Sanders had run an honest and careful administration, a few, including Senator Jimmy Carter, were critical. To eliminate the surplus, Carter favored a tax cut, as did Representative Daniel Grahl who grumbled, "We're not in the savings business." Even though this was Sanders's last year in office, he gave no indication of slowing down or relinquishing the initiative. Many legislators praised his leadership and refusal to act like a lame duck. Representative Janet Merritt of Americus observed that a lame-duck governor in the last year of his administration usually cannot even get a bellboy to carry his bag, but Sanders "still expects his suitcase to be carried."[8]

After getting his program underway, Sanders made a quick trip to Washington, D.C., on January 28 to receive the 1965 Professional Trophy from the Society of Industrial Realtors. The Society bestowed the award on the state judged to have the most effective industrial development programs. Under Sanders's leadership Georgia had made impressive gains—more than 40,000 new industrial jobs added in three years, over $1 billion in new construction in 1965, 134 new manufacturing firms in 1965, plus over $136 million expansion of operations by manufac-

[7]*Atlanta Constitution*, January 12, 1966.
[8]Ibid.

turing firms. Having made industrial development one of his priorities, Sanders appreciated the national recognition. In accepting the award, he stressed the role of the Department of Industry and Trade and the leadership of Director James Nutter.[9]

In contrast to the three previous legislative sessions, which had grappled with biennial budgets, the Minimum Foundation for Education, reapportionment, constitutional revision, and other controversial measures, the governor's agenda in 1966 offered no major innovations. Since the legislature already had enacted practically all of his platform, he concentrated on refining his program. Generating little controversy, his measures sailed through the legislature with ease. As in previous years, Sanders completely dominated the General Assembly which enacted his program routinely. When the session moved into its last week, all of Sanders's major pieces of legislation had passed or were in the final stages of adoption. The only issue that lagged was the constitutional amendment allowing school consolidation across county lines. School authorities considered it an essential first step in implementing the McClurkin Report which called for reducing the number of school districts in the state from two hundred to about sixty. Sanders, who favored consolidating small schools, understood that some legislators bitterly opposed any school consolidation. To minimize the controversy, his proposal did not require consolidation, it merely allowed it. Even in that passive form the measure had opposition, but the governor pushed it through the legislature.[10]

On February 17, next to the last day of the forty-day session, the House, in a rare display of legislative independence, gutted the governor's antigambling bill. By approving a substitute bill drawn up by former member Denmark Groover, who represented some private clubs in Macon, the House shocked Sanders. The Governor's bill, already approved by the Senate, made possession of gambling stamps prima facie evidence of guilt in a state court, but Groover's substitute exempted all fraternal and private clubs. An infuriated Sanders immediately called a press conference and announced that the original bill will "pass over-

---

[9]Ibid., January 29, 1966; *Rome News-Tribune*, January 28, 1966; Daniel, *Addresses of Carl Sanders*, p. 55.

[10]*Atlanta Constitution*, February 15, 1966.

whelmingly" when it is called up for reconsideration. The House action visibly upset Sanders, who normally kept a tight rein on his emotions. Many observers had never seen him so angry over a bill since he had been in office. He instructed Floor Leader George Busbee to force a showdown by demanding a roll call vote. "Either you are for gambling or against it," Sanders asserted. The Governor's efforts produced the desired results. The next day the House passed Sanders's bill by vote of 150 to 19.[11]

A heavy backlog of bills filled the calendars of both houses on the last day of the session. To enact all of the measures, it was necessary once again to stop the official clocks and extend the session an additional three hours beyond its legal deadline. As the session dragged on late into the evening, both houses passed countless bills and resolutions without debate. The families and friends who jammed both houses created a festive mood. While rapidly completing the legislative calendar, the members socialized, wandered around the floor, and munched sandwiches and peanuts. Sanders briefly restored seriousness to the proceedings when he addressed the lawmakers for the last time.

The Governor customarily made a brief farewell address to the General Assembly on the last day of the session, and on three previous occasions Sanders had thanked the members profusely for their contributions to the state. He did so again, thanking them for their service to the state and their friendship and cooperation during his "wonderful and memorable four years as governor." Together, he noted, they had brought progress and growth to Georgia and revitalized the state to meet the challenges of the modern era. But this talk was different. It was his last farewell address, and the finality of it affected him deeply. His era as governor was ending, and he wanted to express his sincere gratitude to the members of the legislature who had contributed so significantly to the success of the Sanders administration. They had enacted every major measure he had presented and had demonstrated remarkable courage in facing extraordinarily difficult issues. Extremely proud of them, he tried desperately to communicate his feelings, but he had difficulty putting his thoughts into words. As he considered the many triumphs of the last four years, he was so filled with pride and sadness

---

[11]Ibid., February 18, 19, 1966; *Savannah Morning News*, February 20, 1966.

that his icy demeanor melted. Overcome with emotion, his voice cracked and he had to pause to regain his composure. With tears in his eyes, the Governor said farewell to his friends and colleagues who had served the state so nobly during the past four years, "the most meaningful years of my life."[12]

In 1966, as in previous years, Sanders controlled the legislature and secured passage of almost every measure he proposed. Although it was a short and generally harmonious session, it failed to produce great legislation. It handled the routine business satisfactorily and adopted several worthwhile measures, but none had the significance of reapportionment, the biennial budget, the Master Plan for Education, or the new constitution. That no single issue stood out from the others in importance was apparent when the *Atlanta Journal and Constitution* interviewed several legislative leaders after the session and asked which issue was most important. Each legislator identified a different bill. Senator Julian Webb rated pension reform the most important measure; Senator Hugh Gillis praised the supplemental appropriations bill; Senator Dan MacIntyre liked the bill requiring auditing of state highway funds sent to cities and counties; Representative Robin Harris was partial to the tax tag bill; Representative Grace Hamilton believed the school merger bill was most important; and Representative Roy Simkins favored the bill allowing a $600 exemption for each child in college. The *Savannah Evening Press* praised Sanders for his leadership in passing the antigambling bill which was "vitally needed." The press universally acknowledged Sanders's control, but generally labeled his 1966 legislative program as "skimpy." After three hectic and very productive sessions, perhaps a respite was needed.[13]

Even though Sanders worked harmoniously with the General Assembly, the forty-day legislative session was a tiring experience. He succeeded in getting his programs adopted because he worked hard communicating with the members and coordinating activities with his legislative lieutenants. His efforts got results, but the session physically

---

[12]*Atlanta Constitution*, February 19, 1966; *Savannah Evening Press*, February 19, 1966; Daniel, *Addresses of Carl Sanders*, pp. 65-67.

[13]*Atlanta Journal and Constitution*, February 20, 1966; *Savannah Evening Press*, February 21, 1966; *Rome News-Tribune*, February 20, 1966.

drained him. He needed a break, and so did Betty. Immediately after the session ended, they flew to Jamaica. Carl had been there previously and was eager to return with Betty. There, far away from the strain and constant pressure of state government, they could relax for a few days. The tropical sun and sandy beaches were especially pleasant in late February after weeks of cold wintry weather in Atlanta. Both Carl and Betty enjoyed travel and the beach, but Carl always insisted on short vacations. With many projects demanding his attention, one week was his limit; after that he became irritable, so anxious to return to work that he could not enjoy longer vacations. Driven to excel in all his endeavors, Carl needed breaks in his routine, but for him one week away from the job was enough.[14]

Upon returning home after the refreshing week in Jamaica, Sanders then directed his attention to a decision that could no longer be postponed. For many months political observers had speculated about Sanders's political future, and everyone wondered if the young governor would challenge Senator Russell. Periodically, columnists, claiming to have inside information, reported that Sanders had decided to run, while other columnists, with equal conviction, reported that he had decided against the race. Actually, Sanders, who remained noncommittal about the race, had not yet made up his mind. When pressed by reporters, he offered the excuse that the legislative session required his full attention. After the session was completed and he had recuperated from it, he knew the time had come to make that decision. Had Sanders relied exclusively on polls, he could have made the decision easily, for the polls consistently showed him far behind Russell. The polls further revealed that Sanders's approval rating was so high he could win any race in the state except the Senate race against Russell. Sanders, however, had stated from the onset that polls alone would not determine his decision. But polls were a factor to be considered, and they revealed that he faced an uphill struggle. A WSB-TV telephone survey of eight hundred persons in the Atlanta area in February, for example, gave Russell a three to one margin.[15]

---

[14]Cook, "Sanders: An Oral History," p. 74.
[15]*Atlanta Constitution*, February 14, 1966.

Senator Russell still enjoyed enormous prestige in Georgia, but advancing age and declining health were factors that made him vulnerable. Both Russell and his advisers kept their eyes on Sanders, trying to discern his political intentions. Clearly, they viewed Sanders as a threat, the first serious competition Russell had encountered in years. Suffering from emphysema, Russell had a tracheotomy in the summer of 1965. While he was recuperating at home in Winder, Roy Harris and Phil Campbell came to see him. Both men expressed concern about his health and wondered if he had the physical stamina to conduct a campaign in 1966, especially a rigorous campaign against an aggressive younger opponent. Harris, not one to mince words, bluntly told Russell that a hard campaign would kill him. To avoid a strenuous campaign, they decided to organize Russell's reelection campaign right away and focus the campaign on 1965 instead of 1966. Their strategy was to build up Russell's support so that he would appear unbeatable, thereby discouraging Sanders or anyone else from challenging the senator in 1966. They went to work immediately, quietly making the necessary contacts. Russell corresponded extensively, letting people know that rumors of his retirement were "baseless" and that he would formally announce his candidacy for reelection at the proper time. In addition, he delivered many speeches in Georgia, developed campaign strategies, and assembled lists of workers on the major college campuses. Russell also mailed copies of the booklet "Senator Richard B. Russell—Georgia's Man in Washington" to political leaders, doctors, lawyers, and various supporters throughout the state. Russell himself remained active in Washington, struggling with civil rights and Vietnam, while his campaign progressed in Georgia. By such means Russell and his friends strengthened the senator's standing, overcame concerns about his age and health, and kept the senator far ahead of Sanders in polls taken in 1965 and early 1966.[16]

Sanders watched the polls with great interest. He knew that polls were accurate indicators of public opinion, but he also knew from experience that effective campaigning changed public opinion. And if he

---

[16]William Bates interview by Hugh Cates, February 25, 1971, J. Phil Campbell interview by Hugh Cates, 1971, Roy Harris interview, February 24, 1971, oral history, Russell Collection; Senatorial Campaign 1966 file, boxes 125, 126, Russell Collection, Russell Library, University of Georgia.

decided to seek the Senate seat, he would campaign as vigorously as he had in 1962—a pace that Russell could not possibly match. As he analyzed his strengths and weaknesses (as well as Russell's), he considered other factors besides polls. Chief among them was his family. He wondered how his election to the Senate would affect Betty and the children. Although Betty had agreed to support whatever decision he made, she clearly had reservations about living in Washington. Lacking political aspirations, she had no desire to participate in politics on the national level. She thoroughly enjoyed living in Augusta and Atlanta and was apprehensive about the hectic pace of life in the nation's capitol. To overcome that problem, they could maintain a home in Georgia for Betty and the children while Carl lived in an apartment in Washington and commuted home on weekends. While many congressmen and senators had adopted that lifestyle, it had no appeal for Carl. He insisted on keeping his family together. The children were another consideration. Naturally, Carl and Betty wanted to provide the best possible environment for their children who were now entering the difficult teen years. In 1967 Betty Foy would be fourteen and Carl Jr. would be twelve. With society unraveling with protests, marches, and violence, and the drug and hippy culture attracting increasing numbers, Betty and Carl worried about the growing temptations and perils confronting teenagers. Neither wanted to rear their children in Washington. Both agreed that Carl Jr. and Betty Foy would fare better spending their vulnerable teenage years in Georgia. In Georgia the children also would confront problems and temptations, but at least they would have a safer and more wholesome environment than Washington provided, their parents reasoned.[17]

Another factor militating against the Senate race was Sanders's realization that he was more effective in the executive branch than he was in the legislative branch of government. While he had served effectively in the Georgia General Assembly, he excelled as an executive. After serving as a governor, he knew that switching back to the legislative branch would would be a difficult transition. A governor can propose and

---

[17]Cook, "Sanders: An Oral History," p. 61.

dispose of things, he later explained, but a senator cannot. He proposes, but "it takes years and years for anything to get disposed of."[18]

After weighing such factors and discussing the matter with his family and close friends, Sanders at last decided what he should do. Before making his final decision and announcing it to the public, however, he sought higher authority. Having no doubt about the existence of an omnipotent Almighty God, he derived great comfort from taking his problems to his Lord. For many years prayer had been a part of his normal routine, and when making major decisions he devoted additional time to prayer. He believed in using all of his earthly wisdom and then seeking supernatural guidance as well. Although Sanders possessed an executive mentality and made numerous important decisions in the leadership positions he held, he nevertheless found decision making a difficult and lonely process. Others provided advice, but ultimately he made decisions and then accepted responsibility for the consequences of his judgments. From prayer and meditation he gained insight, reassurance, and confidence. The assurance he sought in this instance came as he prayed in church on Sunday, March 27. Now convinced that he had made the right decision, Sanders prepared to announce it publicly. Wanting a special setting to announce a decision of this importance, he checked his calendar and found that he was scheduled to dedicate five new buildings at Augusta College the following Wednesday. What better place to announce his decision regarding the 1966 Senate race than in his hometown, where four years before he had announced his decision to run for governor.[19]

After dedicating the new buildings at Augusta College, Sanders then disclosed his plans. Placing political expediency above candor, he explained that his interest in running for the Senate stemmed largely from his concern over Senator Russell's health. Now convinced that Russell's health is again "excellent," he could find no valid reason "why any man in Georgia should oppose our respected senior senator." Instead of challenging Russell, Sanders pledged to support and "actively work for" Russell's reelection to the United States Senate. Regarding his own fu-

---

[18]Sanders, "Interviews in 1990," pp. 130, 180-82.
[19]Sanders, "My Life," p. 51; *Atlanta Journal and Constitution*, March 15, 1964; Daniel, *Addresses of Carl Sanders*, pp. 208-10.

ture, Sanders pointedly left open the possibility of serving the public again. He hoped his tenure in office had proven his "unflinching love for Georgia," and in the future, "when our people again so indicate, I once more will offer these convictions, these hopes, these devotions, these abilities, in service to Georgia." Although most political observers assumed that the ambitious young governor had weighed all the evidence and concluded that he could not defeat Senator Russell, that was not the case. Sanders knew how difficult a race against Russell would be, but he believed he could win. Confident as always, he was convinced that a strenuous campaign would wear down the infirm senator and bring him victory. In deciding against the Senate race in 1966, concern for his family—not fear of defeat—was Sanders's primary consideration.[20]

Two weeks after announcing that he would not be a candidate for the Senate in 1966, Sanders participated in the ceremonies opening Atlanta Stadium to Major League baseball. On April 12 the Atlanta Braves met the Pittsburgh Pirates in the first National League game played in the gleaming new stadium, built in a record fifty-one weeks for $18.5 million. Mayor Ivan Allen, who threw out the first pitch, described the stadium as the symbol of the new Atlanta. In addition to the Atlanta Braves, in the fall of 1966 the stadium also became of the home of the Atlanta Falcons, the city's second professional sports team.[21]

Building the stadium and attracting professional teams to Atlanta resulted from years of hard work by business, political, and civic leaders, and especially Mayor Allen and the Atlanta Chamber of Commerce. When Allen became president of the Atlanta Chamber of Commerce in 1961, it adopted a six-point program of action calling for the following: 1. keeping the public schools open; 2. accelerating the construction of expressways; 3. vigorously supporting urban renewal and expanded housing; 4. building as rapidly as possible an auditorium-coliseum and a stadium; 5. pressing for a large-scale rapid transit system; and 6. conducting a Forward Atlanta program to advertise Atlanta nationally. Sanders supported all of these measures enthusiastically and worked cooperatively with city and business leaders to ensure their completion.

---

[20]Daniel, *Addresses of Carl Sanders*, pp. 208-10; Sanders, "Interviews in 1990," pp. 180-82.

[21]Allen, *Mayor*, pp. 152-60.

Building the stadium at the convergence of Interstate highways 20, 75, and 85 in downtown Atlanta was a complicated undertaking. Governor Sanders used his influence effectively to expedite the process, especially with the Highway Department in constructing an overpass and access roads to the stadium. In his autobiography, Mayor Allen praised Sanders and acknowledged that he did more for Georgia cities "than any governor of Georgia had in recent years."[22]

In addition to helping lure the Braves to Atlanta, Sanders also played a significant role in the origin of the Atlanta Falcons. For several months, Cox Broadcasting Company and several businessmen had attempted to secure a franchise with the American Football League. When at last they finally succeeded in getting a team, Pete Rozelle, commissioner of the older and more prestigious National Football League, suddenly became interested in Atlanta. He appeared at the Governor's Office and informed Sanders that the NFL had decided to expand and wanted to put a team in Atlanta. Sanders asked him about the terms and conditions. Rozelle explained that under NFL policies one person must own more than 50 percent of the team. He asked Sanders to recommend a potential owner and promised to return in a week. After considering the few people who had the necessary capital, Sanders decided that his fraternity brother Rankin Smith would be a good candidate. Since Smith had shown little interest in running the Life of Georgia Insurance Company, had millions to spend, and loved football, perhaps he would like to own a football team. Sanders invited him to the Mansion to find out. At first, Smith expressed only mild interest. When Rozelle returned, they discussed the matter further. Rozelle expected the team to cost about $4 million. A week later Smith informed Sanders that the NFL wanted $6 million. Sanders encouraged him to pay it, arguing that the team would benefit the city and the state and also would be a profitable investment for Smith and his family. Later Smith called again and said the price had risen to $8.5 million. Even though it was a costly investment, Sanders urged his friend to buy the team. He was so convinced that the investment would prosper, he told him, "I think you are crazy not to do it." Swayed by Sanders's arguments, Smith bought the team and named it the Atlanta Falcons.

---

[22]Ibid., pp. 32-34, 135; Sanders, "Interviews in 1990," pp. 171-73.

Despite the Falcons' dismal record of performance, the team has brought great economic benefits to the city of Atlanta, the state of Georgia, and the Smith family, as Sanders predicted. In fact, by 1992 the Atlanta Falcons were worth an estimated $200 million.[23]

During the Sanders years Atlanta enjoyed booming prosperity, as modern hotels and office buildings sprang up along Peachtree Street and other thoroughfares. With the completion of a $22 million improvement program, the Atlanta Airport became one of the busiest in the nation. In addition to becoming a major sports city, Atlanta was the commercial center of the Southeast, adding some 25,000 jobs annually and keeping unemployment below 3 percent, the lowest in the nation. Yet, despite its dynamic growth, pockets of the city remained in poverty. Like all major American cities, Atlanta had its ghettos, as thousands of dispossessed farm migrants gravitated to the city in search of work.[24]

Before World War II, Summerhill had been an elegant residential section, consisting of roomy two-story white frame houses and shady streets. Only eight or ten blocks from the Capitol, it was populated by well-to-do white families. After the war, these substantial white families began moving out of the area, to be followed by lower-class whites and then by blacks. By the mid-sixties, Summerhill had become a ghetto with ten thousand poor Negroes crammed into 354 acres. Almost all new residents who came into Summerhill were migrants without jobs or money, with little hope of finding either. Summerhill was a cauldron of poverty, unemployment, disease, crime, and frustration, located adjacent to the sparkling new stadium. Primed for a riot, all it needed was a spark to set it aflame. The spark came the day after Labor Day, 1966.[25]

Like most riots of the 1960s, the Summerville riot was triggered by a relatively minor incident. An Atlanta police detective cruising through Summerhill spotted a young black man wanted for automobile theft. He placed the suspect, Harold Prather, under arrest. When the young man broke away and tried to escape, the police officer shot him in the leg. Black observers asserted that the white policeman shot Prather again at

---

[23]Allen, *Mayor*, pp. 160-64; Sanders, "Interviews in 1990," pp. 173-75; *Atlanta Journal and Constitution*, July 19, 1992.

[24]Allen, *Mayor*, p. 130; Stone, *Regime Politics*, pp. 55-76.

[25]Allen, *Mayor*, 174-80.

pointblank range, after which Prather collapsed on his front porch. Within minutes of the incident, Stokely Carmichael and other militants were cruising Summerhill in a SNCC sound truck, stirring up the residents. Asserting that the man had been murdered on his mother's front porch, they urged the people of Summerhill to revolt against "whitey" before "he kills us all." Soon thousands of blacks filled the streets, shouting, and screaming in angry confusion. As soon as Mayor Allen learned of the riot, he immediately rushed to Summerville and attempted to calm the rioters by strolling down the street through the howling mob of disenchanted blacks. His courage in walking unarmed among the throng shocked the rioters. They were so disconcerted by the mayor's presence that a hush fell over the crowd. The mayor walked back and forth for nearly an hour, reasoning with them and urging them to elect some leaders to meet with him. Just when his efforts were on the verge of success, SNCC leaders reappeared, shouting "We ain't going to no goddam white man's stadium. . . . They'll get you in there and the po-leeces will shoot you down. . . ." Their inflammatory rhetoric ended rational discussion and conditions deteriorated thereafter. With SNCC leaders chanting "Black Power, Black Power," the crowd began throwing bricks and bottles, attacking the police, and looting anything of value. Mayor Allen then called in the police and gave the order to use tear gas. By prearrangement with Allen, Governor Sanders had dispatched over one hundred state patrolmen to the area in case additional force was needed. They remained out of sight in the stadium, and, fortunately, were not needed. The police quickly restored order and arrested fifty rioters. Compared to Watts, Chicago, and Harlem, the Atlanta riot was mild, as no one died and only nine were injured. Mayor Allen and the police received much praise in the national media for effectively controlling a volatile situation.[26]

Sanders also commended Allen and the police, but expressed outrage at the rioters, calling them "anarchists." In a prepared statement he pointed out that while the Constitution guarantees the right to peacefully assemble and peacefully demonstrate, "there is no right, either legal or

---

[26]Ibid., pp. 180-90; *Atlanta Journal,* September 13, 1966; *Rome News-Tribune,* September 7, 1966; Eliza K. Paschall, *It Must Have Rained* (Atlanta: The Center for Research in Social Change, Emory University, 1975) pp. 155-63.

moral, that permits a gathering to become a mob, and then for that mob to destroy or damage or even threaten property and lives." Appalled by the illegal actions of SNCC, he hoped and expected the courts to deal properly with "these merchants of discord and violence." Although confident that the recent incidents in Atlanta would be resolved by the local officials and leaders of both races, he assured the people that the state government, which had kept in close contact with Mayor Allen, provided one hundred troopers, and alerted units of the National Guard, would take whatever action required to protect the property and lives of all Georgians. Convinced that all responsible Georgians desired peace and public tranquility, he promised that "you will have it." He fulfilled his promise as there were no more riots during his governorship.[27]

On September 14, a week after the Atlanta riot, Georgians cast their ballots in perhaps the strangest Democratic primary in the state's history. At first, the leading contenders to succeed Sanders as governor were former governors Ellis Arnall and Ernest Vandiver. That situation changed abruptly on May 18 when Vandiver, following the advice of his physician, suddenly withdrew from the race because of a recurring heart condition. Senator Herman Talmadge, apprised of Vandiver's health problems, immediately announced that he would be a candidate if the people wanted him. Speculation then arose that Sanders would seek Talmadge's Senate seat. Sanders naturally remained noncommittal about the Senate race and expressed condolences to Vandiver who served Georgia honorably and well with "great courage, character, integrity and dedication." He also sidestepped the draft Talmadge issue by stating that he would support the Democratic nominee, whoever that might be. Talmadge later had second thoughts and decided to remain in the Senate, but several others jumped into the gubernatorial race: Garland Byrd, a former lieutenant governor; Jimmy Carter, a young state senator from Plains; James Gray of Albany, a newspaperman and former chairman of the State Democratic Executive Committee; Hoke O'Kelley, a perennial candidate from Lawrenceville; and Lester Maddox, an Atlanta

---

[27]Press release September 13, 1966, box 35, Sanders Collection, Law Library; *Atlanta Journal*, September 13, 1966.

businessman and archsegregationist who had never held public office—all sought the Democratic nomination.[28]

Sanders did not actively campaign for any of the candidates but quietly threw his support to Ellis Arnall, a brilliant Atlanta attorney who had a very progressive administration during World War II and now sought a political comeback after twenty years. Offering a fifteen-point platform calling for overall tax revision, constitutional revision, a war on crime, and support of education, Arnall quickly jumped into the lead. Gaining endorsements from Congressman Charles Weltner, ex-Governor M. E. Thompson, Georgia's AFL-CIO, many education, business, and political leaders, including William Trotter and Marjorie Thurman, Georgia's two National Democratic Committee members, Arnall maintained a lead throughout the campaign. But polls clearly indicated that a runoff would be required since he had less than a majority of the vote. An Oliver Quayle poll conducted in the first week of August showed Arnall with 32 percent, Maddox with 15 percent, Gray 12 percent, Byrd 8 percent, Carter 5 percent, and O'Kelley 3 percent. Significantly, 25 percent remained undecided five weeks before the election.[29]

Jimmy Carter's platform, promising improvements in education, highways, mental health, and public safety, was similar to Sanders's platform of 1962, and his pledge to appoint a blue ribbon committee, which "will give immediate assistance to the urban areas in the field of crime prevention and juvenile delinquency, parks and recreation facilities, and highways and rapid transit," bore a striking resemblance to the Bowdoin Commission. Campaigning vigorously to make the runoff, Carter launched numerous attacks on Arnall. He accused Arnall of misusing highway funds when he was governor, depicted him as an extremist whose policies would disrupt the state, and charged that his law enforcement proposals were "an attempt to create a police state." Moreover, he claimed that Arnall's candidacy was growing weaker, that he had alienated many Democrats, and that Arnall as the head of the Democratic ticket would be the "kiss of death" in many local elections.

---

[28] *Savannah Evening Press*, May 18, 19, 1966; *Atlanta Constitution*, May 19, 1966; Harold Paulk Henderson, "The 1966 Gubernatorial Election in Georgia" (Ph.D. diss., University of Southern Mississippi, 1982).

[29] Newspaper clippings in Gubernatorial Campaign, 1966 folder, Newsclipping file, Jimmy Carter Papers, Georgia Department of Archives and History, Atlanta.

"Ellis Arnall is an albatross around the necks of the Democratic party," Carter told a Canton audience, and his image "represents everything Georgia voters dislike about President Johnson, the national Democratic party and the Georgia Democratic party." When the votes were counted, Arnall, as expected, came in first with 29.4 percent. Carter's hard-hitting style of campaigning paid off as he surged into third place with 20.9 percent, nosing out Gray with 19.4 percent and easily outdistancing Byrd (5.1 percent) and O'Kelley (1.7 percent). But Carter did not catch Maddox who came in second with 23.5 percent and thereby made the runoff. In the runoff two weeks later, the uneducated and inexperienced Maddox, benefitting from crossover Republican votes, surprisingly defeated Arnall 443,055 to 373,004.[30]

Ordinarily, the Democratic nominee automatically became governor, but this year the Republicans had a strong candidate in Howard "Bo" Callaway, West Point graduate, wealthy heir to a textile fortune, and extremely conservative congressman from the Sixth District. The polls consistently indicated that he had an excellent chance of defeating any of the Democrats and becoming Georgia's next governor. With Maddox, Georgia's most fanatical defender of racial segregation as the Democratic nominee, Callaway's chances seemed promising indeed.

Sanders, accompanied by his wife and her art teacher Ouida Canaday, was in Europe visiting Amsterdam, London, Rotterdam, Brussels, and Paris on a combination business-pleasure tour when the runoff took place. After attending several receptions, including the opening of a Mead Packaging plant in Rotterdam, and making many contacts for future international trade with Georgia firms, Sanders returned home on October 9. The two artists, however, remained in Europe for two more weeks, traveling to Switzerland and Italy where they enjoyed breaktaking scenery and studied some of the world's greatest masterpieces of art. The primary results deeply disappointed Sanders. He always trusted the judgment of the people, but in 1966 something had gone wrong. They had rejected qualified candidates in favor of less qualified men. Undoubtedly the rioting and racial unrest had influenced the outcome, he mused. As a partisan Democrat, Sanders shuddered to think that a Republican, and an archconservative at that, might succeed him. But the

---

[30]Ibid.; *Official Register, 1965–1966*, pp. 1738, 1779.

only other choice was Maddox, a man who had gained international notoriety by refusing to serve Negroes at his restaurant and eventually closed it rather than allow it to be integrated. By training and temperament Maddox was unqualified for the job, and Sanders feared what he would do as Georgia's chief executive. But the governor's commitment to party loyalty was so strong that he had no choice. He felt compelled to support Maddox. Upon returning from Europe, he told reporters, "I am going to vote for the nominee of the Democratic party. I'm a Democrat and I'm going to stay in the Democratic party." When reporters questioned his support of Maddox, Sanders pointed out the obvious—"He beat my candidate in a fair race."[31]

At its convention in Macon on October 15, the Democratic party formally named Maddox as it candidate for governor and installed his ally, Albany publisher James H. Gray, as the new party chairman. The convention honored Sanders by adopting a thirteen-point resolution praising the accomplishments of his administration. Sanders, at the peak of his popularity within the party, made a strong statement of support for Maddox and party unity. He also took the opportunity to deliver some well-chosen barbs at leading Democrats. "I've been a Democrat when it was not popular with a majority of voting Georgians. Some of you here remember those days," he said. Then, looking out into the audience, he got a big laugh when he added: "I'm glad to see a lot of you back." Among those he welcomed back into the fold were both Maddox and Gray who had bolted the party for Goldwater in 1964. Chiding Senator Talmadge, who had indicated he planned to go to Europe before the general election, Sanders commented that some Democratic office holders want to support Maddox "under the cloak of darkness and in some far off place where no one can hear or see them." Emphasizing the importance of party loyalty, he concluded: "A man should be loyal to his country, his family, to his God and to his political party—and don't you ever forget it." After completing his remarks, Sanders, along with outgoing chairman Fuqua, left the city auditorium as the convention gave him a standing ovation.[32]

---

[31]*Atlanta Constitution*, October 14, 1966; undated *Atlanta Constitution* clipping in Foy Newspaper Collection; *Savannah Morning News*, October 1, 1966.

[32]Daniel, *Addresses of Carl Sanders*, pp. 218-20; *Atlanta Journal and Constitution*,

Despite his concerns about Maddox's inadequacies, Sanders remained loyal to his party, but he refused to campaign for the Democratic candidate for governor. Earlier in the campaign he had backed Arnall for governor and George T. Smith for lieutenant governor. Though trailing Peter Zack Geer in the primary, Smith defeated him handily in the runoff. In the general election Sanders concentrated his attention on the amendments, urging the voters to back the educational amendments and the rapid transit amendment. He said as little as possible about the gubernatorial race and undoubtedly wished he had a better alternative. So did thousands of disgruntled moderate and liberal Democrats who, lacking Sanders's strong commitment to party loyalty, agonized over the unappealing choices for governor. Suddenly a movement began to write in Ellis Arnall as a protest vote. Arnall did not participate in the write-in effort, nor did he discourage it. Sanders, by contrast, spoke out against it, but the movement gained momentum nevertheless. On November 8, more than 50,000 voters, unwilling to support either Maddox or Callaway, cast write-in votes for Arnall. Since Maddox and Callaway split the popular vote almost evenly, with only three thousand votes separating the candidates, the write-in votes prevented either from securing a majority. The result was utter confusion. Not since the three-governors controversy twenty years earlier had the state experienced such a constitutional dilemma. Expecting to leave office quietly and resume his law practice, Sanders found himself in the midst of a constitutional crisis that had to be resolved before he could leave the governorship.[33]

October 16, 1966.

[33]*Atlanta Constitution*, October 14, 25, 1966; Cook, "Sanders: An Oral History," p. 62; Harold Paulk Henderson, *The Politics of Change in Georgia: A Political Biography of Ellis Arnall* (Athens: University of Georgia Press, 1991) pp. 232-42.

Governor Sanders faces a stack of 150 bills, part of the 750 measures passed by the General Assembly in 1966.

Georgia's top elected officials: Senator Herman Talmadge, Governor Sanders, and Senator Richard Russell.

Chapter 17

The End of an Era

As soon as the votes in Georgia's 1966 gubernatorial race were tabulated, groups of citizens filed lawsuits challenging the results. Since the Democrats held 183 of the 205 seats in the House and 47 of the 54 Senate seats, the Maddox camp insisted that the General Assembly should make the choice between Callaway and Maddox. Callaway forces countered by arguing that the Republican candidate should be proclaimed governor because he won a plurality of the votes. Any other decision, they maintained, would deny the will of the people. A third argument came from the American Civil Liberties Union. It demanded an entirely new election open to any candidates since neither Callaway nor Maddox had received a majority of the vote. Later a fourth argument reached the courts when a group of citizens brought suit to keep Sanders in office until the next regular election in 1970. How the courts would resolve this legal tangle was anyone's guess. The only certainty during the entire controversy was that Sanders would remain as governor until his successor was properly chosen. In view of the complexities of the issues and the slowness of the courts, it looked as if he might have to remain in office weeks or even months beyond the scheduled end of his term.[1]

On November 11, only three days after the election, Chief Judge Elbert Tuttle of the Fifth Circuit Court of Appeals, speaking for the three-judge federal court, gave a "strong tentative view" that the Georgia legislature cannot choose a governor. A week later, judges Tuttle, Griffin Bell, and Lewis Morgan confirmed the tentative ruling by declaring unconstitutional article 4, section l, paragraph 4 of the Georgia Constitution. That section required the General Assembly to elect a governor from the top two candidates in the event no candidate received a major-

---

[1] *Atlanta Constitution,* December 13, 1966; *Rome News-Tribune,* November 15, 25, December 2, 5, 1966.

ity. Callaway applauded the decision, and so did Maddox who assumed that the decision would allow the people to elect the governor. Governor Sanders, however, reacted negatively to the decision. Convinced that the General Assembly had the constitutional right to make the choice, he instructed Attorney General Arthur Bolton to appeal the decision to the United States Supreme Court as quickly as possible. The Supreme Court accepted the Georgia case and set November 30 as the date for oral arguments. The court's speedy action astonished Bolton, who commented that he had never before heard of the court moving so swiftly. Subsequently the court delayed the hearing until December 5 and rendered its verdict a week later. By a five to four vote the court, agreeing with Sanders, upheld the Georgia Constitution and reversed the lower court ruling. Speaking for the majority, Justice Hugo Black said it is Georgia's duty under its constitution "to proceed to have the General Assembly elect its governor from the two highest candidates in the election."[2]

While the lawsuits worked their way through the courts and the General Assembly prepared to choose a governor, Sanders continued to direct the affairs of state with a steady hand. Realizing that the new administration would have little time to get organized before the General Assembly convened, he prepared a new budget to expedite the transition to the new administration. After assembling his budget, Sanders met with both Maddox and Callaway to familiarize them with his proposals. The purpose of meeting with them, he bluntly explained, was for their information only. It was not to debate issues because "I'm going to put the budget together." Both candidates seemed to appreciate his efforts to have an orderly transition of power, and so did the press. Eugene Patterson of the *Atlanta Constitution* claimed that by courageously staying in charge, drawing a budget, and steadying the state, Sanders was at the "peak of his popularity" and "looks seven feet tall."[3]

In the waning weeks of his administration, Sanders got the opportunity to influence the state for many years by appointing two new justices to the Georgia Supreme Court. In mid-November seventy-three-year-old Justice Joseph Quillian announced his retirement. To replace him,

---

[2]*Atlanta Constitution*, December 12, 1966; *Rome News-Tribune*, November 11, 17, 20, 1966; "Picking Maddox," *Newsweek* 26 (December 26, 1966): 20.

[3]*Atlanta Constitution*, November 15, 16, 1966.

Sanders named H. E. Nichols of Rome, who was then presiding judge of the Second Division of the Court of Appeals. To fill his spot on the Court of Appeals, Sanders named Justice Quillian's son, J. Kelley Quillian, a thirty-six-year-old attorney from Winder. A month later, seventy-six-year-old Justice Tom Candler, a stalwart on the court since 1945, announced his retirement. Actually Candler had offered to retire a year earlier, but at Sanders's urging had remained on the bench. The governor accepted his resignation at this time so he could appoint Hiram Undercofler in his place. By all accounts, Undercofler had done an exceptional job as Sanders's Revenue Commissioner, and his elevation to the Supreme Court was widely praised. Sanders, who had the utmost respect for Undercofler, often relied on him, along with J. B. Fuqua and Bob Richardson, as his most trusted advisers. Knowing the financial sacrifice Undercofler had made to serve in his administration, Sanders wanted to reward him with a federal judgeship, and he fully expected Undercofler to receive one. When Sanders decided against the Senate race, he informed Senator Russell and asked him to secure the next federal judgeship for Undercofler. The old senator, who had been pressuring President Johnson to offer Sanders a federal post to keep him out of the Senate race, was greatly relieved that he would not have to campaign against Sanders. He readily agreed, promising Sanders faithfully that Undercofler would be appointed to the next vacancy on the federal district court in the Northern District. Some months later an opening occurred, but, to Sanders's surprise, the appointment went to Newell Edenfield. Since Russell broke his word, Sanders's respect for him, never particularly high, dropped even lower. In the absence of a federal appointment, Sanders placed Undercofler on the Georgia Supreme Court, where both he and Nichols served with distinction for many years and eventually served as chief justice.[4]

In addition to preparing the budget and making these judicial appointments, Sanders made a host of other appointments, even though he expected the next governor to reject many of them. Later the Senate rejected seventeen of his appointments, including: John Harper to the Pardon and Parole Board, Charles Smithgall to the Board of Regents,

---

[4]Ibid., December 1, 1966; press releases November 15, December 15, 1966, box 35, Sanders Collection, Law Library; Sanders, "Interviews in 1990," pp. 144-45, 190.

Scott Candler, Jr., and Lonnie Sweat to the Board of Education, Bob Richardson to the State Scholarship Commission, and Edgar Dunlap to the Game and Fish Commission. Many other Sanders appointees, however, received Senate approval, including William Morris, III to the Board of Regents, Doug Barnard to the Highway Board, and J. B. Fuqua to the Georgia Science and Technology Commission. In Georgia politics the old maxim "to the victor belongs the spoils" still prevailed, and Sanders was pleased that some of his appointees remained in office in the Maddox administration.[5]

Sanders also was pleased when the bids for leasing the state-owned Western and Atlantic Railroad were opened in mid-December. Controversy had surrounded that railroad, which ran from Chattanooga to the Chattahooche River, ever since the state had built it back in the 1830s and 1840s. When it failed to bring in the expected revenue, many disgruntled Georgians demanded that the state dispose of the "white elephant." The state kept it, however, and by leasing the W and A to a private railroad, managed to recoup its original investment and earn a steady profit year after year. Since 1919, the W and A had contributed $540,000 annually to the state coffers. With his keen business acumen, Sanders thought the payments should be substantially higher. The highest bid came from the Southern Railway, which agreed to pay the state $995,000 annually for the W and A. When taxes and all other aspects of the lease were computed, Sanders expected the state to receive a total of $1,750,000 a year. In the long history of the W and A, this was the first time the lease had been decided by competitive bids, and the results satisfied Sanders.[6]

Early in his administration, Sanders had told a reporter he was determined to move the state ahead—fast. In order to do so he needed every available dollar. Thus, he continually sought to eliminate waste and inefficiency throughout state government and to generate new sources of income. By the end of his term, collections by the Revenue Department passed the $2 billion milestone, thanks in part to the extraordinarily effective job done by Hiram Undercofler as revenue commissioner.

---

[5]Press releases January 4, 5, 1967, box 35, Sanders Collection, Law Library; *Atlanta Constitution*, February 17, 1967.

[6]*Atlanta Constitution*, December 13, 1966.

During the Sanders years state income increased from $445,747,368 in 1962–1963 to $617,279,294 in 1965–1966. The total increase in state income during the four-year period came to $625 million or 42 percent. The revenue increase during the Vandiver years, by contrast, was only 28 percent.[7]

Although Sanders consistently had pumped additional revenue into the prison system, serious problems remained. As soon as new facilities opened they were filled with inmates, as Georgia's high rate of incarceration continually swelled the number of inmates. Despite the efforts of Sanders and his predecessors, many facilities remained terribly overcrowded. One of those overcrowded prisons, the Georgia Industrial Institute at Alto, became an issue in December 1966 when the press reported "widespread brutality and mistreatment of prisoners" there. The charges came from two newly elected legislators who, upon touring the facility, were shown a cache of chains and clubs which, according to inmates, the guards had used on prisoners. Sanders exploded. The Sanders administration "will neither tolerate nor condone such conditions," he asserted. He directed the attorney general to make an immediate investigation and ordered the Georgia Bureau of Investigation to lend its full support. "We will immediately discharge any correctional officer who is found to have mistreated the inmates in his care, and we will discharge any superior officer who would, with foreknowledge, permit such treatment." To reduce overcrowding, Sanders transferred two hundred "honor inmates" to other facilities and promised to seek additional funds from the legislature for upgrading the facility. Having no patience with those who abused their powers, he promised that "those who are guilty will be rooted out."[8]

No previous governor in Georgia's history had traveled as much as Sanders, and he maintained his busy schedule of activities to the end of his term. Since the state was expanding rapidly, he traveled to some part of Georgia practically every day to dedicate a new airport, welcome center, stretch of highway, or building. The schedule was tiring, but the

---

[7]*Atlanta Journal,* December 30, 1966, January 10, 1967; "State of Georgia Summary Statement of Financial Condition, June 30, 1966," Department of Revenue folder, box 3, Augustus Turnbull Collection, Russell Library, University of Georgia.

[8]*Atlanta Constitution,* December 14, 1966; press release December 13, 1966, box 35, Sanders Collection, Law Library.

governor enjoyed meeting the people and seeing the tangible results of his legislative program. He also delivered speeches in various parts of the country, spent much time in Washington looking out for Georgia's interests, and traveled extensively in the South. Recognized as a spokesman for the South, he served as chairman of the Southern Regional Education Board, chairman of the Appalachian Governors' Conference, vice chairman of the Southern Governors' Conference, and as a member of the Executive Committee of the National Governors' Conference.[9] Additionally, Sanders traveled abroad on several occasions as the chief salesman for Georgia. Working with the Department of Industry and Trade, he developed contacts in Europe and the Far East to market Georgia products and lure foreign investors to Georgia. As a result of his efforts, Kagoshima, Japan, became a sister state to Georgia. As the first governor committed to developing Georgia's international potential, his preliminary efforts laid a groundwork for the extensive foreign trade and investment that subsequently developed.[10]

Sanders never complained about the hectic pace he set for himself nor the mundane ceremonial duties he was expected to perform. On the contrary, he thrived on a full schedule and never seemed to mind the ceremonial functions. In fact, four ceremonies near the end of his term brought special pleasure to Carl and Betty. On October 30, they dedicated five new buildings at Georgia Southern College. One of them was the Foy Fine Arts Building, named for Betty's father, Jesse Ponita "J. P." Foy. A week before his term ended, Sanders dedicated two dormitories at the Georgia School for the Deaf in Cave Spring. One of the dorms was named "The Carl E. Sanders Hall," named in his honor because of his firm commitment to education. Not to be outdone by Cave Spring, the University of Georgia, which had grown tremendously during the Sanders years, made November 30 "Carl Sanders Day." The University and the Athens community honored Sanders with a dinner, a number of gifts, and a plaque. Making the event even more special for the

---

[9]*Athens Banner-Herald,* November 27, 1966; Carl E. Sanders, *Age of Change, Time of Decision: A Report to the General Assembly and the People of Georgia on the Administration of Governor Carl E. Sanders, 1963–1967* (Atlanta: State Printers, 1967) p. 7.

[10]*Atlanta Journal,* November 28, 1966; Out of Country (1) folder, box 22, Sanders Collection, Law Library.

former Bulldog quarterback was a ceremony honoring the Sugar Bowl-bound Bulldogs for winning the Southeastern Conference championship with a record of nine wins and one loss. Indirectly, Sanders had contributed to the Bulldogs' success. For several years following the retirement of Wally Butts, the team had floundered under coach John Griffith. Determined to reestablish the winning tradition, Athletic Director Joel Eaves decided to change coaches. He found a promising young coach at Auburn that he wanted to hire, but Vince Dooley refused to take the job unless the University built a new dormitory for athletes. Sanders had never heard of Dooley, but, trusting Eaves's judgment, he agreed to the new dormitory. Dooley then accepted the offer and quickly transformed the moribund program into the SEC championship.[11]

A week before Sanders's alma mater honored him, his hometown of Augusta made November 22 "Carl Sanders Appreciation Day." The governor, serving as grand marshal for the annual Christmas parade, waved to the 50,000 Augustans who lined the streets. In the evening the whole Sanders family—Carl, Betty, the children, and his mother—was honored at a festive banquet. The highlight of the festivities came when Mayor Millard Beckum presented Carl the keys to a brand new Cadillac, a gift from Augusta businessmen and citizens to their favorite son.[12]

Amid all the accolades, gifts, honors, banquets, and awards, the Sanders family's joy suddenly was subdued when the Governor received a death threat. It was not the first one Sanders had received. And, despite all the security precautions that had been taken, he—and all other public officials—remained vulnerable to attack. After all, if President Kennedy could not be protected, could any public official feel completely safe? Every time Governor Sanders appeared in public he knew he might be the target for an assassin, a terrorist, or a mentally deranged person. It was a danger that came with the job, and he lived with it constantly. But since he could do nothing about the situation, he rarely thought about the danger. In November 1963, when Kennedy was

---

[11]*Bulloch Herald,* October 27, 1966; *Athens Banner-Herald,* November 30, December 1, 1966; press release January 4, 1967, box 35, Sanders Collection, Law Library; *Atlanta Constitution,* January 10, 1967; Sanders, "Interviews in 1990," pp. 183-84.

[12]*Atlanta Journal,* November 23, 1966; telephone interview with Carl Sanders, August 26, 1992.

assassinated, Sanders's life also was threatened. Fortunately, nothing came of it, but Mrs. Sanders and the children were frightened until the culprit was apprehended. This latest death threat came while Sanders was addressing a banquet honoring the Bowdoin Commission. As a precaution, the Governor was escorted home by two State Patrol cars and Atlanta detectives. Sanders, who refused to dwell on such matters, had gone to bed when the suspect, a twenty-five-year-old mental patient from Virginia, was apprehended on the grounds of the Governor's Mansion.[13]

On January 6, the day after the death threat, the Georgia Supreme Court by a five-to-two vote upheld a lower court which had thrown out a suit seeking to have a runoff election between Maddox and Callaway. In essence, the ruling authorized the General Assembly to choose the governor. Although Sanders had acknowledged that he would not object if the court ordered a new election, he believed the state constitution allowed the General Assembly to make that decision, and his administration consistently had presented that argument in court. With the last legal hurdle overcome, the General Assembly at last could pick Sanders's successor.[14]

For several years Georgia legislators had sought greater independence from the governor. They grumbled that the governor had so much power they could not function as a coequal branch of government. They especially wanted a greater voice in budgetary matters and the power to select their own legislative leadership. Heretofore, Georgia governors had been so dominant that the General Assembly did little more than rubber stamp their programs. The General Assembly debated each governor's bills and sometimes made minor adjustments in his proposals, but ultimately it adopted the governor's budget and practically all of his legislative program. By appointing the speaker of the house and other key legislative leaders, the governor made sure that his people held the committee chairmanships and the major sources of power in the legislative branch. With his power over the purse strings, patronage, and the construction of highways, the governor had formidable weapons at

---

[13]*Atlanta Constitution*, January 6, 1967; *Atlanta Journal*, November 22, December 2, 1963.

[14]*Atlanta Constitution*, January 6, 7, 1967.

his disposal that enabled him to keep recalcitrant legislators in line. Any legislator bold enough to challenge the governor usually regretted his action. In short, the governor ran the state.

Sanders continued the long-standing tradition of gubernatorial control of the legislature. During his four years the legislature adopted all of the major programs he introduced, and it passed nothing of substance that he opposed. Sanders not only picked the speaker of the house, he communicated with him by installing a direct telephone line from his office to the speaker's podium. Sanders, expecting compliance from the legislature, accepted no deviation from his administration's aims. When Representative Joe Isenberg of Brunswick denounced on the House floor Sanders's plan to cut the pay of shopkeepers for collecting taxes, he learned how tough the governor could be. Since Sanders had appointed Isenberg as the Democratic nominee for the House seat, he was incensed by Isenberg's opposition. Summoning the inexperienced legislator to his office, the governor said to him: "You don't owe me. And I don't owe you anything. Get your ass out of my office. I don't want to ever see you again." Realizing that his district would get no more "goodies" from the Sanders administration, a crestfallen Isenberg trudged back into the House chamber and rose to speak on a point of personal privilege. "Mister speaker, I just want to tell you I have made a serious mistake," he began. He proceeded to reverse himself and even argue in favor of Sanders's compensation reduction for vendors.[15] Young Representative Nathan Dean of Rockmart had a similar experience. He had the audacity to vote against a Sanders budget. Representative James "Sloppy" Floyd, sitting directly behind Dean, nudged him and said: "Nathan, you have just made a bad mistake. Always vote with the governor on the Appropriations bill. Don't ever vote against the Appropriations bill because that is the only thing he really cares about." Soon afterwards, Dean received a visit from an experienced Sanders lieutenant who explained the facts of life to the freshman legislator. Dean, who never again challenged Sanders, later commented that Sanders ran the state "from his hip pocket."[16]

---

[15]Shipp, "Carl Sanders: The Man, The Legend, The Era," pp. 20-21.

[16]Dean interview, October 8, 1985; Nathan Dean interview by James Cook, October 2, 1989, Georgia Government Documentation Project, Special Collections,

A gangly young lawyer from Bremen named Tom Murphy, who would later serve as speaker of the house for many years, also learned the cost of opposing Sanders. Having campaigned enthusiastically for Sanders in the 1962 campaign, Representative Murphy was rewarded with the chairmanship of a standing committee. During the 1964 session, however, Murphy strongly opposed one the Sanders measures on the floor of the House. Learning of his opposition, Sanders called Murphy into his office and urged him to "get on the team." Murphy, stubborn as a Georgia mule, ignored the Governor's admonition and continued to speak out against the measure. Sanders retaliated not only by replacing Murphy as committee chairman but also by moving his seat to the back row of the House. There Murphy remained for the last two years of Sanders's term, learning the cost of opposing a strong governor.[17]

Ordinarily the new governor had a period of four months, from his election in the Democratic primary until his inauguration in January, to organize his administration and prepare his legislative agenda. But when the General Assembly convened on January 9, 1967, the governor had not even been chosen. Legislative leaders, chaffing under gubernatorial control, saw in the peculiar circumstances of the election a golden opportunity to assert their independence of the governor. Taking full advantage of the political uncertainty, while the courts decided how Georgia's next governor would be chosen, the legislature held several meetings and organized itself without any input from the next governor. At a secret caucus, the House chose Sanders nemesis George L. Smith, a former speaker, as the new speaker. When the General Assembly officially convened, the House promptly elected Smith as speaker, and he made the committee assignments. In contrast to Smith, the House then chose two Sanders stalwarts to leadership positions: Maddox Hale as speaker pro tem and George Busbee as majority leader. By choosing its own leadership before the governor was chosen, the House broke away from the governor's control and achieved a degree of independence it never relinquished. Consequently, no subsequent governor dominated

---

Georgia State University, Atlanta.

[17]Sanders, "Interviews in 1990," pp. 187-89; Tom Murphy interview by Cliff Kuhn, March 28, 1988, Georgia Government Documentation Project, Special Collections, Georgia State University, Atlanta.

the legislature as Sanders did. He was the last of Georgia's all-powerful governors. This move toward legislative independence had been building for years, but, as Representative Crawford Ware of Hoganville observed, "The governor's status made it possible."[18]

The next day, January 10, the General Assembly met in joint session for the purpose of canvassing the returns of the general election. Lieutenant Governor Peter Zack Geer presided. Secretary of State Ben Fortson delivered the files and tellers were chosen. Counting the write-in votes proved troubling, and Geer had to resolve several protests. Finally, after eliminating many write-ins, the count was completed. Geer and Speaker Smith certified the vote totals as follows: Arnall 52,831, Maddox 450,626, and Callaway 453,665. Geer then ordered the call of the roll to elect the governor of Georgia. As expected, Maddox won easily, getting 182 votes to Callaway's 66. Eleven members, mostly black legislators, abstained. Following the vote, Geer declared Maddox the governor, and Associate Justice Carlton Mobley administered the oath of office to him.[19]

The next day, January 11, Maddox was inaugurated amid the usual pomp and ceremony. The Great Seal of the State was transferred from Sanders's possession to the new governor, thus symbolizing the transition of power from one administration to the next. After the ceremony, Sanders congratulated the new governor, put on his coat, and slipped out of the Governor's Office. When questioned by reporters, he replied: "I have nothing to say about what has happened. I have turned over the keys of the government to the next governor and am a free man." Thus ended the Sanders years, a remarkable period in Georgia's history.[20]

Sanders had hoped for an orderly transition to the next administration. He also had hoped that his successor would share his political philosophy so that the programs he had initiated could continue without interruption. Unfortunately, that did not occur. Still, Sanders could take pride in what his administration had accomplished. At the beginning of his administration he had pledged to give the people of Georgia "a

---

[18]*House Journal, 1967,* pp. 5-44; *Savannah Morning News,* January 1, 1967; Dean interview, October 2, 1989.

[19]*House Journal, 1967,* pp. 50-59.

[20]Ibid., p. 77; *Savannah Morning News,* January 11, 1967.

competent, honest, morally responsible, fiscally sound, effective, efficient and constructive government." Four years later, he could truthfully tell the General Assembly, "We have fulfilled that pledge." His administration made impressive advances in many areas, and by practically any standard of measurement the political, economic and social condition of Georgia was much healthier when he turned over the reins of government to Maddox than when he had inherited them four years earlier from Vandiver. He left office the way a politician should exit—at the crest of his popularity, basking in almost universal praise from the media. Typical of the press assessments was the *Rome News-Tribune*, which editorialized that the Sanders record "consists of definite progress in every field of state responsibilities—public health, education, welfare, trade and industry." More importantly, it continued, in addition to providing dedicated, honest government, he "projected for Georgia a national image of responsibility, integrity and vision."[21]

Contemporaries recognized that Sanders had been an excellent governor and that his administration had been one of the most successful in Georgia's history, and the passage of time has only reinforced those early impressions. By pressuring the legislature to reapportion the House and congressional districts, allocate more funds to education, produce a new election code and state constitution, and implement the numerous reforms of the Bowdoin Commission for efficiency in government, the Sanders administration addressed the state's most pressing needs and compiled an impressive record of legislation. In addition, amendments adopted by the legislature and approved by the people made possible rapid transit in Atlanta as well as school and county consolidation. The Sanders administration established a new Highway Board and expanded the construction of highways, reorganized the welfare program by establishing a new Department of Family and Children's Services, modernized the Revenue Department and brought record revenues into the state, reorganized the Health Department and greatly improved the treatment of the mentally ill, opened Georgia's first Police Academy to provide instruction in the latest techniques for law enforcement officers, reorganized and expanded the Game and Fish

---

[21]*Atlanta Journal*, January 10, 1967; *Rome News-Tribune*, January 15, 1967; Daniel, *Addresses of Carl Sanders*, p. 54.

Commission and the Parks Department, upgraded the prison system with additional facilities and an emphasis on training and rehabilitation, and built a new Governor's Mansion. In establishing the Water Quality Control Board and the Governor's Commission on the Status of Women the Sanders administration displayed considerable foresight by showing a concern for the environment and women's rights—issues that would become increasingly important in later years.[22]

The most outstanding accomplishments of the Sanders administration, however, came in the areas of education and economic development. Determined to raise the economic level of his state, Sanders directed the Department of Industry and Trade to make long-range plans to attract new industries, and he made sure that other state agencies cooperated fully in the quest for industrial expansion. His efforts achieved impressive results as $1 billion worth of new and expanded industries located in Georgia, 200,000 new jobs were created, employment set a new record, and unemployment remained far below the national average during the Sanders years. Improving the infrastructure was another essential ingredient in economic growth. The Sanders administration spent more money on roads and highways than any previous administration, expanded the port facilities at Savannah and Brunswick, and led the nation in airport construction. Indeed, two-thirds of the paved airports in Georgia were constructed during the Sanders administration. A skilled pilot himself, Sanders recognized that modern industry demanded convenient air transportation. He also understood the economic impact the federal government could make, and he skillfully worked with state agencies and local governments to secure available federal funds. Friendly with both Presidents Kennedy and Johnson, he believed that more could be accomplished through cooperation with the federal government than by blaming Washington for the state's problems, as many of his predecessors had done.[23]

Cooperation was a key feature of his administrative style, not only between the state and federal governments but also within the state bureaucracy. "Working together" toward a common goal was the way Sanders phrased his style. At heart a problem-solver, he wasted no time

---

[22]*Atlanta Constitution*, March 14, 1966; Sanders, *Age of Change*, pp. 21, 23.
[23]Sanders, *Age of Change*, pp. 6, 29-33.

complaining about matters beyond his control. Instead of excuses, he wanted results. And to a large extent he achieved them by forceful executive leadership. As governor, he became the axis around which state government revolved. Yet, even though he had definite goals for the state to attain and was a powerful executive, he was no dictator. Backed by a popular mandate, he sought to implement his program by cooperating with the legislature and patiently convincing members to support him. Ordinarily that approach got the desired results, and judiciously doling out or withholding government favors also smoothed the legislative process. He willingly compromised and made minor concessions to achieve his major objectives, but if conciliatory efforts failed he resorted to more powerful measures. While he preferred the carrot, he used the stick when the occasion demanded it, as Hosea Williams, Denmark Groover, and other opponents found out.

Sanders had promised that education would be the top priority of his administration, and it was. He understood that Georgia was shifting from a rather simple agrarian economy to a more complex urbanized and industrialized economy, and in order for the state to attract new high-technology industries and federal research grants it must transform its educational system quickly or lag behind other states in economic growth. Thus, for Sanders, education was the key that unlocked the door to future growth and prosperity. Consequently, he directed nearly sixty percent of every tax dollar to education. By the end of his term substantial progress had been achieved. His administration raised teachers' salaries $1,400 per year (more than twice as much as any previous governor), added 10,000 new teachers, and built more schools and classrooms than had any previous administration. Not only did the Sanders administration commit more revenue to education, it also adopted noteworthy reforms in the system. It established a Master Plan for Education, set minimum standards, and increased local support for education. In addition, it began the Governor's Honors Program for the brightest students, developed an extensive educational television network, encouraged school consolidation, and greatly expanded vocational training.[24]

---

[24]Ibid., pp. 15-17; "Education Progress in Georgia 1963–1967," Personal (1) folder, box 22, Sanders Collection, Law Library.

Even more impressive than the gains in the public schools were the changes in higher education. More than eight hundred new faculty members were added to the University System and average faculty salaries increased 32.5 percent, moving Georgia from tenth to fourth place among southern states. Under the leadership of Chancellor George Simpson, a network of junior colleges was begun. Four existing junior colleges—Georgia Southwestern, Armstrong State, Augusta, and Columbus—were raised to four-year status. A new dental school was established at the Medical College at Augusta. To accommodate rapidly expanding college enrollments, the Sanders administration appropriated a record $176.5 million for new building construction. To put that amount in perspective, the University System received more state money for building construction in the four years of the Sanders administration than it had received in the previous thirty-one years of its existence. Additionally, the percentage of the state budget allocated to the University System increased from 7.3% to 10% under Sanders. Never before had education received such emphasis in Georgia, and for the University System the Sanders administration was a "golden era."[25]

Sanders was fortunate to be governor in the early sixties, and he enjoyed several advantages that few governors have had. Not only were political changes possible at that time, they also were fashionable, thanks to the climate of reform produced by the Kennedy-Johnson administrations. Sanders also was very lucky that the trauma of racially integrating Georgia's schools had been faced by his predecessor. Had that issue arisen a few years later, his accomplishments probably would have been diminished substantially. In addition to facing the ordeal of integration, the Vandiver administration also had taken preliminary steps toward modernizing Georgia's government, especially in the area of finances. Without this essential groundwork, Sanders could not have achieved all that he did. Since Sanders and Vandiver respected each other and worked together harmoniously, there was continuity of ideas and

---

[25]Sanders, *Age of Change*, p. 20; "Summary of Budget Allotments from State Treasury Receipts," Department of Revenue folder, box 3, Carl Sanders Series, Augustus Turnbull Collection, Russell Library, University of Georgia; University System of Georgia, *Annual Report, 1965–1966*; Dyer, *The University of Georgia*, pp. 335-45; Cameron Fincher, *Historical Development of the University System of Georgia: 1932–1990* (Athens: Institute of Higher Education, University of Georgia, 1991) pp. 53-61.

personnel and a smooth transition of power. Sanders also had the good fortune to be governor during a very prosperous era. Obviously, with more revenue flowing into the treasury, more programs could be funded. Finally, Sanders was the last governor who totally dominated the General Assembly. No recent governor has benefited from the combination of so many positive forces at work as Sanders. These factors contributed substantially to the success of his administration, but his competent and energetic leadership translated opportunity into reality.[26]

Every modern governor of Georgia has achieved some degree of "progress," and in many instances impressive lists of accomplishments could be cited. Governor Carter, for example, reorganized the executive branch of government, while Governor Busbee updated the state constitution, started a kindergarten program, and served two terms. But among modern Georgia governors, only the administration of Ellis Arnall (1943–1947) rivals the Sanders administration for progressive accomplishments. Actually, there were many similarities in the two administrations. Both Arnall and Sanders were energetic young lawyers who, after graduating from the University of Georgia Law School, served in the legislature, rose quickly to positions of leadership, then with aggressive campaigning upset powerful, racist, former governors. Arnall was thirty-five when he defeated Gene Talmadge; Sanders was thirty-seven when he defeated Marvin Griffin. Both campaigned as progressive advocates of a "New South," and both delivered what they had promised. Both leaders, convinced that poverty and ignorance were twin liabilities holding back the state, attempted to establish a new image for Georgia and a more favorable climate for economic expansion. Both understood the pivotal importance of education. Education was the most important issue in Arnall's election, and by promising to take politics out of education he emerged as the champion of education. Sanders emphasized education as his top priority and accomplished unprecedented improvement in Georgia's public schools and colleges.

Both Arnall and Sanders reorganized the Highway Department and reformed the prisons. Arnall hired the first expert to direct the prison system and ended the chain gang and other notorious practices. Sanders opened a new diagnostic center, built new facilities, and emphasized

---

[26]Cook, "Carl Sanders and the Politics of the Future," p. 184.

training and rehabilitation. Both Arnall and Sanders saw the need for constitutional revision; Arnall produced the Constitution of 1945, and Sanders produced the Constitution of 1964, which a federal court refused to allow the people to vote on.

In contrast to the virulent racism of Gene Talmadge, Arnall insisted on accepting court decisions to allow blacks to vote in the Democratic primary. Likewise Sanders, in contrast to Griffin and others, accepted court decisions regarding school integration. Both Arnall and Sanders criticized the Ku Klux Klan and were regarded as moderates or liberals on the race issue. Both governors proved to be honest, efficient, frugal administrators. Arnall managed to pay off the state's indebtedness, while Sanders left an unprecedented $140 million in the treasury for his successor.

Arnall admired Franklin Roosevelt, worked cooperatively with him, and became closely associated with him. After Roosevelt died, he developed an excellent working relationship with President Harry Truman. Sanders also developed an excellent relationship with Presidents Kennedy and Johnson. Both young loyal Democratic governors received much favorable media attention, became nationally known, and frequently were rumored for high federal office.

In many ways Arnall was Georgia's first New South governor. Twenty years later, after an interval of very conservative and racist governors, Sanders picked up where Arnall had left off. The most comprehensive survey to date which evaluated Georgia's governors was compiled in 1985. In it, fifty Georgia historians ranked the governors from Arnall to Busbee in a variety of categories. On urban affairs issues, Sanders received the highest rating; in the field of education, Arnall ranked first and Sanders second; and in the broad category of effectiveness in office, the historians ranked Arnall first and Sanders second. In similar ways both Arnall and Sanders realistically addressed the most pressing problems of their day and brought substantial progress to the state. By implementing a vast array of New South reforms, Arnall and Sanders helped erase Georgia's image as a rural, racist, reactionary state.[27]

---

[27]Ibid., pp. 169-84; Harold P. Henderson, "Ellis Arnall and the Politics of Progress," in *Georgia Governors in an Age of Change*, pp. 25-39; Henderson, *The Politics of Change in Georgia*; Cook, *Governors of Georgia*, pp. 255-59, 283-88.

Sanders returned to private life reluctant to leave the limelight, but satisfied that he had given the state his best efforts for four exhilarating years. In fact, shortly before leaving office, he confided to reporter Sam Hopkins: "I don't know how I could have done much more than I did." In Georgia's long history, no governor had ever worked harder at the job, traveled to more places, given more speeches, or performed more ceremonial duties than Sanders. By training, experience, and temperament, he was ideally suited to lead Georgia during a period of transition, change, and turmoil, and he thoroughly enjoyed the experience. A combination of visionary, planner, and practical politician, he was above all a leader—confident, capable, and tough. Certain that his administration had made a positive impact upon the state, Sanders acknowledged that his four years as governor had been "the most satisfying years of my life."[28]

---

[28]*Atlanta Constitution*, December 12, 1966; *Atlanta Journal*, January 10, 1967; *Athens Banner-Herald*, November 27, 1966; Daniel, *Addresses of Carl Sanders*, p. 66.

Chapter 18

1967–1970

Upon leaving the Governor's Mansion, the Sanders family moved into an expensive townhouse in Westchester Square in Ansley Park. A modern three-story structure, it was conveniently located in an established residential area, close to Piedmont Park and only a few blocks away from the old mansion they had resided in the past four years. Although luxuriously appointed and beautifully furnished with period pieces, it was quite small compared to the massive structure they left. Consequently, not enough space existed to accommodate all the items they had accumulated during the past four years. Even after eliminating nonessentials and storing more valuable possessions, the townhouse remained crowded. Betty Foy and Carl Jr. lived in the dormitory at Westminster School and spent little time at home, but the Sanders "family" now included an additional member, Bessie Matthews, as the Sanders family followed an old Southern tradition by hiring "live-in" domestic help.

Bessie was not the first domestic to become part of the Sanders family, for Helen Lawrence had preceded her by many years. Mrs. Sanders's health was so precarious following the birth of Carl Jr. that she had to have domestic help. Helen, a quiet twenty-one-year-old black woman from Augusta, was hired when Carl Jr. was only two months old. She cooked, cleaned house, helped care for the children, and generally did whatever needed to be done. Hardworking and practical, Helen soon became an indispensable part of the Sanders household. Instead of accompanying the family to Atlanta in 1962, she remained in Augusta caring for Carl's parents. After they died, she rejoined the family in Atlanta, and thus has been continuously employed by the Sanders family for more than thirty-nine years.[1]

---

[1] Sanders, "Interviews in 1990," p. 145; Betty Foy Sanders interview, November 7, 1990.

Originally from Fort Gaines, Georgia, Bessie first became acquainted with the Sanders family when she worked in the Governor's Mansion. Governor Sanders was so impressed by her work ethic and practical skills that he hired her to work for his family when he left office. A short, round-faced black woman with a serious demeanor, she never divulged her age but appeared to be several years older than Governor Sanders. She washed and ironed clothes, cleaned house, and did all of the household chores except running errands, which she was unable to do because she never learned to drive a car. An excellent cook, Bessie prepared a wide variety of foods in the Southern country style that the whole family enjoyed. Carl, in particular, raved about Bessie's cooking and often remarked that he preferred her cooking to the food prepared in any restaurant in Atlanta. In addition to her culinary skills, Bessie also possessed great wisdom which over the years she imparted to the children. Considered part of the family, Bessie moved into the townhouse and lived with Carl and Betty. With three adults and occasionally two teenaged children living under one roof, the townhouse seemed cramped after living in the spacious Governor's Mansion, but they could tolerate the inconveniences for a while since they did not intend to remain there permanently.[2]

Ever since leaving Augusta, the Sanders family had planned to return home when the four-year governorship ended. Betty, especially, eagerly longed to own a large house with high ceilings and plenty of space for the whole family. Assuming they would return to Augusta, she had worked on plans for a gorgeous new home. Betty and Carl purchased a ten-acre lot from the estate of Judge Henry Hammond, Carl's first law partner, and even staked it out in preparation for building when Carl expressed reservations. Like Betty, he had planned to return to Augusta and reestablish his law practice. Certain that he could make a good living there, he looked forward to resuming his practice and enjoying the companionship of old friends. But while Augusta had many attractions for him, so did Atlanta, already a booming city and apparently destined to become the dominant city of the South. As governor he had contributed to the city's growth, and he very much wanted to play a role in its

---

[2]Ibid.; Betty Foy Botts interview, January 28, 1991; interview with Bessie Matthews, Atlanta, May 7, 1991.

future development. Atlanta had so much potential that he was reluctant to leave it. To resolve the dilemma, he decided to remain in Atlanta temporarily and start a new law firm there while maintaining his old law firm in Augusta. After a few months of experimenting, he would then decide on a permanent location.

Betty seemed to realize even before Carl did that after being governor and operating on a national and international level, he would no longer be content living in Augusta. Because so many things had happened to them in the past four years, returning to Augusta would necessitate quite an adjustment. Betty knew that her husband thrived on challenges. He had been that way as long as she had known him. For him to be happy he had to be challenged. Always looking ahead, projecting, building, developing, planning, he could not be satisfied with the status quo. Knowing her husband as she did, she understood that he needed more stimulating challenges than Augusta could provide. Since there were no mountains in Augusta that he had not already climbed, he would be stifled there. But Atlanta, she sensed, was a different story. Building a law firm there, starting it from scratch and competing against the huge established law firms was a challenge Sanders could not resist. Understanding her husband's needs, Betty put aside her house plans, adjusted to the townhouse in Ansley Park, and made plans to remain in Atlanta.[3]

While Sanders was governor, his law firm in Augusta operated under the name Thurmond, Hester, Jolles and McElmurray. Although Sanders was no longer a partner, he kept in touch with the firm and talked with his friend Bert Hester almost every day while he was governor. When Sanders's term as governor ended, the firm was reorganized as Sanders, Hester & Holley. The new partner, Gene Holley, was another ambitious young Augustan. Like Sanders, Holley was a Baptist, a graduate of the Lumpkin School of Law at the University of Georgia, and an accomplished pilot. Bright and aggressive, he was a member of Phi Beta Kappa and a highly decorated veteran of World War II and the Korean War. When J. B. Fuqua decided not to seek reelection to the Senate in 1964, Holley replaced him. Two years later he won reelection, and soon he became one of Georgia's most powerful state senators. Prior to joining

---

[3]Betty Foy Sanders interview, November 7, 1990.

Sanders and Hester, Holley had practiced in Augusta for ten years, most of that period with Bill Congdon.[4]

By coincidence the firm of Sanders, Hester & Holley was located in the Commerce Building in Augusta, and the new firm Sanders started in Atlanta also had an office in the Commerce Building at the corner of Marietta and Broad Street. To run the office Sanders hired two secretaries from the Governor's Office: Mrs. Benny Tackett and Mrs. Kathryn Frierson. Benny, who previously worked for the Game and Fish Commission, began working in the Governor's Office in December 1963. Since she was familiar with all the files and knew his political allies, Sanders used her primarily to help with political activities. Kathryn had been Sanders's personal secretary in Augusta for nine years, but in 1962 she moved to North Carolina with her husband, a medical student, who did his residency at Duke Medical Center. Two years later they were divorced, and Kathryn, a single parent with two small girls, inquired about a job with her former employers in Augusta. Her timing was fortuitous. Hester knew that Sanders's personal secretary was pregnant and did not plan to work after the birth of her child. Instead of returning to her old job in Augusta, Kathryn moved to Atlanta and resumed her position as Sanders's personal secretary. She helped Sanders establish the new law office, kept the books, and did all of his personal work. Unfortunately, cancer tragically ended her short life at age forty. After Kathryn's death in 1971, Benny became Sanders's personal secretary. Demonstrating competence, loyalty, and tactfulness, she quickly gained Sanders's confidence and has remained in that sensitive position, serving as his personal secretary and confidante for more than twenty years. While no employee may be indispensable, Benny came awfully close. Sanders stated many times that when Benny decided to retire he would quit too.[5]

To assist with the legal work, Sanders hired two young lawyers—Norman Underwood and Gerald Burrows. Underwood, from Red Bud, Georgia, did his undergraduate work at George Washington Uni-

---

[4]Sanders, "Interviews in 1990," p. 145; Hester interview, June 5, 1991; interview with Gene Holley, Augusta, April 19, 1991; *Official Register, 1975–1976*, pp. 586-87.

[5]Sanders, "Interviews in 1990," pp. 198-200; Tackett interview, January 23, 1991; Hester interview, June 5, 1991; *Official Register, 1965–1966*, p. 34; *Atlanta Constitution*, February 13, 1971.

versity and received his law degree from the University of Georgia in 1966. His work at the Institute for Government impressed the director, Dr. William Collins, who recommended him to Sanders. After completing his National Guard duty, Underwood began working with Sanders early in 1967. As the first lawyer Sanders hired in Atlanta, Underwood played a pivotal role in developing the firm and remained closely associated with Sanders thereafter. Burrows, by contrast, only stayed with Sanders a few years before moving to south Georgia. Sanders had better luck with Dale Schwartz, another young graduate of the University of Georgia Law School. A native of Winder, Schwartz had worked in the Attorney General's Office before joining the firm. Like Underwood, Schwartz was an excellent addition and became a partner in the firm.[6]

During his four years as governor, Sanders had labored indefatigably to lure new industry to Georgia, expand existing operations, and develop the city of Atlanta. Inevitably the urban-oriented governor developed excellent connections with the corporate leadership of Atlanta. Since he knew many of the CEOs personally, he managed to attract some of Atlanta's top firms as clients for his new firm. His first major client was Coca-Cola. Having earned the admiration of Robert Woodruff, the venerable chairman of the board, Sanders gained that prestigious account. Other substantial clients soon followed. Sanders knew C. E. Woolman, chairman of the board of Delta Airlines, and obtained Delta's business. Subsequently his firm did much legal work for Lockheed, The Mead Corporation, and Union Camp. Among his other clients was the Georgia Railroad Bank in Augusta, which was keenly interested in the passage of the Holding Company Banking Law. In working on that issue, Sanders also gained Citizens and Southern National Bank as a client. Thus from its inception, his firm had a group of very substantial clients. In a short time he had attracted more business than he and his two young lawyers could handle, and more business kept coming in. Another Sanders client was Tom Cousins who, although quite young, had already made an impact as one of Atlanta's biggest real estate

---

[6]Sanders, "Interviews in 1990," pp. 198-200; interview with Norman Underwood, Atlanta, January 23, 1991; Doris Lockerman, *Maestro: The Life and Times of a Law Firm, Troutman, Sanders, Lockerman and Ashmore* (Atlanta: Troutman, Sanders, Lockerman and Ashmore, 1982) p. 101.

developers. Cousins used Sanders for much of his corporate and regulatory work, but he used another lawyer, Jack Ashmore, for his real estate work. Seeing that Sanders had more business than he could handle, Cousins suggested that he communicate with Ashmore and see if they could work together.[7]

Jack Ashmore and Robert Boozer had been partners in the Atlanta firm of Alston, Sibley, Miller, Spann and Shackleford, but they left that prestigious firm in 1965 to form a new partnership. A native of Florida, Ashmore earned both his undergraduate and law degrees at Emory University, and from 1960 to 1965 he had been a lecturer at the Emory University Law School. Boozer, son of a Georgia Power Company executive, also took his A.B. at Emory, where he was elected to Phi Beta Kappa. He earned an LL.B. at Harvard Law School, did additional study in the Netherlands on a Fulbright scholarship, and had practiced for eleven years. Taking two assistants—Richard Newton and Jon Richard Gray—Ashmore and Boozer set up offices at 80 Broad Street, N.W. In addition to Cousins Properties, the new firm represented Railway Express Agency, Bailey Theatres, and several real estate development firms and title insurance companies. In 1967 Richard Newton became a partner and William Epstein was added as a partner. The firm continued to expand, and the next year Mack Butler came in as a partner.[8]

Following Cousins's advice, Sanders called Ashmore and explained that he had additional space in the Commerce Building and more business than his firm could do. He offered to share office space with the Ashmore firm and refer business to them if they wished to joined him. They accepted his offer, and in 1968 the two groups combined to form Sanders, Ashmore and Boozer. The members included Sanders, Ashmore, Boozer, Newton, and Epstein. The associates were William Vance, Mack Butler, James McRae, Gerald Burrows, Norman Underwood, Robert Gerson, and Dale Schwartz. The firm offered a general civil practice to include administrative, antitrust, banking, communications, condemnation, corporate, estate and trust, negligence, probate, public utility, real estate, taxation, transportation, and zoning matters.[9]

---

[7]Sanders, "Interviews in 1990," pp. 198-200.
[8]Lockerman, *Maestro*, pp. 103-104.
[9]Ibid., p. 105; Sanders, "Interviews in 1990," pp. 200-201.

While Sanders was busily developing his practice in Atlanta, his Augusta firm flourished, too, though he had little direct contact with it. Living in Atlanta, he could not keep up with the firm's activities. His major contribution to its success was the use of his name, which undoubtedly brought in business, but he took no money from Sanders, Hester & Holley. Sanders's past had been in Augusta, but his future lay in Atlanta. In little more than a year, through growth and merger, he had started a new firm with only himself and two young associates and had built a highly respected firm of twelve experienced attorneys, with an impressive client list which included Fuqua Industries, J. A. Jones Construction Co., Ryder Truck Lines, Bowman Transportation, Georgia Railway Bank and Trust Co., The Mead Corporation, Martin Theatres, Georgia Milk Producers Association, and Cousins Properties. An impressive accomplishment, the success of Sanders, Ashmore and Boozer demonstrated that Sanders could compete successfully with the old established legal firms in the highly competitive Atlanta market.[10]

While developing his law practice in Atlanta, Sanders expanded his financial investments in many different areas. For many years he had been associated with Fuqua enterprises and regarded J. B. Fuqua as one of his closest friends. Sanders had served Fuqua as legal counselor and board member before his term as governor. Four days after leaving office, Sanders was elected to the board of directors of Natco Corp., a diversified holding company which soon became Fuqua Industries. The Augusta-based firm's operations then included five radio and television stations, manufacturing grain drying and storage equipment, and large-scale production of structural clay products and clay conduits. In 1966 the company was a money loser with annual sales of $19 million; by 1970, Fuqua Industries, now headquartered in Atlanta, had become a major conglomerate with annual sales of more than $300 million.[11]

Sanders and Hester had several investments together, mostly real estate in the Augusta area as well as some land in Florida and North Carolina. In some cases, such as the Cherokee Shopping Center in

---

[10]Sanders, "Interviews in 1990," pp. 200-201.
[11]*Augusta Herald*, January 15, 1967; *Augusta Chronicle*, August 15, 1971; Fuqua interview, April 4, 1991.

Augusta, they actually developed the land they purchased. In other instances they acquired land which they expected to appreciate in value and sold it to developers. The Regency Mall in Augusta was built on land they sold. In 1963 they acquired a large tract of undeveloped land a few miles north of Augusta and started West Lake Estates. They graded the land, built a golf course, and began developing the real estate around it. Eventually West Lake became one of Augusta's most prestigious communities and a successful investment for Sanders. In 1968 Sanders, Hester, and Holley purchased a 1,700-acre tract of undeveloped land in Aiken county, South Carolina, adjacent to the City of North Augusta. The newspapers reported the total cost of the purchase as more than $3 million.[12]

Because Sanders was ever alert to new opportunities and possessed a good grasp of land values and potential growth patterns, he generally made sound investments. Some provided almost immediate profits while others he kept for many years as long-term investments. Not all of his investments flourished, however. Some were major disappointments, and his investments in Texas oil wells were disastrous. Gene Holley, who had a penchant for risky ventures, convinced Sanders to invest in Texas oil. Month after month they continually poured money into the project, but very little oil ever came from the wells. Moreover, the man they hired to look out for their interests probably was a crook who pocketed much of the money they sent for drilling. That failure taught Sanders to avoid risky speculative investments that he could neither see nor control. He preferred putting his money into land, buildings, and stock.[13]

In addition to his numerous Augusta investments with Fuqua, Hester, and Holley, Sanders also worked closely with Tom Cousins and helped him bring professional basketball to Atlanta. Acquiring professional basketball for Atlanta, he believed, would enhance the city's Major League image, stimulate downtown economic activity, and put pressure on the city to construct a large coliseum. Thus he willingly invested his time and money in the project, and in 1968 the National Basketball

---

[12]Sanders, "Interviews in 1990," pp. 205-206; Hester interview, June 5, 1991; *Atlanta Constitution*, October 26, 1968.

[13]Sanders, "Interviews in 1990," pp. 212-13, 220-22; Holley interview, April 19, 1991.

Association gave its approval to transfer the St. Louis Hawks to Atlanta. Initially the Hawks played at the Georgia Tech Coliseum, but its seating capacity of approximately 7,000 was inadequate for a professional team. A much larger facility would have to be built to keep the team in Atlanta. Indeed the N.B.A. agreement authorizing the move stipulated that Atlanta could use the Georgia Tech Coliseum temporarily, but the city must show firm plans for a larger coliseum "in the near future." For many years the city had considered building such a structure, and surveys and marketing studies already had been completed and several private and public officials had endorsed the concept. Convinced that a coliseum would be a bonanza for the city, Sanders did everything he could to nudge the process along. Since Atlanta was emerging as the premier city of the South, he envisaged large political conventions and other large events coming to Atlanta, once a suitable coliseum was in place. No other city in the South except Miami Beach had such a facility, he pointed out, and Atlanta's geographical location was more desirable than Miami's. Neither Sanders nor Cousins had the time or inclination to operate the Atlanta Hawks, and at the time of the purchase Sanders, who owned ten percent of the team, made his intentions clear. "I don't propose to remain a member of the ownership beyond the point that I feel I am essential to its successful operation," he remarked. That point was reached early in 1970, and Sanders disposed of his interest in the Atlanta Hawks, just when the team had the potential of making a profit for its owners. By then, plans for the new coliseum were well advanced and the gubernatorial race was underway. By removing himself from ownership of the Hawks, he eliminated the possibility of charges of political involvement that might jeopardize the coliseum project. Thus Sanders played a significant role in bringing all three major professional teams—the Braves, Falcons, and Hawks—to Atlanta. His involvement in the Hawks also shows that motives other than simply making a profit determined some of his investments.[14]

While building a successful law practice in Atlanta and making numerous business investments, Sanders continued to maintain a high political profile. Unless something better turned up, he expected to seek the governorship again in 1970. To do so, it was necessary to maintain

---

[14]*Atlanta Journal,* May 4, 1968, March 26, 1970.

his political contacts, deliver speeches from time to time, and generally keep his name before the public. It also meant defending his administration from partisan attacks.

During the 1966 campaign for lieutenant governor between Peter Zack Geer and George T. Smith, Geer's South Georgia campaign manager charged that he had received a $1,230 insurance premium kickback from Doug Barnard, Sanders's executive secretary. Later, after losing the election, Geer made a public announcement of the allegation. Four state senators—two Democrats and two Republicans—then claimed they had "shocking" evidence of wrongdoing in state government. Rumors also circulated about irregularities in the Department of Industry and Trade, including charges that the director had overspent his budget. Critics also charged that Representative Crawford Ware of Troup county, chairman of the powerful State of Republic Committee, had received much of the state's insurance business during the Sanders years. These accusations led to an investigation by the Senate Committee on Economy and Reorganization and Efficiency in Government. The chairman, Senator Stanley Smith of Perry, brought in Attorney General Arthur Bolton to determine if any civil liability was involved.[15]

After investigating the charges, the committee found "no evidence" to substantiate them. Indeed, the Albany insurance man who claimed he received the kickback from Barnard told state investigators that "the affidavit was made primarily for political purposes during a political campaign." Investigations also revealed that instead of having a deficit the Department of Industry and Trade actually had a surplus of $50,000. Regarding the insurance complaint, the committee found that the state contract was determined by competitive bidding and the LaGrange agency had submitted the lowest bid. As a result, the committee concluded that "no further investigation of this complaint would be justified." Doug Barnard summed up the whole affair as nothing but "political sour grapes." Rather than embarrassing the Sanders administration, the investigations exonerated it of any wrongdoing and revealed what most Georgians already knew, namely, that the Sanders administration had conducted the state's business in a very efficient and honest manner.[16]

---

[15]Ibid., February 5, 1967; Sanders, "My Life," p. 49.
[16]*Atlanta Journal,* May 4, 1967; Sanders, "My Life," pp. 49-50.

The findings of Senator Smith's committee silenced the critics for awhile, but Governor Maddox, chaffing under the influence Sanders continued to wield in the legislature, attempted to embarrass his predecessor. His efforts were even less successful than the earlier attempts. In June 1969, Wright Lipford, a Newnan attorney and former solicitor general of Coweta county, announced publicly that Governor Maddox had directed him to "embarrass" former Governor Carl Sanders. In resigning his $25,000-a-year job as assistant attorney general assigned to the governor's office, Lipford stated: "I do not intend to be hatchet man for Gov. Maddox or anybody else." Maddox, he continued, is obsessed with Sanders, and his whole purpose was "to embarrass Carl Sanders." Lipford admitted conducting the investigation as Maddox had directed, but instead of uncovering corruption he found the Sanders administration "to be absolutely spotless." Sanders was "delighted" that his administration had been given "a clean bill of health by a man whose lifetime career has been investigative work." Maddox, by contrast, denied ordering the investigation and called the charge "a bald-faced lie."[17]

This was not the first time nor would it be the last time that Sanders and Maddox clashed. Though both strong-willed governors were native Georgians and Southern Baptists, their personalities, beliefs, and styles were quite different. Indeed it is hard to imagine a greater contrast than these two Democrats. Where Sanders was polished, sophisticated, and urbane, Maddox was uneducated, crude, and earthy. Sanders, always immaculately dressed, moved comfortably at country clubs and in executive suites; Maddox, unconcerned about fashion, was in his element shaking hands on street corners and attending fundamentalist church services. Sanders, aloof and thoughtful, excelled at planning, mastering details, and bringing people together. Maddox, the most impulsive of men, acted instinctively and created turmoil wherever he went. Sanders appealed to the intellect, Maddox to the emotions; Sanders was calm and reserved, Maddox was flamboyant and uninhibited; Sanders spoke softly, Maddox shrieked. Inevitably conflicts divided the two men, especially since Sanders was oriented to the future while Maddox attempted to preserve the past.[18]

---

[17]*Atlanta Constitution*, June 14, 1969.

[18]Bruce Galphin, *The Riddle of Lester Maddox* (Atlanta: Camelot Publishing Co.,

Despite their obvious differences, Maddox endorsed Sanders for the vice presidency in 1968. Whether Maddox supported him because he thought Sanders was the best man for the job, or because the vice presidency would remove him from Georgia is conjectural. But when many leaders within the Democratic party in Georgia suggested that Sanders would make a good running mate for either Hubert Humphrey or Bobby Kennedy, both Governor Maddox and party chairman James Gray endorsed him. At the Democratic National Convention in Chicago the Georgia delegation endorsed Sanders, and he gained additional support from the region. Southern Democratic party officials, seeking regional unity, recommended Sanders and six other southern leaders for the vice presidency. Ever the realist, Sanders did not expect to win the nomination. It was flattering to be considered and he enjoyed the attention, but he doubted that he would be selected. Out of office and unable to control the Georgia delegation, he clearly was a longshot. Although he allowed his name to be considered, he neither encouraged nor discouraged his backers. He simply allowed the movement to run its course. Had Senator Robert Kennedy secured the presidential nomination, Sanders certainly would have received serious consideration, since Kennedy had genuine admiration for him. But realistically, his candidacy ended with the assassination of Senator Kennedy. None of the candidates proposed by the Southern leaders made presidential nominee Hubert Humphrey's short list of potential running mates, and eventually he selected quiet and respected Senator Ed Muskie of Maine.[19]

During the 1968 campaign, Sanders's relationship with Maddox, never particularly warm, grew noticeably cooler as Maddox first considered seeking the presidency himself and then threw his support behind the third party candidacy of George Wallace of Alabama. As always, Sanders remained loyal to his party, and he urged Maddox and other Democratic officials to do the same. His often-repeated message was: "Get in the ring and fight." Because Southern Democratic officials had

---

1968); Cook, *Governors of Georgia*, pp. 289-95; Bradley R. Rice, "Lester Maddox and the Politics of Populism," in *Georgia Governors in an Age of Change*, pp. 193-210.

[19]*Augusta Herald*, August 15, 1968; *Atlanta Journal*, April 4, 29, May 17, 1968; Theodore White, *The Making of a President 1968* (New York: Atheneum Publishers, 1969) pp. 304-305.

failed to speak up for this party, Sanders complained, "George Wallace is slowly and surely killing the Democratic Party in the South." Stung by Sanders's criticism, Maddox did not include Sanders as a delegate to the Chicago convention, and Sanders declined to attend as a "distinguished guest."[20]

In September the Georgia political world was stunned by the announcement that five top Democratic officeholders had switched from the Democratic to the Republican party. The defection of Agriculture Commissioner Phil Campbell, State Treasurer Jack Ray, Comptroller General Jimmy Bentley, and Public Service Commissioners Crawford Pilcher and Alpha Fowler to the Republicans revealed deep divisions within the majority party. After recovering from the shock, most commentators concluded that the Democrats had suffered a major loss and the Republicans had gained established leadership. Perhaps, they added, this was merely a preview of things to come and other defections soon would follow. If so, then Democratic domination of Georgia would end and the state finally would have two viable parties. Almost alone among Democratic leaders, Sanders seemed unconcerned by the defection of the five Democrats. In fact, he said their defection would be good for the Democratic party and would "provide a lot of opportunities for new young people." When Sanders also stated on a television interview that Maddox's lack of leadership had contributed to the Democrats' problems, the feisty governor exploded. Calling Sanders's criticism "ridiculous," he pointed out that the defectors were Sanders's opponents, not his. Although no mass exodus of Democratic officeholders followed the defection of these five, party loyalty continued to be a serious concern. And, as Sanders had feared, George Wallace carried five southern states including Georgia in the November election, and Richard Nixon carried the remainder of Dixie.[21]

As he had done for many years, Sanders continued to speak out on issues that concerned him. In discussing Georgia's future, he often spoke in broad, general terms, such as the blending of "progress and comfortable living" so that Georgia could achieve the financial and cultural

---

[20]*Atlanta Constitution*, June 18, 1968; *Atlanta Journal*, July 3, 1968.

[21]*Atlanta Journal*, September 20, 1968; *Augusta Chronicle*, September 21, 1968; White, *Making of a President 1968*, appendix A.

success of a New York City without "the accompanying disorder, alienation, and frenzy." He wanted all of Georgia's citizens to participate fully in the blessings and benefits offered by a "modern, agro-industrial, technical civilization."[22] He frequently stressed the need for continuing the improvement his administration had made in education, transportation, and economic development. But in addition to these general concepts, he also made specific recommendations and addressed controversial topics.

Few Georgia politicians had the courage to advocate county consolidation, but Sanders did so repeatedly. He urged his successor to "work with local officials to accomplish the vital but highly difficult tasks of both municipal and county consolidation" and he took his message directly to the county commissioners. Sanders was the first political leader who dared tell county commissioners to their face that county consolidation was long overdue. That was the message he delivered at the April 1966 convention of Georgia's county commissioners. He told the commissioners bluntly that counties must merge to survive. Surprisingly, the convention gave him a great ovation after his speech, and the next year the Association of County Commissioners gave Sanders its "Man of the Year" award for 1967. In presenting the award, Dr. Bruce Schaefer, president of the association, lauded Sanders for furthering the "regional economic development concept" and for encouraging "greater intergovernmental cooperation for promoting efficiency and economy in government at all levels."[23]

In addition to advocating county consolidation, Sanders also proposed reforms for both the executive and legislative branches. "A predominately part-time legislator with little or no staff assistance, no office but his desk and only a few short weeks on the job is not going to develop much of an expert body of knowledge," Sanders declared at a conference on State Legislatures in American Politics held at Emory University. "It is reform in the areas of staffing, housing and time which will enable legislatures to reassume a truly coordinate role in state government," he insisted.[24]

---

[22]*Atlanta Constitution*, August 30, 1966.
[23]Ibid., April 27, 28, August 30, 1966, March 24, 1967.
[24]Ibid., April 1, 1967.

While suggesting ways to strengthen the legislative branch, Sanders also presented specific reforms to increase the power of the executive branch. The governor, he pointed out in a speech to the Athens Kiwanis Club, is responsible for the entire state government, but his authority is severely limited. He must share executive power with thirteen elected executive officials who are substantially independent of the governor, plus twelve other major departments whose directors are chosen by statutory or constitutional boards. Thus, Sanders concluded, only 2,000 of the 35,000 state employees are under the governor's direct authority. With authority over less than six percent of the state's employees, the governor must use "every bit of indirect authority he possesses" to succeed in his job. His remedy was to give the governor the power to appoint and remove department heads so that he could direct the policy of the major departments of the executive branch. Based on his study of government, as well as his personal experience, Sanders believed that the people's needs were best served by strong governors and that governors should be given authority commensurate with their responsibilities.[25]

As governor, Sanders had shown a concern for protecting the environment, especially the state's water resources, and in the ensuing years his commitment to preserving the natural environment increased. Early in 1970 he called for the establishment of a Georgia Department of Environmental Control to coordinate an all-out war on air, water, and noise pollution. This new department, he argued, would merge existing agencies to alleviate the fragmentation of authority that currently exists. Showing an awareness of the many hazards of pollution, he said the time has come "to move beyond the talking and writing stage, and look at pollution in terms of public policy and governmental action."[26]

Interested in national affairs as well as state politics, Sanders served the public in several appointive positions. Since he had demonstrated a keen interest in developing educational television in Georgia, President Johnson placed him on the Public Broadcasting Board. A member of a commission that looked into the programs of the Office of Economic Opportunity, the federal antipoverty agency, he also served as a member of the National Urban Affairs Commission which studied the problems

---

[25] *Atlanta Journal*, August 22, 1967.
[26] Ibid., March 2, 1970; *Atlanta Constitution*, January 7, 1970.

of cities. Although Sanders participated in national affairs, maintained frequent contact with President Johnson, and often was rumored to be in line for a federal position, his political future was in Georgia. By staking out positions on key issues, he had laid a foundation for another race for governor in 1970.[27]

The years 1967 to 1970 had been productive ones for Sanders. During that period he established a flourishing law practice in Atlanta, enhanced his personal finances through his law practice and numerous investments, helped bring the Hawks to Atlanta, and maintained a high political profile on both the state and national levels. Having accomplished the goals he had set for himself, he was prepared to put aside his private concerns and devote the next four years to full-time public service as governor of Georgia.

---

[27]Sanders, "Interviews in 1990," pp. 146, 193; *Atlanta Journal,* May 27, June 30, 1966; *Savannah Morning News,* September 22, 1966; *Atlanta Constitution,* August 5, 1967.

Campaign Buttons

Baldy (Clifford Baldowski) cartoon in the Atlanta Constitution,
October 27, 1966. (Courtesy of Clifford Baldowski.)

Baldy (Clifford Baldowski) cartoon in the Atlanta Constitution *showing Governor Sanders lighting the way for the South.* (Courtesy of Clifford Baldowski.)

Chapter 19

"Cufflinks Carl" versus the "Redneck"

With glowing confidence Sanders officially announced his candidacy for governor on April 25, 1970, at a rally at Daniel Field in Augusta. Presented by Mayor Millard Beckum, the former governor told the crowd of several hundred supporters that he planned to expand the Medical College and its dental school into a medical complex "that will equal any in the nation." Promising to make education the number one priority, as it was in his first administration, Sanders pledged to "protect and advance the welfare of every Georgia boy and girl." In seeking "educational stability and clarification of the prevailing dilemmas over desegregation policies," he expressed confidence that his goals could be achieved without resort to busing, which he believed was "unworkable and educationally unsound." He also promised to reinstitute the Bowdoin Commission, take a "fresh look at highway construction," and establish a State Department of the Environment and a State Housing Program "to make it possible for more low and moderate income families in Georgia to own their own homes." In contrast to Governor Maddox's bitter clashes with the legislature, Sanders assured everyone that he would work harmoniously with the members of the General Assembly. Finally, he urged the people "to look closely at my record—my performance as a public official—my record of fiscal responsibility and my fidelity to public trust." The best evidence of his effort to achieve economy and efficiency in government, he concluded, "is that I fulfilled every promise to the people and left $140 million in the state treasury at the end of my term."[1]

---

[1]*Augusta Chronicle*, April 25, 1970.

Jumping into a private airplane, the forty-four-year-old candidate flew to Atlanta where he addressed a crowd at a downtown hotel. Repeating his general remarks, he focused on Atlanta's transportation needs, promising "a balanced program of highway construction and some form of rapid transit." Noting that all Georgia cities are facing a financial crisis because of "a very limited tax base," he pledged to "give high priority to working with local government in finding ways to broaden the tax base so cities can provide basic government services."[2]

The next city on the aerial tour was Savannah, where Sanders promised to push for the "immediate completion" of Interstates 95 and 16, preserve the rich historical areas of Chatham county, and protect the coastal marshes. From Savannah he flew to Macon, then to Columbus, Albany, and finally Valdosta. In one hectic day, Sanders had spoken in seven different cities from one end of the state to the other. At each stop he presented in broad outline his plans for the next four years, plus some emphasis on specific local needs. An innovative and impressive way to launch a campaign, it set the tone for what would follow in the months ahead.[3]

Throughout the summer Sanders crisscrossed the state by air, delivering positive addresses in which he identified problems confronting the state and explained how he proposed to remedy them. In each speech, along with the mandatory political rhetoric, he included material of substance, for he believed a gubernatorial candidate should inform the voters as clearly as possible where he intended to lead the state. Knowing the importance of local associations, he also discussed local concerns and invariably pointed out local accomplishments from his previous administration. In practically every county in the state he could allude to some road, building, or project that his administration had provided. Prior to landing, he consulted a thick notebook his staff had assembled which listed by county key supporters and local projects undertaken. With his memory refreshed, he could then greet people by name and speak authoritatively about what his administration had done for that county.[4]

---

[2]Press release April 25, 1970, 1970 Speech folder, box 25, Sanders Collection, Law Library.

[3]Ibid.

[4]Underwood interview, January 23, 1991; interview with Robert Coram, Atlanta,

In contrast to 1962 when Sanders was the underdog, struggling to get his name before the public, wondering if enough money would come in to pay the bills, and improvising as the campaign progressed, this time he ran a highly professional operation. The campaign was organized into six units which operated independently: state organization, youth organization, women's organization, advertising, press, and speechwriting. With plenty of money available from the onset, Sanders hired the respected firm of Burton-Campbell, Inc. to do his advertising. Hugh Wilson, who later gained fame as the creator of the hilarious television program "WKRP in Cincinnati," was the member of the firm who did most of the clever television spots Sanders used. In the previous campaign, Sanders wrote most of his speeches, but now he relied heavily on Norman Underwood and a staff of researchers to provide material. Sometimes Sanders read the Underwood speeches verbatim, more often he revised them, and occasionally he spoke extemporaneously. Serving as press secretary and traveling with Sanders throughout the campaign was Robert Coram, an excellent young journalist. Doug Barnard and John Harper ran the campaign headquarters, supervised the activities of numerous volunteers, and attempted to coordinate the work of the six units. Serving as liaison between the campaign organization and the advertising agency was Remer Tyson, another able young journalist. On Sunday afternoons after church, the key leaders—Barnard, Harper, Underwood, Coram, Tyson, and occasionally J. B. Fuqua and others—met with Sanders at his townhouse to discuss the campaign and coordinate its activities.[5]

Although many capable people were involved in the campaign, Sanders set the tone and direction and made all of the key decisions. He refused to appoint a campaign manager or delegate much authority to anyone else. He rarely sought or accepted advice from his staff, for he knew exactly how he wanted to campaign, and when he felt strongly about an issue he could be so intimidating that few challenged his judgment. Sanders insisted that the campaign take the "high road." Thus it was issue-oriented, stressing his previous record and advancing his

---

April 4, 1991.

[5]Ibid.; Lyons, "A Comparison of Carl Sanders's Gubernatorial Campaigns: 1962 and 1970," pp. 29-55.

ideas on education, the environment, highways, taxes, and other issues. He shunned personal attacks and virtually ignored the opposition. Committed to discussing issues in a realistic manner, he refused to make promises he knew he could not fulfil, especially regarding unpopular court decisions and racial integration. His friends, aware of the growing white backlash and opposition to school integration, urged him to stake out a position for freedom of choice, but he declined, explaining sorrowfully that "the courts have said you can't do that." As far as he was concerned, the Supreme Court was the highest authority, and its rulings, no matter how unpopular, must be obeyed. It was pointless to suggest otherwise. Such rhetoric, he thought, was irrelevant. His campaign would deal with "real" issues that a governor could influence, and it would do so in a rational, straightforward manner. And he expected all other serious candidates to do the same. By comparing the records of the candidates and their views on the major issues, the voters could then choose the best leadership for the next four years. That was the way democracy should function, Sanders believed. And he was convinced that when that process was completed on September 9, a majority of the voters would agree with his campaign slogan—"Carl Sanders ought to be governor again."[6]

A wide variety of candidates sought the gubernatorial nomination in 1970, including some of the most bizarre figures ever to seek elective office in Georgia. In addition to Sanders, other candidates seeking the Democratic nomination included former state senator Jimmy Carter from Plains, who had come in third in the 1966 campaign; Linda Jenness, a twenty-nine-year-old socialist and self-proclaimed admirer of Fidel Castro; Dr. McKee Hargrett, who described himself as a "Wallace-Maddox-Goldwater" Democrat; J. B. Stoner, a Savannah lawyer and white supremist who complained that Hitler had been too "moderate" toward the Jews; C. B. King, an articulate attorney from Albany and the first black ever to run for governor in Georgia; and the strangest candidate of all, Jan Cox, a bearded former carpenter who came on as the "inner man" candidate. On the Republican side, Comptroller General Jimmy Bentley, a former Democrat closely associated with the Talmadge

---

[6]Ibid.; Robert Coram and Remer Tyson, "The Loser Who Won," *Atlanta Magazine* 10 (November 1970): 66.

faction, battled Hal Suit, a popular Atlanta television commentator, for the nomination. Bill Shipp of the *Atlanta Constitution* considered this the "strangest, most complex and crowded gubernatorial contest in Georgia history."[7]

Sanders had little to fear from Jenness, Hargrett, Cox, or Stoner, who had negligible support, but King posed a problem for him. Described by one writer as having "the demeanor of an Oxford-educated African chief," King, who had been involved in many civil rights controversies, was extremely popular among Georgia blacks. He anticipated substantial support from the black community—votes that Sanders otherwise would receive. Sanders hoped to win the primary without a runoff, but King's candidacy made that prospect less likely. Despite King's support among blacks, it soon became apparent that the Democratic primary was a two-man race between Sanders and Jimmy Carter.[8]

Sanders first took notice of Carter in the 1962 Democratic primary when Carter lost his bid for the state Senate to Homer Moore, an old-line politician by only 139 votes. Charging fraud, illegal voting, and other irregularities, Carter challenged the election. After complicated legal battles, and with the assistance of the Sanders administration, he finally gained his seat. Carter kept a low profile in the Senate at first, but his fortunes improved in 1964 when Sanders appointed him to the Governor's Commission to Improve Education. Sharing Sanders's moderate progressive outlook, Carter generally supported the governor's programs. In return, Sanders looked out for Carter's constituents with grants and the elevation of Georgia Southwestern College to four-year status. In the Senate Carter displayed ability, drive, and a remarkable work ethic. Indeed he took pride in reading every bill introduced in the General Assembly—a practice many legislators considered a waste of time. Speaker George T. Smith said members of the House called Carter an "intellectual fool" because he had no common sense. Smith also found him "unyielding," operating on the principle of "my way or no

---

[7]Victor Lasky, *Jimmy Carter: The Man and the Myth* (New York: Richard Marek Publishers, 1979) pp. 73-74. Thomas J. Irwin, Adam B. Matthews, and Charles F. Swint, Sr. also entered the Democratic primary. *Official Register, 1969–1970*, p. 1558.

[8]Reg Murphy and Hal Gulliver, *The Southern Strategy* (New York: Charles Scribner's Sons, 1971) p. 178.

way," as did Ben Fortson who described him "as stubborn as a South Georgia turtle."[9]

What disturbed Sanders was not Carter's ambition or work habits, but rather his failure to keep his word. According to the governor, Carter came to him on several occasions, especially during the writing of the new state constitution, objecting to minor points in proposed legislation. Whenever possible, Sanders worked out the problem to Carter's satisfaction. But to the governor's amazement, shortly thereafter Carter would reverse himself and criticize in committee or on the floor of the Senate the legislation he had previously agreed to support. Sanders did not understand such behavior, and he had little respect for any man who did not keep his word.[10]

Carter began campaigning for the 1970 race almost immediately after losing the gubernatorial primary in 1966. Thus by the time the other candidates had paid their qualifying fees for the 1970 race, Carter already had been campaigning nonstop for more than three years. Assisted by his wife, Rosalynn, and his mother, Lillian, Carter had traversed the state making contacts, listening to people, and greeting ordinary Georgians at service stations, on street corners, in barbershops, and wherever he could find them. By the end of the campaign Carter estimated that he had made 1,800 speeches and had shaken hands with 600,000 Georgians. Yet, his extensive grass roots campaigning seemed to make little headway, for a poll he took in September 1969 showed Sanders leading with 53 percent to Carter's 21 percent.[11]

Vowing that he did not intend to lose again, Carter developed a plan for overtaking the former governor. In March 1968 he jotted down on a yellow legal pad the following characterization of Sanders that he would use again and again in speeches and statements to destroy the reputation of his opponent.

---

[9]Jimmy Carter, *Why Not the Best?* (Nashville: Broadman Press, 1975) pp. 80-87, 139; Jimmy Carter, *Turning Point* (New York: Times Books, 1992) pp. 54-182; Betty Glad, *Jimmy Carter: In Search of the Great White House* (New York: W. W. Norton & Company, 1980) pp. 86-95; Smith interview, April 18, 1991; Sanders, "Interviews in 1990," pp. 66-68.

[10]Sanders, "Interviews in 1990," pp. 186-87.

[11]Carter, *Why Not the Best?*, p. 101; Glad, *Jimmy Carter*, p. 126.

Some images to be projected regarding Carl Sanders . . . more liberal . . . has close connections with Ivan Allen and Atlanta Establishment . . . refuses to let Georgia Democrats have a voice in the Democratic party . . . pretty boy . . . ignored prison reform opportunities . . . nouveau riche . . . refused to assist local school boards in school financing . . . excluded George Wallace from the state. . . . You can see some of these are conflicting but right now we just need to collect all these rough ideas we can. Later we can start driving a wedge between me and him.

Other memos would follow, but the rough outline of Carter's plan to win the governorship was in place.[12]

The Carter strategy against Sanders was revised further by a poll taken by William Hamilton, a Washington-based specialist on southern opinion. Hamilton's interviews with eight hundred select Georgians revealed that Sanders had a favorable rating of 84 percent, one of the best job ratings Hamilton had ever seen. The poll also showed that "both Sanders and Carter were seen as a little more liberal than the electorate" and "this is more true of Sanders than it is of Carter." Hamilton further explained that Carter had a recognition problem since 25 percent of the electorate had never heard of Jimmy Carter and only eleven out of twenty Georgia Democrats had any opinion of him. Carter's low recognition, the pollster pointed out, could be an advantage. "As he becomes better known over the next twelve months, he can emphasize a moderate conservative tone in his campaign and, therefore, put himself between Sanders and the bulk of the electorate." Hamilton found that Carter's strongest supporters were white, between the ages of forty-five and fifty-nine, earned from $6,000 to $12,000 a year, liked George Wallace, and distrusted Atlanta "big shots." He advised Carter to "concentrate heavily on the working man, both skilled and unskilled." The only way Carter could win the governorship, it appeared, was for him to become a "redneck" and wipe out Sanders politically. Following Hamilton's advice, Carter proceeded to do that, methodically and brutally.[13]

---

[12]Carter, *Why Not the Best?*, p. 98; Glad, *Jimmy Carter*, p. 127.

[13]"A Survey of Political Opinion in Georgia," 1970 Jimmy Carter folder, box 24, Sanders Collection, Law Library; Lasky, *Jimmy Carter*, pp. 57-58.

Assisted by a capable group of advisers which included Atlanta attorney Charles Kirbo, campaign director Hamilton Jordan, media director Gerald Rafshoon, and press secretary Bill Pope, Carter shifted his campaign sharply to the Right. Carter took on a redneck image and Sanders became known as "Cufflinks Carl," a term coined by Jimmy Bentley but used effectively by Carter throughout the campaign. Depicting himself as a "working man" who would speak up for ordinary Georgians, Carter characterized Sanders as a wealthy elitist, out of touch with the common people and closely tied to Atlanta bankers and the Atlanta newspapers. The term "Cufflinks Carl" perfectly incorporated the image Carter wished to convey. Moreover, Sanders had misused the office of governor to enrich himself and his friends, Carter charged, and was more interested in Washington's problems than Georgia's. For his billboards and brochures Carter used the ugliest picture his staff could find, a black and white photo of Carter dressed in work clothes. "It made Jimmy look like an average working man," an aide said. "He had a little fear in him. He was proud, a little wary perhaps." The caption read: "Isn't it time somebody spoke up for you?" It made a perfect contrast to the colorful Sanders billboards which showed the handsome former governor dressed in a stylish business suit with the caption "Carl Sanders ought to be governor again." Although the two candidates shared a similar political philosophy and offered nearly identical platforms, their billboards presented starkly contrasting images.[14]

Television commercials presented equally contrasting images. Sanders was shown in many different situations—delivering speeches, working with legislators, campaigning, jogging, boating, and relaxing with his family—but regardless of the setting, he always was fashionably dressed and appeared dignified and affluent, which he was. Carter's commercials, by contrast, presented a highly distorted view of reality. They frequently showed Carter toiling on his farm, although, given his campaign schedule, it seems unlikely that he had spent much time in recent years

---

[14]Bill Shipp, "How He Won It," *Atlanta Constitution*, November 8-11, 1970; James Clotfelter and William R. Hamilton, "Electing a Governor in the Seventies," in *The American Governor in Behavioral Perspective*, Thad Beyle and J. Oliver Williams, eds. (New York: Harper & Row, Publishers, 1972) pp. 32-39; *Augusta Chronicle*, July 14, 30, 31, 1970; Katheryn Hayes, "The Comeback of Cuff-links Carl," *Georgia Trend* 1 (June 1986): 48.

shoveling peanuts. Another commercial showed a man wearing a yellow hard hat crawling out of a manhole. As he looked up, there was Jimmy Carter, smiling with his hand outstretched wanting to know what he can do to help the working man because he is a working man, too. Perhaps Carter's most effective effort in waging class warfare was a twenty-second television commercial devised by Rafshoon. It opened with a picture of a closed country club door. Then a voice said: "This is the door to an exclusive country club, where the big-money boys play cards, drink cocktails, and raise money for their candidate—Carl Sanders. People like *us* aren't invited. We're busy working for a living. That's why our votes are going for Jimmy Carter . . . *our* kind of man, *our* kind of Governor."[15]

When Carter formally announced his candidacy on April 3 at the State Capitol, he told a group of supporters, "Georgians never again want a Governor who will use the tremendous power and prestige of the office for his personal wealth." A week later in Rome, Carter poked his head into a spacious money vault at a bank and quipped, "Looks like Carl Sanders's basement."[16] For Carter to run against Sanders's wealth was odd to say the least because Carter may have been more affluent than his adversary, and he also received backing from the affluent. His inner circle included the type of people his campaign scorned, such as wealthy Calhoun banker Bert Lance; Charles Kirbo, a senior partner in the prestigious law firm of King & Spalding; Philip Alston, Jr., Carter's finance chairman and a senior partner in another prestigious Atlanta law firm, Alston, Miller & Gaines; and David Gambrell, Carter's treasurer, who also was a lawyer and the scion of a very wealthy Atlanta family. In June Carter released a statement showing his personal wealth at $366,000, and he continually chided Sanders to reveal his wealth, which was rumored to be as much as $15 million. In refusing, Sanders declared, "I have a perfect record so far as my public stewardship is concerned." Carter repeated the demand so often that finally J. B. Stoner, in a statewide television debate, challenged Carter to "stop dragging a red herring across the road." Tired of Carter's innuendoes, Stoner told him to "come out and say what it is or apologize." Carter

---

[15]Clotfelter and Hamilton, "Electing a Governor in the Seventies," p. 36; Lasky, *Jimmy Carter*, pp. 60-63.

[16]Glad, *Jimmy Carter*, p. 127; Lasky, *Jimmy Carter*, p. 61.

did neither. When a newsman asked Carter to elaborate on his accusation that Sanders "used political influence to get rich," Carter declined, saying he preferred to wait until late in the campaign.[17]

In addition to the wealth issue, Carter leveled many other charges against Sanders. He asserted that "Cufflinks Carl" had "abused" the Democratic party in Georgia by using it as a vehicle to gain favors from Washington. "No public official should use the party for his own interests," Carter said. Returning control of Georgia government and parties to the people is, he insisted, "the most important issue of the campaign." Attempting to attract Wallace supporters who held Sanders's support of Lyndon Johnson and Hubert Humphrey against him, Carter stated, "I don't think Hubert Humphrey has a right to come into Georgia and tell us who our next governor should be."[18]

At a meeting of the Georgia Press Association at Jekyll Island on June 28, Carter charged that Sanders was more interested in winning the ailing Richard Russell's Senate seat than in being elected governor. As evidence, he called attention to the registration number on Sanders's airplane—6272 Victor. Carter interpreted the number as a symptom of Sanders's Senate ambitions, since "1962 was the year he was elected governor and 1972 is the year Senator Russell's term expires." Sanders, who was at the meeting, denounced this attack as "smear tactics" and pointed out that the numbers were already on the plane when he leased it, which was true. Nevertheless, the attack received press coverage, drawing attention to Sanders's affluence and reminding Russell supporters that Sanders had considered running against Russell in 1966.[19]

A few days later Carter blamed his 1966 defeat on Sanders's interference in the campaign. He claimed that if Sanders and Fuqua had stayed out of the race instead of backing Ellis Arnall, "I would have been elected." Carter's assertion greatly exaggerated the impact of Sanders and Fuqua in that election, but, as Carter's biographer Betty Glad noted, "it linked Sanders to the liberal Arnall, exaggerated the strength of his own earlier candidacy, and suggested that such opposition was somehow

---

[17]Lasky, *Jimmy Carter*, pp. 63-69; *Atlanta Journal and Constitution*, May 17, 1970; *Macon Telegraph*, June 16, 19, 1970.

[18]*Columbus Ledger*, April 10, 1970; *Columbus Enquirer*, April 10, 1970.

[19]Glad, *Jimmy Carter*, p. 129.

wrong, rather than politics as usual." Sanders responded to the charge by stating that Carter "is becoming known as Jimmy the Fabricator. He has absolutely no credibility as a responsible candidate."[20]

Taking a page from Lester Maddox's book, Carter lambasted the *Atlanta Journal* and the *Atlanta Constitution*, claiming repeatedly that their coverage was biased and that they refused to publish his speeches or press releases. The charge was utterly false, as Carter had received ample coverage in both papers, but his criticism played well with the constituency he courted. Carter neglected to point out his close relationship with Anne Cox Chambers, owner of both papers, who was the largest single contributor to his campaign ($26,000). His criticism of the *Atlanta Constitution* was close to the mark on one point, however. Both publisher Ralph McGill and editor Eugene Patterson detested Carter. According to Reg Murphy, McGill referred to Carter as the "pissant."[21]

In his 1975 autobiography Carter stated, "I don't know how to compromise on any principle I believe is right," but in this campaign he managed to do so. He assured Georgians that he was "basically a redneck," and to prove his redneck credentials he made a point of visiting a segregationist academy, cozying up to George Wallace and Lester Maddox, and injecting profanity into his speeches. Such tactics appealed to archsegregationists Marvin Griffin and Roy Harris, who strongly endorsed him. Having used all the proper symbols throughout the campaign to attract the racist and segregationist vote, Carter then, with apparent sincerity, stated, "I have never made any insinuation of hatred or prejudice toward anyone, privately or publicly."[22] Many scholars, however, have reached other conclusions. In *The Southern Strategy*, Reg Murphy and Hal Gulliver explain that while Carter avoided overtly racist statements, he used "code words," which southern voters well understood, to attract the Wallace vote. Writing shortly after the election, Bill Shipp observed race was the "silent issue." Professor Gary Fink, a Carter biographer, concluded, "It would be difficult to find anything highminded about Carter's campaign. He stirred up both class and race prej-

---

[20]Ibid., p. 130; *Atlanta Constitution*, July 10, 1970.

[21]Glad, *Jimmy Carter*, p. 132; Lasky, *Jimmy Carter*, pp. 64, 84; *Savannah Evening Press*, June 29, 1970.

[22]Carter, *Why Not the Best?*, p. 139; *Atlanta Constitution*, June 21, 24, 1970; *Atlanta Journal*, July 28, 1970.

udices to skewer his primary opponent, Carl Sanders." Victor Lasky, a
more critical biographer, quotes Bill Pope, Carter's press secretary, conceding some years later that he had run a "nigger campaign" for Carter
against Sanders.[23]

For months Carter claimed he had evidence to prove how Sanders
had used his office for personal gain, but not until August 26, did he
release his "proof package." His timing was perfect, coming only days
before the primary. At a news conference in Atlanta, Carter made four
specific charges. He claimed that Sanders had teamed up with J. B.
Fuqua to acquire five broadcast stations; that Jones and Fellers, Archi-
tects, received a disproportionate share of state business during the
Sanders years; that state deposits were shifted to favored banks, especially
the Georgia Railroad Bank in Augusta; and that Sanders received over
$100,000 in special retainers from Delta Air Lines which, Carter said,
"will be greatly affected by state actions during the next four years."
While admitting that Sanders had not violated any laws, Carter solemnly
stated, "These documented facts show a consistent pattern of combining
political and business interests on behalf of Mr. Sanders."[24]

Although backed by a sheaf of documentation, the charges, as Bill
Shipp noted, "seemed more like firecrackers than bombshells." In
lengthy press conferences, Sanders denied any impropriety and easily explained away the charges. He pointed out that Fuqua's applications before the Federal Communications Commission were noncontested, that
neither the architectural firm nor the Georgia Railroad Bank received a
disproportionate share of state business, and that his law firm was counsel for Delta between 1967 and 1969 when the airline was seeking a
trans-Pacific flight from Atlanta to Honolulu. Sanders admitted collecting $104,000 in fees from Delta for legal services even though the Civil
Aeronautics Board awarded the flight to Braniff. Sanders described
Carter's accusations as "wild, groundless," and "obviously politically
motivated." He called Carter "the penny-anteist politician I've ever come
across."[25]

---

[23]Murphy and Gulliver, *The Southern Strategy*, p. 186; *Atlanta Constitution*,
November 8, 1970; Gary M. Fink, "Jimmy Carter and the Politics of Transition," in
Georgia Governors in an Age of Change, p. 248; Lasky, *Jimmy Carter*, p. 75.

[24]*Savannah Evening News*, August 27, 1970; *Macon News*, August 27, 1970.

[25]*Atlanta Constitution*, August 27, 1970; *Savannah Morning News*, August 27,

After making these charges against Sanders, Carter piously promised that he would never use the governor's office to grant any special favors and that he would never feel obligated to anybody, no matter how large his campaign contribution. When newsmen asked Carter to identify large contributors to his campaign and how much they contributed, he declined. He also admitted that if elected he would not divest himself of his own business interests.[26] Apparently Carter had one set of standards for himself and a different—and substantially higher—standard for Sanders.

The next day Sanders said he was glad Carter finally made his presentation and "I think it has already backfired." He has not charged me with doing anything illegal, nor has he proved a single instance of conflict of interest, Sanders observed. It is just the same old "smear-type tactics" that he has been using against me all summer long. Regarding the tactics used against him, Sanders promised that he would not forget them and "I've got a memory like an elephant."[27]

The press reacted negatively to the Carter campaign tactics. The *Macon News* summed up the Carter campaign as "a classic example of a good man whose high standards have been undermined by political ambition." Having claimed all summer to have some terrible revelation about Sanders, he admitted that Sanders had done nothing illegal. His long awaited bomb was a "dud." Carter's "great revelation was that Sanders had made money as a businessman and had a client as a lawyer." Carter is basically a liberal who has been trying to remake himself in the conservative image and his campaign "has gone steadily downhill from the moment it was launched."[28] The *Atlanta Constitution* found the "most reassuring thing about Carl Sanders's four years as governor is that nobody can find anything crooked about it." What Carter has provided this summer has been "a shameful character assassination." He "threatened over and over again to expose the Sanders administration, and he has not done so."[29]

1970.

[26]*Atlanta Constitution*, August 27, 1970.

[27]*Columbus Enquirer*, August 28, 1970.

[28]*Macon News*, August 31, 1970.

[29]*Atlanta Constitution*, August 28, 1970.

In the last days before the September 9 election, the campaign took on a "murky aspect," to use Betty Glad's description. Thousands of "fact sheets" suddenly were mailed to white Baptist ministers, lawmen, barbershops, and filling stations across the state. One showed a photograph of Sanders being doused with champagne by a black basketball player—Lou Hudson. The picture, which had first appeared in the sports section of the *Atlanta Journal*, had been taken in the dressing room of the Atlanta Hawks, of which Sanders was a part owner. It was the usual photo of a member of the team giving one of the owners the traditional treatment after a winning season. The picture was distributed to show Sanders socializing with blacks, and evidently was quite effective, especially in south Georgia. As Bill Shipp noted in the *Atlanta Constitution*, "in the context of this political campaign, it was a dangerous smear that injected both race, alcohol, and high living" into an already heated contest.[30]

And there was more. Another "fact sheet" told how Sanders attended the funeral of Martin Luther King, Jr., which, in fact, was true. Unlike Sanders, Carter did not pay his respects to Dr. King. Another widely distributed leaflet claimed that Sanders, as governor, had kept George Wallace from speaking in Georgia. The most ridiculous of the "fact sheets" contended that Sanders and Julian Bond had formed a political alliance. This was utter nonsense, as the two men detested each other. Bond, like many black leaders, supported the candidacy of C. B. King, not Sanders. Collectively, these "fact sheets" had a devastating effect and convinced large numbers of undecided or wavering voters to support Carter.[31]

Another attack on Sanders came from the Black Concern Committee, an organization no black Georgian had ever heard of. It reportedly mailed 50,000 brochures to black barbershops, pool halls, funeral homes, and churches, falsely alleging that Sanders, as governor, had reneged on promises to make black appointments. The brochure went on to praise Governor Maddox for having done more for blacks than Sanders. At the same time, radio spots plugging C. B. King were broadcast. King did not buy the time and knew nothing about the spots or who financed

---

[30]Glad, *Jimmy Carter*, pp. 134-35; Lasky, *Jimmy Carter*, p. 75.
[31]Lasky, *Jimmy Carter*, pp. 78-79; Coram and Tyson, "The Loser Who Won," p. 96.

them. Since Sanders was the only white candidate with appeal in the
black community, strengthening King's candidacy worked to Carter's
advantage. Essentially, every vote for King meant one vote fewer for
Sanders, and in the primary King received 8.8 percent of the total vote.
Carter had played the redneck role so convincingly that he garnered only
5 percent of the black vote.[32]

Carter and his staff have denied responsibility for any of these
tactics, but their protestations have a hollow ring. Why would anyone
else do them? Moreover, former associates of the Gerald Rafshoon
Advertising Agency have suggested that some Carter supporters were
responsible for them. Bill Abernathy, a former vice president of the
agency, says that the leaflet showing Sanders being showered with
champagne was prepared by Bill Pope, then Carter's press secretary.
Dorothy Wood, another former Rafshoon vice president, corroborated
Abernathy's claims, saying she saw the leaflet being boxed "in groups of
several hundred or so in the office." Bill Shipp says he saw Pope
distributing the handbills at a Ku Klux Klan rally. Abernathy confessed
to journalist Stephen Brill that "I personally prepared all of King's radio
ads while I was on Rafshoon's payroll and supervised the production."
Wood backs him up and speculates that Carter must have known about
the King commercials because "he had his finger on every aspect of the
campaign." King admitted it would not be surprising if "Carter people"
did his ads. With keen insight he added, "Carter is a highly opportunis-
tic man. Regrettably, his face is a facade which reveals little of the
inward person. His feet are not only made of clay, they're mired in it."[33]

Had the election been decided by the newspapers, Sanders would
have trounced his opponent, for he won the battle for the press hands
down. Shortly before the election, a Sanders press release listed fifty-one
newspapers that had endorsed the former governor. Daily newspapers
which had endorsed Sanders included: the *Athens Banner-Herald*, *Athens
Daily News*, *Augusta Chronicle*, *Augusta Herald*, *The Columbus Ledger*,
The Daily Times of Gainesville, *The Courier Herald* of Dublin, *Macon*

---

[32]Lasky, *Jimmy Carter*, p. 79; Murphy and Gulliver, *The Southern Strategy*, p. 185;
Leslie Wheeler, *Jimmy Who?* (Woodbury, N. Y.: Barron's Educational Series, 1976) p.
57; *Official Register, 1969–1970*, p. 1558.

[33]Lasky, *Jimmy Carter*, pp. 75-83; Glad, *Jimmy Carter*, pp. 134-35; Steven Brill,
"Jimmy Carter's Pathetic Lies," *Harpers* 252 (March 1976): 79.

News, Marietta Daily Journal, Rome News-Tribune, Savannah Evening Press, Savannah Morning News, Times-Enterprise of Thomasville, and the *Waycross Journal-Herald.* Later, despite Anne Cox Chambers's ownership, the *Atlanta Journal* and the *Atlanta Constitution* endorsed Sanders. By contrast, Carter received the endorsement of only one major daily newspaper—the *Columbus Enquirer.*[34]

With overwhelming backing from the press and the support of community leaders throughout the state, Sanders had good reason to expect to win. On Sunday, September 6, three days before the primary election, Carl and Betty celebrated their twenty-third wedding anniversary. Talking to reporters that day, Carl commented that "there is every indication we can win without a runoff." Our opposition, he continued, "got bogged down in a mudhole at the beginning of this campaign and just kept sinking deeper until he got in over his head. I think Georgia voters will let him stay buried."[35]

Further bolstering Sanders's confidence were polls which showed him comfortably ahead. Sanders's last poll, taken three weeks before the primary, showed Sanders with 54 percent of the vote. For his part Sanders had conducted what he thought was an effective campaign. Although he had not campaigned as strenuously as he did in 1962, he had saturated the state with Sanders buttons, literature, billboards, and radio and television ads, and he had addressed issues in a statesmanlike manner. On television and radio ads alone, he had outspent Carter $290,207 to $170,238. His family and supporters had worked hard getting his message to the people. Numerous endorsements as well as polls indicated that the effort was successful. Despite Carter's constant mudslinging, he had maintained his composure, though it had not been easy. He had traveled the "high road" while Carter, he felt, had disgraced himself with scurrilous attacks and appeals to Wallace-type segregationists. Sanders knew Carter was no redneck, and he felt certain the voters would reject his opponent's false image and negative cam-

---

[34]Undated press release, 1970 press releases 1 folder, box 25, Sanders Collection, Law Library; *Atlanta Journal*, September 1, 1970; *Atlanta Constitution*, September 3, 1970; *Columbus Enquirer*, August 25, 1970.

[35]Press release September 6, 1970, 1970 press releases 2 folder, box 25, Sanders Collection, Law Library.

paigning. Furthermore, unlike Carter, Sanders had already proved that he could do the job, and he assumed his experience would carry a lot of weight with the voters. In addition to all of those factors, Sanders could count on his famous luck. In five previous races he had always won. The 1970 race, he believed, would be no different.[36]

Unfortunately for Sanders, 1970 was different. When the votes of the September 9 election were counted, it was Carter who won, almost without a runoff, winning 48.6 percent of the vote to Sanders's 37.7 percent. Carter received 388,280 votes; Sanders won 301,659. The results shocked Sanders and left him dumbfounded. He could not believe what he saw. How, he wondered incredulously, could it have happened?[37]

With hindsight it is easy to discern what went wrong for Sanders. From the beginning he assumed that being a decent man, running on his excellent record, and offering a solid platform and strong leadership was enough to elect him, but that approach failed to excite the public and proved disastrous against the wily Carter. Sanders later remarked, "I was talking about needs and programs and things I knew the state must do something about. Most people were not really interested in those." By 1970 the public had grown increasingly disgusted with the endless war in Vietnam and domestic unrest, including student rioting, antiwar demonstrations that disrupted college campuses, rising inflation, crime, and drug use. And in the field of civil rights, the attitudes of Georgia voters had changed significantly since 1962 when Sanders trounced archsegregationist Marvin Griffin. Passage of the Civil Rights Act of 1964 and the Voting Rights Act of 1965, as well as numerous federal court decisions, had imposed vast social and economic changes on the South which particularly affected middle and lower class whites. As a result, a strong white backlash had developed, but the Sanders campaign failed to take into account the growing public anger and frustration over forced integration. The decisive factor in the election, Murphy and Gulliver observe, was probably the racial issue, and Sanders refused to capitulate to it. In reality Carter was more liberal than Sanders on the

---

[36]*Atlanta Constitution*, September 13, 1970; *Atlanta Journal*, June 25, 1971; Cook, "Sanders: An Oral History," pp. 63-68.

[37]*Official Register, 1969–1970*, p. 1558.

race issue, but in the campaign Carter shrewdly branded Sanders as the liberal and cast himself in the role of spokesman for white Wallace-Maddox segregationist-oriented voters. Carter may not have offered plausible or realistic remedies to the problems they faced, but by appealing to their emotional and psychological needs, he gained their votes. The clearest evidence of the white backlash can be seen in the election of Lester Maddox as lieutenant governor. Georgia's most notorious segregationist received more votes in the 1970 Democratic primary than did Sanders or Carter. Maddox easily defeated George T. Smith and two other candidates, and he did it without a runoff.[38]

Overconfidence was another problem that plagued the Sanders campaign. Being the frontrunner from the beginning and having a great approval rating among Georgians, Sanders underestimated the Carter candidacy. He simply did not campaign as hard or as viciously as his opponent. Moreover, relying largely on his own experience and "instincts," Sanders made little use of political research. Robert Coram and Remer Tyson found his reluctance to obtain elementary research the "most baffling part of the campaign." Even when Sanders received useful information and advice from Oliver Quayle or his own campaign staff, he seldom used it. Early in the campaign, Quayle urged him to disclose his finances and concentrate his campaign on voters thirty-five and under who live in the cities and suburbs. He also told him Highway Director Jim Gillis was a political liability. Sanders rejected his advice. On April 8 his campaign staff recommended unanimously that Sanders disclose his personal finances. He refused, responding indignantly, "You're asking me to cut my throat from ear to ear. You're just being naive. I've worked this road before. You haven't." By failing to take any polls during the last three weeks of the campaign, he had no evidence to indicate the dramatic shift of voters to Carter. Evidently the highly publicized Carter press conference of August 26 coupled with the wide distribution of "fact sheets" gained Carter thousands of votes, but Sanders was unaware of the erosion of his support. He thought the charges Carter leveled against him were so absurd that anyone could see through them.

---

[38]Ibid., p. 1562; Coram and Tyson, "The Loser Who Won," pp. 41-42; Murphy and Gulliver, *The Southern Strategy*, 187; Lyons, "A Comparison of Carl Sanders's Gubernatorial Campaigns: 1962 and 1970," pp. 29-39.

Convinced that the voters would repudiate such negative campaigning, he simply could not imagine losing to Carter. At various times throughout the campaign, intimates such as Bert Hester, Gene Holley, Bob Sanders, and others told Sanders his campaign was in trouble, but to no avail. Thus, in addition to underestimating Carter's candidacy, he also overestimated his own political expertise and instincts.[39]

In contrast to Sanders, Carter relied very heavily on political research and developed his strategy accordingly. By taking full advantage of modern public opinion polls and computerized voter lists, coupled with his own knowledge gained from extensive grass roots campaigning, Carter molded his image to conform to the public mood. It was a false and utterly deceptive image, as later events proved, but it brought him the Wallace-Maddox vote. With uncanny skill, Carter also managed to alter the public perception of Sanders. By constantly attacking the frontrunner, Carter made "Cufflinks Carl" the chief issue in the campaign, relegating all other issues to insignificance. Never once did Carter prove that the former governor had done anything illegal or unethical. Rarely, in fact, did he even make such accusations. Instead, he slyly attributed sinister motives to practically everything Sanders did and repeatedly implied that Sanders had misused the power of his office to get rich. By resorting to false charges, dubious reasoning, innuendo, and disreputable "fact sheets," he conveyed the message that Sanders had violated the public's trust. Carter practiced the tactic commonly used in modern advertising—if you repeat the same message often enough, people will believe it. It was a remarkable performance, a brilliant example of character assassination carried out ruthlessly by the boyish-looking forty-five-year-old "born-again" Christian candidate whose sincere and innocent expression perfectly masked his Machiavellian intentions. Disregarding morality, the Carter campaign was one of the most brilliantly conceived and skillfully executed campaigns in Georgia's history. Conducting it with almost flawless precision, Carter campaigned relentlessly and achieved an upset victory that few—including Sanders—thought possible.[40]

---

[39]Coram and Tyson, "The Loser Who Won," pp. 64-65; Coram interview, April 4, 1991; Holley interview, April 19, 1991; Hester interview, June 5, 1991; Bob Sanders interview, May 7, 1991; Cook, "Sanders: An Oral History," pp. 67-68.

[40]Murphy and Gulliver, *The Southern Strategy*, pp. 184-87; Shipp, "How He Won It," *Atlanta Constitution*, November 8-11, 1970.

By forthrightly discussing issues in preference to name calling and by waging a slick media campaign instead of a grassroots approach, Sanders unwittingly contributed to the Carter victory. The warm, caring, sometimes humorous Sanders whom family and close friends knew was not conveyed to the public by his campaign. Nor was his intense love of family and home. Sanders was so home-oriented that he spent only two nights away from home during the entire campaign. He insisted on spending the night at home even when it meant arriving at 2:00 or 3:00 a.m. and leaving early the next morning. But this warm, compassionate side of Sanders rarely was seen in the campaign. Instead, the public saw a formal, somewhat aloof and unemotional leader, who never seemed to perspire or even have a hair out of place. By projecting this "perfect" image and displaying the trappings of wealth—living in an exclusive neighborhood, wearing expensive clothing, driving a new Thunderbird, flying, boating, etc.—the campaign fell flat. Carl, as one of Sanders's close friends expressed it, "is not overburdened with modesty," and his expensive media campaign, designed to stress his experience, competence, and professionalism, made him appear rich and somewhat arrogant. By doing so, it reinforced the "Cufflinks Carl" image that Carter was trying to project. The Carter people were delighted with the Sanders campaign, and they could not have devised a Sanders campaign that would have served their purposes better.[41]

Finally, there is a dynamic in Georgia politics that militates against a governor's returning to office. Since 1942, when Georgia lengthened the term of governor from two years to four years, no one except Gene Talmadge had managed to win the office a second time. And Talmadge won on the basis of county unit votes, not popular votes, and he died in 1946 before taking office again. Subsequently, Marvin Griffin, Ellis Arnall, and Ernest Vandiver sought reelection, but none succeeded. Sanders appeared to have a better chance, but he failed, and four years later Lester Maddox suffered the same fate. For whatever reason, Georgia voters do not seem to want former governors to return to that office.

---

[41]Ibid.; Coram interview, April 4, 1991; interview with J. W. Weltch, Augusta, April 19, 1991; Holley interview, April 19, 1991; Bill Shipp interview by Cliff Kuhn, April 22, 1987, Georgia Government Documentation Project, Special Collections, Georgia State University, Atlanta.

Shocked into reality by the vote in the primary, Sanders went on the offensive. Since "high road" campaigning had failed, in the two weeks before the runoff election he resorted to the kind of tactics Carter had used against him all summer. The super-cool, well-dressed, level-voiced former governor gave way to a tieless, coatless, loud, name calling "new" Sanders. Instead of "my opponent," Carter became a "smiling hypocrite," a man against God and in favor of organized crime, a man "without conscience, integrity or character," a "grinning chameleon." Carter, he said, had nothing to offer the people but "a grin, a handshake and a pack of lies."[42]

During the runoff, Sanders did many things he had refused to do earlier. He released "fact sheets" on Carter attempting to show how Carter had exploited workers on his farm, and he finally released his financial statement which placed his wealth at $685,624—not a great deal more than Carter's wealth. And Sanders charged that if Carter had used "fair market value" for the 2,000 acres of south Georgia farmland he owns, "he'd be worth more than me." Sanders pointedly rejected Carter's charge that he had used the power and prestige of the governor's office for his own personal profit by releasing figures which showed that instead of getting rich while he was governor, his net worth actually had declined during those years. By releasing his financial statement, Sanders insisted that Carter was now obligated to meet him in a face-to-face debate.[43]

Carter, however, would have none of it. Now in the driver's seat with momentum shifting in his direction, he refused to debate and ridiculed the "new" Sanders. "Taking off his tie and cuff links does not make him a working man," Carter stated. Calling Sanders "a desperate bitter man," Carter claimed that he would not debate him on television because Sanders's "state of mind and attitude are not conducive to rational debate." "He has started taking off his clothes a piece at a time. I'm glad the runoff campaign is only two weeks long," Carter quipped.[44]

Having restrained himself throughout the campaign, Sanders launched a barrage of attacks against Carter during the runoff, but his

---

[42]Lasky, *Jimmy Carter*, pp. 89-90; Coram and Tyson, "The Loser Who Won," p. 96.

[43]*Atlanta Constitution*, September 18, 1970.

[44]*Savannah Evening Press*, September 18, 1970; *Macon Telegraph*, September 15, 1970.

heart was not really in it. If nothing else, the campaign showed that Carter was far more adept at slinging mud than Sanders. In public Sanders was a slashing, attacking man, but in private, according to Coram and Tyson, "he became human for the first time in the campaign." He became more humble and more gentle. He listened. He turned to his children for consolation and immersed himself in Betty Foy's preparations for college. He grew quiet and introspective when not on the stump and became emotionally prepared for whatever might happen on September 23. Sanders has never been a man for whom one feels sorry, Coram and Tyson observed, "but he came close in those days."[45]

Once a frontrunner loses his lead and momentum shifts to the underdog, it is almost impossible to reverse the trend. Sanders could not. Nothing changed from September 9 to September 23 except Carter picked up more support. Carter received 506,462 votes (59.4 percent) to Sanders's 345,906 votes (40.5 percent). Early in the evening, long before the count was finished, Sanders realized the outcome. With a stoic expression masking a heavy heart, he went to the Carter headquarters and congratulated his opponent. Returning to the Dinkler Plaza Hotel shortly after 10 p. m., he stood with his family before the glare of TV lights and a battery of microphones. Humbled by his first political defeat, he said, "My only disappointment is that I have not been able to convey to the people of Georgia what I had in my heart and in my mind."[46]

Although deeply disappointed that he would not get the opportunity to lead Georgia's government for the next four years, Sanders could at least take comfort from the fact that he had waged an honorable campaign and had come through the ordeal with his character and integrity in tact. The same could not be said of the victorious Carter, who ended the campaign with a troubled conscience. Afterwards he told friends that he "felt bad" about his actions and had prayed for forgiveness for the things he had said and done to get elected. He has been conspicuously reticent about discussing the race, and aside from a few references in his book *Why Not the Best?*, he has made no mention of the campaign in his writings. Moreover, he has sequestered his 1970

---

[45]Coram and Tyson, "The Loser Who Won," p. 97.
[46]Ibid.; *Official Register, 1969–1970*, p. 1660.

gubernatorial papers in his presidential library in Atlanta, where they remain unprocessed and unscheduled for processing. For Carter, who later gained worldwide acclaim as a moralist and humanitarian, his campaign of expediency in 1970 has remained an embarrassment.[47]

---

[47]Lasky, *Jimmy Carter*, pp. 96-97; Howard Norton and Bob Slosser, *The Miracle of Jimmy Carter* (Plainfield NJ: Logos International, 1976) pp. 47-48; Randy Sanders, "'The Sad Duty of Politics': Jimmy Carter and the Issue of Race in His 1970 Gubernatorial Campaign," *Georgia Historical Quarterly* 76 (Fall 1992): 637.

Opponents in 1970: Carl Sanders and Jimmy Carter.

Chapter 20

From Politics to Business

After entering the legislature in 1954, Sanders advanced steadily up the political ladder, rising from representative to senator, and then to floor leader, president pro tem, and finally governor. Having gained an enviable reputation as a legislator and state executive, he stood out as one of the bright and attractive new leaders emerging in the South. Ambitious and hard working, he seemed poised for political greatness. A victory in the 1970 election and another successful term as governor would have positioned him for leadership in the Democratic party. As a handsome and popular moderate Southerner with a proven record of accomplishment and a wide circle of prominent contacts and not yet fifty years old, he certainly had formidable assets for high national office. But that was not to be. Instead, his rival, Jimmy Carter, advanced to national leadership. The gubernatorial campaign of 1970 marked a major turning point in the life of Carl Sanders. His first political defeat, it also was his last political race. After 1970, he never again sought public office. Practically speaking, Sanders's promising political career ended at age forty-five. Although he already had achieved success as a lawyer and businessman, for sixteen years his political accomplishments overshadowed his other endeavors. Up to 1970, Sanders's priorities had been politics, law, and business, in that order; after 1970, they shifted to law, business, and politics.

Although Sanders enjoyed serving the public and used his political skills to great advantage, he was not obsessed with holding office. He rejected President Johnson's offers to make him a judge of the Fifth Circuit Court of Appeals or the ambassador to the Philippines. At other times he had been seriously considered for the positions of attorney general, secretary of commerce, and chairman of the Federal Communications Commission.[1] Accepting no other political office, he left the political arena so that he could expand his law practice and numerous business investments. Yet he continued to maintain a keen interest in political affairs after 1970 and even considered running for office again. He was strongly tempted to enter the United States Senate race in 1972, especially when polls showed him far ahead of incumbent Senator David Gambrell (who had been appointed by Governor Carter to succeed Senator Russell), former Governor Vandiver, young state Representative Sam Nunn, and the other candidates. According to Benny Tackett, only the forceful opposition of Edwin Hatch, president of Georgia Power Company, prevented Sanders from running. On the last day for qualifying, after a press release announcing his entrance into the race had been prepared and a check for the qualifying fee written, Hatch explained that Sanders's candidacy would harm Georgia Power Company. His political opponents, Hatch pointed out, would campaign against the giant utility and Sanders's connection to it. Determined to keep his company out of the political contest, Hatch hinted that if Sanders entered the race Georgia Power might transfer its legal business to another firm. Unwilling to lose a client that paid his law firm $498,051 in 1971, Sanders decided against the race. He threw his support to Nunn, the eventual winner. Although frequently rumored by the press to be planning a political comeback as a candidate for governor or mayor of Atlanta, Sanders never seriously considered entering any race after 1972.[2]

After 1970, Sanders's political activity consisted primarily in working behind the scenes for candidates he favored. An adept fund raiser, he drummed up support for George Busbee in his races for governor in 1974 and 1978, for law partner Norman Underwood's unsuccessful gubernatorial race in 1982, for Zell Miller's successful gubernatorial campaign in 1990, and for Doug Barnard's numerous campaigns for Congress. He also backed Sam Nunn and Wyche Fowler for the Senate, Pierre Howard for lieutenant governor, Andrew Young for mayor of

---

[1]*Atlanta Journal,* May 27, June 30, 1966; *Savannah Morning News,* September 22, 1966; Sanders, "Interviews in 1990," pp. 146, 193.

[2]Benny Tackett interview, June 19, 1991; Sanders, "Interviews in 1990, p. 231; *Atlanta Constitution,* June 1, 1972, June 27, 1977, May 6, 1986.

Atlanta, and Marvin Arrington for president of the Atlanta City Commission. Always loyal to the Democratic party, he continued to provide generous financial contributions to the party and served as its finance chairman during Busbee's eight years as governor. He always voted a straight Democratic ticket with but one exception. Still bitter over the 1970 campaign, he could not in good conscience cast his vote for Jimmy Carter for president. To avoid the hypocrisy of voting for a man he did not respect, he cast a write-in vote in 1976 and 1980.[3]

In addition to supporting Democratic candidates, he used his influence to secure passage of key measures, especially those affecting the future of Atlanta, such as the sales tax to finance MARTA and the development of the World Congress Center. He also spoke out forcefully on critical issues affecting the city and state in hopes of arousing the populace and prodding political leaders to act. He recognized that a major stumbling block impeding growth in the metropolitan Atlanta area was the unusually large number of local political units. Given their different political and economic needs as well as their divergent racial composition, it was always difficult and sometimes impossible to get the various counties, towns, and cities to agree on major policies affecting the metropolitan area. In 1975 Sanders presented a comprehensive plan for a metropolitan government for the whole Atlanta area. Noting that many whites had "given up" on Atlanta as a black city with a black power structure, he stated, "if Atlanta is to expand into one of the world's great cities, racial divisiveness simply has no place." He suggested reorganizing the five counties and forty-five cities and towns into a "super city." Using a two-tiered approach, he called for a Greater Atlanta Federation to oversee police services, mass transit, construction and maintenance of major highways, traffic management, and water systems, while local governments would operate sanitation, parks, libraries, local road construction and maintenance, and fire services. Avoiding the emotional school issue, his plan left the drawing of school district lines to the federal courts. Sanders's plan was a thoughtful and farsighted attempt to overcome the confusion, inefficiency, and parochialism of the existing situation, but it was too radical for the political leaders of that day. Lacking his vision for the future and jealously guarding their own

---

[3]Sanders, "Interviews in 1990," pp. 231-35.

prerogatives, they rejected his plan immediately.[4] Unfortunately, eighteen years later, Atlanta still lacks the kind of metropolitan government Sanders envisaged, and the problems which he addressed so prophetically in 1975 have only intensified.[5]

Atlanta's growing crime rate also deeply concerned Sanders. He understood that all major American cities faced the menace of crime, but in Atlanta the crime problem had become acute. Violent crime continued to escalate in the 1970s, and the city government had done little to combat it. Though troubled by the growing crime rate, Sanders made few public statements about the problem until it affected him directly. When two employees of his law firm became victims, however, he then spoke out with a vengeance. In the fall of 1979 hoodlums attacked a twenty-year-old college student who worked in the file room. As the young man waited for a bus on Peachtree Street, assailants stabbed him sixteen times and left him for dead. Miraculously he survived. Three weeks later, Patti Barry, a lovely twenty-six-year-old secretary in the firm, was killed. Filled with rage by the senseless violence, Sanders sent a blistering letter to Mayor Maynard Jackson, accusing him of being soft on crime and questioning his willingness to pay the political price to rid the city of criminals. Sanders pointed out that the criminals now believe they can "commit crimes of the most heinous nature and get away without being caught." He called for an adequate police force which would strictly enforce the law, ferret out the undesirable elements, and bring them to the bar of justice. No issue, he asserted, is more important than "the personal safety of the citizens." Atlanta could be cleaned up, the angry Sanders concluded, if the leaders are willing to "pay the price." Up to then he believed Jackson was fully capable of doing this job, but "as of today my confidence is beginning to wane."[6]

Several commentators suggested that Sanders was merely raising an issue that he could use in a political campaign for mayor of Atlanta or governor, and many blacks considered his charges a racial attack on Atlanta's black mayor.[7] Both were wrong. His outburst was neither

---

[4]Ibid., pp. 231, 236; *Atlanta Journal,* August 24, 25, 1975.

[5]Shipp, "Carl Sanders: The Man, The Legend, The Era," p. 26.

[6]*Atlanta Journal,* October 18, 1979; *Atlanta Constitution,* October 19, 1979.

[7]*Atlanta Journal and Constitution,* November 25, 1979; Leroy Johnson interview,

politically nor racially motivated. It was an expression of outrage by a private citizen who had "had enough" and now demanded action. Although he and a host of others continued to speak out on crime thereafter, the problem persisted. Indeed, in many parts of the city it grew worse. Sanders himself became a victim in 1992. In the wake of the controversial Rodney King verdict, angry blacks went on a rampage in Los Angeles, and racial tension increased in cities throughout the country, including Atlanta. Four young black males, committing random acts of violence, happened to encounter Sanders as he walked from his office to his car. They knocked him down and ran away. Fortunately, Sanders was not seriously injured, but the attack confirmed his earlier decision to move his office from the Candler Building to a safer and more prestigious location.[8]

The leadership of Georgia's state government in the 1980s impressed Sanders no more than the leadership of Atlanta's city government. He found it bland and uninspiring. What particularly bothered him was that the leaders had allowed the state's infrastructure to decay gradually, an infrastructure he had vastly improved as governor. In a highly publicized speech to the Buckhead Rotary Club on March 5, 1990, he issued a clarion call for Georgia's political leaders to come to grips with the state's decaying infrastructure. If something is not done soon about the state's roads, bridges, classrooms, airports, and sewer systems, Sanders asserted, "the state is going to look like a third world nation in the near future." Citing facts and figures, he noted that only fifty miles of interstate highways had been added in the last ten years, at least 5,000 bridges are obsolete or structurally deficient, cities are desperately seeking $2 billion to build new sewage plants, and Georgia ranks near the bottom in per capita spending for highways and public schools. The total costs of repairing the infrastructure will be so enormous that taxes must be increased to generate the revenue, he pointed out. Acknowledging that no one wants to raise taxes, he added that "further delay will become more devastating to Georgia and Georgians in the future."[9]

February 20, 1991.

[8]Interview with Carl Sanders, Atlanta, September 16, 1992.

[9]"Georgia: A State of Fast Decay," Speech by Carl E. Sanders to Buckhead Rotary Club, March 5, 1990, Sanders Personal Papers; Shipp, "Carl Sanders: The Man, The Legend, The Era," p. 26.

Streamlining government for greater efficiency, improving education, providing law and order, creating jobs, and developing the state's transportation system were issues he had dealt with as governor, and as a private citizen he continued to express his concerns about them.

Although clearly interested in political developments, he relegated politics to the back burner after losing the gubernatorial race in 1970 and immersed himself in business and professional endeavors with the same intensity he had previously directed to politics. The same leadership qualities he had displayed in politics served him equally well as a lawyer and businessman, and he quickly achieved striking success in both fields. His advancement as a lawyer and businessman was so rapid that by 1974, only four years after his humiliating defeat, he remarked that Carter actually had done him a favor by winning the gubernatorial race.[10]

Through the influence of an old friend in Augusta, Sherman Drawdy, who was chairman of the First Railroad & Banking Company of Georgia, Sanders had gotten into the banking business before the 1970 campaign. Drawdy, like practically all other bankers in the state, wanted to expand into the Atlanta area. When the legislature finally passed the Bank Holding Company Law, which allowed banks to go outside their county and acquire other banks in the state, Drawdy with Sanders's help bought the American Bank, a small Atlanta institution with assets of $10 million, from the General Acceptance Corporation of Allentown, Pennsylvania. It was located in the Candler Building, one of Atlanta's first skyscrapers, built in 1906 and rising seventeen stories in height. Soon they acquired a second bank in the business district of Atlanta, the Peoples Bank, which had close to $15 million in assets. The Fulton Bank, which also had assets of nearly $15 million, became their third acquisition. It was located in East Point, a suburb which contained Atlanta's busy airport. Together the three banks had combined assets of approximately $40 million, and they operated them as the First Georgia Bank. Under their leadership the bank flourished and its assets increased substantially. When Drawdy died in September 1973, Sanders, who then chaired the Executive Committee, succeeded Drawdy as chairman of the board. Since 1972, he also served on the board of directors of First Rail-

---

[10]*Atlanta Constitution*, December 2, 1974.

road & Banking Company of Georgia, which had controlling interest in First Georgia Bank.[11]

At the same time Sanders entered the banking business with Sherman Drawdy, he got heavily involved in real estate with his law partner Jack Ashmore. Together they bought 3,000 apartments in north Atlanta from Hardy Kilgore for $20 million. They bought the Candler Building, renovated it, and moved their law firm there. In 1972 they bought Peachtree Air Service, an aviation operation at Peachtree-DeKalb Airport. Sanders, who loved flying and had owned a plane in the late-1960s, thought the business would enable him to fly whenever he desired. To run the business Ashmore hired Jack Minter, a former director of the Department of Industry and Trade in the Vandiver administration. The personable Minter proved to be an ineffective salesman. Consequently, the aviation business never made any money for Sanders. In addition to these investments, Ashmore had several others on the Georgia coast which Sanders was not involved in. Ashmore bought the King and Prince Hotel on Jekyll Island and the Sea Palms Country Club on St. Simons Island. He also purchased land on St. Simons Island and built the Island Club, which was a country club with a golf course, a shopping center, and residential housing.[12]

Sanders, having previously made extensive real estate investments in the Augusta area, continued to invest in his hometown. In May 1973 he announced a $7 million program to revitalize downtown Augusta. The plan called for the renovation of the Richmond Hotel, renovation and expansion of the Southern Finance Building, and construction of a new $5 million hotel on Broad Street. The new 200-bed hotel, Sanders told civic, business, and government leaders, would be "first class in every way" and will provide Augusta with badly needed downtown accommodations, including facilities for conventions.[13] The Southern Finance Building project, which featured a glass penthouse placed atop the existing building, was solely the work of Gene Holley, Sanders's former law partner. Designed by noted architect I. M. Pei, it cost over

---

[11]Sanders, "Interviews in 1990," pp. 202-203; *Augusta Chronicle*, October 12, 1972, September 19, 1973.

[12]Sanders, "Interviews in 1990," pp. 203-205.

[13]*Augusta Herald*, May 30, 1973.

$1 million and afforded a panoramic view of Augusta. Sanders was not involved in that project, but he was a major investor, along with Holley, Bert Hester, and others, in renovating the old Richmond Hotel and in building the new hotel which became the Augusta Hilton. Sanders and the other investors hoped that these substantial investments would stimulate business activity in downtown Augusta, for Augusta, like so many American cities, had been losing business to the convenient new shopping centers popping up in the outlying areas. They expected these major projects to reverse that trend and bring renewed activity to the downtown section, and to some extent they did.[14]

All of these investments were highly leveraged, for Sanders, having an excellent reputation and credit rating, had no trouble borrowing vast sums of money. With his flourishing law firm providing a substantial income, he managed to make the costly monthly payments. Unfortunately for Sanders, investments which appeared so promising in the booming 1960s and early 1970s lost their appeal when the economy slowed down in the mid-1970s. As interest rates, inflation, and unemployment all rose simultaneously, the economy nosedived. Sanders then had difficulty meeting his monthly obligations. Failing to anticipate the economic slump, he soon realized that he was terribly overextended, and his partners were even worse off.[15]

The first sign of trouble came when Ashmore told Sanders that they had to raise $1 million for taxes, insurance, and repairs on the Atlanta apartments. Scattered throughout north Atlanta, the apartments, with 99 percent occupancy, seemed to be a wonderful investment, but neither Sanders nor Ashmore could raise the necessary capital. Sanders suggested that they try to get the bank which held the note on the apartments to take them back. With so many investors defaulting on loans, however, banks hesitated to accept property they could not easily sell. Sanders went to see his old friend Bennett Brown, who was then a senior official with C & S Bank. He explained that bankruptcy loomed for the corporation that held the apartments unless the bank would take over the notes. Sanders considered the apartments first-rate property and hated to lose them, but he saw no alternative. After thinking about the propos-

---

[14]Ibid.; Holley interview, April 19, 1991.

[15]Sanders, "Interviews in 1990," pp. 204-206.

al for a while, Brown agreed to take the apartments. "That was the happiest day of my life," Sanders later recalled. Overjoyed that the huge burden had been removed, he slept soundly that night for the first time in weeks. Within a year, C & S Bank swapped the $20 million apartment notes to Manufacturers Hanover for a $35 million debt. The $15 million profit C & S made from the apartments did not bother Sanders because he was so relieved to be free of the $20 million obligation. He did get a little sick, however, when a year later Manufacturers Hanover sold the apartments to a California group for $75 million in cash.[16]

As the financial crunch worsened, Jack Ashmore suddenly had an aneurysm and died on August 13, 1976, a tragedy that complicated Sanders's financial situation. Jack's brother, Walter Ashmore, attempted to operate his projects but was unable to do so. Trying to make the best of a bad situation, Sanders relinquished to Walter his interest in Peachtree Air Service and some other investments. In return, he received Ashmore's interest in the Candler Building and his stock in First Georgia Bank. At that time the Candler Building was heavily mortgaged and First Georgia Bank, like practically all banks in Georgia, was stuck with a portfolio of bad loans. Eager to reduce his liabilities, Sanders offered the Candler Building to his law firm, but his partners rejected the offer. Their unwillingness to assume the debt ultimately benefitted Sanders, because in April 1978 he sold half-interest in the building to David N. Smith, a client of his law firm and owner of International Horizons Inc., and fourteen months later they sold the Candler Building for $12 million. After paying off the mortgage, Sanders and Smith split a profit of several million dollars.[17]

When Sherman Drawdy died, Sanders as chairman of the board assumed chief responsibility for First Georgia Bank. But, unlike his predecessor, Sanders was not a banker. He had no professional training and little direct experience in banking when he began directing the affairs of First Georgia Bank. Moreover, with a busy law firm to direct, he had limited time to devote to banking. Despite such handicaps, he took charge of the bank and did what was necessary. Confidence in his

---

[16]Ibid., pp. 206-208.

[17]Ibid., pp. 208-209; Jill Abramson, "'Cuff Links Carl' Builds An Empire," *The American Lawyer* (September 1982): 15; *Atlanta Constitution*, February 15, 1978.

own ability to do the job probably was his greatest asset. Possessing inordinate common sense and a talent for grasping the big picture, he selected capable subordinates, established realistic goals, learned all he could about banking from experienced bankers, focused on essential issues, dealt with the staff in a tough but fair manner, and above all made firm decisions and stuck with them. In short, his leadership qualities overcame his inexperience and lack of training.

Fearful that the bank would collapse and thereby damage his reputation, he worked furiously to prevent that from happening. Attempting to gain time so that he could work through the crisis, he met with Monroe Kimbrell, president of the Federal Reserve Bank in Atlanta. He frankly told Kimbrell: "If you made us write off every bad loan we had today, we'd be out of business. But if you made C & S, which is twenty times bigger than us, write off all their bad loans, they'd be out of business too. I don't believe you are going to shut them down, so, for God's sake, don't shut us down." Kimbrell agreed to cooperate as much as possible, which was all Sanders had hoped for. To raise badly needed capital, Sanders convinced First Railroad & Banking Company, which owned a substantial portion of First Georgia, to put $3 million into the smaller bank in the form of a convertible debenture which could be converted into stock ownership. Finding a competent and experienced banker to run the bank was his next priority. Sanders dismissed several executives before he found the leader he wanted in Richard D. Jackson. Sanders lured Jackson from First National Bank, not with a high salary but with the challenge of turning the struggling bank around and the promise that he would be his own boss. Jackson was an excellent choice.[18]

Under the leadership of Sanders and Jackson, First Georgia aimed at the corporate middle market, with emphasis on locally owned companies with annual sales of up to $50 million. In addition to providing services for these customers, First Georgia opened several branch banks in Fulton and DeKalb counties. It became the first bank in Atlanta to offer simple interest consumer loans, and the first in the nation to offer a 12 percent credit card. It also offered Atlanta's first Women's Banking Department, which provided financial seminars, credit conferences, and counseling to women in all walks of life. By electing Tom Cordy to its

---

[18]Sanders, "Interviews in 1990," pp. 209-10.

board of directors, First Georgia broke another barrier, as Cordy was the first black to serve on the board of a major bank in Atlanta. With Sanders and Jackson at the helm, the bank survived the crisis and grew rapidly when the economy improved. In 1978 First Georgia passed the $100 million mark in assets and then ranked as the twenty-second largest bank in the state. Four years later it was the eleventh largest bank in Georgia with more than $200 million in assets.[19] In August 1986 it achieved the milestone of having $1 billion in assets, a remarkable feat since none of Atlanta's largest banks at that time had more than $4 billion in assets. At that point, First Railroad and Banking Company, which owned several small banks around Augusta, acquired Sanders's and other shareholders' interest in First Georgia Bank. Shortly afterwards, First Union Bank acquired First Railroad and Banking Company. From that merger Sanders received 200,000 shares of stock in First Union Bank, all of which he has retained.[20]

While Sanders was struggling to keep First Georgia afloat, operate his law firm, and make monthly payments on investments in Atlanta, he also faced financial difficulties in Augusta. He managed to get through the financial crisis in Augusta unscathed, but his former law partners Hester and Holley did not. Both Hester and Holley, starting from modest beginnings in Augusta, had prospered beyond their wildest dreams. Orphaned at an early age, Holley eventually amassed a fortune of $30 million, much of which he squandered in extravagant living. Spending money as fast as he could make it, he filled his Augusta mansion with expensive furniture and art works from Europe. He bought four airplanes, a helicopter, a huge yacht (the sister ship to the presidential yacht), a mountain in Tennessee, and a whole island off the coast of South Carolina. He directed his financial empire from an office in the I. M. Pei-designed penthouse atop the Southern Finance Building. Being very religious, Holley placed a thirty-six foot lighted cross on top of his penthouse on December 25, 1975, as a "Christmas present to Jesus on his birthday." What Jesus thought of the gift is unknown, but many Augustans complained that it was a garish eyesore. Never satisfied

---

[19]Norman Shavin and Bruce Galphin, *Atlanta: Triumph of a People* (Atlanta: Capricorn Corporation, 1982) p. 378.

[20]Sanders, "Interviews in 1990," p. 211.

with what he had accomplished, Holley continually sought more. But in his insatiable quest for greater wealth, he lost everything. His downfall came as a result of risky investments in oil in Qatar. Expecting to reap a fortune in Middle Eastern oil, he pushed his credit to the limit. His four wells produced oil, but the oil had a high sulphur content. The cost of purifying the oil proved prohibitively expensive, and Holley's lease expired before he realized any returns. Greatly overextended, his whole financial empire collapsed.[21]

On a smaller scale the soft-spoken Hester also amassed a magnificent fortune of $15 million. Although he shunned the ostentatious lifestyle of his friend Holley, he allowed ambition to cloud his judgment and he too lost everything.[22]

In 1979, following a probe of Holley and Hester's activities by the Justice Department under President Carter, a federal grand jury indicted them and two other men for fraud and related offenses in connection with loans of nearly $2 million issued by the First Augusta State Bank in 1975. The bank, which Holley and Hester owned, was declared insolvent in May 1977. Both Holley and Hester denied the accusations, but a jury found them guilty, and Judge Anthony Alaimo sentenced them to ten years in prison.[23] He later reduced the sentences, and they actually served sixteen months at the minimum security facility of Eglin Air Force Base in Florida. The trial left both Hester and Holley financially ruined and disbarred. Holley left the practice of law and went into consulting, but Hester gained reinstatement in the Georgia State Bar and resumed his practice in 1984.[24]

Sanders never believed that his friends had intended to do anything illegal or that they should have spent time in jail. He and J. B. Fuqua had hired a lawyer to represent Hester, but at the last minute Hester decided to represent himself. Similarly, Holley fired his attorney, Edward

---

[21]Holley interview, April 19, 1991; *Augusta Chronicle*, December 5, 1980, August 5, 1981.

[22]Hester interview, June 5, 1991.

[23]*Augusta Chronicle*, November 17, December 7, 1979, February 19-28, April 5, 1980.

[24]Holley interview, April 19, 1991; Hester interview, June 5, 1991; *Augusta Chronicle*, December 2, 1980, March 19, August 3, 5, September 8, 1981, October 4, 1984.

Bennet Williams, and represented himself. Judging from the outcome of the trials, both decisions were mistakes. Sanders had no financial interest in the First Augusta State Bank or Qatar oil. Holley had tried to convince Sanders to invest in additional oil projects by assuring him that they would make millions of dollars, but Sanders, having learned his lesson from Texas oil, wisely refused. He did, however, have several investments with Holley and Hester, and their downfall added additional burdens for him. Eventually he assumed their notes on the Augusta Hilton, West Lake Development, the Richmond Hotel, and a large tract of property in North Augusta. At that time he was so heavily mortgaged that the last thing he needed was more debt. But he had little choice if he wanted to salvage his own investments in those projects.[25]

At some point everyone reaches his physical limit, and in this financial crisis Sanders reached his. Having worked day and night to keep his creditors at bay, his extraordinary stamina began to weaken. Exhausted by the ordeal, he was tempted to give up the struggle. When his burdens were especially heavy and his financial situation seemed utterly hopeless, he often wrote PITHOL, his anagram for "Put in the hands of the Lord." Many advised him to declare bankruptcy, but Sanders refused to consider it. Declaring bankruptcy, he believed, would destroy both his reputation and career. "Money is a replenishable commodity," he often remarked, "your character and your name are not." Convinced that with sufficient time he could satisfy his creditors, he somehow found the strength to persevere.[26]

Overwhelmed with debt, Sanders desperately needed to reduce his obligations. He well understood that if he did not eliminate some of his liabilities, he might lose all of his assets, as Holley and Hester did. Having no desire to stay in the hotel business, he attempted to dispose of both the Augusta Hilton and the Richmond Hotel. Few investors, however, showed any interest in the old Richmond Hotel and its big parking garage. Thus, when B. G. Sanders & Associates of Atlanta expressed an interest in converting the facility into a home for the elderly, Sanders jumped at the opportunity. Since the sale hinged upon securing federal assistance, Sanders contacted everyone who might

---

[25]Sanders, "Interviews in 1990," pp. 211-13.
[26]Ibid., pp. 134-37; Hayes, "The Comeback of Cuff-links Carl," p. 47.

possibly be involved in the transaction. His efforts succeeded and the sale took place in 1980. The new owners converted the old hotel into a successful home for the elderly, and from the sale Sanders paid off notes for $1.5 million plus another $500,000 in interest. Two years later the Augusta Hotel Associates, Ltd. purchased the Augusta Hilton, a transaction that relieved Sanders and his partner Peter Menk of an obligation of nearly $5 million. Although Sanders did not profit from either transaction, he was delighted to be rid of both properties. Having reduced his debt to manageable proportions, he decided to hold on to the West Lake project and the North Augusta property as long-term investments.[27]

Although West Lake had been a disappointment to its investors, Sanders saw great potential in the project. Over a period of several years he secured the notes and stock from all of the investors and managed to pay off all of them with interest by 1985. By doing so, he acquired all of the land surrounding the country club. He then placed the whole operation in the hands of a capable manager, Harry Crosby, and let him run it. Soon West Lake began to show a profit. Carl Jr., who had become disenchanted with banking and was anxious to get into real estate, moved to Augusta in 1986 and learned the business from Crosby. When Crosby retired in 1988, Carl Jr. replaced him. He continued to develop West Lake, Inc., selling from twenty-five to thirty-five lots each year at an average cost of $50,000; by 1992 West Lake consisted of more than 600 homes. Thus, West Lake eventually became the exclusive residential development Sanders envisaged many years before, and his son became a successful businessman directing a flourishing operation.[28]

After several years of extraordinary effort, Sanders managed to put his financial house back in order. It had been a stressful ordeal, but he survived the experience and came out of it a stronger man. From his mistakes he learned valuable lessons. In buying real estate, for example, he learned to avoid buying property unless he had a plan to develop or sell it. He also learned to avoid business partnerships if at all possible. He had placed too much confidence in his business partners and had suffered the consequences. Thereafter he operated on his own. In buying

---

[27]Sanders, "Interviews in 1990," pp. 213-15.
[28]Ibid., pp. 215-17; Carl Sanders, Jr. interview, February 15, 1991.

stocks and bonds, he learned to seek quality companies and buy the stock for the long term. As a mature investor he followed the old theory of "buy right and sit tight." Having neither the time nor the desire to be a stock trader, he favored keeping stock for many years in the belief that stock in good companies will increase in value. Sanders knew that any investment involved risk, and he willingly took risks, but he learned to avoid high risks. A brief experience with buying eggs on the commodity market convinced him that he never wanted to invest in the commodity business again. Likewise, after he got out of the oil deals with Holley, he resolved to avoid the oil business and any other business where he really did not know what he was buying. As a result of the financial ordeal of nearly losing everything, Sanders became a more conservative investor.[29]

One of the most embarrassing moments in Sanders's life occurred in 1978 when he had to resign from the board of directors of First Railroad & Banking Company. At that time he was so overwhelmed with debt that the board thought he was ruined financially. For a man of noted pride, it was a humiliating experience. When First Georgia Bank was sold, one of the provisions stipulated that he would go back on the board of First Railroad & Banking Company. Few events have given him more satisfaction than the day he returned to the board and told the directors: "I'm finally out of trouble. I don't owe you any more money. I've paid all my debts. I'm back on the board and I'm delighted to be here." When First Union Bank purchased First Railroad & Banking Company, he became a member of that board. Since 1987 Sanders has served as chairman of the board of First Union National Bank of Atlanta, and in 1992 became chairman of the Executive Committee of the board of directors of First Union National Bank of Georgia.[30] Thus in a relatively short period of time, Sanders emerged as a powerful and respected force in the banking field.

When Sanders left the governor's office in 1967, he indicated that he wanted to serve on some boards and develop his law practice. In the intervening quarter of a century he did both. Unlike many ex-governors who have their names attached to law firms but do not really practice,

---

[29]Sanders, "Interviews in 1990," pp. 220-23.
[30]Ibid., pp. 213-14.

Sanders remained an active partner in Troutman, Sanders, Lockerman
& Ashmore. Indeed for many years he was the chief executive officer of
the firm and its driving force. Through mergers and the addition of new
lawyers it grew steadily and consistently to become one of the largest
and most prestigious firms in Atlanta. In September 1993 the firm
expanded beyond Atlanta by opening an office in Washington, D.C.
After operating from the Candler Building for twenty years, in 1992
Sanders moved the firm to the new NationsBank Plaza at 600 Peachtree
Street and shortened the name of the firm to Troutman Sanders. From
his spacious office on the fifty-second floor, which overlooked the
skyline of Atlanta, he directed the work of 175 attorneys who brought
in more than $40 million annually.[31]

In addition to developing the law firm, Sanders also helped build up
several companies. He had been heavily involved with J. B. Fuqua for
many years, serving on the board of Fuqua Industries since its inception
in 1967. In recent years he expanded his involvement in other companies. Healthdyne, Inc., an Atlanta company that produced sophisticated
medical equipment, was in difficulty when Sanders went on the board
in 1986. Having made too many acquisitions in a short period of time,
the company had become overextended. Sanders helped restructure it
and return it to profitability. Its revenues increased from $103 million
in 1989 to $191 million in 1991, and its operating profit increased from
$6.8 million to $24 million during the same period.[32] Sanders also made
substantial investments in Carmike Cinemas, a company headquartered
in Columbus, Georgia. Started in 1982, it expanded rapidly, and after
ten years owned more than 1,400 movie theaters, making it the fourth
largest motion picture screen exhibition company in the country. In
1991 it showed an operating profit of $19.5 million on revenues of
$145.7 million.[33] Since 1989 Sanders has served on the board of the
Norrell Corporation, a temporary services company predominantly
owned by Guy Millner of Atlanta. Through his law practice Sanders got
involved in a company called Learning Technologies, Ltd. Started by
David Smith, the man who purchased half-interest in the Candler

---

[31]Interview with Carl Sanders, Atlanta, October 12, 1992.
[32]Sanders, "Interviews in 1990," p. 217; *Healthdyne Annual Report, 1991.*
[33]Sanders, "Interviews in 1990," p. 217; *Carmike Cinemas Annual Report, 1991.*

Building, the company initially sold encyclopedias and books under the name International Horizons. Later it developed audio cassettes to teach English to Japanese preschoolers. When Smith died, the company went into bankruptcy, and Sanders represented the company in the bankruptcy proceedings. After a difficult battle with the government, the company got back on its feet. Sanders made substantial investments in Learning Technologies, Ltd. and was elected to the board. It grew steadily and by 1992 was selling $100 million worth of audio and video programs annually in Japan and Taiwan. With videotaped programs made at Harvard University, it has been a very profitable company and continues to expand. Sanders served on the board of Advanced Telecommunications, Inc. from 1983 until it merged with LDDS Communications Company in 1992, at which point he sold his stock. He also made a substantial investment in Resurgens Communications Group, Inc. and became a member of its board in May 1989.[34]

Thus, after abandoning a very successful political career in 1970, Sanders achieved remarkable success in both business and law. Starting from scratch, he built Troutman Sanders into one of Atlanta's largest and most prestigious firms. At the same time, he took over a fledgling bank and, without the benefit of specialized training or banking experience, expanded it into a $1 billion institution. Ambitious and aggressive, he overextended himself and very nearly lost all of his investments, but through extraordinary effort overcame the crisis and paid off his creditors. Forging ahead, he later made substantial investments in several well-chosen companies and served effectively on numerous boards of directors. By achieving conspicuous success in three different careers— politics, law, and business—Sanders became a wealthy, respected, and influential member of the Atlanta elite with membership in Peachtree Golf Club, Piedmont Driving Club, The Commerce Club, Atlanta City Club, and Ravinia Club as well as Sea Island Golf Club, Augusta Country Club and Augusta National Golf Club, where the Master's Tournament is held. In the 1960s and 1970s he played a pivotal role in making Atlanta a Major League city. In the 1980s and 1990s, as one of Atlanta's "Big Mules," he labored to make his adopted home an international city.

---

[34]Sanders, "Interviews in 1990," pp. 217-18; *Resurgens Communications Group Annual Report, 1992.*

Though he focused much attention on Atlanta, his legendary clout extended far beyond Georgia's capital. His business interests had an international flavor and his name consistently appeared on *Georgia Trend*'s list of "The 100 Most Powerful People in Georgia."[35]

---

[35]"The *Georgia Trend* 100," *Georgia Trend* 7 (January 1992): 41.

Chapter 21

Past, Present, and Future

Having grown up in a close-knit family, Sanders wanted his own family to enjoy the same love and mutual respect that he experienced. Consequently, throughout his public career he placed a high priority on the needs of his family. His love for Betty and the children was obvious to all who knew them, and family concerns often affected his political decisions, such as rejecting races for the Senate in 1966 and 1972. A loving and protective father, Sanders shed his icy and formal public image at home and freely and openly displayed emotion with his family. His home not only provided a respite from the pressures of his demanding jobs, it also strengthened and encouraged him and nourished his soul. From the beginning Betty supported his political ambitions. She and the children campaigned vigorously for him and did all that they could to make his political career a success. The enthusiastic support of his family strengthened Sanders's resolve and contributed substantially to his success in public life.

Like most fathers, Sanders worried about his children during their teenage years. In the late-1960s the hippie, counterculture movement was at its peak, and the Sanders condominium was located near Atlanta's chief hippie districts—14th Street and Piedmont Park. Newspapers reported many instances of children, including well-adjusted affluent teenagers, who simply disappeared or suddenly rejected society and joined a hippie commune. Deeply concerned that such a fate might befall Betty Foy and Carl Jr., Sanders had many fatherly talks with them, alerting them to the dangers teenagers faced. His fatherly efforts, however, failed to protect Betty Foy and Carl Jr. completely from society's pressures. To the discomfort of their father, they played loud rock music, sometimes wore bizarre clothing, and often affected unusual hair styles, as the custom of that day demanded, but they survived the teenage years without any permanent scars.[1]

Carl Jr., who was always fun-loving and mischievous, did not over-exert himself in academic pursuits. In fact, he wore out his welcome at Westminster by the end of the eight grade. Hoping to change his attitude, his parents sent him to Culver Military School near South Bend, Indiana, where he completed the ninth and tenth grades. The military environment had a positive effect on him. Gaining maturity and self-discipline, he returned to Westminster for his junior and senior years of high school. In 1971 he entered Presbyterian College, a small liberal arts institution in Clinton, South Carolina. Showing little interest in academics, he dropped out before completing his freshman year. His father, disappointed in his behavior, insisted that he get a job. After working at a record shop for a year, he entered the University of Georgia and followed his father's footsteps by joining the Chi Phi fraternity. As a student at the University, he served as assistant manager of the Village Apartments, a project owned by Jack Ashmore, his father's law partner. Carl Jr. thrived on the many social activities on the Athens campus, but he also applied himself enough to earn a bachelor's degree in political science in 1976.[2]

The same year he received his degree, Carl Jr. married Debbie Wood, daughter of a Marine colonel. The birth of their daughter Caroline on August 26, 1978, made Carl and Betty grandparents for the first time. Unfortunately, as so often happens in modern marriages, problems developed. In May 1980 they divorced. Five years later Carl Jr. married Christy Brock from Winchester, Kentucky. Their daughter Keaton Marie was born on July 1, 1988, and Carl Edward Sanders III arrived on October 16, 1992.

Resisting parental pressure to attend law school, Carl Jr. started working at First Georgia Bank. Although his father was chairman of the bank, Carl Jr. started at the bottom and even swept floors. After learning all of the routine functions of banking, he advanced to more responsible positions. Bright and personable, Carl Jr. seemed to have a promising

---

[1]Sanders, "Interviews in 1990," pp. 132-33; Betty Foy Botts interview, January 28, 1991; Carl Sanders, Jr. interview, February 15, 1991.

[2]Carl Sanders, Jr. interview, February 15, 1991.

future in banking, but he had other ambitions. After ten years in banking, he left the profession, moved to Augusta, and learned real estate development from firsthand experience at West Lake. When Harry Crosby retired two years later, Carl Jr. had learned the business well enough to succeed him as director of West Lake. At West Lake, he provided the infrastructure and marketed lots. In contrast to his father, Carl Jr. preferred working out of doors, wearing work clothes, getting his hands dirty, driving a pickup truck, and using a small Spartan office with neither a secretary nor a fax machine. Finding his niche in real estate, he developed around 150 lots in his first five years. A successful businessman, he continued to acquire land for West Lake and also helped develop some of his father's property in the Augusta area. Never driven to excel like his father, he insisted on doing things his own way, which was casual and "laid back" with a touch of rebelliousness—traits that caused his father much anxiety. But even during his rebellious period, Carl Jr. had his father's affection; after maturing and settling down, he gained his father's trust and respect too.[3]

After graduating from Westminster, Betty Foy entered Georgia State University in Atlanta where she planned to major in art. Full of wanderlust and curious about other parts of the country, she transferred to Mount Vernon, a small women's college in the Washington, D.C. area. After earning her associate degree, she moved to the University of Arizona where she continued to study art. Growing tired of college, she left before graduating to take a job with the Georgia Chamber of Commerce. Working on the bicentennial program "Stay and See America in Georgia," she traveled extensively, speaking to civic groups and raising money for the program. She also did much public speaking on her next job, which was with Georgia Power Company. A petite blond, pretty and vivacious, she excelled in public relations work and thoroughly enjoyed her jobs.

One of Betty Foy's friends, attempting to play matchmaker, arranged for her to go on a blind date with a lawyer named David Botts. Neither Betty Foy nor David was eager to go on a blind date, but the friend, certain that they were ideally suited for each other, insisted. The mutual friend, it turned out, was right. Betty Foy and David started dating in

---

[3]Ibid.; Cook, "Sanders: An Oral History," p. 75.

January, got engaged during the summer, had their announcement party in September, and got married in November 1977. She was twenty-five and he was thirty. They now have three children: Austin Sanders, born January 1, 1981; Michael David, born June 4, 1985; and Alyssa Betty Foy, born May 31, 1991. David has his own law firm, and they reside in Vinings, only a short distance from the Sanders home so that Carl and Betty get to see their grandchildren frequently.[4]

Shortly after the 1970 election, Carl and Betty moved into a beautiful red brick, white-columned mansion on Tuxedo Road. A spacious two-story structure which once had been the home of Atlanta's great golfer Bobby Jones, it was located on a large wooded lot in Tuxedo Park, Atlanta's most prestigious residential area. Their neighbors included Rankin Smith, Ivan Allen, and Jimmy Carter, for the Governor's Mansion was only a few hundred yards away. Numerous tall pines and hardwoods shaded both the front and back yards and gave the family more privacy. After four years in the condominium, Betty was thrilled by the move. She had become accustomed to twelve-foot high ceilings in the Governor's Mansion and always felt cramped in the modern condominium. The high ceilings in the new home pleased her, as did the large yards and spacious rooms. Even with a swimming pool and bath house in the back, plenty of space remained for Betty to grow beautiful flowers. Since tour buses stopped at both the front and rear of the house, keeping the yards manicured became a necessity, as Betty insisted on keeping up appearances. In 1973 they sold the property in Augusta they had planned to build on and purchased a second home on Sea Island. There, away from the crowds and busy activities of Atlanta, Carl and Betty could relax and enjoy the quiet seashore. Betty, in particular, loved the coast and spent much time there. As the grandchildren grew older, the beach house became the favorite spot for family gatherings.[5]

After the children were off to college, Betty had more time to herself. Determined to develop her artistic talents, she cut back on her commitments to civic activities so that she could have large blocs of time to paint. She converted one large room on the first floor of their home into a studio and spent many hours there perfecting her techniques.

---

[4]Betty Foy Botts interview, January 28, 1991.
[5]Betty Foy Sanders interview, November 7, 1990.

Always a keen observer of nature, she painted many landscapes and pastoral scenes. She enjoyed doing scenes that reminded her of her youth in Bulloch county, such as a dilapidated old farm house, a red clay country road, a shrimp fleet at Brunswick, two old mules, flower beds, etc. Having great respect for Indians and their role in Georgia's history, she did a three-year study of the Cherokees which became her favorite exhibition. A lover of flowers, Betty did an exceptional collection of paintings called "Wildflowers of Georgia," which was first shown in 1985 as the inaugural exhibit at Day Hall, the presentation area of The Atlanta Botanical Garden's new $3 million Gardenhouse. "Wildflowers are nature's gift for men to enjoy," Betty explained. "Our state is blessed with so many and they are ours to see each year. Art is the medium I use to reflect the beautiful things around us and express the subjects woven into my life, past and present."[6]

Working in both oils and watercolors, Betty continually experimented with new subjects and new techniques. She also experimented with different shapes and sizes of canvases, including unusual fan-shaped canvases. Over the years her style evolved from the traditional to an imaginative abstract style featuring vivid colors and pieces of rock and gems mixed into the paint to create a three-dimensional effect. By continuing to explore new ways of expressing her feelings, Betty became a respected and imaginative artist. In addition to exhibiting her work at galleries, universities, and museums, she also served on many commissions including the Georgia Commission of the Arts. Appointed by Governor George Busbee, she served seven years until his term expired in 1982. For her contributions over the years to the arts in Georgia, Betty received the Governor's Award in the Arts in 1984.[7]

Dedicated to promoting art throughout the state, she encouraged her husband to make art a higher priority in state government. During his governorship, the University System constructed seven fine arts buildings, including the Foy Fine Arts Building in Statesboro, named for her father. In 1967 she started the Betty Foy Sanders Art Collection of outstanding Georgia artists at Georgia Southern University. Each year thereafter she contributed an object of art to the collection which is

---

[6] *Statesboro Herald*, September 29, 1985.
[7] Ibid.; *Atlanta Journal*, September 19, 1985.

housed in the Henderson Library. The excellent collection now includes work by Joseph Perrin, Wilbur Kurtz, Lamar Dodd, Ouida Canaday, Edward Moulthrop, Mattie Lou O'Kelley, and many other Georgia artists. Betty's painting "I Will Lift Up Mine Eyes . . ." hangs in the lobby of the Foy Fine Arts Building. In 1991, Carl and Betty donated a large modernistic sculpture by Caroline Montague which was placed in front of the Foy Fine Arts Building. Following the dedication of the sculpture, guests enjoyed "A Three Generation Exhibition," showing works by Betty Foy Sanders, Betty Foy Botts, and young Austin Sanders Botts. That exhibition clearly demonstrated that some of Betty's talent and love of art has been passed on to her daughter and grandson.[8]

When Betty Foy and Carl Jr. were growing up, their father was so busy with politics and his law practice that he had little time for his children. But if he was deficient in spending time with them in their early years, he made up for it in later years. Long ago he developed the practice of telephoning his children almost daily, and he frequently arranged for the family to get together for meals, sporting events, fishing outings, and the like. Typical of many Southern families, the Sanders clan celebrated Christmas, Easter, Thanksgiving, and birthdays together, enjoying each other's company. In addition, since Betty Foy lived so close, she saw her parents regularly. When Carl Jr. lived in Atlanta, he too spent much time with his parents, but since moving to Augusta their contacts naturally diminished. Nevertheless, he and his father still managed to get together often for hunting and golfing.

Proud that their children are now settled and happily married, Carl and Betty have become typical doting grandparents. Spending time with the grandchildren is now a key priority. During the summer months Betty stays busy with grandchildren at the beach home. And Carl has become an avid baseball fan who rarely misses a game in which his grandsons participate. Austin Botts already has shown good athletic potential and, like his grandfather, is lefthanded.[9]

In recent years Sanders's law practice and business interests required him to travel extensively, and he also took many trips abroad for pleasure. As a result he has seen much of the world, including the Soviet

[8]Betty Foy Sanders interview, November 7, 1990.
[9]Ibid.; Sanders, "Interviews in 1990," p. 143.

Union, Japan, China, Vietnam, the Holy Lands, and Europe on many occasions. Betty often accompanied him on trips. For the past several years he has arranged for the whole family, including the grandchildren, to take summer vacations together. Since the board of directors of Learning Technologies meets at interesting sites throughout the world, he scheduled family vacations around those meetings. In 1989 they had a grand time in Alaska. In 1990 they spent a week in the Canadian Rockies, and the following year the family vacationed in Switzerland. In 1992 they enjoyed Acapulco, and in 1993 they toured Greece and Turkey. Sanders believes that leaving his family happy memories is more important than leaving them vast sums of money, and these family vacations at delightful locations throughout the world have provided some of their happiest moments.[10]

Without the benefit of inherited wealth or family prestige, Sanders rose from ordinary circumstances to great wealth and influence. Blessed with a keen mind, a strong body, and an indomitable will, he took advantage of the opportunities that came his way. Eager to get as much out of life as possible, from early youth onward he set high goals for himself and pursued them with unrelenting vigor. When he attained them, he set ever-higher goals to strive for. Never completely satisfied with anything he achieved, he invariably undertook new challenges to satisfy a deep-seated longing to be the very best at whatever he attempted. By never resting on his laurels, he continued to grow intellectually and materially.[11]

In time he achieved conspicuous success in politics, law, and business, and common threads can be discerned in all three careers. Confident of his own ability, he boldly took risks that others avoided. In 1962 he could have become lieutenant governor with ease, but he challenged the odds and ran for governor instead. In 1967 he could have returned to a successful law firm in Augusta, but he preferred starting a new one in Atlanta. In business he took so many risks that he nearly lost all of his investments, but he overcame that crisis and pushed ahead to greater success. In addition to taking risks in all three professions, he also

---

[10]Betty Foy Botts interview, January 28, 1991; Carl and Betty Sanders interview, October 12, 1992.

[11]Sanders, "Interviews in 1990," pp. 141-47.

thrived on the competition each profession offered. Always extremely competitive, he thoroughly enjoyed pitting his abilities against the talents of others, whether on the football field, in the courtroom, in a political contest, or in business. He did not always win. Indeed, sometimes he made mistakes and lost badly. But he always competed fiercely, displayed remarkable resilience, and won far more contests than he lost.

Imbued with a powerful work ethic, he applied himself diligently to whatever challenges he faced and also demonstrated remarkable self-discipline throughout his life. Nowhere was self-discipline more evident than in physical conditioning. Sanders never smoked and seldom consumed alcohol for, like Abraham Lincoln, he always wanted to be in control of his senses. Even at political socials where practically everyone imbibed, Sanders usually nursed one drink for hours or drank water. Despite an extremely busy schedule, he made time for regimented exercise, including jogging, daily workouts at the YMCA, handball, tennis, golf, and other activities. He also consistently practiced sensible eating and sleeping habits. Consequently, he always has enjoyed remarkably good health and looked younger than his age. In 1992 he weighed 175 pounds, just as he did a half-century ago when he played football at the University of Georgia. His excellent physical condition stood out noticeably at the fiftieth reunion of the great 1942 Bulldog team that won the Rose Bowl. At the ceremony at Athens in September 1992, several of Sanders's teammates were terribly overweight. Some were infirm, others had undergone serious surgery, and a depressingly large number already had died. Few members of the team were as physically fit as Sanders.[12]

Another aspect of self-discipline was Sanders's ability to avoid distractions and concentrate attention on the task at hand. The most focused of men, he seldom lost his temper and never lost sight of his objectives. Even in the midst of chaotic political situations, when others reacted emotionally, he remained calm and resolute. In 1961, when most of Georgia's political leaders wanted to close the public schools to avoid integration, Sanders insisted that they remain open. When the House of Representatives became incensed over Julian Bond's rhetoric, Sanders

---

[12]Ibid.; Carl Sanders interview, October 12, 1992; Reg Murphy, "How Governor Sanders Keeps Fit," *Atlanta Journal and Constitution Magazine* (September 15, 1963): 6-7, 34.

urged the members to seat the controversial young legislator. He served effectively as a legislator and as governor because he understood that the system demanded compromise. He willingly made concessions on minor points but always remained focused on his priorities. His ability to cut through extraneous matters and quickly grasp the crucial point of a legal brief amazed his colleagues. The ability to concentrate attention on a given subject is a trait many outstanding leaders possess. Napoleon Bonaparte had it in abundance. Napoleon claimed that his mind was like a chest of drawers. When he finished with one subject, he closed that drawer and opened a new one. In similar fashion, Sanders said his mind was like a bathtub. He filled it with a subject. When he finished with that subject, he pulled the plug and then filled it with another subject.[13]

Sanders advocated change throughout his public life, as a moderate reformer in politics and as a builder and innovator in business and law, yet his worldview, the moral and ethical values formed in his youth, remained fixed and constant. Indeed, in the ethical and moral realm, Sanders has lived a life of extraordinary consistency. His family, the Baptist church, and the YMCA inculcated principles in him in his youth that have guided him thereafter. He experienced no midlife crisis or traumatic experience that radically affected his thinking or behavior. According to close friends, the ambition, competitiveness, work ethic, self-discipline, and high ethical standards that characterized his adult years were evident in his high school and college years. He joined the YMCA as a child and has remained a member throughout his life. He joined the Baptist church at age twelve and has remained in that faith thereafter. He started his political career as a Democrat and consistently has supported the party without wavering. Even his love of fashionable clothing, which was so evident throughout his career, began in his youth. Friends chuckle about the time during his early married years when he came to a pool party outrageously overdressed. His outfit included expensive new alligator shoes, of which he was inordinately proud. His attire made such an impression on the group that several

---

[13]Sanders, "Interviews in 1990," p. 144; J. W. Weltch interview, April 19, 1991; J. B. Fuqua interview, April 4, 1991; Doug Barnard interview, February 16, 1991; Norman Underwood interview, January 23, 1991.

friends grabbed him and threw him unceremoniously into the pool, alligator shoes and all.[14]

With family roots imbedded deeply in the red clay of Georgia, Sanders manifested many Southern traits. As a product of the Depression South, he adhered to the mores of his region. In time he overcame the racial prejudice and provincialism of Augusta, but he retained the typically Southern evangelical faith and traditional love of family, friends, and region. Although he traveled extensively throughout the world and eagerly learned about the customs of other people, Georgia always remained his home. Moving to Atlanta when he became governor, he established roots there and lived in the same home after 1970. When his brother retired as a vice president of Nehi soft drink company in Nashville, Tennessee, in 1991, Sanders completely renovated their boyhood home on Helen Street in Augusta for Bob and his wife to live in. Sanders made frequent trips to Augusta not only to see Carl Jr. and his family but also to visit lifetime friends, such as Ross and Betty Snelling, Frenchie Bush, and Gould and Mary Hagler. Similarly, he made close and lasting relationships with several employees. Both Bessie Matthews and Helen Lawrence worked with him so long that they became part of his family, as did Grady Washington and Josh Lee who maintained the yards and automobiles. After Bessie reached the age of seventy, she has often talked about going home, but Carl and Betty doubt that she ever will leave. Sanders also developed many lasting relationships at work. Norman Underwood and several other attorneys have remained with his firm for many years, and Benny Tackett, in whom Sanders placed absolute trust, has been his personal secretary and friend for thirty years.

The decor of the new facilities of Troutman Sanders also reveal Sanders's commitment to Southern traditions. In 1992 the firm leased seven complete floors (floors forty-six to fifty-two) of the new NationsBank Tower. Sanders's office is on the fifty-second floor, from which he enjoys a panoramic view of the entire city of Atlanta. The only other personnel on that floor are Benny Tackett and a receptionist. The remainder of the floor is devoted to an expansive lobby, conference

---

[14]Weltch interview, April 19, 1991; interview with Doug Barnard, Washington, D.C., June 10, 1992; "Frenchie" Bush interview, August 29, 1991; telephone interview with Ross Snelling, September 3, 1991.

rooms, small meeting rooms, and a library. Tastefully placed in each room are modern paintings and pieces of sculpture. Although they range in style from traditional landscapes to modern abstract designs, they were carefully chosen to depict aspects of Southern culture and to provide an atmosphere of elegant simplicity. A huge specially designed carpet in the lobby depicts Georgia's state flower and bird, the Cherokee rose and brown thrasher. The firm commissioned Southern artists to do the paintings displayed throughout the offices and a large percentage were done by native Georgians. Altogether Troutman Sanders has an outstanding art collection, featuring the work of rising young Southern artists, plus a few pieces by older established artists, such as Lamar Dodd, Allen Tiegreen, Geneive Arnold, and Joe Perrin. For many years both Betty and Carl have attempted to advance the interests of Georgia and advertise their homestate to the world, and their commitment to developing Georgia art has been especially noteworthy.

Having reached the age when most people retire or at least slow down, Sanders has made few concessions to advancing age. Instead of jogging before breakfast as was his custom, he now begins his mornings with a brisk walk around his neighborhood but still gets to his office by 8:15. He works a full day and returns home at 6:00 or 6:30. During his lunch break, he still works out rigorously at the YMCA or the Plaza Health Club as he has done for many years, except when important business meetings disrupt his schedule. He could spend his time on the golf links and let someone else take over Troutman Sanders, but he is not yet ready to do so. He continues to work not to accumulate vast sums of money which he does not need but simply because he enjoys it. Having worked all his life, he has no desire to retire. Realizing that many people lose interest in life after they retire, he intends to work as long as his strength and energy permit. As he expresses it, "I want to wear out, not rust out."[15]

Sanders frequently receives offers from friends and associates to undertake new business projects. Many of the proposals show promise, and in previous years he would have pursued them, but now he invari-

---

[15]Sanders, "Interviews in 1990," pp. 145-47; Betty Foy Sanders interview, November 7, 1990; Bob Sanders interview, May 7, 1991; Hayes, "The Comeback of Cufflinks Carl," pp. 44-50.

ably rejects them. He no longer is interested in developing more real estate or building new companies. He already has plenty of activities without adding new ones. In addition to his law firm and the various boards he serves on, he has more professional, civic, and philanthropic meetings than he can possibly attend and more requests for speeches than he can honor. Throughout his life Sanders has given generously of his time and resources to many civic and charitable causes. Deeply committed to improving education, for many years he has supported Augusta College, Clayton State College, the United Negro College Fund, and especially the University of Georgia. He served as president of the University of Georgia Alumni Association in 1969–1970, and for many years he has been a key fund raiser for his alma mater. Currently he is engaged in raising $2,500,000 for a special project at the University of Georgia Law School. In recognition of his accomplishments the University has bestowed many awards on Sanders. At a special ceremony at Sanford Stadium on October 2, 1993, Sanders and developer Tom Cousins received the prestigious Bill Hartman Award, the highest honor a former student-athlete can receive from the University Athletic Association. In addition to educational concerns, his other favorite charities include his church (Second Ponce de Leon Baptist Church), the YMCA, the Boy Scouts, and the United Fund. He also has given consistently and generously to the Democratic party as well as to individual candidates for office.[16]

Generally optimistic about the future, Sanders believes that Georgia has a "great future" ahead and that the metropolitan area of Atlanta is going to become "one of the great productive and dynamic markets of America." During his lifetime Georgia experienced remarkable growth, and he expects the state to continue to progress. With his friends Zell Miller serving as governor and Pierre Howard as lieutenant governor, he has confidence in the state's political leadership, even though he disagreed with Miller's attempt to replace the state flag and had little enthusiasm for Miller's pet project, the lottery. Sanders thought the

---

[16]Sanders, "Interviews in 1990," pp. 229-33; Lynda Stewart, "The Possible Dream," *Georgia Alumni Record* (summer 1969): 4-9.

former created unnecessary turmoil and doubts that the latter will be a panacea for education.[17]

To Sanders, the most serious problem confronting Georgia is the grossly uneven distribution of wealth in the state. While many urban and suburban areas have prospered, much of rural Georgia has not. Many rural counties have such a depressed economic base that they cannot provide adequate schools or government services. Sanders has long maintained that Georgia has too many counties, and he still believes that the number should be drastically reduced. In seeking a more efficient delivery of services, he recommends that Georgia establish new counties that are "representative of the people" and have the ability to provide "reasonable services" to the people who live in them.[18]

More troubling to Sanders than state issues are several national trends. During the 1980s his beloved Democratic party lost touch with mainstream, hard working Americans. In his view, it veered sharply to the Left, nominated unappealing candidates, and as a result lost the presidency in 1980, 1984, and 1988. Also, during the 1980s and 1990s the federal government accumulated an overwhelming national debt that now must be passed on to the next generation. But what Sanders finds most disturbing of all are the attacks on the free enterprise system. Clearly the country has adopted much socialism in the past sixty years, and Sanders expects that trend to continue, for he sees no way to stop it. Most people today, he observes, believe that the country owes them a job, owes them a comprehensive health program that will take care of them from birth to death, and owes them a retirement at age sixty-five which will provide all of their needs and wants. Such attitudes are foreign to Sanders's thinking. Adhering to traditional political beliefs, he thinks ablebodied people should earn their own way and that welfare programs should be limited to those incapable of working. A staunch defender of the capitalistic system, he fears that if the American people lose their entrepreneurial spirit and incentive to work, they will lose fundamental rights, including much of their liberty as well. Sanders

---

[17]Sanders, "Interviews in 1990," pp. 234-37.
[18]Ibid., pp. 237-39.

shares the Founding Fathers' belief that political freedom can exist only in conjunction with economic freedom.[19]

In a life filled with extraordinary success, Sanders finally has achieved the most elusive of goals—contentment. Now, more than ever before in his sixty-eight years, he seems satisfied with his accomplishments. At last, the forces that have driven him to strive continually for excellence have subsided a little. Although still busy and productive, his ambitions are no longer obsessive. In recent years he has mellowed. More relaxed, he is at peace with himself. "I am completely happy with my life. I have accomplished what I set out to do. And I am satisfied," he said convincingly in 1992.[20]

For Sanders, life has been an exciting adventure, and he always has looked forward to the challenges of each new day. He still does, but he knows the time inevitably will come when he cannot work. Before that day arrives, however, he intends to continue living life to the fullest, and there are many things he wants to do in whatever time remains.

Although he has traveled much, there are still places in the world he wants to visit. Atlanta, now a modern metropolis with shiny skyscrapers, one of the world's busiest airports, and ribbons of concrete expressways extending in all directions like the tentacles of an octopus, faces the enormous task of preparing for the Olympic games in 1996. As a member of the Atlanta Chamber of Commerce, he supported the effort to secure the Olympics for Atlanta. And, although not a member of the Committee to Organize the Olympics for Atlanta, he has worked with Billy Payne and other officials in soliciting support. When the world casts its spotlight on Atlanta in 1996, he wants his city to be prepared. He directs a huge law firm, but he wants it to grow even larger. Always a goalsetter, Sanders recently confided that when his firm reached the milestone of two hundred attorneys and $50 million in income, it might be time for him to step down and let someone else lead it. When that goal is reached in a few years, he may change his mind. But for Sanders even to contemplate retirement is a striking development. More important to him than travel, Atlanta, his law firm, or his many corporate interests, however, is his family. He still has a wife, two children, and

---

[19]Ibid., pp. 239-41.
[20]Shipp, "Carl Sanders: The Man, The Legend, The Era," p. 18.

now six grandchildren to care for. Realizing that he was extremely fortunate to live in a country that provided wonderful opportunities for those willing to work hard and persevere, he sincerely hopes that the same kind of opportunities he had will be available for his grandchildren and great-grandchildren.[21]

---

[21]Sanders, "Interviews in 1990," pp. 144-47, 218-19, 241-43.

The Sanders home on Tuxedo Road.

Betty Sanders with one of her fan-shaped paintings.

Carl Sanders addressing a luncheon honoring Mac Barber on his being sworn in as Public Service Commissioner, January 11, 1991.

Carl Sanders in his office in 1993.

The whole Sanders family in December 1992.
From left to right, back row: Caroline Montgomery Sanders (daughter of Carl
Jr.); Christy Sanders (wife of Carl Jr.); Betty Sanders Botts; David Botts (Betty's
husband); Austin Sanders Botts (son of Betty and David); and Carl Sanders, Jr.
Front row: Keaton Marie Sanders (daughter of Carl Jr. and Christy); Betty Foy
Sanders (Mrs. Carl E.) holding Alyssa Botts (daughter of Betty and David);
Carl E. Sanders holding Carl Edward Sanders III (son of Carl Jr. and Christy);
and Michael David Botts (son of Betty and David).

Bibliography

Primary Sources

Unpublished Interviews by Author

Barnard, Doug. Augusta, February 16, 1991.
_____. Washington DC, June 10, 1992.
Botts, Betty Foy. Atlanta, January 28, 1991.
Bush, Mrs. William "Frenchie." Augusta, August 29, 1991.
Coram, Robert. Atlanta, April 4, 1991.
Dean, Nathan. Rockmart, October 8, 1985.
_____. Georgia Government Documentation Project. Georgia State University, Atlanta, October 2, 1989.
Fite, Gilbert C. Bella Vista AR (telephone interview), March 13, 1992.
Fuqua, J. B. Atlanta, April 4, 1991.
Geer, Peter Zack. Albany (telephone interview), September 5, 1991.
George, Elmer. Griffin (telephone interview), March 13, 1992.
Groover, Denmark. Georgia Government Documentation Project. Georgia State University, Atlanta, September 12, 1989.
Harper, John. Atlanta, May 7, 1991.
Harris, Roy V. Augusta, April 10, 1970.
Hester, Bert. Atlanta, June 5, 1991.
Holley, Gene. Augusta, April 19, 1991.
Johnson, Leroy. Atlanta, February 20, 1991.
Lowe, Yvonne Redding. Cedartown GA, July 2, 1991.
Matthews, Bessie. Atlanta, May 7, 1991.
Neal, Henry. Atlanta, August 28, 1985.
_____. Atlanta (telephone interview), September 5, 1991.
Sanders, Betty Foy. Atlanta, November 7, 1990.
_____. Atlanta, March 25, 1991.
_____. Atlanta, October 12, 1992.
Sanders, Bob. Atlanta, May 5, 1991.
Sanders, Carl, Jr., Augusta, February 15, 1991.
Sanders, Carl E. Atlanta, August 15, 1985.

_____. "Interviews with James F. Cook, June 26, July 9, 16, 18, 23, 1990," unpublished manuscript.

_____. Atlanta (telephone interview), February 28, 1991.

_____. Atlanta (telephone interview), August 26, 1992.

_____. Atlanta, September 16, 1992.

_____. Atlanta, October 12, 1992.

Smith, George T. Atlanta, April 18, 1991.

Snelling, Ross. Augusta (telephone interview), September 3, 1991.

Tackett, Mrs. Benny. Atlanta, January 23, 1991.

_____. Atlanta, June 19, 1991.

Underwood, Norman. Atlanta, January 23, 1991.

Vandiver, Ernest. Lavonia (telephone interview), August 26, 1991.

Weltch, J. W. Augusta, April 19, 1991.

York, Glenn. Cedartown, April 9, 1991.

Published Interviews by Author

"Governor Carl E. Sanders: An Oral History." Georgia Government Documentation Project. Georgia State University, Atlanta, June 1988.

"Governor George Dekle Busbee: An Oral History." Georgia Government Documentation Project. Georgia State University, Atlanta, November 1988.

Other Interviews

Bates, William. Interview by Hugh Cates. Oral History, Richard B. Russell Collection, Richard B. Russell Memorial Library, University of Georgia, Athens, February 25, 1971.

Bentley, James L. Interview by Hugh Cates. Oral History, Richard B. Russell Collection, Richard B. Russell Memorial Library, University of Georgia, Athens, February 18, 1971.

Campbell, J. Phil. Interview by Hugh Cates. Oral History, Richard B. Russell Collection, Richard B. Russell Memorial Library, University of Georgia, Athens, 1971.

Harris, Roy V. Interview by Hugh Cates. Oral History, Richard B. Russell Collection, Richard B. Russell Memorial Library, University of Georgia, Athens, February 24, 1971.

Knox, Wycliffe A., Jr. Interview by Hugh Cates. Oral History, Richard B. Russell Collection, Richard B. Russell Memorial Library, University of Georgia, Athens, February 24, 1971.

Murphy, Tom. Interview by Cliff Kuhn. Georgia Government Documentation Project, Georgia State University, Atlanta, March 28, 1988.

Shannon, Margaret. Interview by Hugh Cates. Oral History, Richard B. Russell Collection, Richard B. Russell Memorial Library, University of Georgia, Athens, March 31, 1971.

Shipp, Bill. Interview by Cliff Kuhn. Georgia Government Documentation Project, Georgia State University, Atlanta, April 22, 1987.

Special Collections

Carter, James E. Papers. Georgia Department of Archives and History, Atlanta.

Foy Newspaper Collection, Carl and Betty Sanders Personal Papers, Atlanta.

Russell, Richard B. Collection. Richard B. Russell Memorial Library, University of Georgia, Athens.

Sanders, Carl and Betty. Personal Papers, Atlanta.

Sanders, Carl E. Collection. Law Library, University of Georgia, Athens.

Sanders, Carl E. Executive Department Correspondence. Georgia Department of Archives and History, Atlanta.

"This Is Your Life" scrapbook. Carl and Betty Sanders Personal Papers, Atlanta.

Turnbull, Augustus Collection of Carl Sanders Speech/Press Materials. Richard B. Russell Memorial Library, University of Georgia, Athens.

Autobiographies

Abernathy, Ralph David. *And the Walls Came Tumbling Down.* New York: Harper & Row, Publishers, 1989.

Allen, Ivan, Jr. *Mayor: Notes on the Sixties.* New York: Simon and Schuster, 1971.

Carter, Jimmy. *Why Not the Best?* Nashville: Broadman Press, 1975.

Hunter-Gault, Charlayne. *In My Place.* New York: Farrar, Straus & Giroux, 1992.

King, Martin Luther, Sr. *Daddy King: An Autobiography*, with Clayton Riley. New York: William Morrow, 1980.

Sanders, Carl E. "My Life." Unpublished manuscript, 1969.

_____. "Story of My Life." Unpublished manuscript, 1987.

State Government Documents

Board of Regents of the University System of Georgia. *Annual Reports.* 1962-1967.

Daniel, Frank, ed. *Addresses and Public Papers of Carl Edward Sanders.* Atlanta: Georgia Department of Archives and History, 1968.

Department of Archives and History. *Georgia's Official and Statistical Register.* 1959-1960, 1961-1962, 1963-1964, 1965-1966, 1969-1970.

Department of Education. *Annual Reports.* 1966, 1968.

General Assembly. *Acts and Resolutions.* 1963-1967.

_____. *Journal of the House of Representatives.* 1963-1967.

_____. *Journal of the Senate.* 1963-1967.

Sanders, Carl E. *Age of Change, Time of Decision: A report to the General Assembly and the People of Georgia on the Administration of Governor Carl E. Sanders 1963-1967.*

Business Reports

Carmike Cinemas, Inc. *Annual Report.* 1991.

Fuqua Industries, Inc. *Annual Report.* 1991.

Healthdyne, Inc. *Annual Report.* 1991.

Resurgens Communications Group, Inc. *Annual Report.* 1992.

Newspapers

The Advocate-Democrat (Crawfordville)   *Greensboro Herald-Journal*
Albany Herald   *Jackson Herald* (Jefferson)
Americus Times-Recorder   *LaGrange Daily News*
Athens Banner-Herald   *Macon News*
Atlanta Constitution   *Macon Telegraph*
Atlanta Daily World   *Moultrie Observer*
Atlanta Inquirer   *New York Times*
Atlanta Journal   *Red and Black* (University of Georgia)
Augusta Chronicle   *Rome News-Tribune*
Augusta Herald   Savannah Evening Press
Brunswick News   Savannah Morning News
Bulloch Herald   Statesboro Herald
Carroll County Georgian (Carrollton)   *Thomaston Times*
Columbus Enquirer   *Thomasville Times-Enterprise*
Columbus Ledger   *Tifton Daily Gazette*
The Daily News (Athens)   *Valdosta Daily Times*
Gainesville News   *Waycross Journal-Herald*
Griffin Daily News

Secondary Sources

Dissertations and Theses

Bolster, Paul Douglas. "Civil Rights Movements in Twentieth Century Georgia." Ph.D. dissertation, University of Georgia, 1972.

Cobb, James C. "Politics in a New South City: Augusta, Georgia, 1946-1971." Ph.D. dissertation, University of Georgia, 1975.

Henderson, Harold Paulk. "The 1966 Gubernatorial Election in Georgia." Ph.D. dissertation, University of Southern Mississippi, 1982.

Lyons, Margaret Spears. "A Comparison of Carl Sanders' Gubernatorial Campaigns: 1962 and 1970." Master's thesis, University of Georgia, 1971.

Pyles, Charles Boykin. "Race and Ruralism in Georgia Elections, 1948-1966." Ph.D. dissertation, University of Georgia, 1967.

Sanders, Randy. "The Sad Duty of Politics: Jimmy Carter's 1970 Gubernatorial Campaign." Master's thesis, University of New Orleans, 1990.

Books

Bartley, Numan V. *The Creation of Modern Georgia*. Athens: University of Georgia, 1983.

Bartley, Numan V., and Hugh D. Graham. *Southern Politics and the Second Reconstruction*. Baltimore: Johns Hopkins University Press, 1975.

Bass, Jack, and Walter DeVries. *The Transformation of Southern Politics: Social Change and Political Consequence Since 1945.* New York: Basic Books, 1976.

Baylor, Ronald H. "A City Too Busy to Hate: Atlanta's Business Community and Civil Rights." In *Business and Its Environment: Essays for Thomas P. Cochran,* ed. Harold Issadore Sharlin, pp. 145-59. Westport CT: Greenwood Press, 1985.

Bell, Earl L., and Kenneth C. Crabbe. *The Augusta Chronicle: Indomitable Voice of Dixie, 1785-1960.* Athens: University of Georgia Press, 1960.

Bernd, Joseph L. "Georgia, Static and Dynamic." In *The Changing Politics of the South,* ed. William C. Havard, pp. 294-365. Baton Rouge: Louisiana State University Press, 1972.

Black, Earl. *Southern Governors and Civil Rights.* Cambridge: Harvard University Press, 1976.

Bowdoin, William R. *Georgia's Third Force.* Atlanta: Foote & Davies, 1967.

Carter, Jimmy. *Turning Point.* New York: Times Books, 1992.

Cashin, Edward J. *The Story of Augusta.* Augusta: Richmond County Board of Education, 1980.

Clotfelter, James, and William R. Hamilton. "Electing a Governor in the Seventies." In *The American Governor in Behavioral Perspective,* Thad Beyle and J. Oliver Williams, eds., pp. 32-39. New York: Harper & Row, 1972.

Cobb, James C. *The Selling of the South: The Southern Crusade for Industrial Development, 1936-1980.* Baton Rouge and London: Louisiana State University Press, 1982.

Coleman, Kenneth, ed. *A History of Georgia.* Athens: University of Georgia Press, 1977.

Coleman, Kenneth, and Charles Stephen Gurr, eds. *Dictionary of Georgia Biography.* 2 vols. Athens: University of Georgia Press, 1983.

Cook, James F. *Governors of Georgia.* Huntsville AL: Strode Publishers, 1979.

Dyer, Thomas G. *The University of Georgia: A Bicentennial History, 1785–1985.* Athens: University of Georgia Press, 1985.

Faircloth, Adam. *To Redeem the Soul of America: The Southern Christian Leadership Conference and Martin Luther King, Jr.* Athens: University of Georgia Press, 1987.

Fincher, Cameron. *Historical Development of the University System of Georgia, 1932–1990.* Athens: Institute of Higher Education, University of Georgia, 1991.

Fite, Gilbert C. *Richard B. Russell, Jr., Senator From Georgia.* Chapel Hill & London: University of North Carolina Press, 1991.

Galphin, Bruce. *The Riddle of Lester Maddox.* Atlanta: Camelot Publishing Company, 1968.

Garrow, David J., ed. *Atlanta, Georgia, 1960-1961: Sit-Ins and Student Activism.* Brooklyn: Carlson Publishing, 1989.

_____. *Bearing the Cross: Martin Luther King, Jr. and the Southern Christian Leadership Conference.* New York: William Morrow, 1986.

Glad, Betty. *Jimmy Carter: In Search of the Great White House.* New York: W. W. Norton, 1980.

Henderson, Harold Paulk. *The Politics of Change in Georgia: A Political Biography of Ellis Arnall.* Athens: University of Georgia Press, 1991.

Henderson, Harold Paulk, and Gary L. Roberts, eds. *Georgia Governors in an Age of Change*. Athens: University of Georgia Press, 1988.

Hunter, Floyd. *Community Power Succession: Atlanta's Policy-Makers Revisited*. Chapel Hill: University of North Carolina Press, 1980.

King, Martin Luther, Jr. *Why We Can't Wait*. New York: Harper & Row, 1963.

Lamis, Alexander P. *The Two-Party South*. New York: Oxford University Press, 1984.

Lasky, Victor. *Jimmy Carter: The Man and the Myth*. New York: Richard Marek Publishers, 1979.

Lockerman, Doris. *Maestro: The Life and Times of a Law Firm*. Atlanta: Troutman, Sanders, Lockerman and Ashmore, 1982.

Martin, Harold H. *Atlanta and Environs: Years of Change and Challenge, 1940-1976*. Athens: University of Georgia Press, 1987.

Meier, August, and Elliott Rudwick, eds. *Black Protests in the Sixties*. Chicago: Quadrangle Books, 1970.

Murphy, Reg, and Hal Gulliver. *The Southern Strategy*. New York: Charles Scribner's Sons, 1971.

Neary, John. *Julian Bond: Black Rebel*. New York: William Morrow, 1971.

Norton, Howard, and Bob Slosser. *The Miracle of Jimmy Carter*. Plainfield, N.J.: Logos International, 1976.

Oates, Stephen B. *Let the Trumpet Sound: The Life of Martin Luther King, Jr.* New York: Harper & Row, 1982.

Paschall, Eliza K. *It Must Have Rained*. Atlanta: The Center for Research in Social Change, Emory University, 1975.

Peirce, Neal R. *The Deep South States of America*. New York: W. W. Norton, 1974.

Saye, Albert B. *A Constitutional History of Georgia, 1732-1968*. rev. ed. Athens: University of Georgia Press, 1970.

Shavin, Norman, and Bruce Galphin. *Atlanta: Triumph of a People*. Atlanta: Capricorn Corporation, 1982.

Stone, Clarence N. *Regime Politics: Governing Atlanta, 1946-1988*. Lawrence: University Press of Kansas, 1989.

Trillin, Calvin. *An Education in Georgia*. New York: Viking Press, 1963.

Wheeler, Leslie. *Jimmy Who?* Woodbury, N.Y.: Barron's Educational Series, 1976.

White, Theodore. *The Making of a President 1968*. New York: Atheneum Publishers, 1969.

Periodicals

Abramson, Jill. "'Cuff Links Carl' Builds An Empire." *The American Lawyer* (September 1982): 14-15.

"The Bond Issue." *Time* 87 (February 18, 1966): 24.

"Bond's Word." *Newsweek* 68 (December 19, 1966): 27.

"A Break in Deadlock on Georgia Election." *U.S. News and World Report* 61 (December 26, 1966): 11.

"Break in Georgia." *Time* 77 (January 13, 1961): 64.

Brill, Steven. "Jimmy Carter's Pathetic Lies." *Harpers* 252 (March 1976): 77-88.

Cleghorn, Reese. "No Seat for the Negro Who Won." *New Republic* 154 (January 29, 1966): 11-12.

Cobb, James C. "Colonel Effingham Crushes the Crackers: Political Reform in Postwar Augusta." *South Atlantic Quarterly* 79 (Autumn 1979): 507-19.

Coram, Robert, and Remer Tyson. "The Loser Who Won." *Atlanta Magazine* 10 (November 1970): 41-43, 60-68, 92-99.

"Georgia Legislature's New Look for 1966." *Ebony* 20 (September 1965): 48-55.

"Georgia and the Pursuit of Reasonableness." *New Republic* 155 (October 1, 1966): 11-13.

"The *Georgia Trend* 100." *Georgia Trend* 7 (January 1992): 33-43.

"Grace in Georgia." *Time* 77 (January 27, 1961): 64-65.

Hayes, Katheryn. "The Comeback of Cuff-links Carl." *Georgia Trend* 1 (June 1986): 44-50.

Hein, Virginia. "The Image of a City 'Too Busy to Hate': Atlanta in the 1960s." *Phylon* 33 (Fall 1972): 205-21.

Hibbs, Ben. "Progress Goes Marching Through Georgia." *Saturday Evening Post* 236 (February 16, 1963): 69-73.

Hornsby, Alton, Jr. "The Negro in Atlanta Politics, 1961–1973." *Atlanta Historical Bulletin* 21 (Spring 1977): 7-33.

"Jubilation in Atlanta." *New Republic* 146 (May 7, 1962): 6-7.

"The Legislative Elite." *Atlanta Magazine* 5 (March 1965): 60-66.

Mertz, Paul E. "'Mind Changing Time All Over Georgia': HOPE, Inc. and School Desegregation, 1958–1961." *Georgia Historical Quarterly* 77 (Spring 1993): 41-61.

Meyer, Sylvan. "Georgia Happening: The Election Nobody Won." *Nation* 203 (December 12, 1966): 640-44.

Murphy, Reg. "Governor Sanders' Brain Trust." *Atlanta Journal and Constitution Magazine*, March 3, 1963, pp. 9, 26.

————. "How Governor Sanders Keeps Fit." *Atlanta Journal and Constitution Magazine*, September 15, 1963, pp. 6-7, 34.

"The Negro in College." *Newsweek* 57 (January 23, 1961): 50-51.

"One Word Too Many." *Time* 87 (January 21, 1966): 20.

"Out of the Smoke House." *Time* 80 (September 21, 1962): 24-25.

Pennington, John. "Carl Sanders: The First Year." *Atlanta Magazine* 3 (January 1964): 44, 46, 55-56.

"Picking Maddox." *Newsweek* 68 (December 26, 1966): 20.

"Politics." *Time* 80 (August 24, 1962): 11-12.

"Politics: The White Backlash, 1966." *Newsweek* 68 (October 10, 1966): 27-28.

"Pulling a 'Huhmun'." *Newsweek* 66 (September 20, 1965): 26-28.

"Redrawing the Lines." *Time* 83 (February 28, 1964): 19-20.

"Retreat in Georgia?" *Newsweek* 57 (January 30, 1961): 51.

"Right to Speak." *Time* 88 (December 16, 1966): 31.

Sanders, Carl. "What Football Taught Me." *Atlanta Journal and Constitution Magazine*, November 3, 1963, pp. 18-20.

Sanders, Randy. "'The Sad Duty of Politics': Jimmy Carter and the Issue of Race in His 1970 Gubernatorial Campaign." *Georgia Historical Quarterly* 76 (Fall 1992): 612-38.

"Senselessness in Georgia." *Time* 84 (August 14, 1964): 18.

"Shame in Georgia." *Time* 77 (January 20, 1961): 44.

Shepherd, Jack. "Gov. Carl Sanders and 'Miss Emma'." *Look* 29 (February 23, 1965): 46-49.

Shipp, Bill. "Carl Sanders: The Man, The Legend, The Era." *Georgia Trend* 7 (June 1992): 18-28.

————. "How He Won It." *Atlanta Constitution*, November 8-11, 1970.

Smith, Charlotte Hale. "Boyhood of Gov. Sanders." *Atlanta Journal and Constitution Magazine*, September 13, 1964, pp. 12-14, 54.

Sparks, Andrew. "Hopes and Dreams of the Sanders Family." *Atlanta Journal and Constitution Magazine*, January 13, 1963, pp. 18-19, 22, 25.

Stewart, Lynda. "The Possible Dream." *Georgia Alumni Record* (Summer 1969): 4-9.

"Times Have Changed." *Newsweek* 65 (June 28, 1965): 24-27.

"Two-Time Loser." *Newsweek* 67 (January 24, 1966): 26-28.

"Up to the Legislature." *Time* 88 (December 23, 1966): 20-21.

Velie, Lester. "Strange Case of the Country Slickers vs. the City Rubes." *Reader's Digest* 76 (April 1960): 108-12.

Watters, Pat. "It's Nearly All White in the South." *New Republic* 150 (June 13, 1964): 11-12.

"Winners Wanted." *Time* 88 (November 25, 1966): 32-33.

Index